SHAKESPEARE ON FILM: A

by Marcus Pitcairn

MMX

To Thomas and Lula

First published by Marcus Pitcaithly, July 2010
© Marcus Pitcaithly 2010
ISBN: 978-0-9556864-2-9

CONTENTS

Acknowledgements

I am of course heavily indebted to those who have gone before. This book was put together in too haphazard a fashion (over a period of several years) to make detailed footnoting possible: but I must mention the writings of Robert Hamilton Ball, Kenneth S. Rothwell, Luke McKernan, and Olwen Terris, which have been invaluable to me. Direct quotations have been footnoted.

The plays

For the convenience of my readers, I have included synopses of the plays featured in this volume.

N.B.:

1 – Of the forty surviving plays currently recognised as canonical by the Oxford editors (*Love's Labour's Won* is sadly lost, while *Cardenio* survives only in a heavily adapted eighteenth century version[1]), there are eleven which, as of July 2010, have never been shown in the cinema: *Coriolanus*; *Edward III*; *Henry VI, Parts 1-3*; *Pericles*; *Sir Thomas More*; *Timon of Athens*; *Troilus and Cressida*; *The Two Gentlemen of Verona*; and *The Two Noble Kinsmen*. However, *Henry VI, Part 3* has been used extensively in adaptations of *Richard III*, while *The Two Gentlemen of Verona* is a partial source for *Romeo se fait bandit* (1910) and referenced in some detail in *Shakespeare in Love* (1998), with the result that each warrants a synopsis. The only film of *All's Well That Ends Well* to have been seen on the big screen is the recording of the live broadcast made from the National Theatre to selected cinemas on 1st October 2009; since I have not seen it, and my article barely touches on the plot of the play, I have included no synopsis of this play. Ralph Fiennes' film of *Coriolanus* is due out later this year or in 2011.

2 – Those of the plays which were revised before 1623 appear in their later forms in the First Folio. Minor revisions (e.g. the excision of profanities from several plays after the censorship laws tightened in 1606) have not been mentioned in the synopses below. Where no adaptor is credited, it is because Shakespeare is believed to have been personally responsible for the revisions. *Hamlet* and *King Lear* survive in their probable original forms in quarto texts (a conflated text is conventionally used for *Hamlet*, but the revisions to *Lear* are too substantial to make this practicable); *Macbeth*, *Measure for Measure*, and *Titus Andronicus* in their revised forms only.

---

[1] The identification of *The Second Maiden's Tragedy* with *Cardenio* is erroneous. *Double Falsehood*, the eighteenth century adaptation by Lewis Theobald, has now been published in the Arden Shakespeare series.

3 –   The Henriads are the eight history plays from *Richard II* to *Richard III*. *Henry VI* and *Richard III* constitute the First Henriad, *Richard II*, *Henry IV*, and *Henry V* the Second, this being the order in which they were written.

4 –   As some films use forms of the titles other than those conventionally employed, I have included in my synopses all variant titles recorded in the First Folio or earlier sources.

Antony and Cleopatra (1606)
Full title: *The Tragedie of Anthonie, and Cleopatra* (First Folio)
Setting: Rome, Greece, Sicily, Egypt; 40-30 B.C. (time compressed)
Background: The events of *Julius Caesar* have left the Second Triumvirate (Marc Antony, Caesar Octavian – the former Octavius – and Marcus Lepidus) as rulers of the Roman world. While Antony and his lieutenant Enobarbus are in Egypt at the court of Antony's lover Queen Cleopatra (formerly the lover of Julius Caesar), Antony's wife Fulvia has stirred up a rebellion against his fellow triumvirs, and Sextus Pompey has set up a pirate base in Sicily.

News is brought to Antony of Fulvia's rebellion and death. He parts in typically tempestuous style from Cleopatra and returns to Rome, where he makes his peace with the other triumvirs and agrees to marry Caesar's sister Octavia. Pompey is persuaded to abandon piracy and rebellion without a fight and Antony leaves, ostensibly for Greece. In fact, he returns to Egypt, thus freshly antagonising Caesar.

Eventually their tensions boil over into war. Against all advice, Antony insists on fighting at sea against Caesar's great admiral Agrippa, off Actium on the Greek coast. Outfought, and abandoned by Cleopatra and her flotilla, Antony is defeated. One by one his supporters leave him, including, finally, Enobarbus, who later kills himself out of remorse. Caesar's forces hunt the lovers back to Egypt, where they inflict another defeat on them. Antony attacks Cleopatra for her supposed betrayal; she flees to her tomb and sends him word she has killed herself. Antony falls on his sword but does not die. He is carried to the tomb and dies in front of Cleopatra.

The Queen surrenders to Caesar, but secretly has a

poisonous asp brought to her in a basket of figs. She and her waiting-gentlewomen Charmian and Iras kill themselves with the aid of the snake.

As You Like It (1599)
Setting: France
Background: Sir Rowland de Boys has died, charging his eldest son Oliver to bring up his brothers Jaques and Orlando as gentlemen; but Oliver treats Orlando like a servant. Sir Rowland's patron Duke Senior has been overthrown and banished by his younger brother Frederick, and lives the life of Robin Hood in the Forest of Arden with a few friends (including, confusingly, a second Jaques, a melancholic gentleman; also the musically inclined Lord Amiens).

Oliver and Orlando quarrel. Frederick's wrestler Charles visits Oliver: he has heard that Orlando intends to challenge him at the next day's wrestling match, and does not wish to harm him: but Oliver tells him "I had as lief thou didst break his neck as his finger". At the wrestling, watched by Frederick, his daughter Celia, and Senior's daughter Rosalind, Orlando defeats Charles. He and Rosalind become smitten with each other but do not speak. Frederick banishes Rosalind; Celia and the clown Touchstone decide to accompany her to seek Senior in the Forest; Rosalind disguises herself as a man, calling herself Ganymede, with Celia as "his" sister Aliena. They buy a cottage on the edge of the Forest.

Oliver's servant Adam warns Orlando that Oliver plans to kill him, and they too flee to the Forest, where they fall in with Senior. Orlando hangs verses on the trees declaring his love for Rosalind. "Ganymede" offers to cure him of love if he will woo "him" by the name of Rosalind; Orlando accepts. Meanwhile a shepherdess, Phoebe, who scorns her own suitor Silvius, has fallen for "Ganymede"; and Touchstone woos a goatherd, Audrey.

Furious at Celia's flight, and suspecting Orlando of involvement, Frederick summons Oliver. When he proves unable to hand over his brother, Frederick seizes his lands and turns him out. Oliver too goes to Arden, where he is nearly killed by a lioness but is rescued by Orlando. The brothers become reconciled and Oliver and Celia fall in love. At the end, Rosalind reveals her identity and marries Orlando with Senior's blessing; Phoebe accepts Silvius; and Frederick repents and retires to a hermitage.

The Comedy of Errors (before 1594)
Setting: Ephesus
Background: The Syracusan merchant Egeon and his wife Emilia had twin sons, both called Antipholus, and bought them twin slaves, both called Dromio; but in a storm Emilia was washed off her husband's ship with one of each set of twins. Egeon brought up the other two children to the age of eighteen then set out to search for his lost wife and son; after seven years he has arrived in Ephesus, little suspecting that not only is this where they fetched up, but his other son is in town looking for him. (Antipholus of Ephesus has a wife, Adriana, a mistress and a string of debts. He lives with Adriana, her sister Luciana, the Ephesian Dromio and the latter's wife Luce or Nell – the text is confused.) But the Ephesian law requires all Syracusans to pay an exorbitant fine for entering the city or be put to death: Syracusan Antipholus manages to pass himself off as an Epidamnian, but Egeon has been arrested.

Duke Solinus gives Egeon one day to find somebody to stand him the ransom money. Meanwhile the two pairs of twins are repeatedly mistaken for one another, and even mistake each other (master for master, man for man). The Dromios receive several unearned beatings; the Ephesians are locked out of their own house while their women entertain the wrong men; Syracusan Antipholus falls for Luciana, who is shocked to be wooed by the man she thinks is her sister's husband; the Ephesian Antipholus' creditors get drawn into the confusion.

Adriana concludes that her husband and Dromio have gone mad, and summons the quack Dr Pinch to cure them. They are confined, but Adriana meets the Syracusan pair and thinks they have escaped: they seek sanctuary in a nunnery. Meanwhile, the Ephesians do escape. The comedy nearly turns to tragedy when Egeon recognises his son, not realising that this is the Ephesian Antipholus, and appeals to him, only to be told "I never knew my father in my life": but at the end all is revealed, Egeon is released, Syracusan Antipholus becomes engaged to Luciana, and the Abbess who gave the Syracusans sanctuary turns out to be Emilia.

Cymbeline (1610, possibly with an unidentified collaborator)
Full title: *Cymbeline King of Britaine* (First Folio contents page);
The Tragedie of Cymbeline (First Folio)
Setting: Britain, Rome; first century A.D.
Background: Twenty years earlier, the banished nobleman Belarius kidnapped Guiderius and Arviragus, the infant sons of King Cymbeline of Britain. The King has now remarried and hopes to marry off his sole remaining child, Imogen, to his stepson Cloten: but Imogen has secretly married the poor gentleman Posthumus Leonatus.

Cymbeline discovers the marriage and banishes Posthumus, who flees to Rome, leaving his servant Pisanio to attend on Imogen. The Queen begs poison of the physician Cornelius, but he, mistrusting her, gives her a draught which will produce only the semblance of death; she gives it to Pisanio saying that it is a cordial, in the hope that he will die, leaving Imogen isolated and her son's way free.

Posthumus boasts of Imogen's beauty and virtue; the Roman nobleman Iachimo goads him into wagering a diamond ring on her fidelity. Iachimo travels to Britain with the Roman ambassador Lusius[2], who has been sent by the Emperor to demand tribute. Iachimo fails to seduce Imogen, so he has himself smuggled into her room in a trunk, writes down a description of the room, steals her bracelet, and notes a mole on her left breast. Meanwhile, Cymbeline refuses to pay the tribute. Returning to Rome, Iachimo uses the details he has gathered to convince Posthumus that he has slept with Imogen. Posthumus sends a letter to Imogen asking her to meet him at Milford Haven, and another to Pisanio ordering him to kill her on the way; he embarks with Lusius, who is now leading a Roman invasion force.

Cloten tries to woo Imogen but she tells him that Posthumus' "meanest garment" is worth more to her than he is. Receiving Posthumus' letter, she flees the court with Pisanio; Cloten decides that he will avenge the insult by dressing in Posthumus' clothes to pursue and rape her. Pisanio reveals his real commission to Imogen, and gives her the "cordial", then

---

[2] The text calls the character "Caius Lucius": but, as Lucius is a forename, it is reasonable to assume that this is a misspelling of the family name Lusius.

writes to Posthumus that he has killed her. For her safety Imogen disguises herself as a boy, calling herself Fidele, but she becomes lost in the Welsh mountains where she is taken in by a local family – Morgan, and his adopted sons Polydore and Cadwal, who are in fact Belarius, Guiderius, and Arviragus, the princes being ignorant of their heritage. Cloten arrives and picks a fight with Guiderius / Polydore, who cuts off his head. Finding "Fidele" apparently dead after drinking the "cordial", the princes lay "him" by Cloten and sing a lament. Waking to find a headless body in Posthumus' clothes by her side, Imogen assumes that her husband is dead. Lusius' army arrives on the spot, and he takes pity on "Fidele" and takes "him" into his service.

    In the battle between Britons and Romans, the remorse-stricken Posthumus fights for both sides in turn, seeking death: along with the three mountaineers, he helps turn the tide in the Britons' favour, but he then gives himself up as a Roman prisoner. The raging Cymbeline plans to slaughter the captives, but Lusius tells him that Fidele is a Briton, and Cymbeline not only frees the "boy" but promises him any boon he shall choose, expecting him to ask for Lusius' liberty: but, recognising Posthumus' ring on the captive Iachimo, Imogen instead demands to know how he got it. The whole truth comes out, Cornelius reports the death of the Queen, and Guiderius is reinstated as Cymbeline's heir; the prisoners are released and peace made with Rome.

Hamlet (1600)
Full title: *The Revenge of Hamlet Prince Denmark* (Stationers' Register); *The Tragicall Historie of Hamlet Prince of Denmarke* (First Quarto); *The Tragedie of Hamlet Prince of Denmarke* (Second and subsequent Quartos); *The Tragedy of Hamlet* (First Folio)
Setting: Denmark
Background: Hamlet, King of Denmark, has died. Although he has an adult son also named Hamlet (who has been paying court to Ophelia, daughter of the Lord Chamberlain, Polonius), his brother Claudius has taken over both the throne and the Queen, Gertrude. The kingdom is menaced with invasion by Prince Fortinbras of Norway.

    The old King's ghost appears to the sentries at his castle of Elsinore. Prince Hamlet's university friend Horatio tries to speak to it, and, after its departure, convinces the sentries' officer Marcellus that Hamlet must be told. Claudius meanwhile sends an embassy to divert Fortinbras, who goes off to invade Poland instead. Claudius and Gertrude try to rouse Hamlet from his melancholy but fail. Polonius' son Laertes departs for Paris, his father sending the spy Reynaldo to keep an eye on him.

Hamlet watches with Horatio and the guards and encounters the ghost, who tells him that he was murdered by Claudius. Hamlet swears the others to secrecy. His behaviour thereafter convinces the court that he is mad. Polonius finds a letter from him to Ophelia, and persuades himself that love is the cause of the Prince's madness; he and Claudius set Ophelia to talk to Hamlet, watched by them; Hamlet berates and then rejects her. Claudius decides to send him to England to recuperate (and to keep him out of the way). He places two more university friends, Rosencrantz and Guildenstern, to spy on Hamlet.

A company of players comes to Elsinore and Hamlet gets them to put on a play depicting in thin disguise the murder of his father. Claudius is smitten with guilt. The play is abandoned. Gertrude sends for Hamlet. On his way to her room he overhears Claudius at prayer and considers killing him, but decides that it would be no revenge to send him to Heaven. Polonius hides in Gertrude's room to hear what Hamlet says; but when Hamlet frightens Gertrude and she cries for help, Polonius echoes the cry, and, thinking that the eavesdropper is Claudius, Hamlet stabs him through the curtain, killing him. He upbraids Gertrude and makes her promise to stop sleeping with Claudius. The ghost appears to Hamlet but Gertrude cannot see it.

Claudius brings forward his plan to send Hamlet to England, but now he writes new letters ordering that he should be killed on arrival. Hamlet finds these letters and substitutes ones ordering the deaths of Rosencrantz and Guildenstern, from whom he is then separated in a pirate attack. Ophelia goes mad, and Laertes returns seeking vengeance for Polonius' death. Ophelia drowns herself. On learning that Hamlet has returned to Denmark, Laertes and Claudius plot to kill him in a fixed fencing match: Laertes' foil will be unbated and poisoned, and Claudius will poison the wine set by for refreshment. Hamlet and Laertes fight at Ophelia's funeral; later the fop Osric delivers Laertes' supposedly amicable challenge.

11

While they are fighting, Gertrude drinks the poisoned wine. Both fencers are wounded with the unbated blade. Laertes confesses the plot, and Hamlet kills Claudius. Before Hamlet dies, word is brought that Fortinbras and his army are at the gates; Hamlet approves Fortinbras' succession, then expires.

Henry IV, Part 1 (1596)
Full title: *The Historie of Henry the Fourth* (all Quartos); *The First part of King Henry the fourth* (First Folio contents page); *The First Part of Henry the Fourth with the Life and Death of Henry Sirnamed Hot-spvrre* (First Folio)
Setting: England, Wales; 1402-03
Background: See *Richard II*. Hal, Prince of Wales, has taken up with a disreputable crowd at Nell Quickly's Boar's Head Tavern in Eastcheap, led by the fat knight Sir John Falstaff. "Hotspur" Percy has captured Scottish noblemen whom he wishes to keep for ransom, but the King takes them from him. Owen Glendower is leading a rebellion in Wales.

Hotspur appeals for the ransom of his brother-in-law Edmund Mortimer, captured by Glendower. The King spurns him.

Falstaff and the Prince banter, before agreeing to go to Gadshill the next night to rob a group of merchants. Hal and his friend Ned Poins secretly plan to let Falstaff and his cronies carry out the robbery and then rob them.

Worcester reminds Hotspur that Mortimer was Richard II's chosen successor. The Percies join forces with Glendower in a rebellion to put Mortimer on the throne; the Archbishop of York and Earl of Douglas join them; Mortimer marries Glendower's daughter. Meanwhile Hal and Poins carry out their plan; Falstaff spins an heroic yarn about the robbery before they reveal what happened. The Sheriff arrives, pursuing Falstaff, but Hal fobs him off.

Glendower boasts about the portents that attended his birth, but Hotspur mocks him. The King reprimands Hal for his wild ways. Falstaff and his hanger-on Lieutenant Bardolph go recruiting men for the war. The two armies face one another at Shrewsbury. Sir Walter Blunt disguises himself as the King to confuse the rebels. Douglas kills Blunt, then attacks the real King, but is driven off by Hal; he then attacks Falstaff, who feigns death. Hal kills Hotspur and mourns Falstaff, who not only proves alive but tries to claim the credit for Hotspur's death. Worcester is captured and executed.

Henry IV, Part 2 (1597)
Full title: *The second part of Henry the fourth, continuing to his death, and coronation of Henry the fift* (Quarto); *The Second part of K. Henry the fourth* (First Folio contents page); *The Second Part of Henry the Fourth Containing his Death: and the Coronation of King Henry the Fift* (First Folio)
Setting: England; 1403-13 (time compressed)
Background: See *Henry IV, Part 1*

Following directly on from *Part 1*, Northumberland receives word that his son and brother are dead. Falstaff cheeks the Lord Chief Justice and dissuades Nell Quickly from an attempt to have him arrested for debt. He roisters at the Boar's Head with the prostitute Doll Tearsheet, and introduces the swaggerer Pistol to the inn. Hal and Poins listen to Falstaff dispraising them to Doll, but, when challenged, he wriggles out of it. The King falls sick. Falstaff and Bardolph are set on the recruiting trail again; Falstaff goes to the estate of his old friend Justice Shallow in Gloucestershire, where they reminisce about old times and Falstaff drafts a sorry crowd of peasants into the army. Shallow's cousin Silence lives up to his name until he gets drunk.

At Gaultree Forest, Hal's brother Prince John and cousin the Earl of Westmorland trick the Archbishop and his cohorts into surrender; they are then put to death. The remaining rebels are defeated, and the dying King sends for Hal. Arriving late and finding his father unconscious, Hal thinks him dead and takes the crown. The King wakes up and berates Hal, who manages to justify himself. The King dies.

Pistol arrives in Gloucestershire and reports the King's death. Falstaff is delighted and takes his followers to London to greet the newly crowned Henry V; but Hal rejects his old friends. Doll and Nell have already been arrested, and Falstaff is carted off to the Fleet prison.

Henry V (1599)
Full title: *The Chronicle Historie of Henry the fift: with his battle fought at AginCourt in France. Togither with Auncient Pistoll* (both

Quartos); *The Life of King Henry the Fift* (First Folio contents page); *The Life of Henry the Fift* (First Folio)

Setting: England, France; 1414-20

Background: See *Henry IV, Part 2*. The House of Commons has brought forward a bill to expropriate bequests made to the Church, but the Archbishop of Canterbury has made an offer to King Henry: if the King will refuse to sign the bill, the Archbishop will provide legal justification for Henry's claim to the throne of France. Since the end of the last play, the Eastcheap fellowship have been released from prison, and Nell Quickly has married Ensign ("Ancient") Pistol.

A Chorus gives heroic narration to the tale of Henry's reign. The Archbishop gives the King the case he wants; immediately afterwards there arrives a French herald, Montjoy, with a scornful message and a gift of tennis balls from the Dauphin. Henry declares his intention to conquer France.

In Eastcheap, Sir John Falstaff dies, mourned by Nell, Pistol, Bardolph, Nym, and his page. The men make ready to leave for France with the army.

After thwarting a plot against his life by his erstwhile friend Lord Scroop and others, Henry leads the invasion of France, making a stirring speech at the siege of Harfleur and then threatening the Governor with dire reprisals if the town should hold out longer. Harfleur surrenders. Meanwhile, there are interspersed comic scenes in which the French princess, Katherine, attempts to learn English, and Welsh and Irish captains in the English force quarrel.

Bardolph is hanged for robbing a church.

The French King Charles VI and his nobles are confident of victory. A massive army is sent out to crush the English force. They face each other at Agincourt. The night before the battle, Henry wanders through his camp in disguise to find out what his soldiers think of him and his cause, and gets mixed messages. In the morning another burst of rhetoric (St Crispin's Day) stiffens English resolve, and the battle is an overwhelming victory; but it is soured by an attack on the English camp-followers, in which Falstaff's page is killed. (Nym and Nell, we learn, are also dead.)

Eventually peace is made and Henry woos and wins Katherine.

Henry VI, Part 3 (1592)

Full title: *The True Tragedie of Richard Duke of Yorke, and the Good King Henrie the Sixt* (Quarto); *The Third part of King Henry the Sixt* (First Folio contents page); *The third Part of Henry the Sixt with the death of the Duke of Yorke* (First Folio)

Setting: England, France; 1460-71 (time compressed)

Background: Henry VI has proved a weak King, losing France and gaining only a harpyish French wife, Margaret, by whom he has a young son, Edward, Prince of Wales. His cousin Richard, Duke of York, who believes himself to have a superior claim to the throne thanks to his descent from the Mortimers (see *Henry IV, Part 1*), has begun a rebellion, supported by the powerful Earl of Warwick, and has defeated the King in battle, personally slaying the loyalist Lord Clifford, whose son has sworn vengeance.

Warwick, York, and the latter's four sons (Edward, Earl of March; George; Richard Crookback; and Edmund, Earl of Rutland – historically the second but in the play the youngest) pursue Henry to London, and force him to make York his heir. Furious at her son's disinheritance, Margaret raises an army of her own to continue the war. Battle is joined; trying to flee the field, Edmund is cornered by Clifford, and butchered despite his pleas for mercy. York is captured, and Margaret taunts him with a handkerchief dipped in his son's blood before Clifford kills him.

March assumes leadership of the Yorkist cause. In the next battle (Towton, during which Henry overhears the lamentations of a son who has slain his father and a father who has slain his son) the Yorkists triumph, and Clifford dies. Henry's young cousin the Earl of Richmond is spirited away into exile, but not before Henry has foretold that he will one day be King. Henry is captured and March becomes King Edward IV, making George Duke of Clarence and Richard Duke of Gloucester. Margaret and the Prince flee to France, whither Warwick is sent as ambassador to negotiate Edward's marriage to Princess Bona of Savoy: but Edward becomes infatuated with Elizabeth Woodville, and, unable to persuade her to become his mistress, marries her. Warwick and the French are alike insulted, and throw in their lot with the Lancastrians; Clarence also deserts to them. Warwick's daughters, Anne and Isabel Neville, are married to the Prince and Clarence respectively. Henry is freed and recrowned; Edward is captured but rescued by Gloucester; Clarence is persuaded to rejoin his brothers;

15

Warwick is killed and Henry recaptured.

In the final battle at Tewkesbury, Margaret's forces are heavily defeated. The three York brothers stab the Prince to death; Gloucester rides back to London and kills King Henry. Queen Elizabeth bears a son.

Henry VIII (1613, with John Fletcher)
Full title: *All is True* (all pre-Folio references); *The Life of King Henry the Eight* (First Folio contents page); *The Famous History of the Life of King Henry the Eight* (First Folio)
Setting: England; 1521-33 (time compressed)
Background: The power of the Lord Chancellor, Cardinal Wolsey, is resented by the nobility; the Dukes of Buckingham and Norfolk head a faction opposed to the Cardinal. Queen Catherine has failed to present King Henry with a son.

Buckingham is arrested and charged with treason. Catherine and Norfolk plead with the King for mercy, but Henry will not listen and sentences Buckingham to death. At a ball, Henry meets and falls for Anne Boleyn, and decides to divorce Catherine; Cardinal Campeggio (Campeius) is sent from Rome to help adjudicate the case. Wolsey is alarmed by the King's liaison with Anne, as the divorce will mean the end of Henry's Spanish alliance, and he wants to marry the King off to a French princess instead: he and Campeggio plot to delay the divorce until this can be arranged, but Catherine sees through them and will not cooperate; their intrigues are exposed and the King dismisses Wolsey.

Abetted by Archbishop Cranmer, Henry declares himself head of the Church, grants himself the divorce, and marries Anne; Catherine falls sick. She receives news that Wolsey has died, and forgives him before herself giving up the ghost. A Privy Council plot against Cranmer is foiled. Anne bears a daughter, who is christened Elizabeth.

Julius Caesar (1599)
Full title: *The Life and death of Julius Caesar* (First Folio contents page); *The Tragedie of Julius Caesar* (First Folio)
Setting: Rome, Lydia, Greece; 44-42 B.C.
Background: Julius Caesar, last surviving member of the First Triumvirate, has defeated the sons of his old rival Gnaeus

Pompey, and been made Dictator-for-life of the Roman Republic.

The tribunes berate the people for idolising Caesar. Caesar voices his distrust of Gaius Cassius to his lieutenant Marc Antony, who dismisses his fears. A soothsayer warns Caesar to beware the Ides of March, but he laughs this off. Caesar's friend Brutus worries that Caesar will make himself King. Cassius works on these fears. Another friend, Casca, brings them news that Antony has publicly offered Caesar a crown and Caesar has refused it, but that it was really a show for the mob.

Two weeks later, on the eve of the Ides of March, there is a thunderstorm and many portents. Cassius, Casca, Brutus' kinsman Decius (historically Decimus), and others visit Brutus: he has agreed to join them in assassinating Caesar, but persuades them that there is no need to kill Antony. His wife Portia reproaches him for keeping secrets from her.

Caesar's wife Calpurnia has had bad dreams, and begs him not to go to the Senate, but Decius says that he is to be made King and the opportunity may pass if he stays at home. Caesar goes, brushing off an attempt by the freedman Artemidorus to warn him, and is killed. Antony arrives and begs leave to make Caesar's funeral oration; Brutus grants it. Brutus makes a speech first and is well received, but Antony's speech stirs the people up against the conspirators. In the ensuing riot, innocents die (including the poet Cinna, who happens to share a name with one of the conspirators). Brutus and Cassius flee to Lydia and raise an army.

Antony joins forces with Caesar's adopted son Octavius. They override Caesar's will, and draw up death lists. Portia kills herself. Brutus is haunted by Caesar's ghost. At the battle of Philippi the conspirators are defeated and both leaders commit suicide.

King John (1595)
Full title: *The Life and Death of King John* (First Folio)
Setting: England, France; 1199 – 1216 (time compressed)
Background: King Richard the Lionheart has died leaving no legitimate children, and predeceased by his brother Geoffrey. Their youngest brother John has been crowned King, but Geoffrey's young son Arthur, Duke of Brittany, arguably has a better claim, and his mother Constance has won the support of

King Philip of France and "Limoges, Duke of Austria" (historically Ademar, Viscount Limoges, but Shakespeare has confused him with the Austrian Duke Leopold).

Count Chatillon arrives at the English court bearing a declaration of war. Philip will attack John's lands in France to claim them for Arthur. John and his mother Eleanor of Aquitaine defy Chatillon. An inheritance dispute reveals Philip of Falconbridge as King Richard's illegitimate son, and he enters John's service. John squeezes money out of the Church to finance his invasion of France.

The kings clash at Angers in an inconclusive battle. The citizens of Angers refuse to take sides so the armies threaten to combine against them. Peace is made by the marriage of John's niece Blanche to Philip's son Louis. Constance denounces this treachery. Cardinal Pandulph arrives and excommunicates John for pillaging the Church. The French turn against John but Falconbridge kills Limoges and Arthur is taken prisoner, and placed in the care of Hubert de Burgh. Pandulph persuades Louis to invade England, ostensibly in Arthur's support but really to claim the crown for himself. John, left isolated by Eleanor's death, panics, and orders Hubert to murder Arthur. Hubert has not the heart to do it but reports it done. The English nobles, led by the Earl of Salisbury, defect to Louis; they are nearly won round by a report that Arthur still lives, but it is no longer true – the boy has died trying to escape.

Louis is proclaimed King, but his ally Count Melun, mortally wounded in battle, confesses to the English nobles that Louis means to have those who have betrayed John put to death when he rules England. They return to John's side and the French are defeated, but John dies, reportedly poisoned by a monk in revenge for the wrongs he has done the Church. His son Henry III succeeds him.

King Lear (1605, revised c. 1610)
Full title: *M. William Shak-speare his Historie, of King Lear* (both Quartos); *The Tragedie of King Lear* (First Folio)
Setting: Britain; an unspecified period of pre-Roman antiquity
Background: The Earl of Gloucester has two sons, legitimate Edgar and bastard Edmund. King Lear has three daughters – Goneril, Duchess of Albany; Regan, Duchess of Cornwall; and the still unmarried Cordelia. Cordelia's suitors, the King of

France and the Duke of Burgundy, attend Lear's court.

Lear announces his intention of dividing his kingdom between his daughters, then asks them which loves him most. Goneril and Regan flatter him but Cordelia has nothing to say. Lear disowns her, and tells the suitors she will have no dowry. Burgundy loses interest; she marries the King of France. The Earl of Kent is banished for speaking up for Cordelia.

Edmund frames Edgar (whose position as heir he resents) for an attempt on Gloucester's life; Edgar flees and disguises himself as a mad beggar, "Poor Tom".

Lear retires from power to divide his time between the homes of Goneril and Regan, with his retinue of a hundred knights. He takes into his service a man named Caius, who is in fact Kent in disguise. Goneril demands that he dismiss half his knights; he is furious and says he will go to Regan's court (which she is holding at Gloucester's castle). He sends "Caius", who overtakes Goneril's servant Oswald, also on a message to Regan; they fight, and the Duke of Cornwall has "Caius" put in the stocks. When Lear arrives, Goneril is close behind him; the daughters close ranks and demand the dismissal of all his knights; Lear storms off onto the heath with his Fool, and they are caught in a thunderstorm. Gloucester goes out and shows the King to a hovel where he can shelter; Lear is by now quite mad. Edgar is in the hovel but his father does not recognise him.

Cornwall puts out Gloucester's eyes as punishment for helping Lear, but is mortally wounded by a horrified servant. Edmund becomes the lover of both Goneril and Regan. The wandering blind Gloucester is taken in hand by Edgar, who foils his attempted suicide and kills Oswald when he attacks them; from letters on the body he discovers Edmund's entanglements. He sends these to the Duke of Albany.

Cordelia invades Britain, and finds and is reconciled with her father; but they are defeated in battle by her sisters' forces, and captured. Edmund secretly orders their deaths. Albany denounces Edmund and challenges him to trial by combat. Edgar comes forward, masked, as Albany's champion, and mortally wounds Edmund, who rescinds the order to hang Lear and Cordelia before he dies. Goneril and Regan kill each other. The reprieve arrives too late to save Cordelia, and Lear dies of despair.

Love's Labour's Lost (c. 1593)

Setting: Navarre

Background: King Ferdinand of Navarre and his friends Berowne, Dumaine, and Longaville have sworn to spend three years together in study, in the care of the tutor Holofernes and the pastor Nathaniel, during which time they will eat frugally, sleep little, and have no conversation with women.

Berowne objects to the strictures, and points out that the King of France's daughter is coming on a diplomatic mission and must be talked to. Ferdinand says he will make an exception in her case, but she and her ladies must camp outside his court because no woman is to be admitted. The Spanish knight Don Adriano de Armado, a guest at court, turns in the clown Costard for consorting with a country girl, Jaquenetta, contrary to the King's edict. Ferdinand claps Costard in jail.

The Princess has with her a mocking lord, Boyet, and three ladies, Rosaline, Maria, and Katherine – each previously acquainted with one of the Navarrese lords and already fond of them. When they meet again, romance is almost instantly in the air, the King and Princess falling for each other as well. Armado, who has fallen in love with Jaquenetta, releases Costard so that he can carry a letter to her: Berowne gives him a letter for Rosaline and the clown confuses them. When the illiterate Jaquenetta takes "her" letter to Holofernes to have it read, the tutor realises that Berowne has broken his vows and sends Costard to inform the King.

Meanwhile, the Navarrese lords each in turn overhear the others confessing that they are in love. Berowne, the only one not found out, berates his companions, but then Costard arrives and exposes him. They decide, for a sport, to visit the ladies disguised as Russians, but Boyet overhears them and tells the ladies in advance; they come out masked, having exchanged the tokens by which the men are to know them, and dance with each other's partners, then mock the lords for being so easily fooled. The commons of Navarre stage a pageant of the Nine Worthies, which the lords make fun of. It is revealed that Jaquenetta is pregnant; although Costard is probably the father, Armado agrees to marry her.

It is reported that the Princess' father has died. She and her ladies return to France, imposing a year's penance on their foresworn suitors, after which time they will return and *perhaps* marry them.

Macbeth (1606, expanded by Thomas Middleton c. 1616)
Full title: *The Tragedy of Macbeth* (First Folio)
Setting: Scotland, England; 1040-57 (time compressed)
Background: King Sueno of Norway has invaded Scotland in the east, supported by rebellions in the west (led by Macdonwald) and the north (led by the Thane of Cawdor). King Duncan's generals Macbeth, Thane of Glamis, and Banquo, Thane of Lochaber, have defeated Sueno and Macdonwald but are unaware of Cawdor's rebellion.

Cawdor is executed and Duncan decides to give his title to Macbeth. Returning from the battle, Macbeth and Banquo encounter the Weird Sisters, three witches who hail Macbeth as Thane of Glamis, Thane of Cawdor, and king hereafter, and Banquo as the father of kings. The witches vanish and a messenger brings the news that Macbeth is indeed the new Thane of Cawdor.

Duncan announces his intention of visiting the Macbeths at their castle. Arriving first, Macbeth is welcomed by his wife, and they discuss how to bring about the prophecy – by murdering the King. Duncan arrives; after some hesitation, spurred on by his wife, Macbeth kills him in his sleep. The body is found by Macduff, Thane of Fife. Suspected of the crime, the King's sons Malcolm and Donalbain flee, and Macbeth becomes King.

Tormented by the fear that Banquo's family will supplant his, Macbeth arranges (without Lady Macbeth's knowledge) to have Banquo and his son Fleance killed: but Fleance escapes and Banquo's ghost haunts Macbeth, breaking up a royal banquet and alienating his nobles. Macbeth goes back to the Weird Sisters, who tell him that he will never be vanquished until Birnam Wood comes to Dunsinane, and that no man of woman born shall harm him, but that he is to beware of Macduff. Hearing that Macduff has fled, Macbeth orders the slaughter of his family.

Lady Macbeth, driven mad by guilt, walks in her sleep and obsessively washes her hands; she later kills herself. Malcolm, Macduff, and Seyward, Earl of Northumberland, march on Dunsinane, hiding their numbers with branches cut down from Birnam Wood. In the battle Macbeth kills Seyward's son, but Macduff, who reveals that he "was from his mother's womb untimely ripped", kills Macbeth.

Measure for Measure (1604, possibly with Thomas Middleton, probably "mended" by Middleton c. 1621)
Setting: Vienna
Background: Under the lax reign of Duke Vincentio, Vienna has become decadent, her strict laws unenforced.

Amid rumours of impending war, the Duke departs on a supposed diplomatic mission, leaving his puritanical deputy Angelo to govern Vienna, on the understanding that he will revive the laws against fornication. Secretly, the Duke disguises himself as a friar to remain in the city and observe what happens.

A young man named Claudio is arrested for impregnating his fiancée Juliet, and sentenced to death. He sends his disreputable friend Lucio to beg his sister Isabella, a novice nun, to appeal to Angelo for mercy. Angelo turns Isabella away, but then receives her and, smitten by her beauty, offers to reprieve Claudio in return for sex. She angrily refuses, and, when Claudio begs her to consent, upbraids him. They are overheard by the disguised Vincentio, who tells them of a woman named Mariana, who was once engaged to Angelo but whom he abandoned when she lost her money. A plan is laid: Isabella will agree to Angelo's demands, but Mariana will take her place in his bed.

The plan goes ahead but in the morning Angelo orders Claudio's death anyway. The Duke and jailer plot to kill another prisoner, Barnardine, in his place, but Barnardine is too drunk to make confession: then, fortunately, the pirate Ragozine dies of a fever in his cell. His head is sent to Angelo. Both he and Isabella think that Claudio is dead. Meanwhile, Lucio dispraises the absent Duke to the "friar", and confides that he himself has begotten a bastard – by a prostitute.

The Duke returns in his own person to take up power again, and Isabella denounces Angelo. The Duke sentences him to death. Mariana comes forward to tell her story and beg for Angelo's life, and persuades Isabella to ask for mercy too. All is revealed; Claudio is set free, Angelo marries Mariana, Lucio is forced to marry the prostitute, and Vincentio proposes to Isabella. She does not reply.

The Merchant of Venice (1596)

Full title: *The comicall History of the Merchant of Venice, or otherwise called the Jew of Venice* (both Quartos)

Setting: Venice, Belmont

Background: By a provision of her father's will, Portia, a rich young lady of Belmont, must choose a husband by a lottery of three caskets, one gold, one silver, and one lead, one of them containing her picture: she must marry the man who makes the right choice. (To prevent too many trying, all who fail are bound by oath to lifelong celibacy.)

The Venetian nobleman Bassanio plans to woo Portia. He asks his merchant friend Antonio for a loan to cover his trip to Belmont in suitable style. Antonio's money is tied up in shipping so he goes to the Jewish moneylender Shylock to request a loan. Although there has been bad blood between them in the past, Shylock agrees, and "in a merry sport" offers to lend without interest if the forfeit for non-payment is made a pound of Antonio's flesh.

Portia is wooed by the Princes of Morocco and Aragon, who each choose the wrong casket.

Shylock's servant Launcelot Gobbo leaves his service for Bassanio's. Bassanio's friend Lorenzo elopes with Shylock's daughter Jessica, to Shylock's misery. He becomes vengeful on realising that Antonio had prior knowledge of it. Bassanio and another friend, Gratiano, arrive at Belmont and are welcomed. He correctly chooses the lead casket, and marries Portia, Gratiano marrying her maid Nerissa; but news is brought that Antonio's ships are lost and Shylock means to claim his pound of flesh. Lorenzo and Jessica take refuge at Belmont; Bassanio and Gratiano return to Venice, followed soon thereafter by Portia and Nerissa disguised as men. Portia arranges for herself to be appointed to decide the case between Shylock and Antonio. Shylock refuses the offer of three times his money, but when Portia points out that the bond does not mention blood, thus preventing him from taking the flesh, he is convicted of seeking Antonio's life. Shylock's possessions are confiscated and he is forced to convert to Christianity. Bassanio offers the "judge" any reward he will choose; Portia insists on taking his wedding ring, and Nerissa similarly wins Gratiano's.

Back at Belmont, after berating their husbands for giving away the rings, the women reveal what truly happened, and the couples are reconciled.

The Merry Wives of Windsor (1597)

Full title: *A pleasant conceited Comedie, of Syr Iohn Falstaffe, and the merry Wiues of Windsor* (both Quartos)

Setting: Windsor and environs

Background: Anne Page has many suitors. Her parents each have their favourites but her choice is young Fenton. (Her suitors include Justice Shallow's kinsman Slender and the French immigrant Dr Caius. Nell Quickly, who in this play is Caius' housekeeper rather than an innkeeper, acts as go-between for all of them.) Meanwhile Sir John Falstaff (who is attended by Pistol, Bardolph, and Nym, staying at the Garter Inn) plans to woo not one but two Windsor ladies for their money: Anne's mother Mrs Page, and her best friend Mrs Ford.

Shallow brings Slender to the Pages' house with the blessing of the Welsh parson Hugh Evans, tutor to Anne's younger brother William. They send Slender's servant Simple to request Nell's help; he hides when Dr Caius comes home but is found. The furious doctor writes a challenge to Evans. Meanwhile Falstaff writes to both ladies; they compare letters and realise what he is about, and decide to play along so as to punish him. Pistol and Nym, dismissed from Falstaff's service because he cannot afford to keep them, warn the husbands of his intentions; Page laughs it off but Ford is wracked with jealousy.

Mrs Ford writes to Falstaff to arrange an assignation. Mr Ford visits Falstaff in disguise and the knight brags about his conquest.

The parson and doctor meet, but the Host of the Garter persuades them to make peace. Mrs Ford and Mrs Page arrange for Falstaff nearly to be caught by Mr Ford; he escapes by hiding in a laundry basket, from which he is thrown into the Thames. Convincing him that it is no fault of hers, Mrs Ford arranges another tryst, and again Falstaff is surprised: this time they dress him as a woman, and pass him off as the witch of Brentford, whom Mr Ford hates. He beats "her" out of doors. The women confess the pranks to their husbands, and arrange one more trick on the unrepentant Falstaff, summoning him to Windsor Park at midnight in the guise of Herne the Hunter, where Anne and William and their schoolmates will dress as fairies and torment him. Mr and Mrs Page each make secret arrangements (he with Slender, she with Caius) for their preferred suitor to carry off and

24

marry their daughter: she pretends to agree with each but has arranged to run off with Fenton instead.

Falstaff is humiliated; Slender and Caius find that their "brides" are boys in drag; Anne and Fenton marry, and the Pages are reconciled to her choice.

A Midsummer Night's Dream (1595)
Setting: Athens and environs; thirteenth century B.C.
Background: Demetrius, formerly the suitor of Helena, has transferred his affections to her best friend Hermia. Her father Egeus favours his suit but Hermia loves Lysander. Meanwhile Oberon and Titania, King and Queen of the Fairies, have quarrelled over a changeling boy.

Duke Theseus tells Hermia to obey her father. She and Lysander decide to elope and marry outside Athens. They tell Helena, but she is so desperate for some approval from Demetrius that she betrays the scheme to him.

Meanwhile, Peter Quince has assembled a crew of craftsmen (the "mechanicals") to put on a play to celebrate Theseus' wedding. The chosen theme is the tragedy of Pyramus and Thisbe. The weaver Nick Bottom wants to play every part. The mechanicals agree to rehearse in the Forest.

When Titania refuses to give up the changeling, Oberon sends the imp Puck (or Robin Goodfellow) to fetch the flower love-in-idleness, whose juice is a powerful love-philtre. He plans to punish Titania by making her fall in love with something monstrous. Seeing Helena pursue Demetrius, who scorns her, Oberon takes pity on her, and decides to use the flower on Demetrius as well; when Puck returns, he gives him this task.

Puck mistakenly lays the juice on the sleeping Lysander's eyes. Happening on the mechanicals at rehearsal, he turns Bottom's head into that of a donkey, and the others flee. Titania wakes and falls in love with the transformed Bottom; Lysander first sees Helena and falls in love with her. Angry at the mistake, Oberon uses the juice on Demetrius, who also falls for Helena. She thinks she is being mocked, and fights with Hermia. Eventually all the lovers fall asleep in exhaustion. Having acquired the changeling, Oberon undoes the enchantments, though Demetrius remains in love with Helena.

A triple wedding (the four lovers, plus Theseus and his Amazon bride Hippolyta) ends the play. The mechanicals' play is performed to much jollity, and the fairies bless the marriage-beds.

Much Ado About Nothing (1598)

Setting: Messina

Background: Don Pedro, Prince of Aragon, and his officers are returning from a campaign against rebels; with them comes his half-brother Don John, who led the rebellion but has been forgiven. (Don John brings his two henchmen, Borachio and Conrade. Borachio's mistress Margaret is waiting-gentlewoman to Leonato's daughter Hero.) They have decided to call on Leonato, the Governor of Messina, and his family: but one of Pedro's officers, Signor Benedick of Padua, is in a state of "merry war" with Leonato's niece Beatrice – "they never meet but there's a skirmish of wit between them".

Leonato welcomes the Princes and their trains. Benedick spars with Beatrice. Another officer, Count Claudio of Florence, confesses to Benedick that he has fallen in love with Hero. Benedick mocks him but Don Pedro is sympathetic. Pedro agrees to woo Hero on the shy Claudio's behalf; he is overheard by Borachio, who reports back to Don John. At that night's masked ball John, pretending to mistake Claudio for Benedick, confides to him that Pedro is in love with Hero. Claudio is smitten with jealousy but is quickly set right. He and Hero become engaged; Pedro, who has been turned down by Beatrice, plots with Claudio, Leonato and Hero to set her up with Benedick.

They arrange for Beatrice and Benedick each to "overhear" that the other is desperately in love with them, which spurs them to realise their own feelings. But Borachio and Don John have another plot: John tells Pedro and Claudio that Hero is unfaithful, and arranges for them to see Borachio and Margaret together, thinking that Margaret is Hero. At the wedding, Claudio rejects Hero, backed up by the Princes; she collapses, and most of the party leaves. Friar Francis convinces those who remain (the family, plus Benedick) to give out that Hero is dead. Benedick confesses his love to Beatrice; she demands that he kill Claudio. After some objections Benedick challenges his friend to a duel.

Unknown to all, the mystery has already been solved: the incompetent City Watch, led by Constable Dogberry and

Headborough Verges, have almost accidentally captured Borachio and Conrade. On hearing of Hero's "death", Borachio is conscience-stricken and confesses all. Claudio begs Leonato's forgiveness; Leonato pardons him and says he must fulfil his obligation by marrying his (Leonato's) niece (a fictional niece, not Beatrice). Claudio agrees; he swears to marry the veiled lady, who then reveals herself as Hero. Don John, who has fled, is recaptured. Benedick and Beatrice, after yet more bickering, also get married.

Othello (1603)
Full title: *The Tragedy of Othello the Moore of Venice* (First Quarto; First Folio)
Setting: Venice, Cyprus; *circa* 1569
Background: The greatest general of the Venetian republic, the Moor Othello, has secretly married Desdemona, daughter of Senator Brabantio. He has also recently appointed Michael Cassio as his lieutenant, to the secret fury of Ensign Iago, who coveted the position for himself. Othello, however, trusts Iago implicitly.

Iago goes incognito with Desdemona's rejected suitor Roderigo to inform Brabantio of his daughter's marriage. Brabantio flies into a rage, and seeks to have Othello arrested, but the Doge overrules him: news has just come of a Turkish fleet preparing to invade the Venetian colony of Cyprus and Othello must hasten to its defence. Othello entrusts Desdemona to Iago to bring her after him; Roderigo disguises himself and goes with them, encouraged by Iago to think that he still has a chance of becoming Desdemona's lover. (Iago is fleecing Roderigo for his money.)

The Turks are beaten and scattered, and Othello takes over the governorship of Cyprus from Montano. Iago gets Cassio drunk and sets up a quarrel between him and Roderigo; Montano, trying to break up the fight, ends up fighting with Cassio himself while Roderigo escapes. The angry Othello dismisses Cassio from his service. Iago suggests to Cassio that he should ask Desdemona to appeal on his behalf; he then plants in Othello's mind the idea that Cassio and Desdemona are lovers.

Othello is reluctant to believe it but Iago gets his wife Emilia to steal a handkerchief that Othello gave Desdemona, and plants it on Cassio, then arranges for Othello to hear Cassio talking about his mistress Bianca, in such a way that it sounds as if Desdemona is meant; Othello eventually succumbs. He makes Iago his lieutenant and orders him to kill Cassio. Iago sets Roderigo to do it but the attempt fails; Iago kills Roderigo to keep him quiet.

Desdemona is haunted by the mournful Willow Song. Othello comes to her and announces that he means to kill her. She pleads for mercy but he smothers her in her bed. Montano and others come to arrest him; Emilia reveals the truth. Iago kills her but it is too late. Othello stabs Iago and then himself; Iago survives, but is a prisoner, and will presumably be executed. Cassio becomes governor.

Richard II (1595)
Full title: *The Tragedie of King Richard the Second* (all Quartos); *The Life & death of Richard the second* (First Folio contents page); *The life and death of King Richard the Second* (First Folio)
Setting: England, Wales; 1398 – 1400
Background: King Richard has alienated his nobles and sits uneasily on his throne. His uncle the Duke of Gloucester has been murdered, and the King is suspected of complicity. His cousin Henry of Bolingbroke has accused the Duke of Norfolk of the murder, and they are due to face one another in trial by combat.

A date is set for the duel, but when it comes Richard stops the fight before it has begun, and banishes Norfolk for life, Bolingbroke for ten years. Bolingbroke's aged father John of Gaunt, Duke of Lancaster, pleads for mercy, and Richard reduces the term to six years: but Gaunt knows he will be dead before that time is out.

Soon Gaunt falls ill. Richard and his favourites, needing money for a campaign in Ireland, eagerly anticipate his death. Gaunt prophesies that Richard will bring disaster to England, and dies. Richard, to the horror of his last surviving uncle the Duke of York, seizes Gaunt's estate. While Richard is in Ireland, Bolingbroke invades England, ostensibly to reclaim his inheritance – but it soon becomes clear that he aims at the Crown. With the support of the powerful Percy family (the Duke of Northumberland, his brother the Earl of Worcester, and Northumberland's son Harry "Hotspur"), Bolingbroke forces York to join him, kills several of Richard's favourites, and finally accepts the surrender of the King himself. Richard surrenders his crown and Bolingbroke becomes King Henry IV. Richard's queen, Isabel, goes into exile.

York's son Aumerle tries to restore Richard but is betrayed by his father. The King forgives him but realises that he will never be safe while Richard is alive. He mutters "Have I no friend will rid me of this living fear?" and is overheard by Sir Pierce of Exton. Exton rides to Pomfret Castle, where Richard is imprisoned, and after a fight in which two of his accomplices die he kills the ex-king: but the conscience-stricken Henry has no thanks for him.

Richard III (1592)
Full title: *The Tragedie of King Richard the third* (all Quartos); *The Life and Death of Richard the Third* (First Folio contents page); *The Tragedie of Richard the Third with the landing of Earle Richmond, and the Battell at Bosworth Field* (First Folio)
Setting: England; 1471-85 (time compressed)
Background: See *Henry VI, Part 3*. Although this play follows directly from the previous one, Shakespeare's compression of historical time means that the future Edward V, who was a newborn baby when *3H6* ended, is now an adolescent with a younger brother, the little Duke of York. (They also have an elder sister, the Princess Elizabeth, for whose birth there was no time in *3H6*; and the exiled Richmond is now an adult.) King Edward IV is sick. The Queen's family, the Woodvilles, have formed a political faction resented and mistrusted by the old nobility.

Richard of Gloucester reveals to the audience that the end of the civil wars has left him out of place in England, and that he plots to become King. He has persuaded Edward to arrest their brother George of Clarence. He meets Clarence going to the Tower and the recently released Lord Hastings coming from it: Hastings blames his imprisonment on the Woodvilles and Richard persuades Clarence that his is also due to them. Hastings is appointed Lord Chamberlain; Richard interrupts the funeral of Henry VI to woo the now widowed Lady Anne Neville. She eventually succumbs, and they marry.

Richard and the Woodvilles quarrel. The dispossessed Queen Margaret appears and attacks all the court except the Duke of Buckingham, who alone was never yet her enemy: but

Buckingham scorns her and lines himself up with Richard. Learning that Edward has rescinded Clarence's death sentence, Richard sends assassins who drown Clarence in a butt of Malmsey wine. The news strikes Edward down, and he dies. Since the Prince of Wales, now Edward V, is a minor, Richard is made Lord Protector of England. He and Buckingham, with Hastings' approval after the event, have several leading Woodvilles seized and put to death. Sounded out by Richard's henchman Catesby, Hastings reveals that he is implacably opposed to Richard becoming King. Richard traps him into an utterance that can be construed as treasonable and has him executed. Buckingham brings the Lord Mayor and prominent London citizens to "persuade" Richard to accept the crown; after a show of reluctance he does so. An unofficial opposition of royal women is formed – Queen Elizabeth, Anne, Richard's mother the Duchess of York, and on its fringes mad Margaret.

Richard feels unsafe while his nephews are alive. Buckingham will not countenance their murder and flees the court. Richard has the princes smothered, and poisons Anne so that he can marry his niece, but her mother spirits her away. Richmond lands with a French army and is joined by English rebels. The Duchess curses Richard. Buckingham is captured and put to death. Richmond marries the Princess Elizabeth. Richard is haunted by the ghosts of his victims. In the battle of Bosworth Field, Richard is killed, and Richmond becomes Henry VII.

Romeo and Juliet (1594)
Full title: *The most excellent Tragedie of Romeo and Juliet* (First Quarto); *The most excellent and lamentable Tragedie, of Romeo and Juliet* (Second and subsequent Quartos); *The Tragedie of Romeo and Juliet* (First Folio)
Setting: Verona, Mantua
Background: The Montague and Capulet families are at feud and frequently battle in the streets of Verona. Lord Montague's son Romeo pines for love of Capulet's niece Rosaline.

A brawl between servants of the rival families quickly becomes a full-blown battle, broken up by the arrival of Prince Escalus, who threatens the heads of the families with death if they disturb the streets again. They disperse. Romeo's cousin Benvolio and their friend Mercutio persuade him to join them in crashing the Capulets' ball to help him forget Rosaline. At the ball, he meets Capulet's daughter Juliet. It is love at first sight. He comes to her balcony later that night and they plight their troth.

Romeo goes to his confessor Friar Laurence to ask him to marry them. The Friar agrees, hoping to make peace between the two houses. With Juliet's nurse acting as a go-between, the couple manage to get to the church, and marry. Juliet's cousin Tybalt, meeting Romeo later, tries to pick a fight; Romeo is conciliatory but Mercutio takes on Tybalt. When Romeo tries to break up the fight Mercutio is killed; Romeo kills Tybalt and is banished from Verona. The Friar and the nurse arrange for the lovers to spend one night together before Romeo flees to Mantua.

Juliet's parents have arranged a marriage for her with Count Paris. She turns to the Friar for help. Laurence gives her a potion that will temporarily simulate death, and sends another friar, John, with a letter to tell Romeo of the plan. Juliet "dies" and is placed in the family vault, but John is detained, and overtaken by Romeo's kinsman Balthazar, who tells him Juliet is dead. Romeo buys poison and rides to the tomb. There he meets the mourning Paris who thinks he is there to desecrate the vault, and attacks him; Romeo kills Paris and then himself. Juliet wakes up only to find her husband dead; she stabs herself. The Friar tells their story and their parents are reconciled.

The Taming of the Shrew (c. 1591)
Setting: Padua, a house outside Verona
Setup: *Shrew* is actually one long play-within-a-play. The framework involves a drunken tinker, Christopher Sly, who is fooled into believing that he dreamed his former life and is in fact a lord; a company of players stages the main story for his amusement. It is usually performed without the framing device.
Background: Bianca Minola has many suitors, including Hortensio and the elderly Gremio, but her father Baptista refuses to marry her off before her elder sister Katherine. But Katherine, though beautiful, is sharp-tongued, bad-tempered, and violent.

The Pisan student Lucentio falls in love with Bianca but is dismayed to have two rivals already. He and his servant Tranio arrive at a complicated plan: Tranio will pose as Lucentio and woo Bianca formally, while the real Lucentio gets himself a job as her tutor so as to get more time alone with her than her suitors.

Hortensio also has a plan: to persuade his gold-digging Veronese friend Petruchio to woo Katherine. Petruchio and his clownish servant Grumio roll up to the Minola household and, ignoring all Katherine's insults and threats, Petruchio blithely ploughs on with his wooing and then declares himself successful. A wedding is arranged. Meanwhile, Hortensio attempts a similar scheme to Lucentio's, without success.

Petruchio turns up late and fantastically dressed to the wedding, and carries Katherine off to his Veronese house immediately after the ceremony. There he bullies the servants and finds fault with everything; Katherine tries to moderate his tone, but he will hear nothing until she confesses that the moon is the sun if he says it is.

Tranio persuades a Mantuan, referred to as "the Pedant" (i.e. schoolmaster), to pose as his father, so that he can (as Lucentio) gain Baptista's consent to marry Bianca before the real Lucentio's real father turns up. Thus it is arranged, and Lucentio and Bianca marry; Hortensio goes off to woo a rich widow. At the end all come together for a banquet; the ladies withdraw, and Hortensio wagers that if their husbands summon them again Katherine will not come. But it is Bianca and the widow who refuse to be bidden; Katherine not only obeys Petruchio but lectures the other two on marital obedience. Lucentio and Hortensio are astonished.

The Tempest (1611)
Setting: an unnamed island somewhere between Tunis and Naples
Background: Prospero, Duke of Milan, devoted all his time to study and let his brother Antonio govern the city, little realising that Antonio was plotting against him, until he was overthrown with the help of King Alonso of Naples (to whom Milan became a tributary state). Prospero and his young daughter Miranda were cast adrift in an open boat, but the Neapolitan lord Gonzalo made sure he had his most valued books with him; they were cast up on an island, deserted apart from the monster Caliban and aery spirits. They have lived there for years, served by the spirit Ariel whom Prospero freed from confinement in a tree; Caliban has become a degraded slave as punishment for his

attempted rape of the now teenage Miranda, while Prospero is now a mighty wizard and absolute master of the island. Then one day Alonso's ship passes, returning from his daughter's wedding in Tunis.

Prospero has Ariel raise a storm which wrecks the ship. Alonso, Antonio, Gonzalo and the King's brother Sebastian are cast up on one part of the island, while Alonso's son Ferdinand, his butler Stephano and his jester Trinculo are each cast up alone on other parts of the island. Everybody thinks their companions have drowned.

Miranda asks Prospero why he has done this and he tells her his story, which she is too young to remember. Alonso mourns the supposed death of Ferdinand, then music made by the spirits on Prospero's orders puts Alonso and Gonzalo to sleep. Antonio suggests to Sebastian that he should kill Alonso and take the throne; the quid pro quo for his assistance will be Milan's release from tribute. They draw their swords but the sleeping men suddenly awake. The drawn swords are explained away.

Ferdinand meets and flirts with Miranda, but Prospero insults the prince and sets him to menial labour. Meanwhile, Trinculo and Stephano have found each other, Caliban, and a crate of wine cast up from the shipwreck. Caliban is so enchanted by the taste of wine that he takes Stephano for a god. He plots with the two drunken servants to kill Prospero and take over the island. Like the royal party, they are tormented by Ariel.

Eventually Prospero, persuaded by Ariel to show mercy, reveals himself. All are reunited and the ship magically rendered seaworthy; Ferdinand and Miranda become engaged, and Prospero frees Ariel and his other spirit slaves, and abandons magic to return to Milan.

Titus Andronicus (c. 1589, with George Peele; probably substantially revised by 1594)
Full title: *The most lamentable Romaine Tragedie of Titus Andronicus* (Third Quarto); *The Tragedie of Titus Andronicus* (First Folio)
Setting: Rome and environs; roughly late imperial period
Background: In the long war between Rome and the Goths, the great Roman general Titus Andronicus has lost 21 of his 25 sons (the survivors are Lucius, Quintus, Martius, and Mutius, and his

daughter Lavinia). The war is at last over, and the Gothic Queen Tamora, her three sons (Alarbus, Demetrius, and Chiron), and her Moorish lover Aaron, have been captured and brought to Rome. The Emperor has recently died, and his sons Saturninus and Bassianus are competing for the succession.

The tribunes, led by Titus' brother Marcus, decide to bypass both princes and offer Titus the throne. He refuses, asserting the right of Saturninus as elder son of the dead Emperor. Despite Tamora's pleas, Titus kills Alarbus as a sacrifice to the shades of his dead sons. Lavinia, who is engaged to Saturninus against her will, elopes with Bassianus, assisted by her brothers; Titus, attempting to prevent the elopement, kills Mutius. Saturninus has become infatuated with Tamora, and marries her.

Chiron and Demetrius have both become obsessed with Lavinia. Aaron offers to arrange for them to rape her. When Bassianus and Lavinia discover Aaron and Tamora at a tryst in the forest, and threaten to tell Saturninus, the princes surprise them, kill Bassianus, rape Lavinia, and cut off her hands and tongue so that she can tell nobody. Aaron frames Quintus and Martius for Bassianus' murder. Saturninus sentences them to death, and Lucius to banishment for trying to defend them. Lucius goes to the Goths, who resent Tamora's entanglement with Saturninus. Titus, tricked by Aaron into thinking he can ransom his sons this way, lets his right hand be cut off, but they are killed anyway.

Tamora bears an obviously mixed-race child, whom Chiron and Demetrius wish to kill to hide their mother's adultery. Aaron saves the baby and flees Rome, but is captured by Lucius and his Gothic army as they advance on the city. Lavinia manages to tell Titus and Marcus who her attackers were. Titus, feigning madness, captures and kills Chiron and Demetrius, then serves them up in a pie to Saturninus and Tamora. He kills Lavinia (who no longer wants to live) and tells the world what has happened before killing Tamora. Saturninus kills Titus and is killed by Lucius, who then declares himself Emperor and sentences Aaron to be buried alive. Aaron dies defiant.

Twelfth Night (1601)
Full title: *Twelfe-Night, or what you will* (John Manningham's

1602 reference; First Folio)
Setting: Illyria
Background: The Countess Olivia has vowed to mourn her brother's death for seven years, much to the dismay of her suitor Count Orsino. Another suitor, Sir Andrew Aguecheek, is entertained (and fleeced) at her house by her uncle Sir Toby Belch. They, the jester Feste, the retainer Fabian, and the waiting-gentlewoman Maria are allies against Olivia's puritanical steward Malvolio. Meanwhile the twins Sebastian and Viola have been separated in a shipwreck, each believing the other dead. Sebastian has been rescued by the sailor Antonio, who is outlawed in Illyria for having served against Orsino's fleet.

Viola disguises herself as a boy, calling herself Cesario, and enters Orsino's service. She falls in love with him but he sends her to woo Olivia on his behalf. Olivia falls in love with "Cesario". After Malvolio breaks up a drinking party, Maria lays a plot against him: she forges a letter from Olivia to make Malvolio think his lady is in love with him, and commands him to appear in yellow stockings and cross-garters.

Olivia thinks Malvolio mad and has him locked up. Sir Toby, delighted with this result, agrees to marry Maria. Sir Andrew is going to leave because he sees "Cesario" as a rival; Sir Toby talks him into challenging "him" to a duel. Toby and Fabian talk up the prowess of each duellist to the other, terrifying both. Antonio arrives, takes Viola for Sebastian, and intervenes, but is then recognised and arrested. He appeals to Viola for the money he has lent Sebastian, but she doesn't understand. Sir Toby encourages Sir Andrew to go after "Cesario" and restart the fight, but Sir Andrew runs into Sebastian instead. Sebastian clouts the heads of the two knights, then Olivia arrives, takes Sebastian for Cesario, and drags him off to church. They get married; Malvolio is mocked by Feste but eventually released; at the end the twins are reunited, Viola revealing herself as a woman and becoming engaged to Orsino. Malvolio leaves, swearing vengeance.

The Two Gentlemen of Verona (c. 1590)
Setting: Verona, Milan, the forest
Background: Despite the protestations of his best friend Proteus, the Veronese youth Valentine is determined to go forth and seek

his fortune at the court of the Duke of Milan, while Proteus remains behind and woos his beloved Julia.

Proteus prospers with Julia, while Valentine, who used to scorn at love, falls for and woos the Duke's daughter Silvia, whose father wants her to marry the foolish knight Thurio. Proteus' father Antonio sends him to Milan; he is loath to part with Julia, but goes, and is welcomed by Valentine, who confides in him his plan to elope with Silvia. Proteus, who has become infatuated with Silvia, betrays the plan to the Duke, and Valentine is banished. He joins a band of outlaws in the forest.

Julia has followed Proteus to Milan disguised as a boy and entered his service. She is shocked at his infidelity. Silvia gets her friend Sir Eglamour to help her escape the court. She is pursued by the Duke and Thurio, and also by Proteus, who is in turn pursued by Julia. Valentine captures Proteus and Julia, but cannot harm or even remain at odds with his friend. Julia reveals her identity and the lovers are reconciled. Thurio and the Duke are left with no choice but to accept this and pardon the outlaws.

Throughout comic relief is provided by Valentine's roguish servant Speed, Proteus' dull-witted servant Lance, and the latter's dog Crab.

The Winter's Tale (1609)

Setting: Sicily, Bohemia; an unspecified period of pre-Roman antiquity

Background: King Polixenes of Bohemia is about to head home after a long stay with his lifelong friend King Leontes of Sicily and Leontes' heavily pregnant wife Hermione.

Hermione, at Leontes' entreaty, persuades Polixenes to stay. Leontes falls into a sudden madness and becomes convinced that Polixenes is Hermione's lover and the father of her child. He suborns his courtier Camillo to poison his "rival", but Camillo warns Polixenes and they flee the court. Hermione is arrested and brought to trial; only her lady-in-waiting Paulina is brave enough to speak up for her. She bears a daughter but Leontes will not acknowledge the child and orders its death. Paulina's husband Antigonus begs mercy for the baby, so Leontes orders him to put to sea and abandon it on some distant shore. Antigonus departs. Meanwhile, Leontes' son Mamillius falls ill.

The Oracle of Apollo reveals that Hermione is innocent,

but Leontes refuses to believe even the god. Mamillius is reported dead and Hermione is carried out in a swoon. Paulina reports that the Queen has also died; Leontes at last recovers his wits and repents. Hermione appears to Antigonus in a dream, and tells him to name the child Perdita and leave her in Bohemia. Antigonus does so, but is eaten by a bear, while his ship is wrecked with all hands. An old shepherd and his son take Perdita in.

Sixteen years later, Perdita has become the sweetheart of Polixenes' son Florizel. While the trickster Autolycus robs Perdita's foster-brother of his purse, Polixenes and Camillo plot to infiltrate the shepherds' shearing festival in disguise to spy on Florizel's amours. Florizel and Perdita reveal their plans to marry, whereupon Polixenes throws off his disguise and utters bloodcurdling threats against Perdita and the shepherds. Camillo offers to help Florizel and Perdita elope to Sicily; Florizel changes clothes with Autolycus. The shepherds determine to tell Polixenes the truth about Perdita's adoption, but before they can reach the palace they meet Autolycus in Florizel's clothes and mistake him for a courtier. He tells them that Polixenes has put to sea to chase the lovers, and accompanies the shepherds to follow the King. In Sicily all is revealed and the kings reconciled; Autolycus is exposed but the shepherds forgive him.

Paulina invites the kings and their children to witness the unveiling of a statue of Hermione; the "statue" turns out to be the Queen herself, who is still alive. Paulina marries Camillo and all ends well.

The Sonnets (c. 1593 – c. 1604) also have a plot of a kind, although matters unconnected with the narrative do intrude into them. Since they have served as the basis for experimental films their narrative is worth recording here. Collectively, they concern a love triangle between three characters: the Poet, the Fair Youth, and the Dark Lady. In Sonnets 1 – 17, the Poet urges the Fair Youth to marry and beget children, so as not to leave the world with no copy of his beauty; 18 – 126 express the Poet's burgeoning love for the Youth, and pain that age and class separate them, while their relationship is further complicated by the attentions of a rival versifier and the Youth's affair with the Poet's mistress; 127 – 154 are addressed to the mistress herself, the Dark Lady, with whom the Poet is obsessed despite his self-disgust. Much ink has been spilled by those who take the sonnets as autobiography on the possible identities of Shakespeare's two beloveds.

Neither of Shakespeare's narrative poems (*The Rape of Lucrece; Venus and Adonis*) has yet been the basis for a film.

Note on entries:

Language is English unless otherwise stated, except in the case of silent films, where for obvious reasons no language listing has been given.

The "headline" title of each film is that of the first release, which is not always that by which it is best known in the English-speaking world. "A.k.a." does not cover every alternative title under which a film has been released: only English language titles and those used in countries involved in the production of the film are listed.

Stars and languages have not been listed for animated films, as these are conventionally dubbed for foreign release: in the index, however, credits for voice work on animated versions of the plays have been included. No lists of stars are provided for films which I have not seen, but actors named in the articles dealing with those films are of course indexed in the normal fashion.

The names of artists in whose native language surnames come first have been given in their Westernised forms, with the surname last.

Although television and straight-to-video adaptations have been omitted, films which have done the festival circuit without a commercial release have generally been included, as long as they were screened at more than one festival. Filmed excerpts from stage productions used in newsreels and cinemagazines in the period before television ownership became widespread in the 1950s have been omitted.

Many works that some might expect to find here have been excluded. Some films that cover much the same historical ground as works by Shakespeare (e.g. *Cajus Julius Caesar* (1914), *Tower of London* (1939/1962), *Coriolano: Eroe senza patria* (1964), etc.) have been omitted because they have too little in common with the plays.

A number of early pictures based on Victorien Sardou's *Cléopatre* (1890) and similar nineteenth century sources have been confused with Shakespeare's *Antony and Cleopatra*: so *Cléopatre* (1910), *Miss Helen Gardner in Cleopatra* (1912), *Marcantonio e Cleopatra* (1913), etc., find no place here. Likewise, "backstage" films make it only if their main plot significantly reflects that of the play: thus, no *Men Are Not Gods* (1936:

39

Othello), *It's Love I'm After* (1937: *Romeo and Juliet*), *In the Bleak Midwinter* (1995: *Hamlet*), etc. – nor, indeed, Popeye's turn as Romeo in *Shakespearian Spinach* (1940).

Many pre-independence Indian films lifted individual scenes from the plays and used them in completely different stories: these do not qualify. It is also not uncommon for the titles of films to refer to the better known plays, particularly *Romeo and Juliet*, because of superficial similarities which do not warrant inclusion here (e.g. *Romanoff and Juliet* (1961), *Romie-0 and Julie-8* (1978), *Romeo und Julia* (1992), *Romeo Must Die* (2000), etc.). There are, furthermore, many films which quite coincidentally share titles with the plays: e.g. *A Comedy of Errors* (1907) and *All's Well That Ends Well* (1914). Both of these hail from studios which were churning out Shakespeare adaptations at the time – Vitagraph and Thanhouser respectively – but neither of which has any connection with the Bard.

The line between a loose adaptation and an original picture which merely owes elements to Shakespeare is difficult to judge: but if the debt is unacknowledged, the film is unlikely to merit inclusion unless it follows the play very closely. (Thus, the sub-Hitchcockian noir *Strange Illusion* (1945), and the corporate thriller *Warui yatsu hodo yoku nemuru* (1960 – directed by Akira Kurosawa, elsewhere a notable interpreter of Shakespeare), both of which are at least partly rooted in *Hamlet*, nevertheless fail to qualify.)

King John (1899, U.K., black and white, silent)
A.k.a. *Beerbohm Tree, the Great English Actor* (U.S.A.)
Directed by Walter Pfeffer Dando and William K. L. Dickson
Starring: Herbert Beerbohm Tree
Runtime: 2 minutes (surviving footage)

The first work of Shakespeare to be committed to film in any form was *King John*, in 1899. The celebrated actor-manager Herbert Beerbohm Tree appropriated the new art form not primarily to provide a record of his theatrical production of the play, but rather to publicise it. The four separate scenes he filmed – of which only the third survives – were a sort of early trailers, designed to whet the punters' appetites and bring them to the theatre. Until 1899, it must be remembered, all films were single-scene: Georges Méliès' pioneering eleven-scene *L' Affaire Dreyfus*, which first overturned this model, appeared that year, and is unlikely to have been known to Tree when he made *King John*.

The surviving scene depicts the death of John, played by Tree himself. The lost scenes depicted Constance (Julia Neilson) lamenting over her betrayal; John suborning Hubert (Franklyn McLeay) to murder Arthur (Arthur Sefton); and the coronation of Henry III (Dora Senior). The misconception that the film included Tree's interpolated tableau depicting the signing of Magna Carta has now been laid to rest.

Various other actors stand around waiting for the end, but it is entirely Tree's show, and quite a meal he makes of it. It would be tempting to see in this snatch of film a window into nineteenth century acting styles, if one did not know that Tree had a reputation even at the time for excessive hamming. (His half-brother Max Beerbohm, covering *King John* for the *Saturday Review*, heaped praise on the production design, but carefully avoided mentioning Tree's performance.) He half-sits, half-lies in his throne, jerking and convulsing, for a minute and a half, and then it is over. It is hard to imagine being moved to anything but laughter by this display, but the production was apparently a great success.

Being so short and tightly focused, the film does not even serve as much of a record of the original staging, which was reportedly an outstanding example of the lavish style which Tree and his rival Henry Irving had brought to the London theatre in the 1890s in reaction against the relative minimalism of previous decades. The popularity which tub-thumpingly patriotic productions gave *King John* in the nineteenth century did not survive into the twentieth – even during World War Two, when Churchill was plundering this play for quotes, *Henry V* was seen as a better source of cinematic propaganda. *King John*'s neglect is undeserved.

Roméo et Juliette (1900, France, black and white)
Based on *Romeo and Juliet*
A.k.a. *Romeo and Juliet*
Directed by Clément Maurice
Believed lost

The Exposition Universelle, opened in Paris on 15th April 1900, featured among its attractions sound film. This was not an absolute novelty: synchronised sound had been film-makers' primary ambition since the invention of the moving picture, and many earlier attempts had been made: but, in competition with the official offerings, Clément Maurice of the Phono-Cinéma-Théâtre (an early associate of the Lumière brothers) presented seven sound shorts, achieved by recording voices and sound effects on wax cylinders after the actual filming. These included two comic interludes, two musical sequences, one series of tableaux originally designed to be silent, and two duel scenes (from *Cyrano de Bergerac* and *Hamlet*: for the latter, see below). One of the musical pieces was an aria from Gounod's *Roméo et Juliette*, sung by the tenor Emilio Cossira – making him the first actor to perform in a sound picture based on Shakespeare, although the Bard's words were first spoken on film by Sarah Bernhardt.

Le Duel d' Hamlet (1900, France, black and white)
Based on *Hamlet*
A.k.a. *Hamlet*
Directed by Clément Maurice
Starring: Sarah Bernhardt, Pierre Magnier
Runtime: 2 minutes

The seventh and final film in Maurice's cycle featured the greatest star in France, Sarah Bernhardt. It was not her first "breeches" part: she had, indeed, been playing Hamlet since the

1880s. It was, however, "the Divine Sarah"'s first film – and, so much did she dislike the experience, her last until she was tempted back for *Tosca* (1909), making it the only footage existing of the active woman she was before sustaining a crippling leg injury in 1905. The wax cylinder bearing her voice and the clashing of the swords is long since lost, but the film survives. At the time, *Le Figaro* spoke of its "rare perfection", while *Le Gaulois* called Maurice's achievement "prodigious":[3] certainly it is an impressive physical performance, although it is impossible now to recapture the effect on critics who had never encountered a film with sound before.

Burlesque on Romeo and Juliet (1902, U.S.A., black and white, silent)
Believed lost
   A convoluted skit on the balcony scene, *Burlesque* went unreviewed and was never heard of again after 1902.

The Tempest (1905, U.K., tinted, silent)
Directed by Charles Urban and Herbert Beerbohm Tree
Estimated runtime: 2 minutes
Believed lost
   "The shipwreck with all its intense realism is reproduced with startling detail. The lightnings flash, the billows leap and roll... the mast snaps and crashes to the deck... unquestionably one of the greatest triumphs of stage production ever attempted."[4]
   Thus Charles Urban, plugging his film of the opening scene from Herbert Beerbohm Tree's much praised *Tempest*. (Tree himself did not appear in the film, since Caliban, the part he played in the stage production, is not in this scene.) The picture was exported to the U.S.A. and well received.
   Incidentally, this may have been the first production of *The Tempest* to engage with the colonial themes that many modern critics have seen in the play. Unsurprisingly, Tree was entirely on Prospero's side: but whether or not he intended any

---

[3] Quoted by Ball, Robert Hamilton, *Shakespeare on Silent Film: A Strange Eventful History* (New York, 1968), p. 28.
[4] Ibid., pp. 31-32.

parallel with British imperialism, one member of the audience reported that the play aroused "a sting of conscience... for my Rhodesian friends"[5], directly comparing the dispossession of Caliban with that of the Matabele.

Duel Scene from Macbeth (1905, U.S.A., black and white, silent)
Based on *Macbeth*
Runtime: 1 minute

The only name to have come down to us associated with *Duel Scene* is that of the well-known cinematographer G. W. Bitzer, later a regular collaborator of the great director D. W. Griffith. A one minute, single shot scene, filmed in a theatre, can hardly have been a challenge to his talents.

The film was originally released as part of the American Mutoscope and Biograph Company's programme *Fights of Nations*, a filmed history of combat presented with live commentary.[6] Covering the almost instantaneous death of Young Seyward, the confrontation between Macbeth and Macduff, and the killing of Macbeth himself, it is indeed a fair depiction of claymore-and-buckler fighting.

The costumes, like the style of combat, belong more to the Highlands of the eighteenth century than to the era of the play; even the English Seyward wears a kilt and plaid. The huge, horsehair-fronted dress sporrans, however, are more modern still: and Macbeth's plumed helmet would look ridiculous in any era. His moustache and hairstyle would not be out of place in a particularly *outré* 1970s rock band, and it is difficult for the modern viewer to take this piece at all seriously.

Otello (1906, Italy, black and white, silent)
Based on *Othello*
Directed by Mario Caserini and Gaston Velle
Believed lost

---

[5] Quoted by Griffiths, Trevor R., "'This Island's Mine': Caliban and Colonialism", in *The Yearbook of English Studies*, Vol. 13 (1983), p. 160.
[6] *Fights of Nations* was copyrighted in 1907, but appears to have been released earlier; certainly my information is that it was filmed in 1905. It was not unusual in the early days of film for pictures never to be copyrighted at all..

Next to nothing is known about this *Otello*. In 1906, Mario Caserini was still primarily a painter: this is one of only two films he made *before* becoming artistic director of Cines.

Hamlet (1907, France, black and white, silent)
A.k.a. *Hamlet, Prince of Denmark*; *Hamlet and the Jester's Skull*
Directed by Georges Méliès
Estimated runtime: 10 minutes
Believed lost

Méliès' *Hamlet* appears to have consisted of his impressions of the play, rather than a direct adaptation: it opened with the graveyard scene, followed by apparitions not only of the deceased king but of Ophelia, then ended with a version of Act Five in which Laertes' sword was not poisoned, obliging the wounded Prince to commit suicide. A still of Méliès in the title role shows him posing in exaggerated style, his hand to his brow.

If one excepts *King John* (1899), whose four scenes were made to be shown separately, this was probably the first multi-scene picture derived from a play by Shakespeare. Sadly, it has not survived; the researches of Robert Hamilton Ball revealed that the negative had formed part of the mogul Leon Schlesinger's film collection, but had disappeared by Schlesinger's death in 1950, probably discarded in one of his periodic clearouts of decayed stock.

La Mort de Jules César (1907, France, black and white, silent)
Based on *Julius Caesar*
A.k.a. *Le Rêve de Shakespeare*; *Shakespeare Writing Julius Caesar* (international English title)
Directed by Georges Méliès
Estimated runtime: 10 minutes
Believed lost

La Mort de Jules César starred Georges Méliès as Shakespeare, stricken with writer's block two acts into *Julius Caesar*: according to contemporary accounts of the film, after abandoning several drafts, he falls asleep, and dreams the assassination scene; then as he wakes the film dissolves to a bust of the Bard decked with the flags of all nations (a touch typical of Méliès).

An alleged surviving print was last heard of in 1964, when its anonymous owner withdrew it at the last minute from a planned public showing.

Hamlet (1908, France, black and white, silent)
Directed by Henri Desfontaines
Believed lost
    Desfontaines' *Hamlet* for Éclipse starred the then 23-year-old Jacques Grétillat as the Prince and the possibly even younger Colonna Romano as his mother. I am unsure on what basis it is dated by the Internet Movie Database to 1908; Ball, who guessed at around 1910, felt unable to date it conclusively.

Romeo e Giulietta (1908, Italy, black and white, silent)
Based on *Romeo and Juliet*
A.k.a. *Romeo and Juliet* (U.S.A.)
Directed by Mario Caserini
Believed lost
    Although proclaimed by Cines as "the master film production of the year", Caserini's *Romeo e Giulietta* made little mark. The director and his wife Maria played the title roles.

La Bisbetica domata (1908, Italy, black and white, silent)
Based on *The Taming of the Shrew*
Directed by Azeglio Pineschi and Lamberto Pineschi
Believed lost
    The Pineschi brothers founded their own production company to make *La Bisbetica domata*, but no trace beyond the names survives of either the company or the film.

Amleto (1908, Italy, black and white, silent)
Based on *Hamlet*
A.k.a. *Hamlet* (U.S.A.)
Directed by Mario Caserini
Believed lost
    Very little is known about Caserini's first attempt to film *Hamlet*, which is often confused with his surviving (and distinctly unimpressive) 1910 version (q.v.). One remarkably favourable

British review survives, from which it appears that the film concentrated on the revenge plot to the near exclusion of other elements; that it included some picturesque location shooting – the reviewer was particularly charmed by a waterfall glimpsed in the ghost scene – and that the Ghost actually showed the Prince a vision of his murder. It appears that this vision, and the dead king himself, were rendered by double exposure.

Macbeth (1908, U.S.A., tinted, silent)
Directed by J. Stuart Blackton
Believed lost except for paper print
The Vitagraph Company of America, the largest U.S. film studio before Hollywood came into being, assumed the responsibility of making motion pictures respectable. The means was to be a programme of literary adaptations, in particular a number of Shakespearean films: and their first such foray was *Macbeth*. With the movement towards cinema censorship on the rise, it was hoped that the Bard's name would lend a touch of class, while still permitting some fairly racy plots: the offstage murder of Duncan (Charles Kent) was even brought onscreen. The outraged Chicago police censor demanded the deletion not only of this sequence but of the climactic duel, calling the film "worse than the bloodiest melodrama"[7]: less hostile reviewers remarked favourably on the use of double exposure, a technique in its infancy at the time, to show the viewer the visions displayed by the Witches to Macbeth (William V. Ranous).
Vitagraph, unlike many film companies of the pre-WWI era, was scrupulous about copyrighting its work, and routinely submitted paper prints of its films to the Library of Congress. Unfortunately, these prints were rarely stored in any sort of order: if they had been, it might be possible to reconstitute the film by photographing each frame individually, although obviously the result would hardly compare with a film print. In this instance there is a further complication: *Macbeth* by all accounts displayed to the full Vitagraph's unfortunate habit of trying to cram complex plots into very short adaptations – and without, apparently, the use of intertitles. One would have thought that this play, in terms of plot one of Shakespeare's simplest, would not pose such a problem, but there were

---

[7] Quoted by Ball, *Shakespeare on Silent Film*, p. 39.

apparently no fewer than seventeen scenes in only 835 feet of film, and its intelligibility appears to have been limited.

Romeo and Juliet (1908, U.S.A., silent)
Directed by J. Stuart Blackton
Runtime: 15 minutes
Not seen by current writer
      Vitagraph's *Romeo and Juliet*, starring Florence Lawrence and Paul Panzer – the latter wearing, to judge from stills, a somewhat distracting moustache – made considerable use of location shooting, mostly in Central Park. It was publicised as "magnificently staged, gorgeously costumed, and superbly acted"[8]; Ball notes the innovative use of cross-cutting, and that the Chicago censor approved the film – even comparing it specifically, and favourably, with *Macbeth*, on the grounds that "the love element, not the fight element, predominates... When [anyone] pays 5 cents to see *Macbeth* he pays to see a fight... love is fit for children to see, if kept within reason".[9]

Romeo and Juliet (1908, U.K., black and white, silent)
Believed lost
      The Lyceum Theatre's *Romeo and Juliet* was filmed in the open air at Fellow's Cricket Field in Dulwich, by the British branch of the Société des Etablissements L. Gaumont, in the summer of 1908. It starred Godfrey Tearle and Mary Malone; from both contemporary reports and information given by Tearle to Ball in 1947, it appears that a considerable amount of footage was shot before being edited down to one reel. It is reported that the cast availed themselves of their surroundings to play cricket in full costume between takes.

Othello (1908, U.S.A., black and white, silent)
A.k.a. *Jealousy* (U.S.A.)
Directed by William V. Ranous
Runtime: 10 minutes
Not seen by current writer

---

[8] Ibid., p. 44.
[9] Ibid., p. 45.

Vitagraph's *Othello* starred William Ranous and Julia Swayne Gordon, with Hector Dion as Iago, and probably appeared in September 1908. Although it is my understanding that the Library of Congress possesses a print, I can find no record suggesting that anybody has actually seen it.

Richard III (1908, U.S.A., black and white, silent)
Directed by J. Stuart Blackton and William V. Ranous
Estimated runtime: 10 minutes
Believed lost except for paper print
    Vitagraph's *Richard III*, starring, as usual, Ranous, was based on the Colley Cibber version of 1700, including a chunk of text from *Henry VI, Part 3* – actually *adding* material to a four hour play to make a ten minute film. To judge from the company's own quite detailed publicity, the film had seventeen separate scenes, and used several snippets of the play's text (and Cibber's additions) in the intertitles, a new departure for Vitagraph; the Battle of Bosworth was shot on location on Long Island. Thomas H. Ince, later a leading producer-director in early Hollywood, is alleged to have made his acting debut herein.

Antony and Cleopatra (1908, U.S.A., black and white, silent)
Directed by J. Stuart Blackton and Charles Kent
Estimated runtime: 10 minutes
Believed lost except for paper print
    Starring Maurice Costello and Florence Lawrence, rather younger than the mature lovers of the play, Vitagraph's heightened *Antony and Cleopatra* was well received on both sides of the Atlantic, but has survived only as disordered strips of paper.

The Tempest (1908, U.K., black and white, silent)
Directed by Percy Stow
Runtime: 12 minutes
    Although Stow is recorded as having directed nearly eighty films by 1916, little seems to be known about him, and next to nothing about this delightful gem of a film. He apparently had a taste for fantasies, notably *Alice in Wonderland*

(1903) and *Beauty and the Beast* (1905). The former shares *The Tempest*'s dreamlike qualities on a still smaller scale, and is justly highly regarded; *Beauty and the Beast* is believed lost.

Shakespeare's plot has necessarily been simplified, especially given the inclusion of the back-story (Prospero and Miranda arrive at the island, encounter Ariel and Caliban, and so forth): but this has been accomplished with a deft hand. The characters are strongly drawn – a stern, patriarchal Prospero, who bears a disconcerting resemblance to the Calvinist reformer John Knox; a hairy and ragged, but recognisably human and at times almost childlike, Caliban; a pretty Miranda, and quick-footed, magical Ariel.

Unusually for the Edwardian era, it is largely filmed on location – in lush and very English meadows, while the caves and seashore are shot in a theatre. It also makes use of what were in 1908 new, if not quite ground-breaking, special effects: Ariel can vanish, teleport, or shift shape while other characters are on screen, and one can hardly see the joins. (The bemusement of first Caliban and then Ferdinand at this carry-on is priceless.) The toy ship sinking in a cardboard sea is less impressive, but audiences at the time are hardly likely to have seen anything more convincing: and when, at the end, a full-sized version of the vessel appears, it really is hard to spot the lack of a third dimension.

This wonderful little fantasy may have lost some of its power to impress, but it has lost none of its charm.

Amleto (1908, Italy, black and white, silent)
Based on *Hamlet*
Directed by Luca Comerio
Believed lost

No details have survived concerning Comerio's *Hamlet* for Milano Films.

As You Like It (1908, U.S.A., black and white, silent)
Directed by Kenean Buel
Estimated runtime: 10 minutes
Believed lost

The Kalem Company's *As You Like It*, adapted by and starring Gene Gauntier, was heavily puffed by the company themselves on release, as "easily a masterpiece".[10] Filmed on location at the Windygoul estate near Cos Cob, Connecticut, with reportedly beautiful costumes and an accompanying lecture on the play, it should have succeeded – but critics of the time tell us that it was ineptly abbreviated and hard to follow, an effect exacerbated by lacklustre performances. The film was still available for viewing in 1910, but has not been heard of since.

The Taming of the Shrew (1908, U.S.A., black and white, silent)
Directed by D. W. Griffith
Starring: Arthur V. Johnson, Florence Lawrence, Linda Arvidson, Harry Solter
Runtime: 11 minutes

It is remarkable that Griffith, in his extraordinarily prolific career, tackled Shakespeare only once as director, in Biograph's slapstick take on *The Taming of the Shrew*. The film is a far cry from his later epics: the sets are small and enclosed, and each scene is shot from one angle only. Some of the director's trademarks, however, are already in evidence: the delight in constant action, and in crowding the screen with figures whose complex movements are perfectly blocked; and the close attention to detail. The set-dressing, a new concept in 1908, is expertly managed, and adds considerably to the realism of the piece.

Not that this realism passes muster if one is looking for a depiction of Shakespeare's own period. Both sets and costumes are of a later age, roughly the 1660s. Whether this is a deliberate attempt at period analogue, in which case it was considerably ahead of its time, or a mistake by somebody on the design team, the effect is comprehensive.

The film concentrates so exclusively on the Katharina / Petruchio storyline that what is left of the rest of the play makes very little sense; Bianca (played by Griffith's wife, Linda Arvidson) and her suitors have little place here. The dominant figure is a manic, violent Petruchio, played by Arthur V. Johnson in a moustache which makes him look to a modern viewer not unlike Groucho Marx – though his comedic style is altogether broader. In fact, it consists largely of brutalising his unfortunate servants, whom he repeatedly hurls across the

---

[10] Ibid., p. 61.

confined set, piling them into heaps and laying into them with a whip. This is apparently supposed to be amusing. His misbehaviour is given so much more screen time than his bride's (Florence "the Biograph Girl" Lawrence[11]) that the audience receives little sense of the "shrew", and sees only a bullied woman submitting to an unstable husband. The result is extremely distasteful.

Julius Caesar (1908, U.S.A., black and white, silent)
Directed by J. Stuart Blackton and William V. Ranous
Starring: Earle Williams, William V. Ranous, Charles Kent, Florence Lawrence
Runtime: 9 minutes

Julius Caesar may seem an odd choice of play to adapt immediately *after* its sequel, *Antony and Cleopatra*: but that is what the Vitagraph Company did. Though not the first of Vitagraph's Shakespeare shorts – indeed, by the time it appeared the industry critics were becoming slightly jaded with them, and it did not receive the enthusiastic notices of its predecessors – this was the film which finally achieved the purpose of the series, and won round the enemies of the cinema. In December 1908, all nickelodeon licenses in New York were revoked by mayoral order, as the cinema was deemed to be a corrupting influence: the trump card played by its defenders, in a campaign which swiftly resulted in their reopening, was *Julius Caesar*, whose example was held to demonstrate that "the moving picture [was] an artistic triumph of the century, a triumph which no devotee of the liberal arts could ignore and every true artist must celebrate".[12]

It would be hard for any film to live up to that kind of hype. Despite considerable attention to period detail in the set and costume design, *Julius Caesar* is not spectacular: the battle of Philippi, indeed, takes place off screen. It is, however, an intelligently filleted and ably performed version of the play,

---

[11] So called as opposed to "the Vitagraph Girl", Florence Turner, another major star whose career was to dry up with the advent of sound; although Lawrence also worked for Vitagraph.

[12] Quoted by Pearson, Roberta E., and Uricchio, William, "The Bard in Brooklyn: Vitagraph's Shakespeare Productions", in McKernan, Luke, and Terris, Olwen (eds), *Walking Shadows: Shakespeare in the National Film and Television Archive* (London, 1994), p. 205.

dominated by one of Vitagraph's leading lights, William V. Ranous, as a passionate Cassius, and featuring an assassination scene modelled on Jean-Léon Gérome's 1867 painting *The Death of Caesar*: and, as the picture which reopened New York's cinemas, its historical significance can hardly be denied.

The Merchant of Venice (1908, U.S.A., black and white, silent)
Directed by J. Stuart Blackton
Runtime: 9 minutes
Believed lost except for paper print

Tiring of Vitagraph's Shakespeare series, the critics met *The Merchant of Venice* with faint praise and outright sneers. "Shylock himself is not up to standard", declare *Moving Picture World* loftily of ubiquitous leading man William Ranous, "though perhaps he is better than some of the others".[13] The studio sets were, it was conceded, better than the performances.

Otello (1909, Italy, tinted, silent)
Based on *Othello*
Directed by Ugo Falena
Runtime: 11 minutes
Not seen by current writer

Film d' Arte Italiana, the Italian branch of Film d' Art, commenced in 1909 a series of hand-tinted Shakespeare films, beginning with an *Otello* starring Ferruccio Garavaglia, largely shot on location in Venice. Contemporary reviews indicate that it was as gorgeous to look at as the surviving films of the series, but that Garavaglia did not make a convincing lead. Ball relates an anecdote about a local gallant whose unwelcome advances to the film's Desdemona, Vittoria Lepanto, ended in his being thrown into a canal by Garavaglia and Angelo Pezzaglia (who played the Doge).

Giulio Cesare (1909, Italy, black and white, silent)
Based on *Julius Caesar*
A.k.a. *Brutus* (international English title); *Julius Caesar*
Directed by Giovanni Pastrone

---

[13] Quoted by Ball, *Shakespeare on Silent Film*, p. 50.

Starring: Giovanni Pastrone
Runtime: 7 minutes (surviving footage)

It is true that *Giulio Cesare* is a damaged print – lacking, for instance, Antony's funeral oration, although a title card announces it. Even when new, however, Italy's first *Julius Caesar* will have seemed notably unimpressive next to the previous year's American offering, despite touches of imagination such as the dream sequence in which the sleeping Calpurnia witnesses a spectral pre-enactment of her husband's murder. It is hurried and ill thought out, and the exaggeratedly physical performances of the stars (a square-jawed Brutus, a shifty Antony, and an hysterical Calpurnia, none of them identifiable, plus the director Giovanni Pastrone[14] as an excessively jovial Caesar) are laughable.

Its one advantage over the Vitagraph version is that it does include a convincingly staged battle of Philippi: the logistical difficulties of filming a battle scene with a small cast are resolved by having Antony and Octavius attack the conspirators' camp, so that the fighting takes place amid tents and smoking fires which would naturally hide the numbers involved; and its one point of interest is its political angle. In Italy, between unification in 1861 and the Fascist takeover in 1922, there was considerable uncertainty over how to view this period of Roman history: ought a patriot to honour Caesar for expanding the power of Rome, or excoriate him for subverting the Republic? Unlike the 1914 biopic *Cajus Julius Caesar*, this picture comes down squarely on the republican side.

Hamlet (1909, France, black and white, silent)
Starring: Mounet-Sully
Runtime: 1 minute (surviving footage)

Mounet-Sully, considered the greatest French actor of the Belle Époque, was by 1909 in his late sixties, and had been playing the Prince of Denmark for well over thirty years. It was, indeed, his performance that had inspired Jules Laforgue to write "*Hamlet* ou les suites de la piété filiale" in 1887: *vide* the film *Un Amleto di meno* (1973). "Hamletism" itself, that melancholy malady of the French poets, owes much to the actor.

At some point, he recorded a film of at least the

---

[14] Later to make the blazingly innovative epic *Cabiria* (1914).

graveyard scene, a short excerpt of which survives. The whole of the known surviving footage was used in the 1947 film *Paris 1900*, a celebration of life in the city before the catastrophe of August 1914.[15] *Paris 1900*'s quotations from both film and theatre show Parisian acting in the period to have been highly overblown[16]: next to most of the other examples, the *Hamlet* scene appears modest and unremarkable.

Mounet-Sully is frequently, and wrongly, referred to as "Jean Mounet-Sully"; some resources even call his brother Paul (q.v.) "Paul Mounet-Sully". In fact, the elder brother was born Jean-Sully Mounet, and adopted "Mounet-Sully" as his stage name; Paul was only ever Paul Mounet. 1909 appears to be a conjectural date – the film is listed under that year on the Internet Movie Database, but I can find no definite reference for it, and most film historians are non-committal. A date no earlier than 1908, and no later than 1911, is, at least, highly probable.

Othello (1909, Germany, black and white)
A.k.a. *Desdemona*
Directed by Franz Porten
Believed lost

Franz Porten used to film scenes for Oskar Messter, featuring his daughters Henny and Rosa, and sometimes himself, to be shown accompanying operatic recordings. One such was his 1909 film of an extract from the last act of Verdi's *Otello*, in which he played the Moor to Henny's Desdemona. Confusion over the dating of this picture has led some film historians to assume, mistakenly, that *Desdemona* (its alternative title) was a separate film.

Le Songe d'une Nuit d'été (1909, France, black and white, silent)
Based on *A Midsummer Night's Dream*
Believed lost

---

[15] The same film features footage of Firmin Gémier as both Shylock and Julius Caesar, but these are theatre-shot and almost certainly taken from cinemagazine footage advertising stage productions. *Hamlet* was filmed outdoors.

[16] Including Mounet-Sully himself in possibly his most famous role, that of Oedipus.

Le Songe starred British comedian George Footit and Russian *danseuse* Stacia Napierkowska. The identity of the director is unknown.

King Lear (1909, U.S.A., black and white, silent)
A.k.a. *Shakespeare's Tragedy, King Lear* (copyright title)
Directed by J. Stuart Blackton and William V. Ranous
Starring: William V. Ranous, Julia Swayne Gordon, Florence Turner
Runtime: 9 minutes

King Lear is one of the most egregious examples of the difficulty some adaptors had with Shakespearean shorts: viz., how to fit plays meant to last between two and four hours into a few minutes of film? It is difficult to maintain much sense of tragedy when the atrocities are piling on top of one another at this pace; and the picture is not helped by a studio-bound shoot with some of the least convincing painted backdrops ever used, nor by some frankly cartoonish ideas. Edgar hides from the hue and cry in a conveniently placed hollow tree which his pursuers completely fail to notice: this is supported by the text, but when the stage is bare apart from the tree it is quite incredible that they miss it. In the storm scene, rain and lightning have been represented by crude zigzags scratched onto the film. The look of the play is interesting: the costumes have apparently been based on etchings of Gaulish and Frankish warriors from François Guizot's *Histoire de France* and similar works: but the resulting evocation for the modern viewer will be of Asterix and Obelix.

Frenetic performances and hyperactive direction abet the headlong downhill rush through the play, resulting in one of Vitagraph's least successful adaptations.

Macbeth (1909, Italy, black and white, silent)
Directed by Mario Caserini
Not seen by current writer

Caserini's lavish and award-winning *Macbeth* was shown in several countries to notable acclaim, and it is reported that the Library of Congress possesses a surviving print. It starred Dante Cappelli (better known as a director) and Caserini's wife Maria.

A Midsummer Night's Dream (1909, U.S.A., black and white, silent)
Directed by J. Stuart Blackton and Charles Kent
Starring: William V. Ranous, Florence Turner, Julia Swayne Gordon, Gladys Hulette
Runtime: 12 minutes

Like other Vitagraph Shakespeares, notably *King Lear* (1909), this *Dream* suffers from its attempt to cram the entire story of the play into a single reel; the effect is rushed and confusing, and viewers unfamiliar with the original text must have found the film hard to follow. It is made all the more perplexing by the inexplicable replacement of Oberon with the extra-textual character Penelope (Clara Kimball Young), in defiance of the Vitagraph policy of strict fidelity to literary sources. Surely Young could have played Oberon, a part not uncommonly given to women in the early twentieth century. (Puck is played by a girl, twelve-year-old Gladys Hulette, who brings to the role a tremendous energy and sense of fun.)

William V. Ranous stars as an exuberant Bottom, throwing himself into the role with gusto. The art of exaggerating a performance just enough to give it the necessary impact in a silent picture without going risibly over the top is a tricky one, but Ranous was a master of it. (Hulette still steals scenes even from him.)

The effects are surprisingly effective for 1909: the string may be visible by which Ranous operates the jaw of his ass's head, but the head otherwise looks quite convincing; the sets and costumes are authentically Greek, albeit Classical rather than Mycenaean; the location shots (in New York's Prospect Park) are suitably Arcadian; and when Hulette puts a girdle round the earth we are treated to the planet's furious spinning behind her as she flies. For the viewer who knows the play well this is a pleasant, amusing little film: it is just a pity that Vitagraph were so overambitious.

Macbeth (1909, France, black and white, silent)
Directed by André Calmettes
Runtime: 10 minutes
Not seen by current writer

Film d' Art's *Macbeth* starred Paul Mounet (younger brother of Mounet-Sully) and Jeanne Delvair of the Comédie.

Ball reports that it included versions of all major scenes, plus an interpolated coronation sequence in which Banquo refuses to recognise Macbeth's right to rule; also that it was too fast to follow easily, stagily blocked, and that the indoor scenes appear to have been entirely shot in a theatre.

Re Lear (1910, Italy, black and white, silent)
Directed by Giuseppe de Liguoro
Believed lost

Giuseppe de Liguoro directed himself as Lear in this Milano production. No stills, reviews, or publicity material have survived.

Hamlet (1910, U.K., black and white, silent)
Directed by William G. B. Barker
Believed lost

Captain Will Barker, founder of Ealing Studios, filmed the first British *Hamlet* picture in a single day on a lot adjoining his house, with pantomime artist Charles Raymond playing the Prince opposite an Ophelia cast principally for her ability to swim. Robert Hamilton Ball spent years chasing this film to no avail: the negative had vanished, and even Barker was able to provide very little information, most of it unreliable.

Amleto (1910, Italy, black and white, silent)
Based on *Hamlet*
A.k.a. *Hamlet*
Directed by Mario Caserini
Starring: Amleto Novelli, Fernanda Negri Pouget
Runtime: 6 minutes (surviving footage)

It is hard to believe that Caserini's *Amleto* was not intended as a parody; it is reminiscent of nothing so much as the cavortings of the Reduced Shakespeare Company. With little or no help from the title cards, scenes whizz by in seconds; it is true that several of them are incomplete, but considering that the original film ran only to ten minutes – and that what is left of it ends abruptly in the middle of Ophelia's funeral – not much material can be missing from the individual scenes which remain, in which gesticulating hams in clearly brand new costumes chase each other around with murderous intent for no reason that an audience has any hope of grasping.

There exists some confusion over this film. Although researchers at the British Film Institute established in the 1990s that the star was the appropriately named Amleto Novelli (who went on to play both Marc Antony and Julius Caesar in biopics often misattributed to Shakespeare), many reference works still have Dante Cappelli in the role. Others confuse this film with Caserini's first stab at *Hamlet*, made in 1908. If this is what the director made to improve upon his original, the 1908 *Amleto* must have been appalling.

Hamlet (1910, Denmark, black and white, silent)
Directed by August Blom
Believed lost

The first *Hamlet* to be filmed at the real Elsinore (the Kronborg, Helsingör), before the now regular on-location performances of the play were instituted in 1915, appears to have been extraordinarily lavish. A huge cast (including the famous stage Hamlet Alwin Neuss, all white face and mad stare, in the title role) was utilised, and it was rumoured that the equivalent of some ten reels of footage had been shot before it was edited down to the single reel on which the studio insisted for distribution.

Even in this butchered condition, the picture was rhapsodised over by the critics, especially in the U.K.: "splendid... masterpiece... beautiful... magnificent"[17] were some of the more restrained epithets heaped on its head. The unity of story and excellence of photography are alike praised, and it is greatly to be deplored that the film has not survived.

Romeo se fait bandit (1910, France, tinted, silent)
Based on *Romeo and Juliet* and *The Two Gentlemen of Verona*
A.k.a. *Romeo turns bandit* (U.S.A.)
Starring: Max Linder
Runtime: 6 minutes

Pathé's modern dress comedy is more inspired by *Romeo and Juliet* than directly founded on it. It begins as a similar tale of

---

[17] Ball, *Shakespeare on silent film.*, pp. 109-11.

star-crossed lovers, taking the line "The orchard walls are high and hard to climb" as the cue for a parody of the balcony scene in which much comic play is made of the difficulty of climbing high enough to attain the forbidden kiss; but thereafter the plot departs into a different play altogether, as Romeo (comic actor Max Linder, the only member of the cast whose name has survived, playing him as an upper class joker in a straw hat) becomes Valentine in *The Two Gentlemen of Verona*. Like Valentine, he is exiled not for a killing but purely for his love; falls in with bandits and takes to their trade; captures those who stand between him and Juliet / Silvia, and forces a happy ending.

At a time when original text productions were uniformly antiquarian, only a version like this – which appropriates the bare bones of a story but no poetry – could get away with transferring the action to contemporary France, where the young wear boaters and blazers and the old tweed caps, and shotguns are more in evidence than rapiers (although at one point two of Romeo's friends are seen practising their fencing). The most noticeable feature of the French setting, however, is not the twentieth century costumes, but the quite spectacular scenery. Shot entirely outdoors and largely in the countryside, *Romeo turns bandit* utilises a gorgeous backdrop of mountains, forests, and rivers in high summer, all in gently tinted Pathécolor.

Twelfth Night (1910, U.S.A., black and white, silent)
Directed by Eugene Mullin and Charles Kent
Starring: Julia Swayne Gordon, Charles Kent, Florence Turner, Marin Sais
Runtime: 12 minutes

The Vitagraph adaptation of *Twelfth Night* displays the company's bad habit of trying to cram complex Shakespearean plots into very short films, but intelligent pruning and concise title cards help it to achieve this rather better than most of its predecessors. It still helps, however, if the viewer is familiar with the play.

Co-director Charles Kent stars as Malvolio, opposite Julia Swayne Gordon as a dignified Olivia. He displays as well as the silent medium allows a deft comic touch and an understanding of the character, moving with pomp and deliberation; his very appearance is good for a laugh, and demonstrates that Vitagraph could manage without William Ranous, who had left the company at the end of 1909. (Kent had been with them for some time as a director, having retired from the stage in 1906 because his voice was going – not a handicap for a silent movie actor.) Florence Turner makes a charming Viola, and the opera singer Marin Sais, incongruously clad in what looks like an Edwardian maid's uniform while the rest of the cast wear Elizabethan costume, is a joyous and life-loving Maria.

The cast's enjoyment of the play is obvious, and infectious. Even today, the film can still raise a smile.

The Winter's Tale (1910, U.S.A., black and white, silent)
Directed by Theodore Marston and Barry O'Neil
Starring: Martin Faust, Amelie Barleon, Frank Hall Crane, Anna Rosemond
Runtime: 13 minutes (surviving footage)

By 1910, American critics had somewhat tired of the Shakespeare shorts that had been pouring out of Vitagraph's Brooklyn studios for the past two years, and room had opened up for competition: so Edwin Thanhouser decided to add the Bard to the repertoire of Thanhouser Classics, beginning with *The Winter's Tale*. The industry papers responded warmly: "a masterpiece", they declared, "a triumph", "we have never seen better acting... Mr Thanhouser deserves the heartiest congratulations".[18]

In 1917, a fire destroyed some ninety per cent of the Thanhouser Corporation's stock, and it was for many decades believed that *The Winter's Tale* was among the lost films; an incomplete print eventually surfaced, however, and was in due course reacquired by the reconstituted Corporation and released on DVD in 2007. It is indeed a handsome film, and, in its use of multiple Grecianesque sets and location shots, more ambitious than most of Vitagraph's offerings. The ruthlessly pruned plot (Mamillius, the oracle, Autolycus, even the death of Antigonus, all fall by the wayside) is conveyed ably enough through the intertitles, although Shakespeare's dialogue is badly missed. But the broad performances hardly justify the rhapsodies of the critics, and the scene they praised the most, the resurrection of

---

[18] Ibid., p. 69.

Hermione (Anna Rosemond), is missing.

Re Lear (1910, Italy, tinted, silent)
Based on *King Lear*
Directed by Gerolamo Lo Savio
Starring: Ermete Novelli, Francesca Bertini, Olga Giannini Novelli
Runtime: 16 minutes

The casting of *Re Lear* is a marriage of theatre and cinema, with classical stage luminary Ermete Novelli in the title role and the rising young film star Francesca Bertini as Cordelia.

The most instantly striking thing about the film is the detailed colour tinting, done entirely by hand – no other method existed in 1910. The weird and wonderful Ancient Britain created by Lo Savio, with costumes ranging from the Biblical to the Burgundian, is brought to life in vivid pinks, greens and yellows. Occasional surprises notwithstanding – shooting outdoors, Lo Savio could neither simulate nor wait for a thunderstorm (and might not have been able to film in it anyway), so Lear goes mad under a smiling sun – the film is a faithful rendition of the play, though lacking the Gloucester subplot for the sake of simplicity; and its visual sumptuousness, combined with powerfully moving performances by Novelli and Bertini, makes it a treat to watch.

The Merry Wives of Windsor (1910, U.S.A., black and white, silent)
Directed by Francis Boggs
Not seen by current writer

The Selig Polygraph Company's *Merry Wives*, reviewed at the time as "relatively satisfactory"[19], is reported to have been severely truncated, concentrating solely on the Falstaff plot.

Il Mercante di Venezia (1910, Italy, tinted, silent)
Based on *The Merchant of Venice*
Directed by Gerolamo Lo Savio
Starring: Ermete Novelli, Olga Giannini Novelli, Francesca

---

[19] Ibid., p. 68.

Bertini

Runtime: 19 minutes / 10 minutes (surviving footage)

Film d'Arte Italiana's second surviving hand-tinted Shakespearean outing is not of the same standard as *Re Lear* (1910). This is not entirely the company's fault: the film has not survived undamaged, with the result that parts of it (including the ending) are missing. Some of the flaws, however, were present from the start.

The more complex plot of *The Merchant of Venice* proved harder to condense than that of *King Lear*, with the result that the film is difficult to follow, and would surely be so even if it had survived intact. It concentrates very heavily on Shylock's side of the story, with Ermete Novelli playing the moneylender. After the flight of Jessica (the charming Francesca Bertini), he succeeds in raising Shylock to something not far short of the tragic stature he gave Lear: but before this point has been rather too jovial and ingratiating for comfort. This performance may indeed help to make sense of Shylock's "merry sport", but there is an ugly whiff of anti-Semitism about it – although it is certainly less objectionable than some Shylocks that were appearing in the theatre in those days, and for decades afterwards. But Novelli's wife Olga, who had been a competent Goneril in *Re Lear*, is sadly miscast as Portia. Her overblown frame and florid acting style are entirely out of place.

On the credit side, the film is as beautifully shot and expertly painted as *Re Lear*. Made on location in Venice, like *Otello* (1909) it provides one of our earliest filmed records of the city whose destruction was being demanded by the Futurists, and reminds us just how lucky we are that they were not heeded.

Julius Caesar (1911, U.K., black and white, silent)
Directed by William G. B. Barker and Frank R. Benson
Estimated runtime: 10 minutes
Believed lost

In the early spring of 1911, the Co-operative Cinematograph Company of London entered into an agreement with the F. R. Benson Company to film and release commercially all six productions of the latter's season at the Shakespeare Memorial Theatre, Stratford upon Avon. The first of these was *Julius Caesar*, commended in industry papers as "well acted and adapted".[20] Sir Frank Benson directed himself as Antony and his wife Constance as Portia to Murray Carrington's Brutus. The Co-operative films were never more than records of the stage productions; for more details, see *Richard III* (1911).

Macbeth (1911, U.K., black and white, silent)
Believed lost
    Macbeth was the second picture in the Co-operative / Benson series of condensed Shakespeare adaptations. Longer than *Julius Caesar*, it appears to have been a more complete record of the play, but very little is known about it.

Henry VIII (1911, U.K., black and white, silent)
Directed by William G. B. Barker
Estimated runtime: 25 minutes
Believed lost
    Sir Herbert Beerbohm Tree, as the actor-manager had by now become, presented at His Majesty's Theatre in 1910 a three act rearrangement of the first four acts of *Henry VIII*: the inferior fifth act, probably written entirely by John Fletcher, was omitted, so that the end of the play focused on the fall of Wolsey, while the climax of the pageantry was not the christening of Elizabeth but the coronation of Anne (Laura Cowie). The lavish spectacle, and Tree's own flamboyant turn as the Cardinal, ensured the play's success, and Will Barker approached Tree to suggest a film adaptation. A contract was worked out under which Tree would be paid a thousand pounds – the biggest fee the British film industry had yet seen – for Barker's right to make twenty prints which would be leased to selected cinemas for six weeks, then destroyed.
    Replicas of the theatrical sets were built at Ealing, and the cast, including extras, decamped thither with their costumes and weapons by the cartload on 9th February 1911. The eleven scenes to which Tree had reduced the sixteen of the play were further whittled down to five, depicting the fall of Buckingham (Basil Gill), Henry's (Arthur Bourchier) first meeting with Anne, the trial of Catherine (Violet Vanbrugh), the disgrace of Wolsey, and the coronation. The result was a piece that the critics

---

[20] Ibid., p. 84.

adored, and that was still able to be described in 1917 – by which time the cinematic art had advanced considerably since 1911 – as "one of the finest picture-plays ever produced".[21] Surviving stills (and photographs of the stage production, from which the stills of the film are scarcely distinguishable) reveal the picture's large cast, close attention to period detail, and painterly aesthetic.

On 13th April, all twenty prints of what was commonly held to be the greatest British film yet made were ceremonially burned in the presence of the press at Ealing Studios. Rumours persisted that Barker, or Tree, or both, had secreted the negative or an unofficial extra print, but none such ever came to light. Ball, on whose invaluable (if slightly outdated) book *Shakespeare on Silent Film* (1968) I have relied heavily for this picture, contacted Barker just before his death in 1951: he was unable to remember if he had kept a copy, but certainly none turned up among his effects: and we must conclude that *Henry VIII* is lost for good.

La Mégère apprivoisée (1911, France, black and white, silent)
Based on *The Taming of the Shrew*
A.k.a. *The Taming of the Shrew* (U.K.; U.S.A.)
Directed by Henri Desfontaines
Not seen by current writer

Although *Moving Picture World* declared Desfontaines' *Shrew* "well acted and beautifully staged",[22] the magazine's account sounds suspiciously like faint praise; as Ball remarks, this "is hardly a play which should emerge on film as 'graceful and dignified'".[23] Ball could find no surviving prints, but I understand that the Library of Congress now possesses one.

Le Roi Lear au village (1911, France, black and white, silent)
Based on *King Lear*
A.k.a. *A Village King Lear* (U.S.A.)
Directed by Louis Feuillade
Not seen by current writer

The extraordinarily prolific Feuillade, who directed some

---

[21] Ibid., p. 82.
[22] Ibid., p. 129.
[23] Ibid.

seven hundred films over the course of his career, made for Gaumont this curiosity, set in modern France. The Lear figure is a blind farmer and has only two daughters; all subplots have disappeared, and the family is in the end reluctantly reconciled. Without the direct Shakespearean reference in the title, it would hardly merit inclusion here.

Falstaff (1911, France, black and white, silent)
Based on *The Merry Wives of Windsor*
Directed by Henri Desfontaines
Believed lost

Desfontaines' *Falstaff* for Eclipse Films, starring the otherwise unknown Monsieur Degeorge (who appears in stills to have been admirably suited to the part physically, possessing not only a round belly but a full beard and a delightfully expressive face), ruthlessly pruned *The Merry Wives*. The wedding of Anne and Fenton was got out of the way at the beginning, Mistress Quickly was conflated with the Host to economise and bring her closer to her incarnation in *Henry IV*, and all characters not directly related to the main plot appear to have been eliminated.

Falstaff was released internationally, and the acting and photography were widely praised.

The Taming of the Shrew (1911, U.K., black and white, silent)
Directed by Frank R. Benson
Believed lost

Although it attracted the same bland and uninformative praise as its predecessors, very little data has survived about the Benson Company's *Shrew*. Apart from Sir Frank and Lady Benson themselves, it is not even known who appeared in it.

Richard III (1911, U.K., black and white, silent)
Directed by Frank R. Benson
Starring: Frank R. Benson, Alfred Brydone, Murray Carrington, Constance Benson, Kathleen Yorke
Runtime: 23 minutes

The only Co-operative / Benson film to have survived gives us a flavour of what these filmed plays were like, and somewhat belies the generous reaction of the industry press to the earlier adaptations. The camera stays stock still, giving an audience's-eye view of the stage, all of which is visible on screen throughout, with nary a close-up or a varied angle. The only use of cinematic technique is in the ghost scene, where, instead of being seen to enter and exit, the various spirits are made to materialise and vanish at the foot of Richard's bed.

As a record of the British theatre before World War One, however, this is a fascinating document. The version of the play used by Benson, although it represents a return to something slightly more authentic than Colley Cibber's 1700 adaptation, is heavily influenced by it: the film incorporates at the beginning the Battle of Tewkesbury and the murder of King Henry from *Henry VI, Part 3*, scenes which do help to make sense of this play. But in this version, Richard alone must stab Edward of Lancaster, who in the earlier play was slain by all three York brothers: to relieve Edward and George of this guilt makes the play rather more black-and-white than Shakespeare's version, which indeed was what Cibber intended.

The scenes of the film are divided by title cards, telling us where we are in the text and providing an appropriate quotation, as if Benson envisaged his audience watching it with a copy of the script in front of them. (Indeed, if they were not, they might find the film somewhat difficult to follow: an acquaintance with the play is assumed throughout.) Each scene, in keeping with Cibber's melodramatic tendencies, focuses on a fresh atrocity by Benson's crookbacked king. It is hard to believe that this swaggering, flamboyant scoundrel has "no delight to pass away the time", or could ever convince anyone of his virtue: he struts cheerfully through the play, bullying subordinates, butchering his enemies, seducing the tearful Lady Anne (played by Lady Benson) and generally enjoying his own villainy.

The murder of the Princes in the Tower is an undeniably affecting scene: but it is hard to get away from the fact that, like the young Henry III in Beerbohm Tree's *King John* (1899), they are played by women. This reversal of the practice of Shakespeare's day was commonplace in the early twentieth century, but is thoroughly alien to a modern audience.

And so on we go to the finale, when Benson wheels his cast of dozens back onto the stage for the Battle of Bosworth Field, which is handled as well as the limitations under which he laboured permit: but all told, *Richard III* is sadly unimpressive. The fourth in a series of what should have been six Shakespeare films, it became the last when the Co-operative Cinematograph Company pulled out of their unprofitable partnership, leaving Benson's *The Merry Wives of Windsor* and *Twelfth Night* unfilmed.

Bruto (1911, Italy, black and white, silent)
Based on *Julius Caesar*
A.k.a. *Brutus* (U.S.A.)
Directed by Enrico Guazzoni
Runtime: 11 minutes
Not seen by current writer

"Every scene being taken in the open air, the photographic quality is perfect throughout. The action is brisk and easily followed and without a single foot of unnecessary padding, the result being a set of perfect pictures that cannot fail to interest and impress every class of audience."[24] Subsequent reviewers have largely agreed with the verdict of the *Kinematograph and Lantern Weekly* on Enrico Guazzoni's spectacular for Cines, based on Acts III-V of *Julius Caesar*; stills reveal the ambition, visual sensibility and striking set design which went into the picture.

Guazzoni went on to direct *Marcantonio e Cleopatra* (1913) and *Cajus Julius Caesar* (1914), both of which have been mistakenly identified with Shakespeare's plays on the same subjects.

For Åbent Tæppe (1911, Denmark, tinted, silent)
Based on *Othello*
A.k.a. *Desdemona*
Directed by August Blom
Starring: Valdemar Psilander, Thyra Reimann
Runtime: 23 minutes

Blom's *For Åbent Tæppe* is one of the earliest examples of the sub-genre (cf. *Kiss Me Kate* (1953), *Shakespeare In Love* (1998), etc.) of films about productions of Shakespeare plays in which the action onstage is mirrored by events in the lives of the actors. Einar and Maria Lowe (Valdemar Psilander and Thyra Reimann) are a husband-and-wife duo playing Othello and Desdemona while their own marriage falls apart. Their own

---

[24] Ibid., p. 116.

characters do not mirror their roles – Einar is nervous and jumpy, Maria cool and assured – but their lives end up mirroring the play, down to its tragic end.

There is no single Iago figure in Blom's story. Rather, while it is a rejected suitor of Maria – an unctuous low-life more like Uriah Heep than Shakespeare's villain – who first sows suspicion in Einar's mind, he later receives reports from various different characters which suggest that his wife is having an affair with a wealthy patron. It may, indeed, be true: whether deliberately or through careless storytelling, Blom leaves the nature of the relationship ambiguous. (Maria is twice seen to kiss her supposed lover, but in a public place where it would be dangerously indiscreet to flaunt an adulterous affair.)

The vagueness resulting from the paucity of title cards[25] makes the film somewhat difficult to follow, and the constantly changing background colour from scene to scene – the picture is now brown, now green, now purple – is a distraction and of little help in the creation of mood. What Blom has succeeded in doing, however, is to recreate on film the two overlapping but very different worlds of the Danish theatre and the aristocratic high life in 1911. We move from dressing rooms to five-star hotels, both rendered in impressive detail, and are given a strong impression of the social gap between the actors and our moustachioed Cassio figure.

Only after seventeen minutes of this pseudo-*Othello*, with very little time apparently devoted to rehearsal (and, necessarily but implausibly, none together) do we finally reach the play: and, at its climax, the now demented Einar becomes the Moor and murders Maria on stage, before rounding on the audience and furiously pointing out his rival in his box. The police rush in, Einar is arrested, the play is given over – and the film ends. There is no explanatory epilogue, no tying-up of loose ends; anybody unacquainted with *Othello* would be left utterly mystified. *For Åbent Tæppe* may be a useful document for the social or theatrical historian, but it is hardly a satisfying film.

Romeo and Juliet (1911, U.S.A., black and white, silent)
Directed by Barry O'Neil

---

[25] Some of which are almost certainly missing, as contemporary summaries give names to characters unnamed in the surviving intertitles and credits.

Estimated runtime: 30 minutes
Not seen by current user

Thanhouser's *Romeo and Juliet*, starring George Lessey and Julia M. Taylor, was made in two reels: but, owing to technical considerations, the reels were released separately, "so constructed that each tells a complete story"[26] according to *Moving Picture World*; the first reel is now missing. Ball found Lessey too old for the part,[27] but remarked on the striking sets and costumes; it was widely agreed that having extra space in which to tell the story made it a considerable improvement over earlier, more confined efforts.

The Tempest (1911, U.S.A., black and white, silent)
Directed by Edwin Thanhouser
Believed lost

The only Bardic adaptation which Edwin Thanhouser directed in person received mediocre notices, although the "sprightliness"[28] of the unnamed Ariel was remarked, as was the prettiness of the scenery.

Hamlet (1912, U.K., black and white, silent)
Directed by Charles Raymond
Believed lost

Raymond, the star of Will Barker's 1910 *Hamlet*, directed himself in the same role two years later.

Romeo e Giulietta (1912, Italy, tinted, silent)
Based on *Romeo and Juliet*
A.k.a. *Romeo and Juliet* (UK.; U.S.A.)
Directed by Ugo Falena
Runtime: 37 minutes
Not seen by current writer

Film d' Arte Italiana's longest and most ambitious Shakespeare adaptation starred Francesca Bertini and Gustavo Serena as the lovers.

---

[26] Ball, *Shakespeare on silent film*, p. 70.
[27] In fact, at 32, he was a year younger than his co-star.
[28] Ball, *Shakespeare on silent film*, p. 70.

Indian Romeo and Juliet (1912, U.S.A., black and white, silent)
Based on *Romeo and Juliet*
Directed by Laurence Trimble
Believed lost

The only Vitagraph Shakespeare adaptation not to have survived even as a paper print was this reworking of *Romeo and Juliet* (which they had made "straight" four years earlier), the brainchild of Hal Reid, who played the Capulet figure to his son Wallace's Romeo and Florence Turner's Juliet. The story was transferred from Verona to the Mohawk Valley before the Europeans arrived, with Hurons as Montagues and Mohicans as Capulets, and a medicine man (Oyenkwa: Hal Wilson) standing in for Friar Laurence. Vitagraph's publicity, possibly with tongue in cheek, calls the picture "far more Shakespearian than Shakespeare".[29]

Cardinal Wolsey (1912, U.S.A., black and white, silent)
Based on *Henry VIII*
Directed by J. Stuart Blackton and Laurence Trimble
Starring: Hal Reid, Julia Swayne Gordon, Tefft Johnson, Clara Kimball Young
Runtime: 10 minutes

As indicated by the change in title, this is the least textually faithful of Vitagraph's Shakespeare adaptations. Indeed, not a word of the Bard appears until the very last title card ("Had I but served my God with half the zeal / I served my King, He would not in mine age / Have left me naked to mine enemies"). Covering Acts Two to Four of the play, Hal Reid's adaptation is marked by an unpleasant strain of anti-Catholic sentiment. Wolsey (Reid) is always brandishing a crucifix to assert his authority, and thereby retains the trust of Queen Catherine (Julia Swayne Gordon) – a departure from the play, her repudiation of him being excised; and it is he who (in defiance of both history and Shakespeare) pronounces sentence of excommunication on Henry. He is seen as a blight on the realm which can be lifted only by Protestantism, and it is not until his brief final scene that Reid's serpentine characterisation

---

[29] Ibid., p. 136.

is tempered with any humanity. (There is, I suppose, a sort of negative sympathy for the Cardinal, in that his opposition to the equally unlikeable Henry (Tefft Johnson) is exaggerated; some critics have managed to find Reid's Wolsey heroic.) It is hard not to conclude that a desire to glorify the Protestant Reformation was responsible for the distortion of the play.

There is no denying that Reid's performance, and that of Julia Swayne Gordon as a pitiable Catherine, are impressive; less so is Johnson's clowning as a childish King, with bizarre painted-on eyebrows. The film was made on cramped studio sets, but some inventive backdrop painting relieves the claustrophobia, a trick of perspective allowing an in fact two-dimensional cloister to appear to recede for scores of yards behind the actors; the paranoia and intrigue that infest a corrupt court are ably captured. It remains a pity that Reid allowed his prejudices to get the better of him.

The Merchant of Venice (1912, U.S.A., black and white, silent)
Directed by Lucius Henderson
Believed lost

Thanhouser's two-reel *Merchant*, shot largely on location in New Rochelle, was praised for its production design and concise storytelling, although Florence La Badie's Portia attracted less positive responses, being found too frivolous.

As You Like It (1912, U.S.A., black and white, silent)
Directed by J. Stuart Blackton and Charles Kent
Runtime: 30 minutes
Not seen by current writer

The rise of Thanhouser and the advent of the multi-reel film threatened Vitagraph, and compelled a change in their approach to Shakespeare. In the autumn of 1912, therefore, they produced an *As You Like It* in three reels, with the noted stage star Rose Coghlan as Rosalind, filmed in the Flatbush woods. Coghlan was over sixty; attempts to make the play more filmic, with the transposition of some existing scenes and the interpolation of new ones, reportedly left it unevenly paced and frequently dull, while the silent medium was woefully unsuited to a play heavily dependent on verbal wit; while handsome photography failed to rescue it.

A copy still existed in the 1960s, but I have been unable to trace what has become of it.

Richard III (1912, U.S.A., tinted, silent)
A.k.a. *The Life and Death of King Richard III; Mr Frederick Warde in Shakespeare's Masterpiece "The Life and Death of King Richard III"*
Directed by André Calmettes and James Keane
Starring: Frederick B. Warde, Violet Stuart, Robert Gemp, Carey Lee
Runtime: 55 minutes

    Richard III, rediscovered in 1996, was the first Shakespearean feature film[30] ever made, and is the oldest known American feature to survive in its entirety.[31] Although very little of the text reaches the title cards, and major characters vanish or are trimmed to slivers (there is no Queen Margaret or Duchess of York, while Hastings spends only seconds on screen; a smooth Buckingham is present but uncredited, leaving us ignorant of the actor's identity), it provided the fullest and richest realisation yet of any of the plays on film. Shot on location in New York by the specially formed Richard III Film Company, it showcases the grandstanding performance of British-born Frederick Warde, one of the most celebrated actors of the turn-of-the-century American theatre. When it was released, Warde toured cinemas reciting passages from the play and giving lectures on Shakespeare between the reels; he complained that he had thought becoming a film actor would mean he could retire from touring. Footage of Warde from these lectures shows him looking every day of his sixty-one years, in contrast to his youthful appearance as Richard: the makeup department – if any[32] – clearly did a good job.

    A budget of thirty thousand dollars, a fortune by pre-Hollywood standards, was amassed to create an epic picture as far as could be from filmed theatre, from whose limits previous Shakespeare adaptations had struggled to escape. It is visible in richly detailed costumes (by and large authentic, although the Burgundian headdress of Lady Anne (Violet Stuart) was never

---

[30] Defined as a film of more than four reels.
[31] A now incomplete print of *Oliver Twist* slightly predates it.
[32] It was not unknown in the silent era for actors to be required to provide and apply their own makeup.

worn in England, and some characters wield seventeenth century swords); and in the size of the cast (used very effectively in march-past sequences such as that with which the film opens, crowd scenes, and the pageantry of royal funerals and coronations, though they are not quite numerous enough to render Bosworth Field convincingly). When Richmond, played in swashbuckling style by the director James Keane, arrives in England, it is in a replica medieval ship stuffed with men-at-arms and bearing the cross of St George on her sail, filmed on water off City Island.

Clever use is made of the background tinting. For the first half of the film, a simple dichotomy is created between the court scenes, coloured a rich but unhealthy pink, and the drab brown of the outside world, evoking the isolation and decadence of Edward's (Robert Gemp) court and the resulting corruption of the realm. The murder of the Princes (Howard Stuart and Virginia Rankin), however, is coloured in a stark, cold blue, which recurs for the poisoning of Anne and for the ghost scene, while subtler shades creep into the rest of the picture as hope is planted for Richard's overthrow.

Like Frank Benson in the previous year, Warde makes an energetic and gleeful Richard: until Richmond's appearance, he is almost the only character to display vigour. It is as if Edward's sickness has dragged all of England save the Duke of Gloucester into a terrible lethargy. The first sign Warde shows that Richard is occasioned any physical hardship by his crooked back is in his coronation scene, when he struggles to mount the steps to the throne before turning triumphantly to brandish his sceptre at his cowering courtiers: the difficulty of the climb reflects the corpse-strewn path that has brought him thither.

The climactic battle is turned into a series of skirmishes, always with the dashing Keane at the heart of the action: but this device cannot hide the shortage of numbers, impressive though some shots of charging knights and the like are. Interestingly, although outdoors, the battle scene is tinted in pink, previously reserved for the court – until it gives place to a fiery orange for the final shot of Richard lying atop a heap of corpses, with the caption "The death of Richard III, last of the Plantagenets". The orange tinting may well symbolise Richard's descent into the flames of Hell: but one detects a note of sorrow for the passing of the medieval world. Throughout the film the Renaissance décor of the court has stood in marked contrast to the more primitive look of the brown scenes: perhaps the battle is coloured like the court because it marks the final triumph of the Renaissance over the Gothic Age.

The Jewish King Lear (1912, U.K., colour scheme unknown, sound mix unknown)
Based on *King Lear*
Believed lost

The *Kinematograph and Lantern Weekly* for 5th September, 1912, lists *The Jewish King Lear*, filmed at the Pavilion Theatre, as showing at New King's Hall in Commercial Road, London. It was presumably an adaptation of Jacob Gordin's 1892 play *The Yiddish King Lear* (for further information about which, see the entry for Harry Thomashefsky's 1934 film), but nothing else is known of it.

The Tempest (1912, France, colour scheme unknown, silent)
Estimated runtime: 20 minutes
Believed lost

Neither Ball nor any subsequent researcher has succeeded in tracing Éclair's *Tempest* or identifying any of the cast and crew; eyewitness accounts suggest that it dwelt so long on the backstory and the shipwreck scene that the main business of the play was compressed into the last five minutes.

Thirty prints were submitted when the film was registered for copyright in the United States, but all had disappeared by the 1950s.

A Midsummer Night's Dream (1913, Italy, black and white, silent)
Directed by Paolo Azzurri
Runtime: 22 minutes
Not seen by current writer

Ball remarks on the attractive location shots and quite advanced photographic techniques of this obscure Italian *Dream*. Removing the court scenes and the mechanicals to concentrate on the lovers and fairies, it reportedly succeeded in streamlining the action of the play into an enjoyable three reels.

Macbeth (1913, Germany, black and white, silent)
Directed by Arthur Bourchier
Believed lost

At the beginning of 1913, the Film-Industrie Gesellschaft von Heidelberg, newly formed to adapt the classics, lured Arthur Bourchier and his company to Germany for a large fee to make a quartet of Shakespeare films, beginning with an epic *Macbeth*. The production was troubled: Bourchier sent his company home and replaced them with German actors; rain disrupted one scene, which had to be reshot back in England; and the planned adaptations of *Hamlet*, *King Lear*, and *The Merchant of Venice* were quietly shelved. Bourchier himself was very pleased with the end result, as were most of the British critics: but on its American release three years later it met an exceedingly frosty reception. Performances which had in 1913 been hailed as subtle and seductive were damned as weak; photography once thought accomplished appeared amateurish; an ambitious production could not match Hollywood's money.

The film's history post-1916 is tangled. The Educational Film Bureau in London certainly still had a viewable copy as late as 1933, but when Ball set out to hunt it down in the 1950s, the Bureau had closed and there was no means of tracking down their print or any other. It is still missing.

Shylock (1913, France, black and white, silent)
Based on *The Merchant of Venice*
A.k.a. *Shylock, le marchand de Venise*
Directed by Henri Desfontaines
Starring: Pepa Bonafé, Harry Baur, Jean Hervé, Romuald Joubé
Runtime: 22 minutes

Despite the altered title (whose subtitle referring to the play is inaccurate: the Merchant is Antonio), Shylock is not the central figure of this film: merely the most memorable. If anything, indeed, he is marginalised by the excision of Jessica and the concentration on the Bassanio / Portia plot (Pepa Bonafé and Jean Hervé playing the lovers): and what is left of him is not really Shylock at all.

Without Jessica's elopement to avenge, the usurer becomes a motiveless monster (as his original was in Ser Giovanni's *Pecorone*, before Shakespeare made him human): and, in Desfontaines' eyes, his malignity is clearly a direct consequence of his Jewishness. The tone of the film is set in the opening credits, when the four stars appear and make their bows: while the other three are already in costume, Harry Baur appears first in his own guise, a dapper Parisian gentleman in evening dress, before metamorphosing into a gap-toothed, dirty creature. He might make a passable Fagin, but is not recognisable as Shakespeare's Jew – who can be interpreted as a villain, but is written as careful and houseproud, not an animal. This Shylock runs his hands through his gold in an ecstasy of avarice, but is willing to give it up for the pleasure of carving Christian flesh; contrasted to him is the personable Romuald Joubé as an entirely likeable Antonio. And at the end, after he has been thrown out of court (instead of begging leave to go as he does in the play) and the rings scene has taken place, a scene is added which seems to be a hideous parody of Henry Irving's sympathetic take on the moneylender. Irving, directing himself in the part in 1879, had famously added a coda in which Shylock drags himself back to his empty house and moans the name of Jessica; it stunned audiences and won plaudits internationally. But in the equivalent scene with which this film finishes, the audience is invited to sympathise not with Shylock but with the mocking crowd that chases him home.

(Whether or not Baur himself held anti-Semitic views in 1913, we do not know: but in 1936, he married a Jewish actress, Rika Radifé; and it was because of this marriage and Radifé's suspected Resistance activities that Baur was tortured to death by the Gestapo in 1943.)

Desfontaines' *Shylock* has its virtues. It is richly designed, ably blocked and shot, and puts far more Shakespeare on the title cards than most silent versions of the plays. It is at base, however, a vile film.

Bianco contro negro (1913, Italy, black and white, silent)
Based on *Othello*
Directed by Ernesto Maria Pasquali
Believed lost

White Against Black, as it literally translates, was an adaptation of Verdi's *Otello*. Presumably the cinema organist or pianist supplied the music.

Ein Sommernachtstraum in unserer Zeit (1913, Germany, black and white, silent)
Based on *A Midsummer Night's Dream*
Directed by Stellan Rye
Estimated runtime: 45 minutes
Believed lost

Ball refers to the writer of this *Sommernachtstraum*, Hanns Heinz Ewers, as "a third-rate romancer... strongly influenced by E. T. A. Hoffman and Poe but without their ability".[33] Its connection with the *Dream* appears limited: the mechanicals are not mentioned, and the lovers' experience in the woods is explicitly made a dream. How closely the dream-plot corresponded to that of the play is uncertain, although despite the modern setting characters both mortal and fairy retained their Shakespearean names. In the light of Ewers' and Rye's records, it is likely to have been sensationalist schlock.

La Bisbetica domata (1913, Italy, black and white, silent)
Based on *The Taming of the Shrew*
Directed by Arrigo Frusta
Estimated runtime: 40 minutes
Believed lost

Frusta's *Shrew* starred Gigetta Morano and Eleuterio Rodolfi, and omitted all subplots. Stills show that, like D. W. Griffiths' 1908 version, it utilised costumes and wigs of the mid seventeenth century; Rodolfi even sports a moustache not unlike Arthur V. Johnson's in the earlier film.

Julius Caesar (1913, U.S.A., black and white)
Directed by Allen Ramsey
Believed lost

The Edison Film Manufacturing Company was in the vanguard of efforts to endow films with synchronised sound, developing its first Kinetophone system as early as the 1890s. In 1913, Allen Ramsey directed five Kinetophone films for Edison,

---

[33] Ball, *Shakespeare on silent film*, pp. 176-77.

including an extract from *Julius Caesar*, Act Four, Scene Two.[34] The experiment was not a success and Kinetophone did not last.

Cymbeline (1913, U.S.A., black and white, silent)
Directed by Lucius Henderson
Starring: Florence La Badie, James Cruze, William Garwood, William Russell
Runtime: 23 minutes

After their first studio fire in 1913 (which was itself immediately made the subject of a film), the Thanhouser Corporation, though remaining based in New Rochelle, took up premises in the newly settled Hollywood. There is therefore some doubt over which coast *Cymbeline* was filmed on: although, since most of the actors were based in the east, a Californian shoot seems somewhat unlikely.

The only surviving big screen picture of this particular play, *Cymbeline* displays the increasing scale and ambition of Thanhouser projects in its large cast, detailed sets and costumes, and in particular the battle scene. The dress of the Britons owes more to the Arthurian paintings of Morris and Burne-Jones than to archaeology, but at least this furnishes them with plenty of Celtic motifs. Imogen's (Florence La Badie) extremely twentieth century headdress, and the obviously false facial hair of many of the male characters, are distractions; the neatly manicured American parkland on display in the outdoor sequences hardly resembles the wild woods of ancient Britain; and the small size of the opposing armies in the climactic battle is obvious: but overall the film is visually impressive for its time.

The complicated plot is also largely intelligible, although the last two acts are somewhat rushed, the death of Cloten and pseudo-death of Imogen being omitted. Occasional quotations from the play are scattered through the workmanlike title cards, helping to add atmosphere to exposition. It must be remembered, however, that *Cymbeline* lacked the familiarity of, say, *Macbeth*. The average audience member, even if quite well educated, is not likely to have been acquainted with the play, and may therefore have had some difficulty in following the

---

[34] It is likely that Eric Williams' "speaking picture" *Brutus and Cassius* (1918) and DeForest Phonofilms' *Julius Caesar* (1926) were based on the same scene.

film.

The quality of the acting is varied. La Badie's Imogen is affecting in subtler moments, but the actress displays a tendency to overplay scenes of high drama: no doubt the awakening scene, if it had been included, would have included an arm cast across her eyes and much extravagant weeping. William Garwood's reptilian Iachimo is more effective; most other characters are largely concealed behind their hair.

The far more destructive second Thanhouser fire in 1917 was for a long time thought to have claimed *Cymbeline*, but a print surfaced in the 1960s, and eventually made it onto the 2007 DVD *Thanhouser Presents Shakespeare*.

Henry V (1913, U.K., colour scheme unknown, silent)
Believed lost

The Picture House in Stratford upon Avon made much of its money in the years before World War One from local, often amateur, films. Among these was a film of *Henry V* made by the boys of the local grammar school, Shakespeare's own *alma mater*.

Hubert and Arthur (1913, U.K., colour scheme unknown, silent)
Based on *King John*
Believed lost

Eric Williams, who had quit schoolmastering in 1911 to teach elocution and give public recitations, in 1913 dreamed up the idea of filming scenes to go with his dramatic pieces; he later founded Eric Williams' Speaking Pictures to make these himself. He would then accompany the resulting movies on tour, speaking the dialogue in synch with the (silent) film. One of his first such efforts was a film of Act Four, Scene One of *King John*.

Hamlet (1913, U.K., black and white, silent)
Directed by E. Hay Plumb
Starring: Johnston Forbes-Robertson, Gertrude Elliot, Adeleine Bourne, J. H. Barnes
Runtime: 70 minutes

Plumb's *Hamlet* is never sure whether it wants to be epic cinema or filmed theatre, an adaptation of Shakespeare or a showcase for its sixty-year-old star Sir Johnston Forbes-Robertson. Despite many location shoots – a daylight Ghost scene by the seashore; Osric (George Hayes) mincing through the ferns to deliver Laertes' challenge in a forest clearing; and so forth – it contrives to feel stage-bound, mostly because all the interior scenes are filmed on the same (admittedly cleverly designed) set – a castle hall crowded with pillars, closing the cast in and making the play's multiple eavesdroppings very easy – and nearly always from the same angle (and on two occasions with a fly crawling across the lens). It is no surprise that this was an adaptation of a stage production in Drury Lane.

It is certainly not a satisfactory presentation of the play. The constraints of silent film seem not to have been fully understood by those making it: actors talk and talk and talk unheard, while the title cards show only fragments of the speeches they are delivering. Claudius (Walter Ringham) becomes a marginal figure, and the plot would be extremely hard to follow without a prior knowledge of the play. This would be better described as the edited highlights of the Drury Lane *Hamlet* than as a film adaptation.

By no means, however, does *Hamlet* lack redeeming features. The design is impressive: it is set in the twelfth century, when the Hamlet story was first written down, and displays in costume and architecture the Byzantine-influenced stylings of the Romanesque. Frustrating though it is not to hear the long speeches, the acting is mostly solid to fine – although Adeleine Bourne, nineteen years Forbes-Robertson's junior, not only looks but behaves more like his daughter than his mother. The knight himself shows us why he was considered the finest Hamlet of his generation, and why he was still playing the part at twice the Prince's stated age, with a subtle, sensitive performance whose explosions into action are nevertheless entirely convincing. His antic disposition is entirely assumed at least until the play scene, and he clearly wishes he could take Ophelia into his confidence; the agony of mistrust is movingly conveyed. At the close, Horatio (S. A. Cookson) and Marcellus (Robert Atkins)[35] help the dying Prince into the throne and hand him Claudius' crown and sceptre, and the court kneels to honour

---

[35] Remarkably, given his success on stage and his survival until 1972, this bit part was Atkins' only big screen Shakespeare role. He would play Bottom, Falstaff, and Caliban on television between 1946 and 1956.

Hamlet.

The preservation of Forbes-Robertson's performance is welcome: but the film hardly does the same service to the play that the original production must have done.

King Henry V (1913, U.K., colour scheme unknown, silent)
A.k.a. *England's Warrior King*
Believed lost

Filmed in York and featuring men of the Scots Greys, *Henry V* was one of Eric Williams' greatest successes. Its patriotic theme meant that the outbreak of the Great War was a considerable fillip, and Williams was still touring it in 1919.

Amleto (1914, Italy, black and white, silent)
Based on *Hamlet*
A.k.a. *Hamlet* (U.S.A.); *The Mad Prince*
Directed by Arturo Ambrosio
Believed lost

Ball had doubts over the existence of this film: the records are vague and incomplete. A print of an Italian *Hamlet* believed to be this one was in existence as late as 1952, but disintegrated before he could see it. Hamilton Revelle is reported to have played the Prince.

Una tragedia alla corte di Sicilia (1914, Italy, black and white, silent)
Based on *The Winter's Tale*
A.k.a. *Novella d'Inverno: Una Novella di Shakespeare*; *Racconto d'Inverno*; *The Winter's Tale* (U.K.); *The Lost Princess* (U.K.: 1919 re-release)
Directed by Baldassare Negroni
Starring: V. Cocchi, Pina Fabbri
Runtime: 32 minutes

Negroni's adaptation of *The Winter's Tale* adopts a framing device: a prosperous-looking Shakespeare, having just finished composing his play, reads it to an implausibly aristocratic circle of friends, to their delighted applause – although none of the play's actual text reaches the title cards. The main story, which despite the occasional appearance of

Greek-costumed extras has been relocated to a fairly well realised thirteenth century, is told succinctly, though without strict fidelity to the play. Some of the departures are understandable. Mamillius' death appears to have been found too shocking – despite the title's reference to "tragedy", this is a gentle, fairytale film – so he does not appear at all; a bear might be difficult to render convincingly, so Antigonus is murdered by robbers (who throw him into an active volcano, no less!); Autolycus, though a wonderful character, would hold up the progression of the plot in a version as condensed as this, so he disappears.

Other changes make rather less sense. Dramatic tension is reduced by the absence of the film's Hermione from her own trial; Leontes (V. Cocchi with a perpetual scowl on his face) does not reject the Oracle, which rather undermines the sense of divine retribution in his misfortunes; and the statue scene is replaced with a somewhat absurd ending in which, the title card tells us, "Leontes wishes to show his daughter once the face of her mother" (a rather morbid desire, surely) and opens her sarcophagus, only to find it empty. Paulina (Pina Fabbri, the only other cast member credited) then shows them through to a room where the Queen is sleeping on a couch. (Perhaps she has slept for sixteen years. Earlier, she is seen being placed in the tomb: how she escaped it is anybody's guess.)

The acting style is florid, with many expansive hand gestures, although the imperious Fabbri and a charmingly ingenuous Perdita are pleasant to watch; but the real strength of the film lies in the beauty of its sets, costumes and locations, and finely choreographed celebration scenes such as Leontes' banquet at the beginning and the Bohemian sheep-shearing festival. These are enough to make it an enjoyable, and sometimes magical, half-hour.

The Merchant of Venice (1914, U.S.A., black and white, silent)
Directed by Phillips Smalley and Lois Weber
Believed lost

Despite the claims advanced on behalf of *Cymbeline* (1913), it is likely that *The Merchant of Venice* was the first Shakespeare adaptation to be made in Hollywood (by Universal). It is also believed to have been the first feature film with a female director (Lois Weber, who played Portia to her husband Smalley's Shylock). Reviews indicate that it was a well designed picture but that, of the cast, only Weber really rose to her part – Douglas Gerrard's Bassanio being singled out for criticism. Problems with distribution costs, and a campaign against the film on the grounds of perceived anti-Semitism, helped to sink it, and it was a failure.

Otello (1914, Italy, black and white, silent)
Based on *Othello*
A.k.a. *Othello* (U.S.A.); *Othello the Moor* (U.K.)
Directed by Arrigo Frusta
Not seen by current writer

Frusta's lavish *Otello* in four reels, reportedly sticking very closely to the play (though set in the fifteenth century), was a major hit in many countries, and a critical success to boot. It starred Paolo Colaci, Cesira Lenard, and Riccardo Tolentino, and included extensive location shooting in Venice and an exciting dramatisation of the rout of the Turks at sea.

The Taming of the Shrew (1915, U.K., colour scheme unknown, silent)
Believed lost

The British and Colonial Kinematograph Company's "synchronised speaking excerpt" from Act Two, Scene One of *The Taming of the Shrew* featured brother and sister Arthur and Constance Backner as Petruchio and Katherina, and was accompanied to cinemas by actors who endeavoured to speak their dialogue in time with the film. Unfortunately, whenever one character crossed to the other side of the screen, "their" voice would come from the wrong direction to match the picture.

Love in a Wood (1915, U.K., black and white, silent)
Based on *As You Like It*
Directed by Maurice Elvey
Believed lost

In somewhat straitened circumstances as a result of the War, the London Film Company elected to transfer the plot of *As You Like It* to a present day British setting, thereby avoiding both the royalty payments attendant on using modern material and the expense of costuming a conventional Shakespearean piece.[36] These being the days before period analogue, a new script was provided by Kenelm Foss, adhering fairly closely to the story of the play – save that the rival dukes were no longer brothers, but an impoverished squire and the *nouveau riche* neighbour who buys his estate.

Elisabeth Risdon, who played Rosalind, later reminisced: "We had fun doing it, but the press and the public *did not like it*, and the result was a failure."[37] Her recollections (relayed to Robert Hamilton Ball in 1957-58) and the American copyright records contain all the surviving information on this film; all known prints were destroyed to recover their silver nitrate content in the late 1920s, an all too common fate for early pictures.

Macbeth (1915, France, black and white, silent)
Believed lost

Éclair's *Macbeth* was not a self-contained adaptation but a series of the play's major scenes, chiefly noted at the time for its visual effects and for Georgette Leblanc's portrayal of Lady Macbeth. ("Her carriage and every gesture denotes majesty and force",[38] declared the publicity material.) It passed unremarked outside France. Séverin-Mars played the title role.

The Merchant of Venice (1916, U.K., black and white, silent)
Directed by Walter West
Starring: Matheson Lang, Nellie Hutin Britton, Joseph R. Tozer, Kathleen Hazel Jones
Runtime: 20 minutes (surviving footage)

Only two reels survive of the original five of *The Merchant of Venice*, covering the action from the signing of the bond to Portia's (Nellie Hutin Britton, looking incongruously modern) arrival in court. The film was adapted from a stage production at St James' Theatre; although these roots show very

---

[36] There is no connection between this film and William Wycherley's 1671 play of the same title.
[37] Ball, *Shakespeare on silent film*, p. 360.
[38] Ibid., p. 244.

clearly, it is less stage-bound than many such adaptations in silent era British cinema, avoiding the all too common fault of a static camera.

The production is unremarkable, and is of interest chiefly for the sympathy with which Britton's husband Matheson Lang portrays Shylock. This is a pitiable version of the moneylender, who hobbles about with a walking stick, appears reasonably benevolent until Jessica (Kathleen Hazel Jones, playing her as a child-like innocent) elopes, and whose grief is movingly conveyed afterwards. As he bewails his fate to Tubal (Terence O'Brien), he pours dust on his head in a Biblical gesture of mourning, while the picture cuts to his daughter trading her mother's ring for a monkey; his finest speeches, including the whole of "Hath not a Jew eyes?", are given in the intertitles, while the idle and thoughtless Christian nobles – especially the narcissistic Lorenzo (Ernest Caselli) and the violent Solanio (uncredited) – come across much less favourably.

Unfortunately, however, Lang lacks the presence to carry this interpretation through, and by the trial scene his Shylock is merely pathetic. Combined with a somewhat unimaginative production, which was viewed even in 1916 as excessively old-fashioned, this results in a notably unsatisfying film.

The Real Thing at Last (1916, U.K., black and white, silent)
Based on *Macbeth*
Directed by J. M. Barrie and L. C. MacBean
Believed lost

It is not known whether the makers of *The Real Thing at Last* were aware, when they embarked on the project, that a *Macbeth* (q.v.) was about to be produced in Hollywood: but, if this was coincidental, it must have been a godsend. (The Hollywood version's star, Herbert Beerbohm Tree, greatly admired *The Real Thing at Last*, calling it "brilliant" and "remarkable".)

The brainchild of J. M. Barrie and A. E. Matthews (the head of the British Actors Film Company), *The Real Thing at Last* was a spoof of both American cinematic bombast and British understatement, in which Shakespeare (Leslie Henson, who also impersonated Charlie Chaplin and stood in as King Duncan so that filming need not be stopped by Norman Forbes' illness) sells *Macbeth* to movie producers, who proceed to make two completely different films for British and American releases. The former is restrained to a fault (Lady Macbeth (Nelson Keys in drag) having no difficulty wiping off a tiny spot of blood), the latter anachronistic – Macbeth (Edmund Gwenn) and Macduff (Godfrey Tearle) fighting their final duel on top of a skyscraper – and full of all kinds of excess, before a tacked-on repentance and happy ending.

The film was not well received. The British industry press, with an uncharacteristic concern for transatlantic sensibilities, leapt to Hollywood's defence and almost unanimously denounced the depiction as a travesty: but it is hard not to feel that Barrie had succeeded in touching a few nerves with what reads like a moderately insightful comment on the failings of two very different cinematic traditions as they stood in 1916.

Macbeth (1916, U.S.A., black and white, silent)
Directed by John Emerson
Estimated runtime: 80 minutes
Believed lost

His work had been adapted there before, but 1916 was the year in which Hollywood truly discovered Shakespeare. To celebrate the tercentenary of the Bard's death, three of the major studios announced that they would be producing films of his plays: and Triangle pulled off the considerable coup of signing Herbert Beerbohm Tree to star in an adaptation to be helmed by D. W. Griffith, who had recently made headlines with the shockingly racist but technically brilliant *Birth of a Nation* (1915).

Various plays were considered. After the idea of revisiting *Henry VIII* had been rejected, Griffith and Tree toyed with *The Tempest*, *A Midsummer Night's Dream*, and *Richard II*, before deciding that the play best suited to the epic interpretation the studio had in mind was *Macbeth*. Committed to *Intolerance* (1916) – in which Tree and his Lady Macbeth, Constance Collier, appeared as extras – Griffith proved unable to direct in person, and took a back seat to John Emerson: but he continued to supervise production, and by all accounts to imprint his style upon the picture. Both studio publicity and reviews stress the vast scale of the film: "five hundred camp-fires, thousands of torches, great cataracts of boiling pitch... the weird, picturesque witches... the most wonderful electrical and mechanical effects... wild dances of highlanders... and the huge drawbridge of Dunsinane Castle and the terrific battle there, scores of men falling from high walls into the moat below".[39] Meticulous research was reported to have helped create an authentically early medieval look, and the few surviving stills by and large bear this out.

The production generated many anecdotes about Tree's behaviour on set. He reportedly insisted on speaking his lines in full, with the result that the cameraman had to conceal the fact that he had stopped filming after gaining the footage required and run an empty camera until Tree had finished speaking. Despite his age and lack of training, he wanted to perform all his own stunts, forcing the crew to film Macbeth's action scenes secretly when Tree was off set.

Macbeth must have been quite a spectacle. The New York Times lavished praise on Emerson's "imagination... fine sense of composition... prevailing good taste" and called the finished film "among the best things in motion pictures" (though adding that its "beauty is not in any sense Shakespearean")[40]: but it was a commercial failure, leaving Triangle anxious to get rid of Tree, who had hoped to make a series of Shakespeare pictures in Hollywood. Rumour has it that he was offered inappropriate and humiliating parts in a deliberate attempt to drive him into giving up his contract – although Ball investigated these stories and found little evidence. Tree did after a few months return to England, where he died the following year.

Romeo and Juliet (1916, U.S.A., black and white, silent)
Directed by Francis X. Bushman and John W. Noble
Runtime: 135 minutes
Believed lost

Bushman's lavish *Romeo and Juliet* for Metro, with himself and his regular co-star (later his wife) Beverly Bayne in the title roles, was one of the more remarkable cinematic successes of 1916, popular with critics (in the dailies as well as the film press) and audiences alike. Ball quotes almost in full a piece by George F. Blaisdell for *Moving Picture World* in which is praised the film's "unique double appeal – to the eye and to the

---

[39] Ibid., pp. 230-31.
[40] Ibid, pp. 233-34.

mind".[41] In several cities it was the first film ever to play in more than one venue simultaneously, often for the longest runs those cinemas had yet experienced.

Metro retained the negative, but by the 1960s it was in decayed condition and effectively unviewable. Ball expressed the hope that it might one day be restored, but this never proved possible.

Romeo and Juliet (1916, U.S.A., black and white, silent)
Directed by J. Gordon Edwards and Maxwell Karger
Runtime: 70 minutes (U.S.A.)
Believed lost

"Italy, in the period of *Romeo and Juliet*, was no place for a Sunday school girl." ~ Theda Bara.[42]

It seems bizarre today that a studio would deliberately court direct competition by duplicating a rival's project: but William Fox, founder of the corporation which still bears his name, made something of a habit of it in the 1910s. On hearing about Metro's *Romeo and Juliet* he promptly set out to make his own sensational version, to star Theda Bara in a succession of extremely sheer dresses.

A vicious advertising war ensued, which viewed from this distance appears somewhat ludicrous; but it ended with the Metro version being released first, in eight reels, to considerable critical acclaim, while Fox had to reduce his film from seven reels to five for the U.S. release (the longer version was seen in the U.K.), and received a distinctly lukewarm response. Few critics actually attacked it, but such praise as there was focused more on the physical charms of Miss Bara and her co-star Harry Hilliard than on the production or the performances, and showed none of the enthusiasm which had greeted the Metro film. Nor was there any of the controversy for which, judging from the casting and publicity, Fox seems to have been at least half hoping. The public was less indifferent, and Fox's *Romeo and Juliet* appears to have performed respectably at the box office: but it was soon largely forgotten.

---

[41] Ibid., p. 238.
[42] Ibid., p. 240.

King Lear (1916, U.S.A., black and white, silent)
Directed by Ernest C. Warde
Starring: Frederick B. Warde, Lorraine Huling, Hector Dion,
Ina Hammer, Edith Diestel
Runtime: 70 minutes (estimated) / 36 minutes (cut version)

Thanhouser's sole feature length Shakespeare adaptation survives only in what is probably a pirate edition on three reels: had the studio not neglected to copyright it, the picture would probably have been lost in the 1917 fire. With the entire plot of the play still present and correct, the film moves at a sometimes dizzying pace, and would be confusing to anyone ignorant of the play: faults probably absent from the lost five-reel original, which ran at approximately double the surviving version's length.

The growing ambition visible in *Cymbeline* (1913) is near its apex here, taking full advantage of the rapid advances in filming techniques seen during the 1910s: close-ups alternate with wide shots, the editing is far quicker and slicker than would have been possible five years earlier, and the cast is probably the largest Thanhouser had yet employed. (The battle scene, however, like that in *Cymbeline*, still suffers from a lack of numbers.) The earlier film's Morris-inspired vision of ancient Britain has been replaced by a vaguely early medieval look, with occasional grating touches such as Edmund's (Hector Dion) cartoonish horned helmet: but it is suitably primitive and mostly manages not to jar.

Thanhouser, belonging culturally as well as geographically to the East Coast, had largely resisted the burgeoning star system that was developing in Hollywood: its stable existed, but consisted of only three actors. Probably the most prominent was ageing stage star Frederick B. Warde, here seen behind a vast false beard, playing Lear under the direction of his own son, Ernest. (Warde Junior also briefly capers onscreen as the Fool.) Warde displays a suitably savage majesty, but is let down by Lorraine Huling's utterly wooden Cordelia.

With occasional interpolated scenes putting on screen what was left offstage (Edmund's dalliance with the sisters, and even Cordelia's death, intercut with Albany's men racing to save her), *Lear* puts far more Shakespeare on the title cards than any previous Thanhouser effort. The always upmarket studio attempted with this film to make its mark as a producer of heavyweight pictures: but the fire hit its fortunes badly, and it was not long before it went out of business.

Amleto (1917, Italy, black and white, silent)
Based on *Hamlet*
A.k.a. *Hamlet* (U.S.A.)
Directed by Eleuterio Rodolfi
Starring: Ruggero Ruggeri, Helena Makowska, Mercedes
Brignone, Martelli, Armand Pouget
Runtime: 48 minutes

It is immediately apparent on watching *Amleto* that Eleuterio Rodolfi had been much impressed by Hay Plumb's *Hamlet* (1913). The high medieval setting (rendered with rather less period sense than in the British film), the location shots, and in particular a carbon copy of the ending, in which Hamlet (Ruggero Ruggeri) is crowned King before he dies, all bear witness to this. Despite the damage that the surviving print has suffered, *Amleto* is in some ways the more successful of the two films: but its success is far from complete.

Its most obvious advantage over Plumb's version lies in the succinct rendition of the story. Although this is not flawless – Fortinbras (a boisterous turn by an uncredited actor) goes unmentioned until Hamlet encounters his implausibly small army, and even by the time he claims the throne the audience will have been left with little idea of who he is; while Ophelia (Helena Makowska) gets very little chance to display her character before going mad – there is a clarity here which the 1913 film lacked.

The acting is less impressive. Makowska's mad act consists mostly of staring and laughing; Martelli makes an unthreatening Claudius, his one striking moment being the look of horror he gives as Gertrude (the coolly aristocratic Mercedes Brignone) fastidiously dabs her mouth after drinking the poison; the extravagantly bearded Polonius is conventional to the point of self-parody; while Ruggeri, as an at once petulant and self-satisfied Hamlet, plays to the back row without ever finding any depth. The Player King, played for laughs, is depicted as an outrageous old ham, but his overacting is barely to be distinguished from that of the Prince.

Rodolfi does make occasional use of cinematic technique, with a translucent double-exposed Ghost (Armand Pouget) able to walk through walls and disappear in clouds of smoke and flame, flashbacks to the murder of the old King, the face of Yorick superimposed on his skull, and quick cuts between the duel scene and the advance of Fortinbras' army: the last of these touches was used again, to better effect, by Kenneth Branagh in his 1996 *Hamlet*: but *Amleto* still contrives to feel somewhat stagey. Ruggeri is no Forbes-Robertson, and the time passes slowly.

Elfenszene aus dem Sommernachtstraum (1917, Germany, colour scheme unknown, silent)
Based on *A Midsummer Night's Dream*
Believed lost
    Understandably, despite their reverence for him, German film-makers by and large neglected *"unser Shakespeare"* during the Great War; but in 1917 the ballet corps of the Deutschen Opernhausen von Berlin was filmed in a scene set to Mendelssohn's *Sommernachtstraum* (1826), choreographed by Mary Zimmermann and shown with live music.

Die lustigen Weiber von Windsor (1917, Germany, colour scheme unknown, silent)
Based on *The Merry Wives of Windsor*
Directed by William Wauer
Believed lost
    Wauer's setting of Otto Nicolai's 1849 operetta was a somewhat ambitious undertaking: an orchestra had to accompany it to the cinemas. Whether or not singers also travelled with the film, and how the public received it, history does not relate.

Brutus and Cassius (1918, U.K., black and white, silent)
Based on *Julius Caesar*
Directed by Marshall Moore
Believed lost
    Brutus and Cassius was the last of Eric Williams' Speaking Pictures. It is not known who played Cassius.

Othello (1918, Germany, black and white, silent)
Directed by Max Mack

Believed lost

Mack's *Othello*, starring Beni Montano and Ellen Korth, appears to have paralleled Shakespeare's play with some other narrative: the credits show that the leads doubled as non-Shakespearean characters. Possibly it was in fact a "backstage" film, although the title suggests that the play was the dominant element. Unfortunately no information concerning the secondary storyline has survived.

A Sage Brush Hamlet (1919, U.S.A., black and white, silent)
Based on *Hamlet*
Directed by Joseph Franz
Believed lost

George Elwood Jenks put together this Western for his frequent collaborator Joseph Franz: Larry Lang (William Desmond) gets nicknamed "The Sage Brush Hamlet" when he sets out to avenge his father's death at the hands of the bandit Claude Dutton (Edward Peil), and further mimics the Prince by feigning insanity to lull Dutton's suspicions. There the similarities to the play apparently ended, and the film would not merit inclusion here were it not for the fact that Jenks deliberately drew attention to his Shakespearean debt in the title.

'Amlet (1919, U.K., black and white animation, silent)
Based on *Hamlet*
Directed by Anson Dyer
Believed lost

'Amlet was the first in a series of short animated burlesques on Shakespeare filmed by Anson Dyer, and featured an Horatio modelled on the notorious swindler Horatio Bottomley. (Although not actually convicted of conspiracy to defraud until 1921, Bottomley had been a disgraced man and a figure of ridicule since before the War; the mischievous Dyer probably had considerable fun with his reputation.)

Oh'phelia (1919, U.K., black and white animation, silent)
Based on *Hamlet*
Directed by Anson Dyer
Runtime: 13 minutes

Oh'phelia is thought to be the only one of Anson Dyer's Bardic burlesques to have survived in its entirety: a companion piece to the lost *'Amlet*. Made in engagingly primitive style, it is set in a delightfully homely Elsinore, where a washing line hangs in the minstrels' gallery, Claudius can draw himself a pint of beer without getting up from the throne, and Gertrude rolls out pastry during the closet scene. The letters of the intertitles rearrange themselves to spell out appalling puns, and a bowler-hatted censor marches right onto one title card to prevent the word "bloody" from appearing. 'Amlet ("known as the 'Gloomy Dean' on account of his mind being un'Inged") cuts Ophelia's hair into a short post-War style ("To bob or not to bob"), driving her mad and drawing down the wrath of a cowboy Laertes (modelled on Western star "Laughin'" Bill Hart, in keeping with Dyer's practice of inserting celebrity "cameos" into his cartoons); the Prince ends up forced to join the Boy Scouts, but all proves well when the First Aid instructions in his scouting manual enable him to save Ophelia from drowning and change the ending of the play.

It is impossible not to like a world in which, when a thrush eats a snail, a sign pops up by the empty shell reading "This house to let unfurnished"; and those who remember with affection the cartoons of Peter Firmin will recognise in Dyer a precursor of his style. The loss of all his other Shakespeare skits except a two-minute extract from *Othello* (1920) is grievous indeed.

The Merchant of Venice (1919, U.K., black and white animation, silent)
Directed by Anson Dyer
Believed lost
Only the date and title of Dyer's third Shakespeare cartoon are known.

Othello (1920, U.K., black and white animation, silent)
Directed by Anson Dyer
Runtime: 2 minutes (surviving footage)
In his animated burlesque of *Othello*, Dyer moved the action to a seaside pier, making Brabantio the owner of a bathing hut and the Moor a blackface minstrel. (A jibe, perhaps, at the

appearance of some white Othellos in their makeup?) Unfortunately only a fragment of the film now survives, jumping straight from Othello applying his burnt cork to a confrontation with his flapperish Desdemona over a check handkerchief, ending with him "smother[ing] her – with cork and kisses". Between these scenes there was originally an extra ten minutes or so of film, which reportedly stuck quite closely to the play.

Romeo and Juliet (1920, U.K., black and white animation, silent)
Directed by Anson Dyer
Believed lost

For this film, Dyer brought his celebrity portraits into the foreground: instead of having a Bottomley or Bill Hart cameo, he modelled the eponymous lovers themselves on Charlie Chaplin and Mary Pickford (whose real Shakespearean debut would be seen before the decade was out). The Little Tramp and America's Sweetheart in the greatest love story ever told, animated by Dyer, must have been a sight worth the seeing.

The Taming of the Shrew (1920, U.K., black and white animation, silent)
Directed by Anson Dyer
Believed lost

There is some uncertainty over whether Dyer's last Shakespearean effort was ever actually released. No details about the film are known.

Romeo und Julia im Schnee (1920, Germany, black and white, silent)
Based on *Romeo and Juliet*
A.k.a. *Romeo and Juliet in the Snow* (international English title)
Directed by Ernst Lubitsch
Runtime: 45 minutes
Not seen by current writer

Lubitsch's farcical reworking of *Romeo and Juliet* is set in a nineteenth century Alpine village at dead of winter: the names are Germanised as "Montekugerl" and "Capulethofer"; fights are conducted with snowballs; the apothecary substitutes sugared water for the poison so that the lovers (Lotte Neumann and

Gustav von Wangenheim) can leap up after their families have reconciled and shout "Surprise!". The Wagner-inspired costumes at the Capulethofer dance have been particularly praised.

Otello (1920, Italy, black and white, silent)
Based on *Othello*
Directed by Camillo De Riso
Believed lost

Hardly any details survive concerning De Riso's *Otello*; even the cast list does not specify who played which role.

Carnival (1921, U.K., black and white, silent)
Based on *Othello*
Directed by Harley Knoles
Starring: Matheson Lang, Hilda Bayley, Ivor Novello, Clifford Grey
Runtime: 80 minutes

Matheson Lang and his co-author H. C. M. Hardinge had based their play *Sirocco* on the same conceit as the 1911 film *For Åbent Tæppe*: a married couple playing Othello and Desdemona become riven by suspicion and jealousy in real life, with parallels to the play heavy-handedly pointed up. (Silvio, the film's Othello – played by Lang – even discusses the psychology of jealousy, and dismisses the Moor's behaviour as barbaric, before predictably aping it when he begins to suspect his own wife.)

Harley Knoles, a British director who had made his name in the U.S., returned to Britain in 1920 to found his own production company, modestly named H. K. Productions: and he chose *Sirocco*, under the new title *Carnival*, as the subject of its first film. He cast Lang and his stage co-star Hilda Bayley in the leads, pruned the text to its melodramatic essence, and departed for Venice to undertake location shooting.

The necessary trimming of Lang and Hardinge's text has the unfortunate effect of highlighting *Sirocco*'s stilted dialogue and unconvincing characterisation. Silvio's lightning change of character from kind and civilised husband to murderous monster on the basis of passing suspicion is utterly implausible, and all the more so when it is contrasted with *Othello*'s masterly depiction of a similar alteration; his wife Simonetta is a weak-willed booby, whose inability either to reject definitively her would-be lover (Ivor Novello, in his first British film role) or to hold her husband responsible for trying to kill her in front of a vast audience earns her no sympathy whatever. The indoor sets sit ill with the glamorous outdoor shots of a Venice in which gondolas are apparently the only form of transport, and the "happy" ending sits worse with the preceding melodrama.

It is not altogether surprising that H. K. Productions' first film was also its last.

Hamlet (1921, Germany, black and white, silent)
A.k.a. *Hamlet: The Drama of Vengeance* (U.K.)
Directed by Sven Gade and Heinz Schall
Starring: Asta Nielsen, Heinz Stieda, Hans Junkermann, Mathilde Brandt
Runtime: 131 minutes

"Is it a son, good nurse? A prince for Denmark?"
"No, my queen! It is a princess!"

There had been female Hamlets before 1921 – most notably Sarah Bernhardt – but they had been women playing the Prince. Despite the mischievous suggestions of Professor Edward E. Vining in his 1881 book *The Mystery of Hamlet. An Attempt to Solve an old Problem*, there had never been a Princess of Denmark on stage or screen. Asta Nielsen, the greatest Danish star of the silent era, changed that. She formed her own production company with husband Sven Gade to allow her to play Hamlet in a film which is as much knowing comedy as tragedy, and as much Vining as Shakespeare. (Although the film claims to be drawn from "original Norse legends", this means little more than that lumps of Saxo Grammaticus' *History of the Danes* have been crudely tacked onto the play where they hardly belong.)

Although only about a quarter of the title cards are Shakespearean in origin (and none until a full half hour in), unused snippets of text show up visually. Hamlet's "inky cloak" is a flowing black cape that allows Nielsen to make every movement dramatic with the minimum of effort; the "serpent" which in the play doubles as an official explanation for King Hamlet's death and a metaphor for Claudius is here a literal snake used as a murder weapon; and, most crucially, the film follows Vining in picking up on the Gravedigger's remark that

Hamlet was born the day his father overcame the elder Fortinbras. A prologue dramatises the duel: the Danish king is wounded, and the recently delivered Gertrude receives false word that her husband is dying. To preserve the kingdom and her own safety, she gives out that her newborn daughter is in fact a son. Thus Hamlet is brought up as a boy – although Nielsen, even by the androgynous standards of German cinema in the Twenties, never convinces as a man.

This sets us up for subsequent departures from the play: interpolated scenes of Wittenberg student life introduce Horatio (Heinz Stieda) as Hamlet's secret love interest ("Give me that man that is not passion's slave, / And I will wear him in my heart's core, yea, / In my heart of heart, as I do thee") – and, most surprisingly, also make Fortinbras their fellow student and friend. The flattering misconceptions Shakespeare's princes have of each others' characters depend on the fact that they never meet; while no direct equivalent for the Prince of Norway exists in Saxo's account. (Despite emphasising in the prologue that England was subject to Denmark "in the Middle Ages" – in fact, until 1042 – the film moves Hamlet's exile to Norway. Since, despite anachronisms, it appears to be set *circa* 1400, when Norway was indeed under Danish rule but England had been independent for centuries, this makes a certain amount of sense: but the fact that Fortinbras' later invasion and annexation of Denmark occurs at Hamlet's invitation remains a surprise.)

Gertrude is a willing accomplice in her first husband's murder; the Ghost does not appear, nor is it encountered at all by Horatio and the guards, but instead whispers to Hamlet from the tomb (an intimation perhaps that the "Prince"'s madness is genuine?); the heavily cut Ophelia (Lilly Jacobson) is wooed purely to keep her apart from Horatio, who is captivated by her; and the attempt to square Saxo's ending with Shakespeare's ties the film in knots. As in Saxo, Hamlet returns during a feast and burns Claudius alive in his hall. The funeral of Ophelia then *follows* this, without the court yet being aware that their King and several of his retainers are dead (or apparently wondering where they might be); and it is Gertrude who plots Hamlet's murder with Laertes, and finally drinks her poison in a fit of absent-mindedness while an astonished Horatio discovers that his dying friend has breasts. It is hard to tell whether or not we are meant to laugh here; the film constantly mixes a ponderously melodramatic reading of the tragedy with comic interpolations and the upbeat music of Giuseppe Becce.

Convincingly male or not, Nielsen makes an interesting Hamlet. Her playful, kittenish Prince / Princess shows little of the text's melancholy but much of its antic disposition, and rather more subtlety of expression than is usual in silent film: she has the difficult task of conveying whole soliloquies without speech. ("Oh, that this too, too solid flesh would melt" is played out through Nielsen's face without a single title card.) She is well supported by a largely uncredited cast, even if several of the characters are no longer entirely who they were. The rakish, dishevelled Claudius and calculating but lusty Gertrude make a thoroughly dissolute royal couple; the real power in the court, and Hamlet's principal antagonist, is Hans Junkermann's sly, insinuating Polonius, one of the least likeable incarnations of the Lord Chamberlain ever to appear on the screen – but also one of the most convincing. Too many Poloniuses turn the cunning old man into a buffoon. The production is fairly lavish, and the stylised cinematography of Curt Courant and Axel Graatkjaer does full justice to Gade and Nielsen's vision: but it is difficult today, unless one has an academic interest in gender studies relating specifically to Weimar Germany, to regard the film as more than a curiosity.

Macbeth (1922, U.K., black and white, silent)
Directed by Harry B. Parkinson
Believed lost

In 1922, the British film company Master produced a series of six one-reelers under the title *Tense Moments from Great Plays* (following on from *Tense Moments with Great Authors* and *Tense Moments from Opera* earlier the same year). Selected and arranged by Frank Miller, produced by H. B. Parkinson and starring Sybil Thorndike, they included scenes from *Macbeth* (in which Thorndike played opposite her brother Russell, with whom she had frequently acted on stage, as Constance to his King John and the Fool to his Lear) and *The Merchant of Venice*.

The Merchant of Venice (1922, U.K., black and white, silent)
Directed by Challis Sanderson
Believed lost

The *Merchant* segment from *Tense Moments*, in which

Ivan Berlyn played Shylock to Sybil Thorndike's Portia, received mediocre notices. It was remarked that the sets appeared to belong to a later era than the costumes, smacking somewhat of the eighteenth century.

Macbeth (1922, Germany, colour scheme unknown, silent)
Directed by Heinz Schall
Believed lost

Schall's *Macbeth* would be written off as an abortive project, were it not for a reference which gives a specific length of film (916 metres). This is the only evidence that the film was actually made.

Othello (1922, Germany, black and white, silent)
A.k.a. *The Moor* (international English title)
Directed by Dmitri Buchowetzki
Starring: Emil Jannings, Werner Krauss, Ica von Lenkeffy, Lya De Putti, Ferdinand von Alten
Runtime: 80 minutes

Buchowetzki's *Othello* features two of inter-war Germany's most celebrated actors – Emil Jannings, who in 1929 was to win the award for Best Actor at the first ever Oscars, and Werner Krauss – before they became tainted by Nazism (which both enthusiastically embraced). Film was not really their medium, and their near-operatic performances often verge on – or actually cross over into – the comical; but at their best they are a joy to watch.

The film opens with titles and a scene-setting caption over a painting of the Grand Canal, before expending its first ten minutes on a prologue (inspired largely by Shakespeare's original source, Giovambattista Giraldi Cinthio's 1566 novella *The Story of Disdemona*, which was clearly a major influence on the film) filling in the back-story to the play; the title cards cleverly work several of Shakespeare's lines into a scene which covers both the promotion of Cassio (Theodor Loos) and the elopement of Othello and Desdemona (Jannings and Ica von Lenkeffy), while also introducing the main characters and giving us thumbnail sketches of them. These are broad and simplistic, and the characterisation never really attempts to go any deeper; it is assisted by the near-cartoonish appearance of several of the characters, notably Jannings' bulging-eyed Moor, Krauss' bristly, moustachioed N.C.O. Iago, Loos' effeminate Cassio, and Ferdinand von Alten's kiss-curled cream-puff Rodrigo. At times the comedy seems to be deliberate: Rodrigo's disguise in Cyprus is a very obvious false nose, and Cassio's drunken mockery of it becomes Rodrigo's ground for fastening a quarrel upon him – an episode which, despite its seriousness in terms of the plot, is played almost entirely for laughs.

(Incidentally, although a line has been inserted in which Othello claims that "I am the son of an Egyptian prince and Spanish princess – my blood is fair, like hers", Jannings' hair and makeup are clearly intended to make him look sub-Saharan. The "Arab Othello" conjured up by racist critics in the nineteenth century is trying to coexist with the African original, and the result is confusion. His clothing, which mixes Arabic and Persian styles, would not necessarily be inappropriate on an African in the sixteenth century, but would certainly look odd on a general of Venice, whatever his colour.)

The heavy-handedness of the makeup department, if there was one, is all the more regrettable when their work is compared to that of the set and costume designers, who have created a splendidly realised late Renaissance world with a strong feel of authenticity. Interestingly, while other characters change regularly from one period confection into another, Iago retains the same simple black costume throughout: and, if it were not for a discreet earring and the slashes in his lower sleeves, he could almost pass for a soldier of the Great War.

Once we pass from the brightly lit prologue into Act One of *Othello*, Buchowetzki brings the shadows into play. This is our first real taste of a skill for lighting and camerawork which considerably outweighs his talent for directing actors: while it must be admitted that the crowd scenes are ably handled, a really competent director would have known when to rein in Jannings and Krauss. When Brabantio (Friedrich Kühne) swoops into the Senate's midnight meeting like an avenging angel, we are even treated to an upwards-angled shot, letting Kühne loom threateningly over the camera, that takes in the ceiling of the set – something practically unheard of in 1922. (Throughout this scene, Brabantio seems more than human; his final warning to Othello is delivered as if in a prophetic frenzy.)

The script throughout is dealt with cavalierly. This is in part an unavoidable consequence of turning a very long play into an eighty-minute silent film, and most of the interpolated scenes, whether invented, lifted from Cinthio, or based on Shakespeare's hints, work well enough: but the excision of Bianca leaves sizeable holes in the plot, and, perhaps partly as a result of this, the ending seems somewhat rushed. For all that, it is impressive that so much of the play's text did make it onto the title cards – a rare occurrence in silent adaptations of Shakespeare.

Through all this it is impossible not to wonder what effect the memory of the War had on Buchowetzki and his crew – not least upon the politics of the film. *Othello* is one of the most closed of Shakespeare's tragedies, the public life of the characters having far less of a role to play than in *Hamlet*, let alone *Lear* or *Macbeth*: but here the general populace is never far away, washing like waves against the palaces of the great, always shouting for their hero Othello. The Venetians and Cypriots alike love the Moor, their saviour from the marauding Turk: at the end, even as he kills himself, a crowd that has heard of his arrest gathers to demand his release; Cassio steps out onto a balcony and quiets them with a Roman salute before announcing the general's death. The film may slightly predate Mussolini's march on Rome, but its overtones remain disturbing, especially in the light of what was to come.

Juliet and Her Romeo (1923, U.K., black and white, silent)
Based on *Romeo and Juliet*
Believed lost
Beyond the fact that Frank Miller scripted this parody, nothing is known of it.

Falstaff the Tavern Knight (1923, U.K., black and white, silent)
Based on *The Merry Wives of Windsor*
A.k.a. *John Falstaff*
Directed by Edwin Greenwood
Believed lost
Next to no details are known concerning British and Colonial's Falstaff film. The title suggests an influence from Rafael Sabatini's novel *The Tavern Knight* (1904), or from Stoll Pictures' 1920 adaptation thereof: neither of these has any connection with Falstaff or Shakespeare. Roy Byford played the knight, a role to which he returned on stage the following year.

The Taming of the Shrew (1923, U.K., black and white, silent)
Directed by Edwin J. Collins
Runtime: 22 minutes (surviving footage)

Another British and Colonial literary two-reeler, *The Taming of the Shrew* is quite rich in design, includes more text on the title cards than is usual, and puts across the story of the play quite effectively: but there its virtues end. The acting is mannered and artificial: the pudgy and ageing Lauderdale Maitland chortles his way through a one-note portrayal of Petruchio, and Dacia Deane grotesquely overplays Kate, while the rest of the cast is as wooden as the studio-bound sets. They are hardly assisted by a static camera and some of the worst blocking I have witnessed on stage or screen.

The end of the film is missing. Given the approach evident in what survives – in which sympathy for Kate and any attempt to fathom why she has become such a termagant are entirely lacking – this is perhaps just as well.

Der Kaufmann von Venedig (1923, Germany, black and white, silent)
Based on *The Merchant of Venice*
A.k.a. *Shylock, der Jude von Venedig*; *The Jew of Mestri* (U.K.: 1926 re-release)
Directed by Peter Paul Felner
Starring: Werner Krauss, Henny Porten, Harry Liedtke, Lia Eibenschütz, Carl Ebert
Runtime: 95 minutes / 71 minutes (U.K.: 1926 re-release)

This film possesses a significance beyond itself, in that its star, Werner Krauss, would later come almost to personify the uneasy relationship the Nazis had with Shakespeare: which makes his early rendition of so contentious a part a potentially invaluable insight into attitudes surrounding anti-Semitism in Weimar Germany. (The most powerful production of the play that I have yet seen, the 2001 televised version of Trevor Nunn's 1999 production for the National Theatre, starring Henry Goodman, moved the setting to Berlin *circa* 1930, to stunning effect.)

The Nazi regime was dubious about *The Merchant*, recognising the propaganda value of a Jewish antihero but worrying that Shylock's thrift and industry contrasted favourably with the fecklessness of the Christian characters, that his self-justifications were too effective, and, most of all, that the apparently happy and approved marriage of Lorenzo and Jessica constituted an incitement to miscegenation. It was Krauss who was principally responsible for producing a version acceptable to the Propaganda Ministry, judiciously cutting lines to depict Shylock as unsympathetically as possible, and turning Jessica into a stolen Aryan child who was returning to her "true" racial heritage when she married Lorenzo. When "enemy" playwrights were banned in 1939, Shakespeare alone escaped the prohibition, allowing Krauss to return to this role in 1943 for what was probably the most grotesquely racist production the play has ever received: it is fascinating to view an early version, filmed when Krauss had yet to express a single anti-Semitic view in public (and had, indeed, starred only the previous year in a film of Lessing's *Nathan, der Weise*, whose philo-Semitism would secure it a ban under Hitler).

Like the recent German films of *Hamlet* (1921) and *Othello* (1922), *Der Kaufmann von Venedig* makes much of going back to pre-Shakespearean sources. In this case, however, it is untrue: the non-Shakespearean material is almost entirely the invention of the director Peter Paul Felner, and the alternative names given to the characters in the English language print are new. The plot alterations exacerbate the divided nature of the play, making the love-plot more comic and the bond-plot more tragic to the point where one feels that there are two different films here. On the one hand, Ferdinand von Alten camps it up as a much expanded and somewhat tedious Prince of Aragon, and the "rings" episode is played (anticlimactically) as light and frothy comedy; on the other, such coals of fire have been heaped on Shylock's head that anybody in his position might reach for a knife.

This Shylock is part of a more fully realised Jewish community than that of the play. He lives not alone with Jessica (Lia Eibenschütz), but with his still living wife Leah and his mother.[43] At the beginning of the film the family is celebrating Jessica's betrothal to Tubal's (Albert Steinrück) serious, studious son Elias (Friedrich Lobe). To help pay for the wedding, Leah is

---

[43] Confusingly, different cast lists name Frida Richard in both these parts: on balance it seems more likely that she played Leah.

sent to request an early return of some of the money already lent to Bassanio (Harry Liedtke); he and his friends laugh at her, she flies into a fury, collapses, and dies. In what appears to be a deliberate echo of the final scene of *Lear*, Shylock carries her body home through the streets, his grief writ large on his face; from this moment on, the hitherto benevolent and avuncular moneylender becomes a figure of godlike rage comparable to a Lear or a Titus. The "merry sport" of Antonio's (Carl Ebert) bond is here already a vague revenge plot. By the time Antonio forfeits, Shylock has been further tortured not only by Jessica's elopement, but by Elias' subsequent suicide. (Around this time, the mother disappears from the film, leaving Shylock alone.) After the trial, he seeks consolation in the Torah, but is disturbed by trumpets greeting the three married couples as they pole down the canals being showered with flowers from overhead bridges; the final shot of the film is a close-up of the exhausted, solitary Shylock closing his eyes, a man destroyed. What Krauss' later patrons thought of this can but be guessed at: but it is a far cry from the version he gave them in 1943.

The film is quite gorgeous to look at, vast sets and real Venetian locations beautifully photographed by Axel Graatkjaer and Rudolph Maté, while the costumes, though not period accurate – they incorporate into a basically Elizabethan look elements from a century or so either side of it; Felner had set the play neither in the medieval period from which the sources originate, nor during Venice's decline in the 1590s, but, as the first title card tells us, in 1565, to make use of all the pomp and spectacle afforded by the Serene Republic's last age of greatness – are convincing in context and exquisitely designed. Huge crowds are expertly directed in a stunning festival / masque scene and a trial sequence heavy on pageantry; and, despite the silliness of some of the Belmont scenes, the film is overall an impressive achievement.

Cymbeline (1925, Germany, black and white, silent)
Directed by Ludwig Berger
Believed lost

Ludwig Berger, best known for co-directing *The Thief of Bagdad* (1940), is alleged early in his career to have filmed *Cymbeline*. Ball was unaware of the film, and I have been unable to discover any details, or names other than Berger's associated with it.

Ein Sommernachtstraum: ein heiteres Fastnachtsspiel (1925,
Germany, black and white, silent)
Based on *A Midsummer Night's Dream*
A.k.a. *A Midsummer Night's Dream* (U.S.A.); *Wood Love* (U.K.)
Directed by Hans Neumann
Believed lost

Neumann's *Dream* appears, if conflicting accounts can be
trusted, to have been a bizarre affair, full of high-kicking chorus
lines, ballerinas (Valeska Gert and Tamara Geva) playing male
fairies, extra-textual characters, and deliberate anachronisms.
Ball remarks of the reviews that "It is as if we are talking about
not one but several films".[44] (Stills suggest extreme stylisation
and a strong influence from Greek art and ancient comedic
conventions, not mentioned by reviewers.) When shown with
non-Shakespearean intertitles (by Alfred "Klabund" Henschke),
it was deemed crude, overblown, and overacted; the Berlin
censor marked it "forbidden for juveniles", while in Britain the
title was changed to relieve Shakespeare of a dreadful
responsibility; but when the original text was restored for the
American release, critics were more muted, complimenting the
photography but finding the overall effect somewhat dull.

Werner Krauss reportedly made an utterly unrestrained
Bottom.

Julius Caesar (1926, U.K., black and white)
Directed by George A. Cooper
Believed lost

Since the beginning of film, there had been efforts to
endow pictures with synchronised soundtracks, by various
somewhat far-fetched means. The first real breakthrough was
made by Lee DeForest when he developed his Phonofilm mix in
1921, although sound films remained a fringe interest for several
years, as it was not yet practicable to make them at feature
length. DeForest confined himself to single reel shorts for most
of his career.

It was DeForest who produced the first true

---

[44] Ball, *Shakespeare on silent film*, p. 299.

Shakespearean sound film as the term is understood today: an extract from *Julius Caesar*, starring Basil Gill and Malcolm Keen as Brutus and Cassius respectively. It has not survived.

Romeo e Giulietta (1927, U.K., black and white)
Based on *Romeo and Juliet*
Starring: Mary Cavanova, Otakar Marak
Language: Italian
Runtime: 6 minutes

This operatic short from DeForest Phonofilms barely qualifies for inclusion here. I have excluded *Mme Alda Singing "Ave Maria" by Verdi* (1930), despite its use of material from *Otello*: but, although Cavanova and Marak wear modern evening dress and sing to the camera, I have concluded that the fact that the duets they have chosen carry forward the plot of Gounod's *Roméo et Juliette* qualifies this as a Shakespearean film. Marak seems somewhat overwhelmed by Cavanova's considerably more powerful singing voice.

The Merchant of Venice (1927, U.K., black and white)
Directed by Widgey R. Newman
Starring: Lewis Casson, Maurice Farquharson, Torin Thatcher
Runtime: 10 minutes

Newman's uninspired film of Act Three, Scene One of *The Merchant of Venice* – the oldest surviving recording of Shakespeare's words in a sound film – epitomises everything that was most fossilised in British theatre in the 1920s. Its sole points of interests are quickly passed over before the actual scene begins: it opens with a jaunty dance (a modern equivalent, perhaps, to the jigs performed after plays in Shakespeare's day?), followed by outtakes (possibly the first in cinema history) from an attempt to film an entirely different scene. Then, alas, we move into the supposedly dramatic territory, and all is static blocking, wild ranting, camp gestures, and faintly ludicrous upper class accents, with very little apparent understanding of the text. Even the young Torin Thatcher, who might have made a tolerable Solanio had he come to the part twenty years later, is negligible in his first film role; while the uncredited Tubal and Lewis Casson as Shylock play the Jews as ancients so doddery it's a wonder they live to the end of the film.

Khoon-E-Nahak (1928, India, black and white, silent)
Based on *Hamlet*
Directed by K. B. Athavale
Believed lost

No details are known concerning India's first Shakespeare picture, an adaptation of *Hamlet* from Excelsior Films.

The Taming of the Shrew (1929, U.S.A., black and white)
Directed by Sam Taylor
Starring: Mary Pickford, Douglas Fairbanks, Edwin Maxwell
Runtime: 68 minutes / 63 minutes (1966 re-release)

The first feature-length Shakespearean "talkie" (which survives only in its slightly shortened 1966 cut) was undertaken with some trepidation: a possibly apocryphal story relates that an apologetic studio worker promised that Sam Taylor was "turning it into a cah-medy".[45] The result is a slapstick farce containing only a fraction of the original text, and – a common fault with screen adaptations of the *Shrew* – concentrating so heavily on the Katherine / Petruchio storyline that other characters are crowded out: indeed, Lucentio, the second male lead, has disappeared entirely, so that it is Hortensio (Geoffrey Wardwell) whose wooing of Bianca (Dorothy Jordan) succeeds. (It should be remembered that Shakespeare adapted the *Shrew* from George Gascoigne's *Supposes* (1566), in which the equivalent to the Lucentio / Bianca plot is paramount, and characters corresponding to Kate and Petruchio do not appear at all. Taylor, however, was drawing on David Garrick's 1754 adaptation *Catherine and Petruchio* as much as on the original text.)

Taylor's heavy-handed approach to the comedy is at first ineffectual. Exaggerated violence, overplayed tantrums, and the habit of both principals of carrying whips with which they lay about one another and anyone else within reach, do not amuse. The film becomes much more effective, however, when it reaches the wedding night. It has already been hinted that Mary

---

[45] Quoted by Rothwell, Kenneth S., *A history of Shakespeare on screen: A century of film and television* (Cambridge, 2004), p. 28.

Pickford (who also produced the film) is a Kate for the twentieth century, by her first appearance in a very modern dress and hat amid (not especially authentic) Renaissance surroundings; now, unseen by Petruchio (Pickford's real-life husband Douglas Fairbanks), she overhears his "Thus have I politicly begun my reign" speech, and realises how to best him. From then on, Petruchio's frustration is a sight to behold as Katherine obeys and agrees with him whenever he tries to pick a quarrel; and it is he, ultimately, who is tamed, as Pickford signals in a broad wink to Bianca at the end of her final speech.

This conceit may seem to turn the play on its head, but at its heart and those of Pickford's and Fairbanks' (sometimes overblown) performances lies an understanding that the "taming" represents not a template for marriage, but the specific means by which this particular couple forge their way to a loving understanding. From the beginning they feelingly convey the powerful attraction between the two characters. As for what Shakespeare would think of such an interpretation: we already know. The *Shrew* was inverted and Petruchio brought to heel in his lifetime, in John Fletcher's sequel *The Tamer Tamed* (1610) – shortly after which, Shakespeare entered into a partnership with Fletcher to write *The Two Noble Kinsmen*, the lost play *Cardenio*, and *Henry VIII*. He clearly approved.

Carnival (1931, U.K., black and white / colour)
Based on *Othello*
A.k.a. *Venetian Nights* (U.S.A.)
Directed by Herbert Wilcox
Starring: Matheson Lang, Chili Bouchier, Joseph Schildkraut, Brian Buchel, Lilian Braithwaite
Runtime: 87 minutes

Herbert Wilcox's sound remake of *Carnival* (1921) features Matheson Lang once again in the roles of Silvio Steno and Othello, this time with the benefit of his deep and resonant voice; the director makes up for this film's lack of the original's Venetian locations with close-ups, quick cuts, and an extended fireworks sequence filmed in two-tone Technicolor. There are certain distinct improvements – notably an opening shot of Silvio apparently strangling Simonetta (Chili Bouchier), before we learn that they are rehearsing *Othello* – but despite such touches and a much fuller background to the relationship of the central couple, the sound film often struggles even to live up to its not very impressive silent predecessor.

Every character has become more unlikeable. Silvio is jealous sooner, Simonetta more shallow, her money-grubbing brother Lelio (Brian Buchel) more slimy. Silvio's sister Ottavia (renamed Italia and played by Lilian Braithwaite) now appears the voice not of reason but of spite – almost an Iago, sowing doubts in her brother's mind. The presence of sound exposes the inadequacies of the actors, who almost without exception overplay their parts to a ridiculous degree; and the ending, already preposterous, becomes downright offensive – after the attempted murder, it is in this version not Simonetta but Silvio who is laid on a couch and fussed over, before reconciliation with his innocent wife. Making considerably less use of Shakespeare than the silent version does not help.

Remaking *Carnival* was unnecessary, and the resulting film manages the considerable feat of being both ridiculous and dull.

Otello (1932, Portugal, black and white)
Based on *Othello*
Starring: Manuel Salazár, Lelane Rivera
Language: Italian
Runtime: 40 minutes

Until recently, this film of Verdi's *Otello* was thought to have survived only as a single eight minute clip of Rivera singing Desdemona's aria. The full version has now been rediscovered. It features highlights of the opera rather than a continuous version. The lead singers certainly possess powerful voices (let down by the deteriorated soundtrack: the picture too shows its age badly) but lack a little as actors. Rivera simpers, and the very plump Salazár, wearing what looks like a silk dressing gown, makes a sentimental, almost teary-eyed Otello. The production is stage-bound, but the camerawork is mobile and highly competent, and the sets impressive.

The Yiddish King Lear (1934, U.S.A., black and white)
Based on *King Lear*
A.k.a. *The Jewish King Lear*; *Der Yiddishe Koenig Lear* (U.S.A.); *Der Yidishe Kenigen Lir* (U.S.A.)

Directed by Harry Thomashefsky
Starring: Maurice Kroner, Miriam Grossman, Jacob Bergreen, Morris Weisman
Language: Yiddish
Runtime: 83 minutes

The Yiddish King Lear was the first play Jacob Gordin completed after arriving in New York from Vilna in 1892; it is a loose update of *Lear* to the middle class Lithuanian Jewish world he had left behind, with a wealthy merchant (David Mosheles, played by Maurice Kroner) as the Lear figure. (Shakespeare is explicitly evoked, and Mosheles' similarity to Lear pointed out, by Joffe (Jacob Bergreen), a curious combination of Kent and the King of France.) Harry Thomashefsky's film version, one of a number of Yiddish language features distributed in the U.S. by the Jewish Talking Picture Company in the 1930s and '40s, betrays its stage roots with static blocking and long indoor scenes – although it also includes an ambitious sequence depicting Mosheles' pilgrimage to Jerusalem and prayer at the Wailing Wall.

At first, the film seems destined to fail in its bid for our sympathies: Mosheles seems a benign patriarch, Toibelle (Cordelia: Miriam Grossman making the best of an underwritten role) an ungrateful brat: but gradually the father's autocracy, folly, and selfishness become apparent, although he remains both more rational and more likeable than Shakespeare's King. Despite both Kroner's relatively positive characterisation and the respect which Gordin accords Mosheles, however, he is an antagonist – though not the principal one – to the dramatist's ideological points. These are a defence of female education – Toibelle nurtures academic ambitions, which are sneered at by everybody except Joffe – and a celebration of Joffe's modern interpretation of Judaism over the strict orthodoxy of Mosheles, which, although viewed with a certain nostalgic affection, is depicted as stultifying and chauvinistic.

The parallels are not exact. The Gloucester subplot disappears, although Mosheles himself loses his eyesight – only to regain it miraculously in a reconciliations-all-round ending reminiscent of the late romances rather than *King Lear*. Unlike the British monarch, Mosheles has a living wife (Fannie Levenstein); and the only real villain is their snobbish and mercenary son-in-law Abraham (Morris Weisman). Even he is forgiven at the end, and the dark cloud of Tsarist persecution that has hung over the family is simply forgotten. While this treatment is unsatisfying, however, the film achieves on its admittedly small scale a convincing picture of the life that people like the Mosheles lived at the end of the nineteenth century; and, when finally required to, Kroner rises to a truly Lear-like majesty in the title role.

Unfortunately the age of the film has badly affected both picture and sound.

Khoon Ka Khoon (1935, India, black and white)
Based on *Hamlet*
A.k.a. *Hamlet*
Directed by Sohrab Modi
Language: Urdu
Runtime: 122 minutes / 90 minutes (cut version)
Believed lost

Already a giant of the Parsi theatre and one of India's most distinguished Shakespearean actors, Sohrab Modi had avoided film before 1935: but, feeling that the talkies were damaging the theatre, he decided to strike back in defence of high culture by founding the Stage Film Company to adapt plays to the screen. His starting point was *Hamlet*, in which he had already had success on stage in Mehdi Ahsan's translation: in keeping with the traditions of Indian theatre, which have become equally strong traditions in Indian cinema, Ahsan had added seventeen songs to the text. (The odd plot point was also altered: for instance, it is reported that the film explicitly made Gertrude (Shamshadbai) complicit in her husband's assassination.)

No concession was made to a cinematic aesthetic: instead, Modi and his cast simply performed *Hamlet* on stage in front of two static cameras. It is perhaps instructive to contrast this with the visual style that Modi brought to his later historical epics, which remain favourites while *Khoon Ka Khoon* is lost and almost forgotten.

Despite critical praise for the director-star's own performance, the picture was not a success: but, as India's first Shakespearean talkie and the launching pad for the film careers of Modi and Naseem Banu (who, then aged eighteen, made her acting debut as Ophelia), it remains significant. It was followed mostly not by straight adaptations, but by the appropriation of elements from Shakespeare's plays (sometimes including whole scenes transplanted into completely different stories): unsurprising given the magpie habits of Indian cinema in the Thirties and Forties. Modi himself drew on *King John* and *Richard III* in this way for *Said-e-Havas* (1936), and on *Cymbeline* for *Meetha Zaher* (1938); while *Romeo and Juliet* must be one of the most frequently referenced texts in Bollywood.

A Midsummer Night's Dream (1935, U.S.A., black and white)
Directed by William Dieterle and Max Reinhardt
Starring: James Cagney, Mickey Rooney, Victor Jory, Olivia de Havilland, Dick Powell
Runtime: 133 minutes / 117 minutes (U.S.A.: cut version) / 142 minutes (U.S.A.: with overture)
Academy Awards (1936): Best Cinematography (Hal Mohr: write-in candidate); Best Film Editing (Ralph Dawson)
Academy Award nominations: Outstanding Production (Warner Brothers); Best Assistant Director (Sherry Shourds: write-in candidate)

Max Reinhardt was the director whose pioneering modern dress *Hamlet*, performed in Berlin in 1920, restored period analogue to the Western theatre after 150 years' dominance by antiquarian productions. When the Nazis came to power, the Jewish Reinhardt fled his native Germany for Los Angeles, where he continued his love affair with Shakespeare. His 1934 *Dream*, staged in the Hollywood Bowl, took a more traditional approach than *Hamlet*: and its success generated a bidding war among film studios, which was in the end won by Warner Brothers. The result was that Reinhardt received a sizeable budget, but was constrained to make Warner Brothers Shakespeare with a Warner Brothers cast: and it is at best a mixed success.

One certainly cannot complain about the look of the film. The costumes (designed by Max Rée and Milo Anderson) are rich and beautiful: Elizabethan for the aristocrats, with "Greek" armour (whose style is in fact Roman), fantasy for the fairies, near-modern for the mechanicals (who wear trousers, and very Thirties-looking hats). The neo-classical indoor sets and fantasy-realistic wood are very impressive. The latter was designed by Reinhardt himself, who had brought real trees onto the stage when he directed his first *Dream* thirty years earlier. Finding it too gloomy to shoot in, cinematographer Hal Mohr strung cobwebs everywhere and dusted them with aluminium particles to reflect the light: the resultant magical twinkling won him the first ever write-in Academy Award.

Unfortunately, the acting fails to live up to the artwork. A great deal of egregious hamming is on display, particularly from Victor Jory's sinister Oberon and Ian Hunter's lecherous Theseus; the lovers are bland; vaudevillean Joe E. Brown's camp, dim-witted Flute backfires. Mickey Rooney (carried over from the stage production), with horns pushing through his blond mop, is clearly enjoying himself and succeeds in bringing out Puck's childish cruelty, but his shrieking laugh soon becomes grating – and then infuriating. James Cagney, a bold if not eccentric casting choice as Bottom, is hilarious at his best, but often seems uncomfortable with the language.

Nor is the direction as sure-footed as one might expect from a veteran like Reinhardt. Some touches – an extended sequence of the lovers chasing one another round the forest; Quince (Frank McHugh) posing Flute like a mannequin; the painfully unmusical Bottom teaching Titania (Anita Louise) his "ousel-cock" song; Puck shadowing Lysander (Dick Powell) and mimicking his every move (shades of Buster Keaton) – work well; but all too often, particularly in the mechanicals' scenes, jokes are overplayed until the audience feels beaten over the head. The decision (probably at the studio's insistence: Warner Brothers were major musical producers in the 1930s) to have various characters burst into song at random moments was also ill-advised.

In fact, the film is at its best when nobody is speaking, particularly in the two long, effects-heavy, balletic sequences that begin and end the midsummer night. Translucent fairies – Titania's pre-Raphaelite followers in gossamer gowns, Oberon's sharp-nosed dwarfs in bat-wing cloaks – shimmer in and out of the mist, ride on flying branches, and dance up stairways of cloud, to Felix Mendelssohn-Bartholdy's exquisite music, arranged by Erich Korngold. (It is worth reminding the modern viewer that Mendelssohn's Wedding March, now best known out of context and whose frequent use in the picture can strike one as anachronistic, was written for this play.) These scenes are where the skills of Mohr, Reinhardt, co-director William Dieterle, and the effects and choreography teams, truly come to the fore: but it is not enough to compensate for the cast's mangling of the verse.

If some other studio had made *A Midsummer Night's Dream*, Reinhardt would probably have had less money to work with, and perhaps a less talented arts team: but perhaps, if he had not been tied to Warner Brothers' contract stars, he could have assembled a cast capable of doing justice to the text. For all Rooney's joyousness and Cagney's flashes of brilliance, this is not the cast that Reinhardt and Shakespeare required.

Die Lustigen Weiber (1936, Germany, black and white)
Based on *The Merry Wives of Windsor*
A.k.a. *Falstaffs Abenteuer*
Directed by Carl Hoffmann
Language: German
Runtime: 88 minutes
Not seen by current writer
　　　　The only known Shakespeare adaptation made in Nazi Germany, *Die Lustigen Weiber* was a modern dress musical version of *The Merry Wives of Windsor*, adapted by Georg Zoch, with music by Franz Grothe, and starring the celebrated Austrian tenor Leo Slezak. Although it is rumoured to survive, I can find no archive which claims to hold a copy.

Romeo and Juliet (1936, U.S.A., black and white)
Directed by George Cukor
Starring: Leslie Howard, Norma Shearer, John Barrymore, Edna May Oliver, Basil Rathbone
Runtime: 125 minutes
Academy Award nominations (1937): Best Actress in a Leading Role (Norma Shearer); Best Actor in a Supporting Role (Basil Rathbone); Best Art Direction (Cedric Gibbons, Fredric Hope, Edwin B. Willis); Outstanding Production (Metro-Goldwyn-Mayer)
　　　　"Boy meets girl, 1436" ~ tagline to *Romeo and Juliet*.
　　　　George Cukor's *Romeo and Juliet* was post-silent Hollywood's third stab at the Bard, and the most ambitious yet. Set against a lavishly realised late medieval Italy, to the delicate strains of Tchaikovsky, it assembled a stellar Anglo-American cast: Leslie Howard and Norma Shearer (who had earlier played Juliet in a sketch in *The Hollywood Revue of 1929*) in the title roles; classical stage luminary John Barrymore as Mercutio, in his only

Shakespearean screen credit apart from the brief "*Richard III*" sequence in *Show of Shows* (1929 – credited to the wrong play, as the passage in fact comes from *Henry VI, Part 3*; his planned film of *Hamlet* never materialised, although a 1933 screen test survives, revealing just what a powerful Prince he made); and Basil Rathbone as Tybalt.

All were capable actors, who could speak the verse with clarity and understanding: but *Romeo and Juliet* is a play about youth. Howard was 43, Shearer 34, Rathbone 44, and Barrymore 54 when they tackled these parts: unsurprisingly, not one of them convinces as a teenager. Rathbone alone can be said to get away with his age: Tybalt could be anything up to thirty, for which he could easily pass. (The two principals actually look considerably older than even their real ages, never mind those of their characters.) Rathbone's, indeed, is the stand-out performance: while the lovers are somewhat staid, and Barrymore, who was frequently drunk on set, hams with abandon, his proud, dangerous Tybalt realises the character as written. (His duel with Barrymore is also the only onscreen swordfight which Rathbone – in real life an expert fencer – ever won.) One can only dream of what might have been had Cukor's first choice for Romeo, Laurence Olivier, accepted the lead.

Although the fifteenth century setting has been well researched, a couple of anachronisms creep in: Shearer sports a modern hairstyle that sits somewhat incongruously with her costume; and the swords are of seventeenth and eighteenth century designs, to accommodate a more swashbuckling fencing style than the era depicted ever saw. Nevertheless, the art team's fine work and William H. Daniels' excellent cinematography make this a strikingly handsome film. This is especially impressive when one considers how difficult it was to achieve such quality with the still relatively primitive equipment available in the 1930s: *Romeo and Juliet* looks almost good enough to have been made after the War. Cukor's direction, despite a tendency to the kitsch, is never less than workmanlike.

For all that, it was a commercial failure. The effect was to convince the film industry that Shakespeare was box office poison, an idea that lasted until 1944 and the explosive directorial debut of Olivier.

As You Like It (1936, U.K., black and white)

Directed by Paul Czinner
Starring: Elisabeth Bergner, Laurence Olivier, Sophie Stewart,
John Laurie, Mackenzie Ward
Runtime: 96 minutes

Czinner's *As You Like It* is of interest chiefly for the multifarious talents it assembled. It marks the young Laurence Olivier's first Shakespearean film role; it is scored by William Walton, the treatment was written by J. M. Barrie, and the editor was David Lean. The result, however, is far less impressive than one might expect. This is not entirely Czinner's fault: he had to cope with a very limited budget, and Elisabeth Bergner (Czinner's wife and regular star: both were Austrian-born refugees from fascism) as Rosalind was having trouble suppressing her accent. Other flaws, however, were more avoidable.

The sets and, above all, the costumes (designed by John Armstrong and Joe Strassner) are cartoonish, betraying a complete lack of period sense: it is impossible to say in which country or century the film is set. Walton's tunes for the numerous songs (including "Tell me, where is fancy bred", imported from *The Merchant of Venice* as if *As You Like It* did not have enough songs already – more, indeed, than any other play in the canon) make them sound less like pastoral tunes of the Renaissance than like Victorian Christmas carols sung by a church choir. The most serious problem, however, is that, while Olivier and John Laurie are at worst competent as Orlando and Oliver, and Felix Aylmer has fun as the evil Frederick, most of the acting is stilted and unnatural. Bergner, the worst offender, has at least the excuse that English was not her native language; but the woefully unfunny Mackenzie Ward as Touchstone, and the least convincing collection of yokels (all with cut-glass accents) ever committed to the screen, cannot be so easily exonerated.

The text is treated cavalierly. More than a third of the play has been cut, including everything too dark for Czinner's pantomime vision and anything that might have let another actor overshadow Bergner – but, bizarrely, Rosalind's epilogue is quite inappropriately retained. This piece was written for a boy-actor in women's clothing, and makes no sense coming from a woman: some modern stage productions have found inventive ways of dealing with the problem, but Bergner simply recites to camera with little sign of understanding.

117

The production is not without its charm; the homely touch by which farm animals are seldom off the screen, reminding us that the play is pastoral as well as comedy, works well enough, and its very amateurishness is at times endearing. Ultimately, however, it is of only mild interest, far more important as a step in Olivier's career than in its own right. The star himself did not accord it even that significance, omitting all mention of it from his autobiography.

Dil Farosh (1937, India, black and white)
Based on *The Merchant of Venice*
Directed by D. N. Madhok
Language: Hindi
Believed lost

    Dil Farosh (literally "The Merchant of Hearts") was a nineteenth century rendition of *The Merchant of Venice* into the traditional forms of Parsi theatre, with many added songs and a certain reduction in moral complexity: Shylock, in India, is usually a pantomime villain.

    Very little is known about the 1937 film.

Julieta y Romeo (1939, Spain, black and white)
Based on *Romeo and Juliet*
Directed by José Maria Castellví
Language: Spanish
Runtime: 93 minutes
Believed lost

    Castellví was a minor director of romantic and dramatic films whose career had been interrupted by the Spanish Civil War; as it drew to a close in 1939 he returned to cinema with *La Linda Beatriz* and *Julieta y Romeo*. Neither film is well documented or believed to survive.

The Boys from Syracuse (1940, U.S.A., black and white)
Based on *The Comedy of Errors*
Directed by A. Edward Sutherland
Starring: Allan Jones, Joe Penner, Rosemary Lane, Irene Hervey, Martha Raye
Runtime: 73 minutes

Academy Award nominations (1941): Best Art Direction (Black and White) (John Otterson); Best Special Effects (John P. Fulton, Bernard B. Brown, Joe Lapis)

"After 'The Comedy of Errors' by William Shakespeare", the credits proclaim – "Long, Long After!" They are not wrong.

The Rodgers and Hart musical *The Boys from Syracuse* first hit Broadway in 1938, and was soon rushed (as is all too obvious) into a cinematic adaptation, starring Allan Jones as the Antipholus twins and radio comic Joe Penner as the Dromios. Shakespeare's text has been replaced with a deliberately anachronistic script by George Abbott – the first character we see, an emcee played by Larry J. Blake, is puffing on a cigar as he cracks wise in up-to-date American slang. (His opening line, "Citizens of Ephesus, the war is over," had acquired by the time the film was released a black irony not thought of when Abbott was writing it; but the newspaper headline "EPHESUS BLITZKREIGS [*sic*] SYRACUSE", the Roman salutes exchanged by the Ephesians, and the Ephesian Antipholus' Hitlerish staccato hand gestures as he calls for the execution of all Syracusans found in Ephesus, all suggest that events in Europe were not far from the director's mind. American politics get a nod too, with jokes about the illogicality of the Ephesian tax system which could be read as fairly gentle digs at Roosevelt's policies.)

As mentioned above, it is Antipholus – whose heroic war record, glanced at in the play, is here explicitly said to have been gained fighting the Syracusans – who is responsible in the musical for the law that threatens his father's life; Solinus (a sad-sack performance by Charles Butterworth) is portrayed as sympathetic to the law's victims. This is the first of many mostly minor changes to Shakespeare's play: Pinch (Eric Blore) and Angelo (Alan Mowbray) have become a pair of camp, English-accented tailors, whose double act replaces everybody to whom either Antipholus owes money in the play; Luciana has been renamed Phyllis (Rosemary Lane), presumably to avoid confusion with Luce (Martha Raye) – who, though certainly buxom, is far from the "spherical" "fat wench" that Shakespeare made her. Only towards the end does Abbott make major departures from the Bard, throwing in a chariot chase and a threat of execution over all the major characters for added drama: although, if anything, drama is lost by the excision of

119

Emilia. (Interestingly, in the world of the film, Syracuse can apparently be reached from Ephesus overland in a matter of minutes. The Mediterranean must have been a lot narrower, not to say drier, in those days.)

The anachronisms are by and large pointless and without wit, and the majority of the songs forgettable – although Jones' dreamy "Falling in Love with Love" and Lane's catchy "This Can't Be Love" are exceptions, and have deservedly survived. The performances are so broad they belong in a circus. Penner, whose popularity was on the wane and who had failed to break into the movie world, shows us why with every gurn, wink, and pratfall. At 73 minutes, with some not-bad singing to appreciate and attractive female stars to feast the eyes on, *The Boys from Syracuse* passes pleasantly enough; but if it were much longer, the elements that (as things are) merely annoy should become intolerable.

Zalim Saudagar (1941, India, black and white)
Based on *The Merchant of Venice*
A.k.a. *Merchant of Venice*
Directed by J. J. Madan
Language: Hindi
Believed lost

J. J. Madan was the owner of Madan Theatres, Calcutta, whose film division was very active in the pre-independence period, specialising in adaptations of stage productions. He is reported to have drawn on Shakespeare for film before, *Hathili Dulhan* (1932) using elements of *The Taming of the Shrew*, but *Zalim Saudagar* is his only known straight adaptation.

Shuhaddaa el gharam (1942, Egypt, black and white)
Based on *Romeo and Juliet*
A.k.a. *Romeo and Juliet* (international English title); *Victims of Love* (U.S.A.)
Directed by Kamal Selim
Language: Arabic
Estimated runtime: 90 minutes
Believed lost

Selim, who specialised in romances throughout his career, in 1942 directed the greatest of them all, with the title roles going to Ibrahim Hammooda (who formed a film-making partnership with Selim, retiring after the latter's death in 1946) and popular singer-starlet Laila Mourad. The film was released internationally, but its eventual fate is unknown.

La Bisbetica domata (1942, Italy, black and white)
Based on *The Taming of the Shrew*
Directed by Ferdinando Maria Poggioli
Starring: Lilia Silvi, Amedeo Nazzari, Lauro Gazzolo, Rossana Montesi
Language: Italian
Runtime: 81 minutes

Poggioli's *Shrew* transfers the story to Rome in the early part of the War. The Forties, and the War itself, have scarcely yet intruded. The America from which Petruccio (Amedeo Nazzari) has just returned is apparently not yet Italy's enemy, bomb damage is not visible, and no uniformed servicemen appear, though an air raid does interrupt the action early on. The fashions on display, the twinkling stars animated behind the cheery opening credits, and the quickfire dialogue, all smack of mid-Thirties Hollywood, with an Italian touch brought in by Felice Montagnini's bouncy score.

Although the Lucentio plot is somewhat altered, and bulked out with some irrelevant digressions about Battista's (Lauro Gazzolo) tailoring business, the main plotline of the play is fairly closely adhered to, with some additions: and we are clearly supposed to side with the smug Petruccio against the petulant Catina (Lilia Silvi). When Petruccio has his servants stage a haunting to scare his bride, her terror is played for laughs, her attempt to fight off the "ghost" causes a fire, her assumption that the fire is another of Petruccio's tricks nearly gets her killed, and Petruccio is obliged to rescue her. He does at last demonstrate real love in his fear for her safety: but this is also the moment that supposedly sets her on the path to submission. After this, she happily pushes Petruccio's broken-down car, then is seen sitting at his feet, gazing adoringly up and nodding at his every word. "Thy husband is thy lord, thy life, thy keeper" is replaced with a jaunty song about the proper place of a wife.

It is hardly surprising that a film whose characters periodically utter admiring asides about *Il Duce* should espouse a socially conservative view, and the film is too frothy to ever be

121

seriously offensive – it has none of the violent undertones of *La fierecilla domada* (1956), for instance. It remains impossible to warm to.

Dente per dente (1943, Italy, black and white)
Based on *Measure for Measure*
A.k.a. *Measure for Measure* (U.S.A.)
Directed by Marco Elter
Language: Italian
Runtime: 83 minutes
Not seen by current writer

  Dente per dente was reportedly a straight, in-period adaptation of *Measure for Measure*. It received a U.S. release in December 1951, but performed poorly.

Romeo y Julieta (1943, Mexico, black and white)
Based on *Romeo and Juliet*
A.k.a. *Romeo and Juliet*
Directed by Miguel M. Delgado
Starring: Mario "Cantinflas" Moreno, María Elena Marqués, Ángel Garasa
Language: Spanish
Runtime: 104 minutes

  Cantinflas, the "Mexican Charlie Chaplin" whose name has passed into the Spanish language[46], stars in this somewhat hit-and-miss burlesque of portentous Shakespeare productions. An overlong introduction sets up the situation – Cantinflas, a fast-talking jobbing mechanic, poses as a classical actor and blags his way into a production of *Romeo and Juliet* – taking up 32 minutes of the film before the curtain goes up. Unfortunately, the humour lies mainly in complex wordplay – of the sort that delighted Shakespeare himself – which does not translate well. The physical comedy (Juliet knocking flowerpots off her balcony, Romeo falling into a fishpond or obtaining access to the orchard by clobbering a sentry with his mandolin) is not especially funny, although it helps if the viewer appreciates the references to George Cukor's 1936 film, which *Romeo y Julieta* enthusiastically mocks at every turn.

  Although the play – rewritten in rhyming couplets, often

---

[46] "Cantinflear" means "to talk volubly without saying anything of note".

near-translations but with a twist – as used here is more often absurd than tragic, it is played with absolute seriousness by everybody except the gloriously over-the-top Cantinflas. Even when the warring families throw food at each other instead of fighting in the opening scene, it is treated as a deadly matter; when swords do come out, they windmill about in a parody of the bad fencing in Hollywood swashbucklers. Only the first and last scenes take place in the theatre: the matter between is largely location-shot, making use of a colonial-era plaza which may be almost as old as the play but is markedly more Spanish than Italian. (Mexican culture is asserted over that of the Old World: when Romeo plays a mariachi song, waking Juliet's parents, Lady Capulet remarks that she does not recognise the "foreign" music: but her daughter adores it.) At the somewhat anticlimactic end, the death scene is disrupted by Cantinflas' jealous girlfriend bursting onto the stage, and the actors end up in the local Commissar's office.

I suspect that *Romeo y Julieta* would be easier to enjoy if I had a better grasp of Spanish: as it is, only the broader – and, it must be said, less successful – elements of the parody survive translation. Many of Cantinflas' fans, however, regard this as among his finest films.

The Chronicle History of King Henry the Fift with His Battell Fought at Agincourt in France (1944, U.K., colour)
A.k.a. *Henry V*
Directed by Laurence Olivier
Starring: Laurence Olivier, Leslie Banks, Nicholas Hannen, Ralph Truman, Robert Newton
Runtime: 135 minutes
Academy Awards (1947): Special Award to Laurence Olivier for his achievement as actor, director and producer
Academy Award nominations: Best Picture; Best Actor in a Leading Role (Laurence Olivier); Best Art Direction (Colour) (Paul Sheriff, Carmen Dillon); Best Music Score of a Dramatic or Comedy Picture (William Walton)

Arguably the first film to bring original text Shakespeare successfully to a mass audience, Olivier's wartime propaganda piece (at the time the most expensive British film ever made) was certainly the most spectacular treatment the Bard had yet received, and kick-started the Shakespeare boom of the Forties and early Fifties. The 37-year-old star had never directed a motion picture before, and invited William Wyler (with whom he had worked before, on *Wuthering Heights* (1939)) to take the helm: but Wyler reportedly responded "No, if it's Shakespeare, it must be you,"[47] thus (after Terence Young and Carol Reed had also turned the project down) giving the world its first of all too few tastes of Olivier's talent as a film director. (In his long career, he directed only four more pictures, two of them Shakespearean.)

The constraints of filming in wartime, and making a picture dedicated to the British troops who even then were engaged in the D-Day landings with which the film draws a parallel ("To the commandos and airborne troops of Great Britain, the spirit of whose ancestors it has been humbly attempted to recapture in some ensuing scenes"), naturally meant that the darker aspects of the play had to be excised. This is a thoroughly simplistic reading of the text, one that takes the Chorus at his word and ignores anything in the action that contradicts it, presenting us with a bold and stainless English hero in knitted chain mail (real metal was rationed). As a rendition of the play, it is unsatisfactory: but as a piece of cinematic art, it is a great success.

We open with a panorama of Elizabethan London (a model) in glorious Technicolor, then move in on the Globe Theatre, where the first ever performance of *Henry V* is taking place – a clever device to introduce the Chorus (Leslie Banks, who remains in the costume of 1600 throughout), and to prepare us for the stylised nature of what is to follow. Olivier is first glimpsed not as Henry V, but as Richard Burbage standing in the wings, about to become Henry; laughing and jeering groundlings short-circuit any such reactions on the part of the viewers in the cinema, and at the same time let them feel part of the Elizabethan audience. The whole conceit is very cleverly handled.

When we leave the Globe, it is not for a realistic outside world, but for one deliberately drawn from the Middle Ages' most consciously romanticised view of itself, the *Très Riches Heures* of the Duc de Berri. This picture-book medievalism is maintained throughout, never once subverted: the closest we get to any negative reflection on Henry's character is a flashback by

---

[47] Olivier, Laurence, *On Acting* (London, 1986), p. 269.

the dying Falstaff (the former music hall comedian George Robey) to his rejection at the end of *Henry IV, Part 2*, and that is heard and not seen, Olivier himself never appearing in a bad light. The English are stout-hearted and good-humoured, the French buffoonish, and only the Constable (Leo Genn) approaches villainy: he is made responsible for the attack on the English camp-followers, before dying in single combat with Henry – an episode that has no parallel in the play. Episodes such as the treason of Scroop, the bloodcurdling threats made to the Governor of Harfleur, the execution of Bardolph, and Henry's notorious order for the slaughter of the French prisoners, vanish; and the King's rough wooing of Princess Katharine (Renée Asherson, who took over the role when Olivier's then wife Vivien Leigh proved unable to escape her Hollywood contract – the costumes had already been made, and Asherson was cast largely because she happened to have the same measurements as Leigh) is played purely as light comedy. Robert Newton's Ancient Pistol is a lovable clown.

This patriotic fairytale is beautifully shot; the performances are strong if necessarily unsubtle; and the Battle of Agincourt, taking place in bright sunshine instead of the rain which historically made an essential contribution to Henry's victory, was in 1944 one of the most impressive battle scenes yet committed to film. (Many of the Irish extras received a bonus for providing their own horses.) Over the whole plays William Walton's magnificent score, strongly influenced by Prokofiev and described by Olivier as "the most wonderful I have ever heard for a film".[48] Although some French-Canadian servicemen (and even a few Scots) reportedly walked out of screenings for the troops, it was deservedly a great success with the general public; and it is complemented rather than supplanted by Kenneth Branagh's 1989 anti-war version.

Macbeth (1946, U.S.A., black and white)
Directed by Thomas A. Blair
Starring: David Bradley, Jain Wilimovsky, William Bartholmay
Runtime: 73 minutes
The first talking picture of what is probably Shakespeare's most popular play might almost have been better

---

[48] Quoted by Kennedy, Michael, *Portrait of Walton* (Oxford, 1998), p. 125.

as a silent: certainly the look of the film is far superior to the sound. The brainchild of Chicago film student David Bradley, it was a tremendously ambitious project to undertake with a budget of only $5,000: but visually, at least, Bradley's invention pays off.

From the opening shot, as the camera peers down at a bubbling, sulphurous bog, to the final image of a dead tree standing alone on the battlefield of Dunsinane as Malcolm (J. Royal Mills) strides off to be crowned, the film is beautifully photographed (by Bradley himself, an onerous task to take on at the same time as playing the lead). He makes cunning use of the conventions of film noir to disguise the low budget, long shadows hiding the edges of the set while the actors are brilliantly illuminated. The witches first appear atop a mound, silhouetted against the setting sun, while Macbeth and Banquo peer up at them out of the darkness: only later, when they have abdicated their role as apparently neutral Fates to display openly the evil of their natures, does Macbeth see the leprous skin and rotting teeth already momentarily glimpsed by the viewer. Scotland is throughout a realm of low clouds and looming shadows, the sun never seen until the English invasion, while across the border it shines brightly and the birds twitter.

The design does not entirely succeed in supporting Bradley's cinematography. The sets and locations look sufficiently rugged and Scottish, but the costumes (designed by the young Charlton Heston) do not bear scrutiny: the obvious false beards, tinfoil helmets and cardboard crown are merely embarrassing. Moreover, the battle scene brutally exposes the film's budgetary limitations. It begins promisingly: a seemingly peaceful field is slowly defiled as the English soldiers begin to seep out of the woods: but the ridiculously small numbers of the opposing armies, and the unconvincing fight choreography, bloodless in all senses, unfortunately bring the film down in its last few minutes.

Bradley's artistic endeavour had already taken something of a battering from his actors. As was his practice, for reasons financial, pragmatic, and personal, Bradley had packed the cast with his friends from Northwestern University: even so, he could perhaps have shown more discrimination. William Bartholmay as Macduff and the uncredited Banquo in particular plod painfully through the verse, demonstrating an almost total lack of understanding. William Sweeney is tedious as the Porter,

126

whose scene has inexplicably been allowed to hold up the film while far finer, and more important, passages from the play have been cut. The best that can be said about these "actors" is that they make the central performances of Bradley and Jain Wilimovsky appear more impressive: the stars make credible but hardly compelling Macbeths. A clunking score and very poor sound recording lend them little assistance.

Macbeth sank almost without trace, but Bradley was undeterred: and four years later he would launch his friend Heston on the world via *Julius Caesar* (1950).

Othello (1946, U.K., black and white)
Directed by David MacKane
Runtime: 45 minutes
Not seen by current writer

MacKane's condensed *Othello* is believed to have been designed for showing in schools as an introduction to the play. It was studio-bound, shot on a very low budget, and starred John Slater, Luanna Shaw, and Sebastian Cabot.

Romeo and Juliet (1947, India, black and white)
Directed by Akhtar Hussein
Language: Urdu
Believed lost

Hussein's *Romeo and Juliet* is, for some reason, often confused with his better known *Anjuman* (1948), which is frequently (and incorrectly) alleged to be based on the play. The film was a family affair, with the director's brother Anwar – who preferred the spelling Hussain – and sister (born Fatima A. Rashid; known in her films as Nargis, and, since her 1957 marriage to Sanjay Dutt, as Nargis Dutt) both appearing in it.

A Double Life (1947, U.S.A., black and white)
Based on *Othello*
A.k.a. *Inspiration* (working title); *The Art of Murder* (working title)
Directed by George Cukor
Starring: Ronald Colman, Signe Hasso, Shelley Winters, Edmond O'Brien
Runtime: 104 minutes

Academy Awards (1948): Best Actor in a Leading Role (Ronald Colman); Best Music Score of a Dramatic or Comedy Picture (Miklós Rózsa)

Academy Award nominations: Best Director (George Cukor); Best Original Screenplay (Ruth Gordon, Garson Kanin)

Like *For Åbent Tæppe* (1911) and *Carnival* (1921 / 1931), *A Double Life* is the story of an actor (Ronald Colman, in a part originally written for Laurence Olivier) who takes on the role of Othello, only to find his own life mirroring the story of the play: but where the earlier films were far-fetched yarns reliant on coincidence to link life and art, *A Double Life* is an ably photographed, sharply written, and beautifully scored psychological chiller. Unfortunately, under the gloss, it is every bit as implausible as its predecessors.

Colman's character, Anthony John, relies on "character absorption" to an extraordinary degree, making it difficult for him to "switch off" a performance when he leaves the stage. This makes him an excellent actor but also makes tragic parts dangerous for him – and none more dangerous than Othello, a role with which he is obsessed before he even comes to play it. No sooner has the project been mentioned than he begins to hear lines from the play, and to see his reflection assume the makeup and headgear of the Moor: on first viewing this looks like nothing more than the workings of a powerful dramatic imagination, but it later becomes clear that these are the early stirrings of Anthony's mental instability.

His "only friend", as he puts it, and certainly his only serious link to reality, is his ex-wife Brita (Signe Hasso – "engaged during Oscar Wilde... divorced during Chekhov"). Anthony chases other women, and develops an on-very-much-off relationship with waitress Pat (Shelley Winters, who reprised this part in a TV remake for *The Alcoa Hour* in 1957), but always returns to Brita, and is deeply pained by her flirtation with her press agent Bill (Edmond O'Brien). Thus are the seeds of tragedy sown: Brita agrees to star opposite him; Anthony is drawn further and further into Othello's world as the play runs and runs, with the voice of the Moor effectively playing Iago in his head; he injures Brita in an over-energetic performance of the murder scene; finally, he loses his reason and kills Pat, taking her for Desdemona. The film then briefly changes direction, becoming a crime thriller in noirish Forties style, tracing Bill's attempts to prove Anthony's guilt – until, on the last night, seeing the police waiting in the wings, Anthony commits suicide for real.

Put as baldly as this, the film's plot reads like the absurd melodrama it is: but Ruth Gordon and Garson Kanin's razor-sharp script (incorporating large chunks of *Othello*), and Colman's often harrowing central performance, are sufficient to prevent any such thought crossing the viewer's mind. The film revolves around the play: the opening shot is of the curtain going up: the play scenes were filmed in sequence as if the actors were engaged in a real performance of *Othello*. In these circumstances, it is surprising as well as disappointing that Colman's acting is not equal to the Moor, and certainly smacks little of the Method. As Anthony John – even, if not especially, when speaking Shakespeare's lines offstage – he cannot be faulted; but as Othello he is artificial, and it falls short of credibility that the play could run for two years with so weak a lead. Only in his last, fatal performance does he truly rise to what the play demands.

Hamlet (1948, U.K., black and white)
Directed by Laurence Olivier
Starring: Laurence Olivier, Jean Simmons, Felix Aylmer, Basil Sydney, Eileen Herlie
Runtime: 155 minutes
Academy Awards (1949): Best Picture; Best Actor in a Leading Role (Laurence Olivier); Best Art Direction (Black and White) (Roger K. Furse, Carmen Dillon); Best Costume Design (Black and White) (Roger K. Furse)
Academy Award nominations: Best Director (Laurence Olivier); Best Actress in a Supporting Role (Jean Simmons); Best Music Score of a Dramatic or Comedy Picture (William Walton)

Olivier's Hamlet is an icon. His portrayal of the Prince, a gauntly handsome shadow in black velvet and blond pudding-bowl, remains instantly recognisable even to people who have never seen the film; any cartoonist wanting to depict Hamlet draws Laurence Olivier. It is also a landmark in the history of the Academy Awards, being the first picture ever to land a Best Actor Oscar for the director; to date, only Roberto Benigni's *La Vita è bella* (1998) has replicated the feat. (Hammer horror fans might also be interested to know that this was the first film to feature both Peter Cushing, as a flamboyantly camp Osric, and

129

Christopher Lee, in an uncredited role as a guard, with the single line "Light!". However, the two did not actually meet until they worked together on *The Curse of Frankenstein* (1957).)

Constrained by a considerably smaller budget than he had been able to command for his Technicolor extravaganza *The Chronicle History of King Henry the Fift with His Battell Fought at Agincourt in France* (1944), Olivier was forced to shoot in black and white: but he made a virtue of necessity, turning the play into film noir, a genre well suited to the material. ("To me", he remarked, "Hamlet is an engraving, not an oil painting."[49]) Once again, he demonstrated that a theatrical background was no bar to skill with a camera: the long shadows cast in this gloomy Elsinore, and the innovative quasi-Wellesian camera angles (*Citizen Kane* is a clear influence), expertly create a haunting and haunted atmosphere.

The tight budget, incidentally, did not prevent Olivier being the only director yet to include the pirate battle in a film of *Hamlet*. He has a high old time swinging from ropes and playing at being Errol Flynn; but then, his textual changes mean that this incident is rather more important to the plot of his film than it is in the play. For Olivier has cut out Rosencrantz and Guildenstern. They are not the only omission – the Fortinbras plot is trimmed until it is barely noticeable, and everywhere the text has been pruned back as far as can be; this is not only distressing to the textual purist, but also tends towards over-simplification of the play (a fault towards which Olivier was prone in his cinematic adaptations). Some have connected this with his opening announcement that "This is the tragedy of a man who could not make up his mind": but in fact such a description no more does justice to the film than to Shakespeare's play. Possibly it was included to avoid frightening viewers away from what, for all its thrillerish style, remains a more "intellectual" work than his *Henry V*.

At the centre of this, there remains Olivier's stark, powerful performance, and those of his strong supporting cast. Eileen Herlie, thirteen years younger than her "son", plays a languid Gertrude, practically taunting the censors with the play's Oedipal overtones – the film features a full-on kiss between mother and son, something unheard of in the cinema of 1948. (Olivier had sought the advice of Ernest Jones, who was at the

---

[49] Quoted by Rothwell, *A history of Shakespeare on screen*, p. 54.

time working on his *Hamlet and Oedipus*, published the following year.) But Herlie is overshadowed by the lovely Jean Simmons, who portrays perfectly both Ophelia's initial innocence and her descent into scurrility and madness. Both are a joy to behold, while Felix Aylmer's fussy, stuffy Polonius provides comic balance.

There have been other great Hamlets on the silver screen since Olivier's: but none has imprinted itself on the public consciousness in the same way.

Macbeth (1948, U.S.A., black and white)
Directed by Orson Welles
Starring: Orson Welles, Jeanette Nolan, Edgar Barrier, Dan O'Herlihy, Roddy McDowall
Runtime: 107 minutes / 89 minutes (cut version)

"If Laurence Olivier's work is Apollonian... Welles's is Dionysian and passionate" ~ Kenneth S. Rothwell.[50]

Hot on the heels of Olivier's *Hamlet* (1948) came another noir-influenced Shakespearean adaptation from a theatre-trained actor-director with a sizeable ego and talent to spare: but Orson Welles' *Macbeth* was in all other respects a very different beast. While Olivier had set the action in a recognisable Elizabethan-era milieu, Welles, who, since he had exploded onto the world's screens with 1941's extraordinary *Citizen Kane*, had not stopped innovating, went for what has been described as "Mongolia after the Martians have landed":[51] an extremely stylised vision touched with surrealism, and bearing little or no resemblance to any historical setting.

As was his normal practice, Welles had had his cast record the dialogue in advance and mime along to their own played-back voices. This helped speed up the filming process: *Macbeth* was completed in twenty-three days, which was as long as Welles could afford. But when the studio heard the cast's faintly preposterous attempts at Scottish accents, they flew into a panic. A disastrous early screening sealed the film's fate: it was withdrawn, and Welles was forced to cut eighteen minutes of

---

[50] Ibid., p. 69.
[51] Taylor, Neil, "National and racial stereotypes in Shakespeare films", in Jackson, Russell (ed.), *The Cambridge Companion to Shakespeare on Film* (Cambridge, 2007), p. 269.

footage and re-dub the entire picture in American accents. The butchery thus inflicted apparently made *Macbeth* more acceptable to English-speaking audiences – to the bemusement of foreign critics, particularly in France, who had loved the director's bizarre vision. The original version was not restored until the 1980s.

The text is handled respectfully, despite the intrusion of a new character, a "Holy Father" (Alan Napier) who cannibalises lines from various minor characters and comes to represent a stern and lugubrious "good" not especially preferable to the evil of Welles' ethereal witches; but unexpected interpretations are occasionally put on familiar lines. When, for instance, Banquo (a sinister Edgar Barrier) declares that "I fear thou played'st most foully for it," he is in this version speaking directly to Macbeth (Welles) – not articulating a moral doubt so much as apparently threatening his new King with blackmail, which is not only in keeping with Welles' dark vision of the play and of humanity, but makes the imperative for his murder that much more urgent.[52] Turning soliloquies into addresses was to become a hallmark of Welles' Shakespeare adaptations.

Interpolated set-pieces such as the execution of Cawdor and the suicide of Lady Macbeth (Jeanette Nolan) serve to show off Welles' skill with the camera (which, as Jean Cocteau remarked on first seeing the film, "is always placed just where Destiny itself would choose to observe its victims"[53]), but also complement the text; unfortunately, however, the acting – even apart from the Hollywood-Scots accents – fails to give adequate support to the direction. Welles' own skills were often put to better use behind the camera than in front of it: but the worst piece of miscasting is Nolan, who hams her way through the part of Lady Macbeth as if she were playing the Wicked Queen in *Snow White*.

Ultimately, this is a fascinating but deeply flawed picture. Welles was to return twice to Shakespeare on the big screen, in *The Tragedy of Othello: The Moor of Venice* (1952) and *Campanadas a medianoche* (1965): both are, overall, much better films than *Macbeth* (which Welles himself dismissed in later life

---

[52] It is worth remarking that Akira Kurosawa, in *Kumonosu jô* (1957), also makes his Banquo-figure complicit in the first assassination – following Holinshed where Shakespeare departed from him.

[53] Quoted in the sleeve notes for the DVD (2003).

as "a B-movie"[54]), but neither shows quite the same level of invention.

Gunasundari Katha (1949, India, black and white)
Based on *King Lear*
Directed by Kadri Venkata Reddy
Language: Telugu
Runtime: 172 minutes
Believed lost

   Described as "loosely based" on *King Lear*, this offering from the king of Telugu cinema featured parts for the Hindu gods, a McGuffin called the "Mahendramani Jewel", and the transformation of one character into a bear.[55] The title character (played by Sriranjani) was equivalent not to Lear (who was rendered by Govindrajulu Subba Rao), but to Cordelia; and she is married off not to the King of France, but to a crippled boy (comedian Kasturi Siva Rao). By this point the play has been left some distance behind.

Les Amants de Vérone (1949, France, black and white)
Based on *Romeo and Juliet*
A.k.a. *The Lovers of Verona*
Directed by André Cayatte
Starring: Anouk Aimée, Serge Reggiani, Pierre Brasseur, Marianne Oswald, Louis Salou
Language: French
Runtime: 105 minutes

   By 1949, with *A Double Life* (1947) and its Oscars fresh in the memory, the sub-genre of films in which the offstage life of actors mirrors the Shakespeare play in which they are appearing was well established. André Cayatte and his screenwriter Jacques Prévert had therefore to go a step further in search of originality: so *Les Amants de Vérone* centres not on a stage production, but on a film of *Romeo and Juliet*; and it is not the stars but their stand-ins (Anouk Aimée and Serge Reggiani) who become star-crossed lovers. The papered-over divisions in post-

---

[54] Ibid.
[55] Rajadhyaksha, Ashish, and Willemen, Paul, *Encyclopaedia of Indian Cinema* (London, 1994), p. 292.

war Italian society (possibly intended to represent the similar atmosphere of mistrust and recrimination in France) serve as a modern equivalent for family feuds.

Reggiani's character, Angelo, is a Venetian glass-blower; while Aimée's Georgia is the daughter of a snobbish ex-Fascist magistrate (Louis Salou), obsessed with family honour and under the thumb of the bullying, blackmailing tout Raffaele (Pierre Brasseur, overacting outrageously), who wants to marry Georgia – a Paris and Tybalt combined. Although their affair is larded with references to the play, the balcony scene being reprised for real the night after they film it, while Marianne Oswald's malevolent Laetitia is a kind of anti-Nurse, the film does not stick closely to the source material (lacking, for instance, a Mercutio), and even threatens to end happily: but in the last few minutes Georgia's family lure Angelo into a trap which goes badly wrong, leaving Raffaele dead and Angelo mortally wounded. Georgia, in full Renaissance costume from the film, has time for a tearful farewell before slitting her wrists with a piece of broken glass.

There is no denying that the film is sentimental, an effect exacerbated by Joseph Kosma's overblown score: but the Venetian and Veronese cityscapes (and, indeed, interiors, with talc sprayed in the air to capture the light) are beautifully shot, and it is a hard heart that will not be won by Aimée's performance.

Cayatte was one of the "Old Wave" French directors most loudly condemned by the angry young men of the New Wave a decade later. The flaws they identified are real enough: but they were nevertheless unfair to a talented man.

Julius Caesar (1950, U.S.A., black and white)
Directed by David Bradley
Starring: David Bradley, Charlton Heston, Grosvenor Glenn, Harold Tasker
Runtime: 84 minutes

The politics of *Julius Caesar* have always been a matter of debate, but more hotly so since Orson Welles' famously anti-fascist modern dress production in New York in 1937. The first film version after the Second World War took its lead from Welles, but was ambiguous in its attitude to the enemies of tyranny.

Producer-director David Bradley found what most film-makers would regard as an unworkably small budget for this project, with the result that considerable inventiveness was forced upon him. Students from Northwestern University were persuaded to appear in crowd scenes unpaid, causing many commentators to mistake this for a student film; Chicago's neo-classical public buildings stood in for ancient Rome; extreme close-ups and other tricks of the camera were used to disguise the small size of the cast and the fact that Bradley was able to hire only one horse per day. (This last device is not entirely successful. The conspirators appear to constitute the entire Senate, and, during the battle of Philippi, it is obvious that the opposing armies consist of handfuls of men.) Imagery based on fire and water often replaces direct representation; the edges of the screen are burning throughout the scene in which Cinna the Poet (Russell Gruebner) meets his gruesome end.

Memories of the War are repeatedly evoked. The helmets of the Roman soldiers are modern tin hats with plumes and earpieces tacked onto them; the desert setting of the surprisingly bloody final battle, in which almost every shot (and the shots are very brief) records a death, evokes the struggles for North Africa and for the isles of the Pacific; the vindictive and bloodthirsty Antony (Charlton Heston) conjures up memories of Hitler, without letting us forget the manipulative orators of the Allied side; Chuck Zornig's sparingly used score, which was composed and arranged in three days, smacks strongly of the 1940s.

Interestingly, despite his relative inexperience – this was only his second feature film, having debuted at the age of sixteen in the title role in Bradley's *Peer Gynt* (1941) – Heston is by some distance the most impressive actor in the picture. Most of the others are either flatly artificial or grotesquely exaggerated, or veer between the two. Although Bradley's own nervy, self-absorbed Brutus, a man of little nobility in this interpretation, is interesting to watch, Grosvenor Glenn's colourless Cassius is less so; and, while most other characters have been ill-served by the heavy cutting of the text, it is hard to wish to see more of them.

Nevertheless, *Julius Caesar* is a striking achievement, and a fascinating example of how far a talented director can stretch limited resources – to say nothing of its importance as a launching pad for Heston's subsequent career. Hard to find for

135

many years, it is now available on DVD, with the once badly deteriorated soundtrack fully restored.

Die Lustigen Weiber von Windsor (1950, East Germany, black and white)
Based on *The Merry Wives of Windsor*
A.k.a. *The Merry Wives of Windsor*
Directed by Georg Wildhagen
Starring: Sonja Ziemann, Paul Esser, Camilla Spira, Claus Holm, Ina Halley
Language: German
Runtime: 90 minutes

 East Germany's main state-owned studio, the Deutsche Film-Aktiengesellschaft (D.E.F.A.), produced many adaptations of literary and musical classics. One of the earliest was this vibrant and bouncy version of Otto Nicolai's Shakespeare-based operetta *Die Lustigen Weiber von Windsor* (1849).

 It is conventional in producing *Die Lustigen Weiber* to include as much of Shakespeare's dialogue (and / or any interpolations) as one thinks necessary between Nicolai's songs. The only guidance is the placing of the songs and the characters for whom they are written: but this does constrain a director somewhat. Nicolai concentrated first and foremost on the wives, and secondly on the Anne / Fenton subplot (which he lends more weight than Shakespeare accorded it); other diversions receive no musical attention, and are therefore customarily omitted. While Evans, Pistol, Shallow, and the present but drastically cut Caius (here played as a camp fop by Gerd Frickhöffer) cannot but be missed, and Nicolai's rendition of the courtship of Anne (Ina Halley, sung by Sonja Schöner) and Fenton (the impossibly clean-cut Eckart Dux, sung by Helmut Krebs) is somewhat saccharine, this decision allows for considerable streamlining. To do full justice to the original play *and* include Nicolai's songs would take several hours.

 Director Georg Wildhagen moved the action to what looks like *circa* 1630. The cast are a troupe of travelling players (who manage to rustle up an entire orchestra!); but, in the middle of the wives' first duet, Sonja Ziemann and Camilla Spira wander off their mobile stage, through the market and into the Fluth (Ford) house, singing all the while. The camera moves with them, with surprising fluidity. At the end, we will cut back to the marketplace to see the cast taking their bows.

Wildhagen and his cast handle the *Singspiel* ably. Paul Esser (sung by Hans Kramer) plays the Falstaff character, Spenser, as a seedy old soak, difficult to love; Ziemann makes a delightful Frau Fluth, her beauty and vivacity complemented by the singing voice of Rita Streich. The direction falters only at the close: the Park scene is inexplicably shot in daylight, and ends with a misjudged and slightly distasteful sequence in which Spenser is chased out of town. This is not enough, however, to undermine the film's warmth: and the whole remains perhaps the most charming rendition yet of this play for the cinema.

Antony and Cleopatra (1951, U.K., black and white)
Runtime: 33 minutes
Believed lost

Parthian Productions' short *Antony and Cleopatra*, starring Pauline Letts and Robert Speaight, has sunk with little trace; not even the name of the director is known. A print was reported to exist in the early 1970s, but has not, so far as I can discover, been heard of since.

Romeo at Julieta (1951, Philippines, black and white)
Based on *Romeo and Juliet*
A.k.a. *Romeo & Juliet* (Philippines)
Language: Filipino / Tagalog
Believed lost

Despite featuring such names as Erlinda Cortes – a major star in the Philippines – *Romeo at Julieta* has disappeared entirely.

Io, Amleto (1952, Italy, black and white)
Based on *Hamlet*
Directed by Giorgio Simonelli
Language: Italian
Runtime: 103 minutes
Not seen by current writer

Io, Amleto appears to have been something of a vanity project by star Erminio Macario, who founded Macario Films to produce it. It survives now only in a couple of preservation prints.

The Tragedy of Othello: The Moor of Venice (1952, U.S.A. / Italy /
France / Morocco, black and white)
A.k.a. *Othello* (U.S.A.)
Directed by Orson Welles
Starring: Orson Welles, Micheál MacLiammóir, Suzanne
Cloutier, Robert Coote
Runtime: 90 minutes

"*Othello*, whether successful or not, is about as close to
Shakespeare's play as was Verdi's opera." ~ Orson Welles.[56]

No sooner was *Macbeth* (1948) complete, than Welles
launched himself into another Shakespearean project: an
adaptation of *Othello*, starring himself as the Moor. It was to be
an extraordinarily troubled shoot, dogged by lack of money.
Twice Welles had to close down production while he took on
other roles (including his famous turn as Harry Lime in *The
Third Man* (1950)) to earn enough to fund his film, with the
result that it took nearly four years to complete. Occasionally,
however, the problems he faced brought out his talent for
invention: the highly effective notion of setting Roderigo's death
in a bath house was forced on Welles by the fact that it was the
first scene due to be shot, and hardly any costumes had yet been
delivered to his Moroccan base of operations. (Iago (Micheál
MacLiammóir) is the only character clothed in more than a
towel in that scene.)

The text is drastically cut: so much has gone, indeed,
that Welles was forced to add narration at the beginning to
explain a situation that would otherwise have baffled his
viewers. (A full-length *Othello* would run at well over twice the
length of this film.) What remains, however, is dealt with
effectively by a talented cast – even if some major characters
were dubbed by other actors, Welles himself reading most of
Roderigo's lines in place of Robert Coote. Problematic though it
is for modern audiences to see a white man blacked up to play
Othello, Welles carries off the part considerably more

---

[56] Quoted by Guneratne, Anthony R., "Cinema Studies: 'Thou Dost Usurp
Authority': Beerbohm Tree, Reinhardt, Olivier, Welles, and the Politics of
Adapting Shakespeare", in Henderson, Diana E. (ed.), *A concise
companion to Shakespeare on screen* (Oxford, 2006), p. 39.

successfully than he did Macbeth. MacLiammóir's sinister, gravelly-voiced Iago is perhaps a little too obviously evil, but certainly does not lack power.

As always with a Welles film, however, the direction is the star. His trademark stunning camera work is here in spades; the use of *chiaroscura*, and of unconventional angles, is uniformly masterful. Like Olivier's Elsinore, Othello's Cypriot fortress is begirt with cliffs against which the waves crash as if trying to break in, besieging and trapping the characters. Welles here retreated from the surreal realms of *Macbeth* to set the film against a recognisable historical background, projecting the action back to the beginning of Venice's last imperial period in the late fifteenth century.[57] He has recreated the era faithfully, modelling the look of the film on the paintings of Vittore Carpaccio; but he follows his practice in the earlier film of interpolating extra-textual scenes for use as set-pieces – most notably Othello's funeral, with which he begins and ends the film, Iago looking on from a cage hung from the city walls.[58] From the beginning, the audience is left in no doubt that all are doomed.

I do not consider that any cinematic adaptation has yet done full justice to *Othello*. This particular version falls short of ultimate success due to its massive textual cuts, slightly over-hasty editing and perfunctory treatment of the secondary characters: Emilia (Fay Compton) gets particularly short shrift. It remains, however, a powerful, expertly made film,[59] and the best cinematic *Othello* to date.

Julius Caesar (1953, U.S.A., black and white)
A.k.a. *William Shakespeare's Julius Caesar*
Directed by Joseph L. Mankiewicz
Starring: James Mason, John Gielgud, Marlon Brando, Louis Calhern, Greer Garson
Runtime: 120 minutes

---

[57] She first acquired Cyprus in 1489.
[58]This is supposed to have been a traditional Venetian punishment for traitors, although actual instances of it are hard to find.
[59] Despite receiving generally hostile reviews at its first release, it was the first English-language winner of the Palme d'Or at the Cannes Film Festival.

Academy Awards (1954): Best Art Direction (Black and White) (Cedric Gibbons, Edward Carfagno, Edwin B. Willis, Hugh Hunt)

Academy Award nominations: Best Picture; Best Actor in a Leading Role (Marlon Brando); Best Cinematography (Black and White) (Joseph Ruttenberg); Best Music Score of a Dramatic or Comedy Picture (Miklós Rózsa)

In 1953, the age of the Roman epic was at its height. Technicolor behemoths lumbered forth from every major studio. Joseph Mankiewicz's decision, staunchly defended by his producer John Houseman, to film *Julius Caesar* in black and white must, therefore, have seemed a little eccentric: but, to him, it was justified by the dramatic needs of the chillingly silent assassination scene. If Caesar's blood were red, Mankiewicz and Houseman feared, the audience would be looking at that instead of the face of Brutus (James Mason). They were repaid for their determination with five Oscar nominations, one successful, and the declaration of the National Board of Review that they had produced "the best and most forceful adaptation of William Shakespeare that Hollywood has ever accomplished".[60] Critic Bennett Cerf went further, somewhat hyperbolically announcing that *Julius Caesar* was "the most impressive and exciting movie I have ever seen".[61] Orson Welles, meanwhile, decided that his chances of outdoing Mankiewicz were slim, and abandoned his own plans to film the play, which was to have been his next project after *Othello* (1952).

Mankiewicz concentrates very closely on the conspirators' side of the story, and particularly the relationship between Brutus and Cassius (John Gielgud, in his first Shakespearean film role, although cinemagazine footage exists of him playing Romeo as early as 1924: Gielgud had for some years argued strongly that the plays were unfilmable, but changed his mind on seeing *The Chronicle History of King Henry the Fift with His Battell Fought at Agincourt in France* (1944)). Much material extraneous to this is cut. The director has no especial political message, beyond an interest in the moral ambiguities of the assassins' case: he seems to take at face value Antony's judgement of Brutus, that "all the conspirators save only he /

---

[60] Quoted on http://campus.bloomfield.edu.
[61] Quoted by Morley, Sheridan, *John Gielgud: The authorised biography* (New York, 2002), p. 251.

Did that they did in envy of great Caesar". Gielgud's Cassius and John Hoyt's Decius positively seethe with bitterness, in stark contrast to Mason's conscience-racked Brutus.

An effect of this focus, however, is that we never get much chance to compare the conspirators with Antony (Marlon Brando, in a role for which both Richard Burton and Stewart Grainger had been considered) and Octavius (Douglas Watson, in a part trimmed to a sliver). Brando's performance – achieved after hours spent listening to tapes of British classical actors, including his co-star Gielgud – stunned critics at the time, who had earlier lambasted the unconventional casting choice because, as Brando himself put it, "you can't mumble Shakespeare", and is indeed impressive; but his Antony remains an enigma. For such a key character he has received remarkably little of the director's attention. There are occasional nice touches: "Lend me your ears!" becomes an exasperated exclamation when the rabble refuses to shut up; "Mischief, thou art afoot" may have been cut, but Brando replaces it with a crooked smile that says as much as the line. How far these were Mankiewicz's decisions, and how far Brando's, we cannot now know.

The rest of the cast suffer from that tendency to artificiality which is common among actors unused to Shakespeare, and was worse in the Fifties than now. Louis Calhern in particular struggles with the role of Caesar, and never really manages to make the verse sound convincing; Greer Garson as Calpurnia veers into excessive histrionics, while Deborah Kerr as Portia devotes more attention to her diction than to her acting. Gielgud privately dismissed Calhern as "very ham" and the ladies as "simpering and affected";[62] it is hard to disagree.

The film is competently photographed, although it is hard not to wonder whether colour might not have been a wise investment after all, particularly in view of the huge sets and minutely detailed costumes, which are not well served by its absence. Mankiewicz had a considerable flair for crowd scenes; and the climactic Battle of Philippi, although turning it into a John Ford-style ambush in a gully makes a nonsense of the text, is expertly directed and extremely effective dramatically. Tighter focuses too, for instance on Caesar's body falling at the foot of a

---

[62] Gielgud, John, ed. Mangan, Richard, *Sir John Gielgud: A life in letters* (London, 2004), p. 160.

statue of his arch-rival Pompey, or on Brutus' dead face at the end, are handled well. Unfortunately, Miklós Rózsa's militaristic, brass-heavy score, typical of the backing music to Hollywood's Roman epics in this era, is only intermittently appropriate. Several scenes would have benefited from softer music, which is largely lacking.

If the Board of Review's opinion seems a little excessive, it is as well to remember that most Shakespearean films before this time had not come from Hollywood – which, indeed, had not produced a straight original text adaptation since George Cukor's *Romeo and Juliet* (1936). *Julius Caesar* certainly has its faults, and loses intensity at times (the argument between Brutus and Cassius before Philippi seems oddly drained), but it showcases the work of some very fine actors and succeeds, within its limits, in realising the text. It also demonstrated that it was possible to spend considerable amounts of money on a Shakespearean picture and still succeed. Its place in the history of adaptations is an important one.

Le Marchand de Venise (1953, France / Italy, black and white)
Based on *The Merchant of Venice*
A.k.a. *Il Mercante di Venezia* (Italy); *The Merchant of Venice* (international English title)
Directed by Pierre Billon
Language: French
Runtime: 102 minutes
Not seen by current writer

Le Marchand de Venise, which featured Andrée Debar as Portia and Swiss actor Michel Simon as Shylock, made considerable use of location shooting in Venice. The sub-plots were reportedly heavily cut to afford more prominence to these two stars.

Kiss Me Kate (1953, U.S.A., colour)
Based on *The Taming of the Shrew*
Directed by George Sidney
Starring: Kathryn Grayson, Howard Keel, Ann Miller, Keenan Wynn, James Whitmore
Runtime: 109 minutes
Academy Award nominations (1954): Best Scoring of a Musical

142

Picture (André Previn, Saul Chaplin)

Cole Porter's 1948 Broadway smash *Kiss Me Kate* was based on a clever, if confusing, conceit: a musical (called *Kiss Me, Kate*, with a comma) within a musical, based on *The Taming of the Shrew* (which is a play within a play), and with the offstage plot roughly mirroring that onstage – and with himself (played in the movie by Ron Randell) as a character, supposedly the adaptor of the play: which, of course, he was! Conveniently for film, this notion also made it possible to shoot almost entirely within a theatre, with deliberately artificial sets, rather than striving for expensive realism. This meant that the film-makers could afford to shoot no fewer than three different versions, on 1.85-1 widescreen and 3-D as well as the then conventional 1.33-1; no other film is known to have been made this way. After test runs, the widescreen version was chosen for release.

Lilli Vanessi (Kathryn Grayson) and Fred Graham (Howard Keel) are our Kate and Petruchio, formerly married actors reunited for these peculiarly appropriate roles (although at first they are more reminiscent of Beatrice and Benedick). They and the entire cast take the theatrical setting as an excuse for wild overacting: there is not much else that could be done with such a broad-brush script, and it never seems out of place. It is fully in keeping with the lurid, Pierrot-style, cod-Renaissance costumes and the garishly painted plywood set. Of course, the internal musical has been cut down so sharply from the original play that it would in fact be impossible for an audience to follow, but that is an unavoidable consequence of making a 160-minute play plus songs and an offstage plot fit into a 109-minute film, and it is easy to suspend disbelief. Nor, in this obviously unrealistic world, does Fred's "taming" of Lilli become offensive – even when he has recourse to violence.

The weakness, crucially for a musical, lies in the songs. Few seem to belong: twice, indeed, Porter himself draws our attention to this, by making "Too Darn Hot" a number cut out of the show because there is nowhere to put it and "Wunderbar" a reprisal from a previous show Fred and Lilli performed together. Nor are many especially memorable. There are two exceptions. The first is Fred's hummable "Where Is The Life That Late I Led?", based, like one or two others – including "I Come To Wive It Wealthily In Padua", which manages to rhyme the Italian city with "what a cad you are" – on Shakespeare's text. The other, of course, is the hilarious showstopper "Brush Up Your Shakespeare", performed incongruously by a couple of gangsters (Keenan Wynn and James Whitmore), which is on an entirely superior plane to the rest of the film. But these are not enough to build a whole musical upon. "From This Moment On", which was written specially for the film, is not particularly impressive.

One does get the impression that the actors hugely enjoyed making *Kiss Me Kate*, but communicating the same joy to an audience is a tricky business, and they seldom pull it off. Porter could do better than this, and "Brush Up Your Shakespeare" serves only to remind us of the fact.

Hamlet (1954, India, black and white)
Directed by Kishore Sahu
Language: Hindi
Not seen by current writer

Filmindia gave this production an astonishingly vitriolic review, in which "stupid" and "stinking selfishness"[63] were among the milder criticisms. Having managed to see only a couple of three minute clips, it is difficult for me to judge this, beyond noting the fairly unremarkable sets and vaguely Elizabethan costumes, and the surprisingly upbeat music: the film incorporated many songs, often corresponding to songs in the play ("Tomorrow is St Valentine's Day" was replaced with a nineteenth century traditional piece, "In youth when I did love" with something much more modern and carefree). If the music (by Ramesh Naidu) had been in this register throughout the film, it would certainly have been inappropriate: but I have no reason to suppose that this was the case.

Reviewers report slight alterations to the script, Gertrude being explicitly involved in her first husband's murder, Hamlet (Sahu) coveting the throne, and Rosencrantz and Guildenstern being excised: but apart from these tweaks, the play was quite closely adhered to.

Romeo and Juliet (1954, Italy / U.K., colour)
A.k.a. *Giulietta e Romeo* (Italy)

---

[63] Quoted by Rothwell, *Shakespeare on screen: An international filmography and videography* (New York, 1990), p. 64.

Directed by Renato Castellani
Starring: Laurence Harvey, Susan Shentall, Mervyn Johns, Flora Robson, Sebastian Cabot
Runtime: 138 minutes

Romeo and Juliet arrived trumpeted like few films of so literary a bent before, and trailing clouds of tie-in merchandise. Expectations, thanks to the publicity campaign, were very high indeed: they were to be cruelly dashed.

It is generally admitted that the film does at least look good. Certainly the Veronese locations are very beautiful, and no film photographed by Robert Krasker – who won a British Society of Cinematographers Award for his work here – was ever actually unpleasant to look at: but the contrast-heavy Technicolor reminds one more of Twenties experiments in two-tone than of the more vivid look commonplace by the Fifties, an effect exacerbated by the frequent colour clashes of Leonor Fini's costumes. These, modelled on the paintings of Botticelli and Raphael, set the action of the film towards the end fifteenth century: although the black and white scholarly garb of the Chorus (John Gielgud) belongs to the Elizabethan era, creating the impression that the story he is telling is already old. Roman Vlad's pastiche Renaissance score, while overusing sacred music and variations on "Greensleeves", by and large assists the sense of period – although, at the first appearance of the Nurse (Flora Robson), it veers into incongruously modern areas reminiscent of Prokofiev's *Peter and the Wolf.*

Unfortunately, however, the film is ploddingly directed, clumsily edited and poorly acted. Laurence Harvey as Romeo appears to be far more in love with the sound of his own voice than with Juliet, while the inexperienced Susan Shentall brings little more fire to her role; Mervyn Johns' pedantic, donnish Friar is *so* gentle and avuncular as to appear foolish. The only actor to show any kind of passion is Sebastian Cabot, on hammish form as Juliet's father. The cast were not helped by Castellani's butchering of the script, which, while retaining several now obscure jokes in the opening scene, brutally hacks away some of the most beautiful passages, and inserts snippets of unnecessary extra-textual dialogue here and there. Unforgivably, the Queen Mab speech has disappeared entirely, and Mercutio (Ubaldo Zollo, who like Shentall had no acting experience – a casting policy which Castellani imagined lent "authenticity" to his films) is so drastically cut that the audience receives no sense

145

of his friendship with Romeo.

When one adds to this the uneven, often dragging pace of the film and the laughable fight scenes, the result is so far below what had been promised that the Golden Lion awarded to Castellani in Venice is absolutely inexplicable.

Gunsundari (1955, India, black and white)
Based on *King Lear*
Directed by Kamalakara Kameshwara Rao
Language: Tamil
Believed lost

K. K. Rao, screenwriter of *Gunasundari Katha* (1949) – a Telugu *Lear* – presided six years later over a remake in Tamil. Like the original, it featured several songs by popular artist Leela which went on to be more successful than the film.

Otello (1955, U.S.S.R., colour)
Based on *Othello*
A.k.a. *Othello* (U.S.A.)
Directed by Sergei Yutkevich
Starring: Sergei Bondarchuk, Andrei Popov, Irina Skobtseva, Vladimir Soshalsky, Antonina Maksimova
Language: Russian
Runtime: 107 minutes

If Errol Flynn had ever played Othello, with Michael Curtiz directing (and, no doubt, Basil Rathbone as Iago, Olivia de Havilland as Desdemona, and Erich Korngold providing the score – it is perhaps not so difficult to imagine after all!), the end result might not have been so very different from Sergei Yutkevich's lavish swashbuckling epic. At one point Yutkevich even directly references the Flynn / Curtiz *oeuvre*, with a thrilling staircase duel modelled on that in *The Adventures of Robin Hood* (1938). Before the opening credits go up or a word is spoken, the stories of Othello's (Sergei Bondarchuk[64]) past life which so captivated Desdemona (Irina Skobtseva) – sea-battles, shipwrecks, slavery under the Barbary corsairs – are dramatised in front of us on a colossal scale, to a rousing score put together

---

[64] Better known as the director of the four-part *Voyna i mir* (*War and Peace*, 1965-67) than as an actor.

from the music of Aram Khachaturyan.

This *Othello* has been heavily influenced by Orson Welles' 1952 version: pounding waves, billowing cloaks, and unconventional camera angles are all much in evidence: but it is in every way bigger, though not necessarily better. Welles' version was confined to festivals for some years, and did not receive a general release until after the Russian film was completed: but Yutkevich, who had a passion for filmed Shakespeare, had sought it out. Yutkevich seems to have regarded the earlier film as a challenge to be met by deploying the vastly bigger budgets that Mosfilm could command. He could not, of course, buy Welles' skill with the camera and understanding of the text: but, while simplistic, his reading of the play is not unsatisfactory. It is helped not only by a visually stunning picture, but by some fine acting, particularly from Andrei Popov as a mercurially Mephistophelean Iago. Bondarchuk's portentous, self-aggrandising Moor runs the risk of crossing the line into self-parody, but for most of the film succeeds in avoiding this, save where Yutkevich's direction veers into the pompously melodramatic. This, almost fatally, includes the murder of Desdemona – all grasping hands and sinister red lighting – but the film is rescued by Bondarchuk's subdued and sensitive rendition of the final scene.

The cutting of more than half the text undeniably hurts the film: in particular, Act Three Scene Three can barely afford to lose a line if one is to avoid making Othello look foolishly gullible. It is also true that some of the supporting cast are a little stagy: but Yutkevich's confidence in his vision is infectious, and, while hardly the most profound interpretation of the play, this remains one of the most enjoyable.

Joe MacBeth (1955, U.K., black and white)
Based on *Macbeth*
Directed by Ken Hughes
Starring: Paul Douglas, Ruth Roman, Bonar Colleano, Grégoire Aslan, Sid James
Runtime: 90 minutes

Ken Hughes' *Joe MacBeth* is an original take on the *Macbeth* story – or at least, was so when it was made, however hackneyed its premise has since become. The play is transferred to a gangland milieu in an anonymous American city: as

147

envisioned by the British director, this is a stylised world of neon, fedoras and cigarette smoke – perhaps not realistic, but familiar to the movie-going public in the 1950s. The result is uneven, but never uninteresting.

The screenplay, by Hughes and Philip Yordan, draws more heavily on the noir and hardboiled genres than on Shakespeare – although Minerva Pious, as the fortune teller who stands in for the Witches (with a roast chestnut stall for a cauldron), gets a few near-quotes, and there are occasional neat references ("The knife knows where to go, Joe – just follow it"). By and large, this is a good thing: a script too close to that of the play would have been forever reminding the audience of its own inferiority to the original work. Clichés of American noir do intrude from time to time, but they are kept to a minimum, and there are many imaginative touches: the murder of the Duncan figure (Grégoire Aslan) takes place in a lake on the MacBeths' land; the slaughter of the Macduffs is not intentional, but a botched kidnapping – and tips Lily MacBeth (Ruth Roman) into madness when she arrives inopportunely on the scene; Lily's own death is an accident at the hands of her trigger-happy husband (Paul Douglas), who is mourning her when his enemies catch up with him.

The economical combination of characters is also deftly handled: Seyton, the Porter, and several minor Thanes become MacBeth's butler Angus (Walter Crisham); and the King's most formidable enemies, Malcolm, Fleance, and Macduff, are now one man (Bonar Colleano). Extra-textual characters have also been intruded: Harry Green plays a gluttonous rival gangster, whose dismissal of his stuttering food-taster proves fatal, with great comic gusto. The lead performances, however, are less impressive. The hulking Douglas seems out of place as a kingpin, and overplays his dramatic moments; Roman is more assured, but never makes it convincing that the intelligent and attractive Lily would have chosen to marry a fat, unimaginative thug old enough to be her father. They are well supported by Grégoire Aslan as the sleazy, heavily accented Duca, and Sid James in a rare serious role as the Banquo figure (maintaining a quite convincing American accent – most of the time); but there is a gap at the heart of the film.

Dvenadtsataya noch (1955, U.S.S.R., colour)

Based on *Twelfth Night*
A.k.a. *Twelfth Night; The Twelfth Night* (video title)
Directed by A. Abramov and Yan Frid
Starring: Klara Luchko, Alla Larionova, Mikhail Yanshin, Vasili Merkuryev, Bruno Frejndlikh
Runtime: 88 minutes

Yan Frid's romantically conceived and lavishly executed *Twelfth Night* is a high point of the escapist fare that characterised Soviet cinema in the mid to late 1950s (complete with wonderfully over-the-top fight scenes comparable to those in Sergei Yutkevich's *Otello* in the same year); yet, for all its upbeat tone and the heavy cuts made to the script, it never loses sight of the thread of melancholy that runs through the play, instead balancing it perfectly against a glorious sense of fun.

The performances of the handsome and charismatic cast may occasionally veer into the excessively "actorly", but are by and large masterful. (The English dubbing of the dialogue is occasionally slightly flat, but generally expressive enough; the songs are left in rumbustious Russian.) Mikhail Yanshin's boisterous Sir Toby and Klara Luchko's enchanting Viola are the most impressive, but the support they receive from Vasili Merkuryev as an inflated, mincing Malvolio, Alla Larionova as an Olivia with a streak of the tragic in the genuine sorrow she displays for her brother, and Georgi Vitsin as a mournful puppy of a Sir Andrew, is very strong. The costumes are as beautiful as they are authentic; Aleksei Zhivotov's vibrant and varied score may not entirely succeed in avoiding sentimentality, but is nevertheless delightful.

Only one reservation need be made: the passage of the years has not been kind to the sound quality. A restored re-release is sorely needed.

Richard III (1955, U.K., colour)
Directed by Laurence Olivier
Starring: Laurence Olivier, Ralph Richardson, Claire Bloom, Cedric Hardwicke, John Gielgud
Runtime: 161 minutes
Academy Award nominations (1957): Best Actor in a Leading Role (Laurence Olivier)

Olivier's last Shakespearean film as director was also his most ambitious. Working from the Colley Cibber version of the play, as further revised by David Garrick (non-Shakespearean lines such as "Off with his head! – So much for Buckingham" and "Richard is himself again" remain in the script), Olivier set out to make a Technicolor epic to put his own *The Chronicle History of King Henry the Fift with His Battell Fought at Agincourt in France* (1944, also the year in which he had first played Richard on stage) to shame.

One cannot honestly say that he succeeded. His gaudily-coloured view of the Middle Ages, appropriate enough to the upbeat interpretation he brought to the earlier film, seems rather unsuited to this darker work – and is in any case less fully realised here, the sets and costumes having been thrown together in something of a hurry. His own much parodied performance and appearance (both apparently based on the unpopular American director Jed Harris, who was also the model for Disney's Big Bad Wolf) strain credibility. (Incidentally, Olivier modelled Richard's voice not on Harris, but on older actors' impersonations of Sir Henry Irving in the role. It is interesting to compare the result with recordings of Irving's Richard, which Olivier himself never heard.) That this overtly evil bottled spider can deceive not only the vulnerable Lady Anne (played exquisitely by Claire Bloom) but also his hardnosed brothers (Cedric Hardwicke as the King, John Gielgud as an unexpectedly gentle Clarence) is very hard to believe.

The textual cuts are also rather odd. Of course, cuts were necessary, since the play is extremely long and Olivier has followed Cibber in incorporating extra text from *Henry VI, Part 3*: but to lose altogether so powerful a character as the dispossessed Queen Margaret was surely a mistake. Indeed, there is scarcely any female presence in the second half of the film, and it is the poorer for it; Queen Elizabeth (Mary Kerridge) and the Duchess of York (Helen Haye) are cut to mere fractions of their roles in the play.

The main supporting performances are as strong as the screenplay allows them to be – the innocent-looking Ralph Richardson in particular has fun with a much trimmed but still cheerfully villainous Buckingham; but many of the minor characters are stodgily played, and the scheming nobles become interchangeable. All are in the shadow of Olivier's Richard, a thick slice of honey-roast ham. Long before we get to Bosworth Field (which seems to have absorbed more than its share of the budget without ever becoming nearly so impressive as Olivier's version of Agincourt, and without its arid Spanish scenery ever looking remotely English), the film begins to drag; and Olivier fails to save it.

Sad to say, the master's last Shakespearean outing behind the camera was also his weakest. He would almost certainly have gone out on a higher note had philistine money-men not denied him the funding to make his *Macbeth*.

Romeo i Zhulietta (1955, U.S.S.R., colour)
Based on *Romeo and Juliet*
A.k.a. *Romeo and Juliet* (international: English title)
Directed by Lev Arnshtam and Leonid Lavrovsky
Starring: Galina Ulanova, Yuri Zhdanov, A. Yermolayev, Sergei Koren
Runtime: 92 minutes

The collaboration between Mosfilm and the Bolshoi Ballet on the film of Sergei Prokofiev's 1938 piece *Romeo and Juliet*, conducted by Gennadi Rozhdestvensky, produced something so rare as to be almost oxymoronic: a genuinely cinematic ballet. Huge and exquisitely detailed sets (designed by Aleksei Parkhomenko to create a surprisingly convincing vision of sixteenth century Verona), edge-of-the-seat fight scenes, and a larger cast than any stage could hold, all contribute to this effect, the crowning glory being a stunning carnival scene which must have been extraordinarily difficult to choreograph.

Though always stylised, the movement of the characters is often not especially terpsichorean, resulting in a quasi-naturalism that balances the more conventional ballet of the dramatic high points. The latter is expertly danced, in particular by Galina Ulanova, for whom Prokofiev originally wrote the role. Though in her forties by the time the film was made, she convinces as the teenage Juliet thanks to the exuberance of her performance and her superb physical condition (on display in several near-transparent gowns). Beside Ulanova, Sergei Koren's clownish lutenist Mercutio, A. Yermolayev's melodramatically sneering Tybalt, and Yuri Zhdanov's somewhat bland Romeo are shown up in their limitations: she is not only the best dancer but the best actor in the picture.

Mnogo shuma iz nichego (1956, U.S.S.R., black and white)

151

Based on *Much Ado About Nothing*
Directed by Iosif Rapoport and Lev Zamkovoy
Language: Russian
Runtime: 91 minutes
Believed lost

While Russia's major studios were using Shakespeare as the source for elaborate spectacles, Zamkovoy's recording of Rapoport's production of *Much Ado* at the Evgeni Vachtangov Theatre in Moscow fell under the radar. The film has not been heard of since the 1950s.

La Fierecilla domada (1956, Spain / France, colour)
Based on *The Taming of the Shrew*
A.k.a. *La Mégère apprivoisée* (France); *The Taming of the Shrew* (international English title)
Directed by Antonio Román
Starring: Carmen Sevilla, Alberto Closas, Raymond Cordy, Claudine Dupuis, Jacques Dynam
Language: Spanish
Runtime: 80 minutes

Screenwriter Manuel Villegas López' loose adaptation of the *Shrew* to a Spanish setting *circa* 1400 seems unsure of the path it wants to take. It contains a subversive strain, sympathetic to Catalina (the film's Kate, played by Carmen Sevilla): it is hard not to warm to this hunting, shooting, and fencing minx who first appears in male costume, loosing arrows at Don Beltrán (Petruchio: Alberto Closas); especially when her sister (Claudine Dupuis) is so obviously a sly manipulator, one of the least likeable Biancas the cinema has given us. (It is she, rather than Hortensio – to whom no character here exactly corresponds – who suggests to Beltrán that he should woo Catalina.) There are also frequent touches of tenderness between Catalina and Beltrán: but these are indicative less of López' insight into their relationship than of the inconsistency of his writing. Both partners oscillate between cloying faux charm and violent rage without rhyme or reason, and by the third time Catalina initially resists an embrace before melting into her husband's arms, it is clear that López is not describing one couple's expression of their love but prescribing a rough approach to women.

And rough it certainly is. A streak of sadomasochism, perhaps unsurprising in the cinematic tradition that produced

152

Jesus Franco but oddly out of place in a work which otherwise radiates the conservatism of his military namesake, runs through this film. Beltrán kisses and gropes other women, ties Catalina to a pillar in her father's bedroom, carries her off over his shoulder from their wedding, and at one point even plays dice in a country inn with her as the prize – largely to give himself an excuse to start a fight when he loses. She, for her part, destroys a whole party by smashing up tables and food, locks Beltrán in a dungeon, and later knocks him out with the hilt of his own sword. She frequently seems ready to submit long before Shakespeare's Kate does, only to revert to her old ways: but this seems to be less a conscious decision than a matter of sloppy writing on López' part.

For some reason, López and the director Antonio Román have raised the social status of Shakespeare's essentially middle class characters. Beltrán lives in a massive and perfectly kept castle, surrounded by servants to whom he tosses gold when Catalina is out of the room, to compensate for mistreating them in front of her: the impoverished Petruchio would be very much out of his element here. The absent father of the barely more visible Lucentio figure is not a merchant but a marquis; while Bautista (Raymond Cordy, in a somewhat ludicrous goatee and a tabard that looks like a dress, mirroring his daughter's transvestism) is no mere Minola but "de Martos y Ribera". The Grumio figure, Florindo (Jacques Dynam), is a crudely drawn and hapless "comedy servant" compelled to play a mixture of Leporello and Sancho Panza (both semi-explicitly evoked, perhaps by way of Hispanicising the piece) to his wayward master. These alterations look almost like a celebration of social hierarchy, which would perhaps have been to the taste of Spain's Falangist rulers: they make an interesting contrast with the Communist reading of the same play, *Ukroshchenie stroptivoy* (1961).

La Fierecilla domada is quite a handsome film, even in its now badly faded state, and Sevilla's lively performance is certainly enjoyable: but the poverty of the interpolated material and the unpleasantness of the conclusion cannot be got over.

Forbidden Planet (1956, U.S.A., colour)
Based on *The Tempest*
Directed by Fred McLeod Wilcox

Starring: Walter Pidgeon, Anne Francis, Leslie Nielsen, Marvin Miller (voice), Warren Stevens

Runtime: 98 minutes

Academy Award nominations (1957): Best Special Effects (A. Arnold Gillespie, Irving G. Ries, Wesley C. Miller)

Forbidden Planet was one of the most successful science fiction movies of the 1950s. It remains famous for having launched the careers of Leslie Nielsen (now more familiar for his deadpan comic performances in the Zucker-Abrahams-Zucker films) and Robby the Robot; for having been the first film ever to use a soundtrack composed entirely of electronic music (by Louis and Bebe Barron); and as the basis for the stage musical *Return to the Forbidden Planet*, a loose reworking of the film with pop and show tunes inserted and innumerable lines quoted or misquoted from the whole Shakespearean canon ("Wherefore art thou Prospero?").

The set-up is inspired by *The Tempest*. There is a Prospero (Dr Morbius, played by Walter Pidgeon), a Miranda (Altaira: Anne Francis in a succession of very short skirts), a Ferdinand (Commander Adams: Nielsen), and an Ariel (Robby, inhabited by various actors and voiced by Marvin Miller), and even a Stephano (the alcoholic Cook: Earl Holliman). The planet Altair IV is Prospero's island, on which Adams' spaceship is forced to land: but the story quickly diverges from that of the play, never to return. The revenge plotline, which is central to *The Tempest*, is here reduced to an allusion; many of the play's major characters have no equivalents. The monster faced by the crew has been identified with Caliban: there is little or nothing in its storyline or nature to support this, though the final explanation of the creature's origins is one which might well be applied by Freudian critics to Shakespeare's demi-devil.

Irving Block and Allen Adler, who wrote the story from which Cyril Hume's screenplay was adapted, had turned down an offer from Allied Artists to film what was originally entitled *Fatal Planet*: the studio was notorious for churning out cheap, forgettable space operas, and was partly responsible for the low esteem in which science fiction cinema was held in the 1950s: they held out for the film to be made by M.G.M., and were eventually successful. The result was that the picture received the budget necessary for the convincing creation of Altair IV, with its green sky, twin moons, abandoned laboratories, and long-dead civilisation. Much of the film's look was later to become

154

part of the cliché-ridden language of the genre: but in 1956 it was new and spectacular.

Hume was a talented screenwriter, and his script is often sharp, but it suffers from the dead weight of pseudo-scientific jargon and the frequently incongruous humorous scenes upon whose insertion the studio insisted so as to lighten a story considered too dark in its original form for the audiences of 1950s America. Nor, sadly, is it well supported by the cast. Pidgeon has his moments but veers into ham too often; Francis' naivety becomes grating; Nielsen has little to do but square his jaw and hug his girl.

The film's powerful conclusion, with its at once pessimistic and forgiving verdict on human nature, is justly famed – and, while it is spelt out in a most un-Shakespearean fashion, would not necessarily be inappropriate as a critical reading of *The Tempest*. It is also one of the principal reasons for the survival of *Forbidden Planet* when shallower films of the same genre and era have been forgotten.

Kumonosu jô (1957, Japan, black and white)
Based on *Macbeth*
A.k.a. *Cobweb Castle*; *Macbeth* (U.S.A.); *Spider Web Castle*; *The Castle of the Spider's Web*; *Throne of Blood* (U.S.A.)
Directed by Akira Kurosawa
Starring: Toshirô Mifune, Isuzu Yamada, Takashi Shimura, Minoru Chiaki
Language: Japanese
Runtime: 105 minutes

In 2004, in a poll taken among 200 actors of the Royal Shakespeare Company, Kurosawa's first stab at the Bard was voted the best Shakespearean film adaptation of all time. That a version which does not even use the original language could achieve this is a remarkable tribute to the "Emperor" and his long-term collaborator Toshirô Mifune.

Unlike Kurosawa's later effort *Ran* (1985), *Throne of Blood* (as it is most popularly known in English, although *Cobweb Castle* is the literal translation of the Japanese title, and bears a greater relevance to the story: Washizu (Mifune), the Macbeth figure, is a spider who becomes trapped in his own web) sticks very closely to the original play, with the single exception of the excision of the Macduff plotline. Perhaps *Macbeth* was more easily transferred to a Japanese context than *King Lear*. One could dub Shakespeare's text in place of the Japanese dialogue with very little inconsistency.

As was Kurosawa's habit, the film opens with a striking image: a monument on a windswept moor, announcing that a castle once stood here whose lord was destroyed by ambition. A hundred minutes later, the film will close with a shot of this same memorial: after all the power-lust, machinations, and bloodshed that we have seen, nothing is left but a faint folk-memory.

We are in the same feudal-era Japan that Kurosawa had already conjured up in the masterpieces *Rashômon* (1950) and *Shichinin no samurai* (1954) – rather closer to the former, with all the question marks it hangs over the nature of reality and memory, than to the latter. Whenever Washizu ventures into the fog-bound Cobweb Forest, he journeys to the edge of nightmares. The mist swirls around the pine trees, and out of it come the spirits who correspond to Shakespeare's witches and their "masters": the first of these appears sitting at a spinning-wheel, spinning out the future like the Greek *Moirai* or the Scandinavian *Nornir*, spinning another web to entrap Washizu.

Despite its European source, the film draws more heavily on Japanese art forms than much of Kurosawa's earlier work. The influence of the *Noh* theatre, often a factor in his films, looms large here: the actors' make-up is modelled on *Noh* masks; the acting, though never unconvincing, conforms to *Noh* styles and conventions; motifs such as pine branches and shrine-like gateways, drawn from the *Noh* stage, are much in evidence. Japanese classical painting is also referenced, reminding the viewer that Kurosawa himself had been a painter before adopting the art form for which he is better known.

The central performances, by Toshirô Mifune and Isuzu Yamada, complement one another perfectly. The ever charismatic Mifune brings all the fire, violence, and ambition to the role of Washizu that Shakespeare could have wished, while Yamada's quiet, still performance as Asaji (Lady Macbeth), following *Noh* tradition, makes a chilling contrast. Sitting unmoving in the centre of the room, she too is a spider, the most cunning and patient of all: but she too ultimately destroys herself.

Exquisitely photographed and perfectly played from first to last, this is a classic piece of film-making. The best

Shakespeare adaptation of all time? Perhaps not; but surely the best *Macbeth*.

Der Rest ist Schweigen (1959, West Germany, black and white)
Based on *Hamlet*
A.k.a. *The Rest is Silence* (U.S.A.)
Directed by Helmut Käutner
Language: German
Runtime: 103 minutes (Germany) / 106 minutes (U.S.A.)
Not seen by current writer

In 1958, Helmut Käutner helped set up Freie Film Produktion GmbH, with the intent of producing one high-end art film per year. The company's first production, *Der Rest ist Schweigen*, transposed the *Hamlet* story to Fifties Germany: the murder which haunts Ruhr industrialist Paul Claudius (Peter van Eyck) thus serves as a metaphor for the crimes of the Nazi regime, pointed up by giving the family a hidden history of war profiteering. The national sense of guilt was a preoccupation for Käutner, who had himself trodden the finest of lines between non-collaboration and survival in the Nazi years, going no further than refusing to make propaganda, when most other non-Nazi filmmakers had fled the country. Hardy Krüger, in typically neurotic style according to reviewers, played the Hamlet figure, John.

Having premiered at the Berlin Film Festival in the summer of 1959, where it was unsuccessfully nominated for a Golden Bear, the film was released theatrically in Germany and overseas in 1960. Freie Film Produktion, however, folded.

Sen noci svatojanske (1959, Czechoslovakia, colour animation)
Based on *A Midsummer Night's Dream*
A.k.a. *A Midsummer Night's Dream* (U.S.A.)
Directed by Jiří Trnka
Runtime: 73 minutes

Jiří Trnka, puppeteer and founder of Trick Brothers, brought traditional Czech puppet theatre to the screen in the form of stop-motion animation, of which he was probably the greatest European exponent of the twentieth century. Less famous now than his 1949 masterpiece *Cisaruv slavík* (*The Emperor's Nightingale*), but no less beautifully made, his

Midsummer Night's Dream was in its time a critical success, nominated for the Golden Palm in Cannes and redubbed for foreign release by the likes of Richard Burton.

Magic is Trnka's speciality, and the film belongs to the fairies: Oberon, changing in the blink of an eye from horned and fur-draped forest god, to walking cornucopia hung with fruit, to glittering winter king in a crown of icicles, and sinisterly majestic in every guise; the ethereal, dignified Titania, her train not held up by but *composed of* dozens of tiny insectoid elves (one of many ambitious effects carried off seamlessly); the gleeful, Peter Pan-like Puck (who at one point has to ward off the amorous attentions of a ram accidentally dosed with love-in-idleness – careless, given that he has just seen that it can make even statues get off their pedestals and embrace), and assorted walking twigs and acorns who shimmer into other shapes at will.

The humans, however, are not neglected, but benefit as much as the fairies from Trnka's lively imagination. The flamboyant, athletic Lysander is a flautist who turns his instrument into a weapon when he fights the stiff, military Demetrius. Snug makes a very mournful lion, whining like a hurt dog in rehearsal but roaring ferociously on the night (when his tail moves independently!), and is given a wonderful moment in which he and Bottom face each other, two animal-headed men, one real and the other false, before the lion squeals and scampers off.

The play within the play is conventionally comic up to the death of Thisbe: but Trnka, interestingly, brings a true poignancy to Bottom's rendition of Pyramus' suicide, besetting the poor weaver with remembered images of Titania and leaving his fellow mechanicals momentarily afraid that he is really dead, before he gets up to take his bow. Throughout this scene, as through every one except the prologue in which the lovers' history is outlined, the fairies are present in the shadows; Puck even tries to join in the bergomasque. The film ends with Puck sweeping away fleeting images from the earlier action, before the credits go up over a theatrical curtain.

In the original Czech version, this was narrated by R. Pelar, with no other voice artists: soft-voiced and minimal narration went well with the graceful movement of the puppets and the bouncy, varied, perfectly pitched score of Václav Trojan to produce a sort of balletic effect very close to the traditions of Czech puppet theatre (although no live puppeteer could ever work on Trnka's scale, with multiple hugely detailed sets and scores of puppets onscreen at once). However, in the English language dub, dialogue adapted from the play was added, spoken by a very distinguished cast: and this, too – so far as I can tell from the brief excerpts I have seen from the dubbed version and the remarks of contemporary reviewers – worked. The influence of this exquisite film on *Shakespeare: The Animated Tales* (1992-94), in particular on its puppet segments[65], is obvious, and yet another reason to be grateful to Trnka.

The only problem is the difficulty of finding a copy. It is long overdue for restoration and re-release.

Otelo (1960, U.S.S.R., black and white)
Based on *Othello*
A.k.a. *The Ballet of Othello* (U.S.A.); *The Moor of Venice* (international English title); *Venetsianskiy mavr* (U.S.S.R.: Russian title)
Directed by Vakhtang Chabukiani
Starring: Vakhtang Chabukiani, Zura Kikaleishvili, Vera Tsignadze
Language: Georgian
Runtime: 95 minutes

The great Georgian dancer and choreographer Chabukiani devised a ballet version of *Othello*, scored by Aleqsi Machavariani, in 1957, dancing the part of the Moor himself. (Unusually for a ballet, snippets of speech from the play were retained to open major scenes.) It proved popular, and when in 1960 it was re-staged for the Kirov, the production was filmed and released in cinemas.

No attempt was made to render the ballet cinematic: it was filmed on sparse sets, with only basic furniture and a Venetian flag billowing in the background – although an unusually deep stage did permit more movement than would usually be the case. This Chabukiani put to full use, investing his role with an astonishing manic energy: the somewhat crude makeup (by A. Kirvalishvili, probably not designed with close-ups in mind) is easily overlooked in the presence of such fierce conviction and physical drive. The fiery Moor is balanced by

---

[65] *The Tempest* and *Twelfth Night* in the first series, *The Taming of the Shrew* and *The Winter's Tale* in the second.

Zura Kikaleishvili's slimy Iago, who at one point actually slithers like a snake on his belly; Desdemona (Vera Tsignadze), however, comes across as faintly pathetic, more because of the way the part is conceived by Chabukiani than because of any weakness on Tsignadze's part.

The quality of Feliks Vysotsky's filming is basic at best, but Chabukiani's powerhouse performance, Machavariani's music (at its stirring best in the most tempestuous scenes, occasionally straying into the saccharine when something softer is required), and the flawless dancing of the whole cast, carry it along at a fine pace, and the end result is impressive. Unfortunately, the version I saw was missing several scenes, although I understand that a complete print does still exist.

An Honourable Murder (1960, U.K., black and white)
Based on *Julius Caesar*
Directed by Godfrey Grayson
Starring: Norman Wooland, John Longden, Philip Saville, Marion Mathie, Margaretta Scott
Runtime: 67 minutes

An Honourable Murder, partly scripted by Brian Clemens, turns *Julius Caesar* into a boardroom drama: Julian Caesar (John Longden) is the chairman of Empire Petroleum, newly returned from negotiating a merger with Pompey Shipping: but director Cassius (Douglas Wilmer), fearful of Caesar's growing power, determines to remove him from his position – for which he needs the vote of Caesar's friend Brutus Smith (Norman Wooland). Losing the vote gives Caesar a fatal heart attack, and his aide Mark Anthony (Philip Saville[66]) goes to the shareholders to seek their authority to move against the conspirators.

There are slips in the adaptation. The implausibility of the play's bloodbath in this relatively non-violent context means that Cassius and Portia (Marion Mathie) are both still alive at the end. Caesar shows no outward sign of being corrupted by power until after Brutus has joined the conspiracy; hitherto, Cassius has appeared to be little more than a fantasist, especially since Wilmer plays him as semi-deranged. In any case, it is difficult to imagine a company commanding the same kind of

---

[66] Who would go on to direct Christopher Plummer in a TV *Hamlet*, filmed on location at Elsinore in 1964.

loyalty as the Roman Republic. Brutus sacrificing everything else he holds dear, and ultimately his own life, in the name of his country's constitution, is plausible: but for a business?

These flaws aside, however, *An Honourable Murder* is an enjoyable hour. The acting is assured, even if Wooland has to wrestle with an unbelievable character; the writing is as sharp as one would expect from Clemens, complete with any number of references to the play. Caesar hears worrying rumours about the share price from one Sam Sayer (uncredited); when voted down, he gasps "And you, Brutus? The motion is carried". The sound quality has suffered from the passage of the years, but this remains a thoroughly diverting little film.

Hamlet, Prinz von Dänemark (1961, West Germany, black and white)
Based on *Hamlet*
A.k.a. *Hamlet* (U.S.A.)
Directed by Franz Peter Wirth
Starring: Maximilian Schell, Hans Caninenberg, Wanda Rotha, Dunja Movar, Franz Schafheitlin
Language: German
Runtime: 152 minutes

Precisely who decided that an at best unremarkable German television *Hamlet* should be dubbed into English (with the voices of, among others, John "Sergeant Schultz" Banner and Ricardo Montalban, and a quite extraordinary array of different accents) and released in cinemas, and why, is something of a mystery. Nevertheless, decide they did.

It is hardly the fault of the producers that the sound and picture quality are poor, or that the action is confined to a single set (a dingy basement full of concrete pillars). Other weaknesses, however, are less easily forgiven. The contrast between the modern surroundings and the pseudo-Renaissance stylings of Gerd Richter's costumes and Rolf Unkel's underused score is not used inventively, but simply present, creating a strangely inconsistent feel (bizarre when one remembers that Richter designed the set as well); and some of those costumes are out of place, if not downright laughable. The Ghost (Alexander Engel), in vast collar, glittering metallic cloak, and heavy makeup, looks uncannily like Ming the Merciless, while the hedgehog-like hair of Polonius (Franz Schafheitlin) is a fright to see.

161

The blocking is inept, the cutting of the script ham-handed, every directorial decision unimaginative, and most of the acting flat and dreary. Maximilian Schell, a usually capable character actor, is out of his depth as the Prince; Hans Caninenberg's camp Claudius is entirely one-dimensional; Dunja Movar does attain a certain poignancy as Ophelia, but this is perhaps partly because of the viewer's knowledge that the actress did subsequently commit suicide.

It says all that needs to be said that this adaptation was used in a 1999 episode of *Mystery Science Theater 3000*, a series devoted to the worst and most mockable films ever made. It is tortuously dull.

Ukroshchenie stroptivoy (1961, U.S.S.R., black and white)
Based on *The Taming of the Shrew*
A.k.a. *The Taming of the Shrew* (international English title)
Directed by Sergei Kolosov
Starring: Andrei Popov, Lyudmila Kasatkina, Vladimir Soshalsky, Vladimir Blagoobrazov, Olga Krasina
Language: Russian
Runtime: 85 minutes

Like the play, this film offers us an induction before the main action: not the story of Christopher Sly, but director Kolosov in a rehearsal room, explaining to his actors the application of Communist theory to the play. This somewhat tortuous and unnecessary exercise in self-justification is, fortunately, soon over, and the credits go up over a wide shot of Lucentio (Vladimir Zeldin) and Tranio (Vladimir Soshalsky) galloping up to the gates of Padua.

Some effort has certainly been made at a political reading of the text. Kolosov finds something heroic in the non-conformism of both Petruchio (Andrei Popov) and Kate (Lyudmila Kasatkina), who in this version recognise in each other fellow rebels. Servant characters (Sergei Kulagin's earthy Grumio, a lugubrious and uncredited Curtis, and above all Soshalsky's cheeky, confident Tranio) are given their proper due, and much is made of the implications about class inherent in the play's many disguise plots. Tranio, indeed, thanks to the combination of Kolosov's focus and Soshalsky's charisma, dominates the film whenever the central couple are off screen; while the bourgeoisie – Vladimir Blagoobrazov's doddery

Baptista; Antoni Khodursky's pompous, overdressed Gremio; and Mark Pertsovsky's dandyish, slightly effeminate Hortensio – are presented satirically. After their final kiss, Kate and Petruchio pointedly leave Baptista's house and go out into the street, where passers by salute them with a toast.

This reading is not allowed, however, to swamp the text or interfere with the primary purpose of entertainment. While some indoor scenes do tend to drag, finding it hard to match the lovingly created bustle of the streets of Padua, the film is, over all, well paced and quite consistently amusing – although Kolosov has found an undercurrent of darkness prefiguring the middle comedies. Kasatkina's Kate, behind her "curst" behaviour, is clearly desperately unhappy in her father's house: she uses aggression as a shield, and at first turns it against Petruchio, only to drop it as he shows her its effects by turning it back upon her: and her "submission" speech is made an expression of love for the man who has in fact liberated her. In this Kolosov anticipates modern criticism, showing remarkable perception.

While Petruchio is given as much depth as he needs to support this interpretation of his relationship with his wife, Andrei Popov ensures that it never detracts from the flair with which he plays the swaggering, brawling Veronese, who makes his first appearance fighting a duel in the market square. He drinks, fights, smoulders and woos with tremendous energy and considerable charm, and, despite the fact that Kolosov has taken care to give due weight to Bianca's storyline, effortlessly makes the film his own.

Moments of ennui, the under-use of Aleksandr Golubentsev's score, and occasional blips in the editing, prevent *Ukroshchenie stroptivoy* from being as entire a success as, say, *Dvenadtsataya noch* (1955): but it remains a fine adaptation.

Macbeth (1961, U.S.A., colour)
Directed by George Schaefer
Runtime: 108 minutes / 120 minutes (extended edition)
Not seen by current writer

George Schaefer's *Macbeth* for Hallmark Hall of Fame in 1954 was such a success that, six years later, he reassembled the same lead actors, with a significantly bigger budget, to make an on-location version at Hermitage Castle in the Scottish Borders –

using film instead of Hallmark's usual videotape. Although it was made for television, and originally broadcast in November 1960, the new version was deemed of a cinematic standard, and was sent to the Berlin International Film Festival in June 1961 (which I have treated as its release date) before receiving a limited theatrical release in the U.S. in 1963.

Maurice Evans and Judith Anderson, who had first played the Macbeths together on Broadway in 1941, returned to the roles. Imaginative touches such as having Macbeth's bloody hand slip from his wife's grasp when she pulls him toward their chamber after the murder were remarked upon, as was the colourful production design.

West Side Story (1961, U.S.A., colour)
Based on *Romeo and Juliet*
Directed by Jerome Robbins and Robert Wise
Starring: Natalie Wood, Richard Beymer, Rita Moreno, Russ Tamblyn, George Chakiris
Runtime: 151 minutes
Academy Awards (1962): Best Picture; Best Direction (Jerome Robbins, Robert Wise); Best Actor in a Supporting Role (George Chakiris); Best Actress in a Supporting Role (Rita Moreno); Best Art Direction (Colour) (Boris Leven, Victor A. Gangelin); Best Cinematography (Colour) (Daniel L. Fapp); Best Costume Design (Colour) (Irene Sharaff); Best Film Editing (Thomas Stanford); Best Scoring of a Musical Picture (Saul Chaplin, Johnny Green, Sid Ramin, Irwin Kostal); Best Sound (Fred Hynes, Gordon E. Sawyer); Honorary Award to Jerome Robbins for his outstanding achievement in the art of choreography on film
Academy Award nominations: Best Screenplay Based on Material from Another Medium (Ernest Lehman)

Robert Wise and Jerome Robbins' Oscar-sweeping adaptation of Leonard Bernstein's 1957 stage musical (original concept by Robbins), bringing the plot of *Romeo and Juliet* to a setting of inter-ethnic gang warfare in Fifties New York, remains a triumph and a cornerstone in the history of the musical. The very idea of adapting a tragedy into this format, and treating the subject, if not quite realistically, then at least seriously, was a revolutionary one: and the hitherto light and fluffy art form was never the same again. Robbins and Wise became the only directors in history to win joint Best Director Oscars.

From the bold decision to play the overture over a silhouetted cityscape of Manhattan on orange card, through the fade from the card to a helicopter shot of the real thing (Wise – who had to fight hard to get to shoot on location in the city, but proved it worthwhile by his brilliant evocation of young working-class life there as the Sixties began – shows an expensive but effective penchant for overhead shots) to a potently cathartic ending courtesy of William Shakespeare (but with the denunciation of feuds – and, thanks to the new context, of racism – spelt out still more starkly), the film seldom falters. Of course, the combination of the play's plot with Bernstein's music was a powerful one to begin with: but Robbins' brilliant choreography and Wise's direction raise it yet higher. Who but Robbins could have built those pirouettes into knife fights convincingly? It is a testament to his skill that the toughness and menace of the hoodlums is never diminished by their dancing, which could so easily have rendered them risible. (There is also occasional transposition of scenes and songs to more appropriate places than they had occupied in the stage version, most obviously the swapping of "Gee, Officer Krupke" with "Play It Cool".) The intensely stylised, brightly coloured look, created by an art team who were showered with Oscars for their work, is perfect.

Bearing in mind how unusual it was at the time to intrude *any* darkness into musicals, it is quite startling to find that *West Side Story* positively boils with violence; the lyrics, even after they had been censored for cinematic release, are full of hatred (and occasional substitutions for what are obviously supposed to be four-letter words). Between the explosive songs of the gangs and the lighter, but equally energetic, numbers expressing the exuberance of youth, romantic songs such as "Maria" and "There's A Place For Us" sit a little uneasily, always in danger of crossing the line into the saccharine that the movie has largely left behind: but the combination of these elements in the central quintet "Tonight" is masterly.

The standards of the performances are variable. Richard Beymer as Tony, the Romeo figure, is the weak link – not actually bad, but never entirely filling the role. Since he did not do his own singing, and spends rather less time dancing than any of the other major players, one must presume that he was cast principally for his looks. Natalie Wood makes a lovely Maria

(Juliet), playing the finale with extraordinary power – and Marni Nixon, who dubbed her songs, demonstrates not only a great voice but the remarkable ability to retain a Puerto Rican accent while singing at the top of it; Rita Moreno, one of the few genuine Puerto Ricans in the cast, earned her awards as a fire-spitting, scene-stealing Anita.

At two and a half hours – a most unusual length for a film musical: normal practice is to trim the stage versions of everything that can be spared when transferring to celluloid – *West Side Story* is perhaps a little long; but it is hard to see what could have been lost. Even moments that could have been handled better still have a necessary place in building character, atmosphere or both. It is certainly not without its flaws; but the good far outweighs the bad.

Was Ihr wollt (1962, West Germany, black and white)
Based on *Twelfth Night*
Directed by Franz Peter Wirth
Language: German
Runtime: 166 minutes
Believed lost

Wirth's *Twelfth Night*, starring Ingrid Andree as both twins, began life as a TV play before receiving a cinematic release. Very little is known about it.

All Night Long (1962, U.K., black and white)
Based on *Othello*
Directed by Basil Dearden
Starring: Patrick McGoohan, Paul Harris, Marti Stevens, Richard Attenborough, Keith Michell
Runtime: 87 minutes

"Good evening. Tonight I'm giving a party, and I'd like you to come along. You'll meet some fascinating people, and hear some great music."

The opening sentences of the original trailer (spoken to camera by Richard Attenborough) pretty much sum up *All Night Long*, which essentially uses the plot of *Othello* as a clothes-hanger for a jazz concert, celebrating the smoke-filled-warehouse music scene of early Sixties London, with a stylish retro-Twenties Art Deco look created by art director Ray Simm and cinematographer Edward Scaife. The film takes place over one night in the East End apartment of upper class jazz buff Rod Hamilton (Attenborough, in something roughly approximating to the Roderigo role, although Rod is far more sympathetic than his original), at a party to celebrate the first wedding anniversary of Rex (Othello: Paul Harris) and Delia (Desdemona: Marti Stevens), and features such stars of the era as Dave Brubeck, John Dankworth, and Charles Mingus playing themselves.

The updating is well handled: Delia is a former singing star who has given up her career for her husband; Cassio (Cass: Keith Michell) a band manager with a pot problem; Iago (Johnnie: Patrick McGoohan) an ambitious drummer thwarted in forming his own band when Delia, who has also rejected his sexual advances, refuses to sing with him; Emilia (Emily: Betsy Blair) a co-dependent former groupie, who is given the longest speech in the film to describe how she came to marry Johnnie; the handkerchief is a gold cigarette case; the conversation that convinces Rex of Delia's infidelity is not overheard but recorded on tape. (Oddly, Harris' race is never referred to.) The crackling script, by Nel King and Paul Jarrico (credited as Peter Achilles), follows the play closely until the end, but unfortunately loses power by bottling out of the tragedy: not only do Rex and Delia survive, it is even implied that their marriage is not over. But the couple that interests the writers more is Johnnie and Emily: and it is to them that we return. Even after publicly denouncing her husband, Emily cannot leave him until he orders her to; the last line spoken is Johnnie's bitter "Find somebody else to love". As the final credits roll, he is left alone in the club, still playing the drums.

Despite several excellent performances, particularly from McGoohan and Michell, the real star of *All Night Long* is the music. Whether it is Sonny Miller's haunting title song (the film's equivalent for "The Green Willow", accompanied by lingering shots of Rod, Rex, and Cass carried away by Delia's singing while Johnnie doctors the incriminating tape in the next room), the drums sequence in which Johnnie's furious playing mingles with the confusion in Rex's head, or the frequent occasions when the film simply takes a break from plot to watch one of the "name" artists playing, the jazz dominates. The soundtrack is easily the film's greatest triumph.

Ophélia (1963, France, black and white)
Based on *Hamlet*
Directed by Claude Chabrol
Language: French
Runtime: 105 minutes
Not seen by current writer

Chabrol's film is a self-referential, blackly parodic take on *Hamlet*. His protagonist, bored rich youth Yvan (André Jocelyn), finds himself in the prince's situation when his mother (Alida Valli) marries his deceased father's brother (Claude Cerval). He becomes obsessed with the play, watching the Olivier film and adopting the prince's antic disposition. This involves casting his girlfriend Lucie (Juliette Mayniel) as Ophelia, merely to fit his self-dramatisation.

Yvan's obsession creates tragedy loosely mirroring the play for the two families, culminating in his uncle's suicide: only then does he discover that his father died a natural death. He is not the only deluded figure: it is reportedly hinted that the strikers from whom the uncle, an industrialist, hides in his mansion, surrounded by thuggish bodyguards, are entirely imaginary.

Yavas gel güzelim (1963, Turkey, black and white)
Based on *The Taming of the Shrew*
Directed by Memduh Ün
Language: Turkish
Believed lost

Only the names of the major cast and crew are recorded for this Turkish *Shrew*. Director Memduh Ün later went on to produce *Intikam Melegi – Kadin Hamlet* (1977), starring his girlfriend Fatma Girik.

Istana berdarah (1964, Singapore, black and white)
Based on *Macbeth*
Directed by Hussain Haniff
Language: Malay
Believed lost

Next to no details are known about *Istana berdarah*.

Gamlet (1964, U.S.S.R., black and white)
Based on *Hamlet*
A.k.a. *Hamlet* (U.S.A.)
Directed by Grigori Kozintsev and Iosif Shapiro
Starring: Innokenti Smoktunovsky, Mikhail Nazvanov, Anastasiya Vertinskaya, Elze Radzinya, Yuri Tolubeyev
Language: Russian
Runtime: 140 minutes

In the 1960s, Soviet cinema was emerging from decades of strict censorship into a slightly freer mode; and one of the many talented directors to take advantage of this was Grigori Kozintsev. *Hamlet* (which had been banned under Stalin as inconsistent with the "Soviet spirit of optimism, fortitude, and clarity"[67]) was a popular text in Eastern Europe during and following the "Thaw": plays about corrupt courts can always be used as veiled or open satire against current governments, and many directors noted the parallels between Polonius' near-obsessive eavesdropping on Claudius' behalf and the constant surveillance endured by the citizens of Communist states. This element is not absent from Kozintsev's version, but to read it exclusively in such a light would be reductive.

Using a translation by Boris Pasternak of *Doctor Zhivago* fame, Kozintsev whittled the text down to 140 minutes without sacrificing any significant plot elements: much of the poetry is sorely missed, but he did not take the common route of Anglophone directors and cut out Fortinbras. Indeed, an impressive scene has been inserted depicting the landing of the Norwegian forces – whose high-crested helmets give them, intentionally or otherwise, a distinct resemblance to Spanish conquistadors – in Denmark; and, when Fortinbras eventually claims the crown, it appears to be a sign of hope for the kingdom rather than merely a subjection – although Kozintsev gives no easy answers. (The allegorical reading, according to which Fortinbras is Khrushchev to Claudius' Stalin, is an over-simplification: although, as Kozintsev himself made clear in his writings on the film, it is not entirely unwarranted.)

From the beginning, we are reminded that we are in a royal court of the late Renaissance, not, as some directors make Elsinore appear, a dysfunctional family's country house.

---

[67] Quoted by Jess-Cooke, Caroline, *Shakespeare on film: such things as dreams are made of* (London, 2007), p. 21.

Claudius' first speech is read out as a proclamation, with foreign visitors excitedly translating it into French and German for the benefit of their neighbours, before we cut to the King uttering the final lines to his Council; nobles and politicians are seldom far away, and there is a distinct sense that more intrigues are going on than we see on the screen. It is a world in which the philosopher-prince cannot exist: at the end, the dying Hamlet (Innokenti Smoktunovsky, a war hero and former inmate of the Gulag, whose casting had a particular resonance for Russian audiences) staggers out of the prison-like castle to expire on the rocky seashore.

Claudius (Mikhail Nazvanov) himself, in this interpretation, represents not so much what is rotten in the state of Denmark as the state itself, rottenness and all: not until the prayer scene is he seen as a man, and it then becomes apparent that he has ceased to be one. The face that stares back at him out of his mirror is dead; he has killed his own soul along with his brother's body, and, vampire-like, shuns his reflection after this scene. Interestingly, the King is allowed to pray and soliloquise without the threat of death: Hamlet does not appear in this scene. The excision of his refusal to send his uncle to Heaven is one of many minor chips knocked off the play's Christian atmosphere – perhaps unsurprising in a film made in a constitutionally atheist country. The two principal intrusions of Christianity into the film are the vengeful Laertes' (Stepan Oleksenko) dedication of his sword at the altar (an interpolated scene harking forward to his readiness "to cut [Hamlet's] throat i' th' church"), and the priest's refusal to give Ophelia full funeral rites. Kozintsev himself was not hostile to Christianity, but certainly seems to have given his film an anticlerical streak.

And what of the Prince himself? Gone is the doubter he accuses himself of being; gone too is the madman many interpretations make of him. Smoktunovsky's Hamlet is an ice-cool, stone-faced philosopher, who, except when deliberately donning his "antic disposition" and during a handful of strictly controlled explosions, is entirely sane and master of his situation – which makes his treatment of others, especially Anastasiya Vertinskaya's desperately vulnerable Ophelia, appear monstrously cruel. If, as one reviewer inferred, he "uses thought and contemplation as his only weapons",[68] he drives them

---

[68] Quoted in sleeve notes for the VHS (1991).

unflinchingly through more than one heart. In madness, meanwhile, Ophelia finally becomes happy, a state the sane cannot aspire to in Claudius' Denmark.

All this is played out against a lavishly recreated and exquisitely photographed sixteenth century backdrop. Sergei Eisenstein's *Ivan Groznyy* (1945) is an inescapable point of reference, but Kozintsev also evokes Ingmar Bergman in his use of light and shadow, creation of images (notably a chiming clock from which issue forth the figures of the *Danse Macabre*), and strong, detailed sense of period. Earlier influences too are apparent: his players rehearse, and the Aeneas speech is delivered, in a near-circular courtyard, which could almost be a Greek or Roman theatre. And over all this, there plays Shostakovich's wonderful score, always in tune with the mood of the play – and cunningly incorporating the original English tune for "He is dead and gone".

Outside this Elsinore, as with Olivier's, the waves beat incessantly against the cliffs. The unquiet sea is always present in the film, heard when it is not seen: heralding the Ghost's approach, carrying Fortinbras (A. Krevalid) to his throne and Rosencrantz and Guildenstern (Igor Dmitriyev and Vadim Medvedev, providing a rare touch of comedy with their over-the-top costumes, ludicrous hairstyles, and general bewilderment) to their doom; Ophelia drowns herself not in the "brook" of the play, but in a fjord; at the end, as at the beginning, we fade from the shore, to the open sea, to a brazier burning in the wind on the castle walls.

Though political, *Gamlet* is not a "message" film. Even in the marginally more liberal atmosphere briefly flourishing in the Soviet Union, such could not be made unless the message was one that suited the Communist agenda: and, though a sincere Marxist, Kozintsev was no tool of the state. It is, however, all the stronger for that, offering not answers but conundra: will Fortinbras' rule improve anything (as the Soviet people wondered every time a leader fell)? Is the overthrow of Claudius worth the death of innocents? Is this Hamlet's heartless rationalism really superior to the court's amorality, or would he, were he King, prove a logical tyrant like Camus' Caligula? For all the state's approval of the film, few among its original audiences can have failed to ask themselves these questions.

Hamile (1964, Ghana, black and white)
Based on *Hamlet*
A.k.a. *Hamlet* (U.S.A.); *The Tongo Hamlet*
Directed by Terry Bishop
Runtime: 120 minutes
Not seen by current writer

The students of the University of Ghana School of Music and Drama had achieved a striking local success with their stage production of *Hamlet,* transferred to a setting among the Frafra of Tongo in northern Ghana, and starring Kofi Middetan-Mends. It was decided to commit the production to film, and it was fortunate enough to secure a U.S. release; it is reported to have been distinguished by energetic performances. There appears to be some doubt over whether the film has survived in its entirety: the British Film Institute holds only a single reel as preservation material.

Viel Lärm um nichts (1964, East Germany, colour)
Based on *Much Ado About Nothing*
Directed by Martin Hellberg
Starring: Christel Bodenstein, Rolf Ludwig, Martin Flörchinger, Gerhard Bienert, Arno Wyzniewski
Language: German
Runtime: 97 minutes

This pleasant, low-key *Much Ado* is one of the lesser efforts of East Germany's D.E.F.A., but not unenjoyable. With the exception of a few glimpses of rocky sea-shore, it is entirely studio-shot, but none the worse for that: the airy Italianate sets are most effective, and the artificiality of the "outdoor" light becomes obvious only when studio scenes are cut together with genuine outdoor footage.

Although some effort has been made to locate the film geographically in Sicily, its temporal setting is non-specific. The general impression, created by cravated, frock-coated gentlemen and parasol-twirling ladies, is of the early to mid nineteenth century; but both Elizabethan and modern elements have been dropped into the mix. That this is deliberate is evident from the cunning design of the sand-coloured uniforms of Don Pedro (Wilfried Ortmann) and his soldiers: at first glance they appear contemporary, but as the camera moves closer we notice the broad collars and short capes of the sixteenth century. The

Watch, outfitted in pantomimic bright blue, carry antiquated pikes; but amid this Ruritanian world moves an irrepressible Margaret (Ingrid Michalk) in a dress straight from the Sixties, while Borachio (Edwin Marian) wears a T-shirt under his doublet. The stylisation of the brightly coloured costumes (designed by Gerhard Kaddatz and Luise Schmidt) makes this fantastical mixture work, although the apparent intention of pointing up the timelessness of the play is not entirely fulfilled. Almost everybody dons cod-Elizabethan garb for the masked ball, referencing other Shakespeare plays; we are even treated to one partygoer dressed as Falstaff in his Herne the Hunter guise.

Unfortunately, despite some trendily mobile camerawork by Erwin Anders, Martin Hellberg's direction is largely flat and uninteresting. The sexual charge of the film's opening images quickly fades, and what comic energy the picture possesses is supplied by the actors (particularly Gerhard Bienert's blustering Dogberry: it is interesting to see petty authority so enthusiastically mocked in a film from a Communist country) unassisted by Hellberg, if not in spite of him. Dramatic scenes fare still worse, even Benedick's (Rolf Ludwig) challenge to Claudio (Arno Wyzniewski, whose foppish appearance makes him well suited to the part of the petulant count) being drained of nearly all its tension. The director is at his best in near-wordless quasi-fantasy scenes, particularly the ball, into which he incorporates several counter-realistic balletic sequences, foreshadowing the play's later darkness through the diabolic appearance of Don John (Gerhard Rachold); although, with sinister music and red lighting, this effect is carried a little too far. The latter fault emerges again at the end, when the reunited couples actually dance into the sky, watched by the rest of the cast.

Viel Lärm um nichts is mildly diverting, but ultimately a slight and unremarkable addition to the canon of Shakespearean cinema.

Giulietta e Romeo (1964, Italy / Spain, colour)
Based on *Romeo and Juliet*
A.k.a. *Romeo and Juliet* (U.S.A.); *Los Amantes de Verona* (Spain)
Directed by Riccardo Freda
Language: Italian
Runtime: 95 minutes (Italy); 99 minutes (Spain)

Not seen by current writer

Giulietta e Romeo, starring Geronimo Meynier and Rosemary Dexter, opens with a scene straight out of a Western. The brawl between the contending families takes place not in the streets of Verona, but on a ranch, where the Capulets are attempting to steal Montague cattle. It was action sequences such as this which earned the film its reputation for being fast-moving, colourful, and spectacular; unfortunately, to judge from the sixteen minute fragment I have seen, the non-action scenes drag, thanks to static blocking and monotonous shooting. Furthermore, all outdoor scenes were filmed in rural areas, suggesting that the cattle raid was less the result of inspired originality than of budget limitations.

The film received a U.S. release in 1968 on the back of the Zeffirelli version, which had created an appetite for the play.

Hamlet (1964, U.S.A., black and white)
Directed by John Gielgud and Bill Colleran
Starring: Richard Burton, Eileen Herlie, Hume Cronyn, Alfred Drake, Linda Marsh
Runtime: 191 minutes

In 1963, John Gielgud, himself a legendary Hamlet in the 1930s and '40s,[69] brought the play to the Lunt-Fontanne Theatre in New York, starring the hottest theatrical property of the day: Richard Burton. It was an original vision of the play – not set against any defined background, but played in the cast's own clothes on an almost bare stage as if it were a final undress run-through. Even the miniatures of Claudius and King Hamlet that the Prince compares are imaginary. (Only the Players – including Kit Culkin as an authentically Elizabethan boy-Queen – "dress up", resembling the figures on playing cards.) "This is a *Hamlet*... stripped of all extraneous trappings, so the beauty of the language and imagery may shine through,"[70] Gielgud explained. The production was a great success, and Gielgud decided to commit it to film: or, rather, to Electronovision.

Electronovision was, in fact, a very Sixties futuristic

---

[69] His own performance in the role was unfortunately never committed to film in full, although snatches of it are preserved in Humphrey Jennings' 1945 portrait of wartime Britain, *A Diary for Timothy*.
[70] Quoted in sleeve notes for the VHS, 1996.

name for a multi-camera real-time video recording. The idea was to capture a live performance, or "theatrofilm", which would then be shown, four times only, in one thousand selected cinemas around the U.S.A., allowing those who could not make it to the Lunt-Fontanne to share the audience's experience in "the theatre of the future". (The final version was in fact edited together from two nights' worth of filming, which slightly undermines this premise.) There would be no cuts, no corrections, "and the result", said Burton in an interview, "will be certainly unique, possibly extraordinary, and perhaps epoch-making. That is something for the audience to decide."[71] Decide they did: Burton alone made half a million dollars from showings of *Hamlet*. The film was even supposed to be as impermanent as theatre: contractually, all prints were supposed to be destroyed after the four showings. Burton, however, secretly kept one and sent another to the British Film Institute, with the result that *Hamlet* has survived.

Unfortunately, Electronovision was not all it was cracked up to be. Video has never quite been able to compete with film: in 1964 there was no comparison. Bill Colleran's multi-camera work is certainly more complex than had been possible in any previous recording of a live performance, and the sound (with occasional blips possibly caused by the age of the picture) is better than might be expected: but the image is grainy, the very basic theatrical lighting unsuited to the medium, and the lack of colour detracts from the immediate realism Gielgud desired. The presence of an audience means that intimate scenes are played to the gallery. Filmed theatre is seldom if ever a match for either of the media it combines: theatre recorded on Electronovision even less so.

The best thing to be said for *Hamlet* is that it preserves Burton's performance. He makes a vigorous and energetic Prince, an unconventional interpretation in 1964, prefiguring 1990s Hamlets such as Mel Gibson and Kenneth Branagh; he certainly outshines most of the rest of the cast. (Unexpectedly, he delivers "How all occasions do inform against me" in a low key, sitting on a pair of steps throughout the soliloquy. It is curiously effective.) Not all the others are poor: Gielgud himself gives a credible sense of suffering to the voice of the Ghost (who is represented visually by a helmeted shadow on the wall, an image

---

[71] Ibid. The interview is also included on the VHS and DVD.

which has acquired new connotations post-*Star Wars*); Eileen Herlie, Olivier's Gertrude reprising her former role, brings both more energy and greater vulnerability to the part than she had done in 1948, albeit not without faltering; Hume Cronyn, playing Polonius mostly for laughs, dominates the stage whenever Burton is off it in the first half. The rest of the cast, however, are for the most part stilted and unnatural; Linda Marsh's Ophelia in particular is hard to believe in. (Gielgud privately admitted that Marsh "lacks experience and is daunted by the vast theatre", and was scathing about Alfred Drake's Claudius, comparing him to "an ex-croupier from Monte Carlo who has eloped with a fat landlady who keeps a discreet brothel on the Côte d'Azur".[72])

As a record of experimental theatre in the 1960s, and of Richard Burton in one of his finest roles, *Hamlet* is an important picture: as entertainment, it is sadly lacking.

Die Lustigen Weiber von Windsor (1965, Austria / U.K., colour)
Based on *The Merry Wives of Windsor*
A.k.a. *The Merry Wives of Windsor*
Directed by Georg Tressler
Starring: Colette Boky, Norman Foster, Charles Igor Gorin, Mildred Miler, Lucia Popp
Runtime: 97 minutes

Although he did not direct, the driving creative force behind this version of Nicolai's *Merry Wives* (featuring the Zagreb Symphony Orchestra, conducted by Milan Horvath) was Norman Foster, who, in fat-suit and bright red beard, sang the part of Falstaff as well as producing the film and writing the English lyrics (a translation of a translation, back into the original language – although Foster did occasionally turn back to Shakespeare, his principal concern was that the words should fit the music).

While elements of the greater realism that was becoming fashionable in European historical pictures are in evidence, *Die Lustigen Weiber von Windsor* is essentially old-fashioned, with such stylised fifteenth / sixteenth century costumes as to verge on the pantomimic; and where Shakespeare presented Windsor as a small town, and Georg Wildhagen's Windsor in 1950 was

---

[72] Gielgud, *Letters*, p. 307.

suitably urban, in Foster's vision it is positively bucolic, a thatched farming idyll at harvest time – although very little work appears to be going on.

Despite this, the screen is constantly filled with activity: Tressler, perhaps, imposing something of his presence on the film. Whether in the fields, the Garter, the Ford household, or the Park, the film is rarely static; and trendy tricks of photography and editing, reminiscent of Tony Richardson's *Tom Jones* (1963), heighten the effect. Only the Park scene feels clumsy, perhaps because the choreography is less sure-footed than elsewhere; but it is followed up by a non-Shakespearean banquet scene (based on *The Peasant Wedding Feast* by Brueghel the Elder, albeit somewhat sanitised) that recaptures the film's earlier visual flair.

The cast clearly enjoyed making the picture: Colette Boky as a flirtatious Mrs Ford and Charles Igor Gorin as her husband, in particular, attack their parts with gusto: and while Foster's lecherous jolly giant, guzzling chicken and rolling his Rs as if his life depended on it, is hardly the most multi-layered of Falstaffs, he is still enjoyable to watch. It is debateable, however, whether his decision to dispense altogether with spoken dialogue and turn the *Singspiel* into an outright opera was a wise one. Nicolai is not Verdi (whose *Falstaff* has tended to overshadow the earlier adaptation), and his music cannot quite bear the weight of the whole picture.

Foster's writing credit reads "Norman Foster, with reluctant assistance from William Shakespeare". This does the film an injustice, but is not without truth. *Die Lustigen Weiber* is a diverting film, which at 97 minutes does not have time to bore even when the pace and invention flag: but it will not linger in the mind.

Othello (1965, U.K., colour)
Directed by Stuart Burge and John Dexter
Starring: Laurence Olivier, Frank Finlay, Maggie Smith, Joyce Redman, Derek Jacobi
Runtime: 165 minutes
Academy Award nominations (1966): Best Actor in a Leading Role (Laurence Olivier); Best Actress in a Leading Role (Maggie Smith); Best Actor in a Supporting Role (Frank Finlay); Best Actress in a Supporting Role (Joyce Redman)

"I think Shakespeare and Burbage got drunk together one night and Burbage said, 'I can play anything you write, anything at all'. And Shakespeare said, 'Right, I'll fix you, boy!' And then he wrote *Othello*." ~ Laurence Olivier.[73]

In 1964, after nearly thirty years' experience of playing Iago, Olivier finally tackled the Moor in John Dexter's production for the National Theatre, marking the 400th anniversary of Shakespeare's birth. Although the star described the part as a "monstrous burden", the play was a great success, and was hastily adapted into a film helmed by Stuart Burge; its theatrical roots and hurried production are all too evident.

The play was filmed entirely on National Theatre sets, without even the pretence of realism in scenes set outdoors; but, judged as theatrical sets rather than film ones, these are impressive enough, evoking a gloomy Venice and a Cyprus of decaying classical grandeur. Like Orson Welles (1952), Dexter chose to set the play not against its original historical backdrop, the Cypriot crisis of 1568-70, but during Venice's imperial birth pains in the previous century, which suits his somewhat Gothic vision. (The film begins in Hammer horror style, with a shot of a single burning torch and the tolling of a church bell.) The costumes are simple and muted without losing authenticity; Othello at first advertises his convert status by wearing a large crucifix, but loses it as the play progresses.

Unfortunately, problems associated with live performances, which should not have been allowed into a film, do creep in. Olivier's makeup rubs off onto Maggie Smith (Desdemona) and Frank Finlay (Iago) when he touches them; Smith's breathing is visible when Desdemona is supposedly dead. At least once, a fudged line goes uncorrected. This is not professional film-making.

Nor has the usually impressive Olivier succeeded in adapting his stage performance – already somewhat overblown – to the different demands of film. It is not without its strengths: he never lacked presence; in his late fifties, he was able to say more truly than most Othellos that "I am declined into the vale of years"; and he maintains a reasonably convincing accent, and a note far below the usual range of his light voice. However, quite apart from the fact that he never looks like anything other than a

---

[73] Quoted by Holden, Anthony, *Laurence Olivier* (New York, 1988), p. 376.

white man in blackface, and the uncomfortable feeling that he is too jealous too soon – perhaps Dexter and Burge rejected his claim to be "one not easily jealous", but it is, after all, backed up by Desdemona, and surely his suspicions should all be planted by Iago – the performance is constantly in danger of ham, and occasionally crosses the line. It certainly does not justify the picture's tagline, "The greatest Othello ever by the greatest actor of our time".

Other performances support Olivier's well enough. Smith makes a fine, delicate Desdemona, while Derek Jacobi's unconventional portrayal of a flamboyant, egotistical Cassio (overcoming the handicap of one of the worst wigs in cinema history) leaves the viewer with the distinct impression that Iago would indeed have been the better lieutenant: but it is Frank Finlay who dominates the film. His effortlessly malevolent puppet-master is never less than note-perfect. It is all too easy to let Iago steal Othello's play from the hero, but with such a superior Iago it is unavoidable. (One has to wonder what the Academy was thinking in classifying Iago as a supporting role: surely Finlay should have gone head to head with Olivier for Best Actor.)

Burge's *Othello* is a curious affair: a record of an important production, containing at least one excellent performance; but patchy, cheap-looking, and fundamentally unsuited to cinematic release. This was Olivier's last Shakespearean role on the big screen, his Shylock (1973) and Lear (1984), like Welles' (1969 – never screened – and 1953 respectively), having been confined to television adaptations; while he remains a disembodied voice in *Romeo and Juliet* (1968): and that is the real tragedy.

Campanadas a medianoche (1965, Spain / Switzerland, black and white)
Based on *Henry IV, Part 1*, *Henry IV, Part 2* and *Henry V*
A.k.a. *Campanades a mitjanit* (Spain: Catalan title); *Chimes at Midnight* (U.K.); *Falstaff* (Switzerland)
Directed by Orson Welles
Starring: Orson Welles, Keith Baxter, John Gielgud, Jeanne Moreau, Margaret Rutherford
Runtime: 113 minutes (Spain) / 119 minutes (Switzerland) / 115 minutes (U.S.A.)

Orson Welles' favourite of his own films, *Chimes at Midnight* is an elegiac rendition of the Second Henriad, a labour of love that had been decades in the making. Welles had first attempted to condense the history plays into a single work, *Five Kings*, in 1939; although neither that nor his later stage production of *Chimes at Midnight* had achieved commercial success, he managed through sheer determination to raise funding and assemble an excellent cast for the film, shooting in Spain (because, Welles half-joked, "it was the only country where they didn't know that black and white wasn't commercial"[74]), and starring himself in what his biographer Frank Brady called "the role of his life",[75] and he himself had called "the best role that Shakespeare ever wrote":[76] the Bard's most beloved character, fat Jack Falstaff. (It is a little known fact that Jesus Franco worked as a second unit director on the film.)

The Henriads chronicle the end of the Middle Ages: and, to Welles, Falstaff was not only a wonderful character (rounded in every possible sense, "a Christmas tree, decorated with vices"[77] and looking like Santa Claus), but the England of Chaucer, struggling to survive under the cold-blooded monarchy of the Lancastrians (complemented by Angelo Francesco Lavagnino's pastiche medieval music). The film opens with a long shot of Falstaff and Shallow (Alan Webb) limping through the snow, exchanging poignant reminiscences about their wild youth: as with *Citizen Kane*, Welles begins the story near the end of his antihero's life before rewinding a few years. The scene is suffused with a melancholy sense that the merry world the two old men are discussing, if it ever existed, is dead, and that in which they live is harsh and unforgiving. As the opening titles go up, Ralph Richardson[78] reads from Holinshed's *Chronicles*, setting the political scene as we move to the impersonal, echoing, draughty world of the palace, presided over by John Gielgud as a Bolingbroke with frost on his breath and ice in his

[74] Quoted by Leaming, Barbara, *Orson Welles, a biography* (Pompton Plains, 1985), p. 461.

[75] Brady, Frank, *Citizen Welles: a biography of Orson Welles* (New York, 1989), p. 539.

[76] Welles, Orson, ed. Estrin, Mark W., *Orson Welles: interviews* (Oxford, Mississippi, 2002), p. 118.

[77] Ibid., p. 132.

[78] Himself one of the great stage Falstaffs of the twentieth century, much admired by Welles.

veins. This is in fact two locations: Soria Cathedral, and a disused prison in the hills above Barcelona: but they fill the role perfectly. Ingenious use is made of their corridors and interlocking chambers by shooting several scenes from outside the rooms in which they take place, creating a strong sense of the endemic eavesdropping at the corrupt Lancastrian court, and contrasting tellingly with Nell Quickly's (Margaret Rutherford) tavern, which for all its dirt and squalor is warm and alive. (The tavern sets built for *Chimes* can also be seen in Sergio Leone's *C' era una volta il West* (1967).)

As always in Welles' films, the lighting and camera work cannot be bettered: and the latter is perhaps at its best in the battle of Shrewsbury, the most ambitious scene he ever shot. In a sense, this is a reply to Olivier's Agincourt. The difference in approach is indicated early on: where Olivier had shown one knight being winched onto his horse as a pleasing dab of period detail, Welles offers us the surreal spectacle of dozens being lowered from the same tree like grotesque spiders. (The detail is in fact inauthentic for the period, but this is a quibble.) Brilliantly capturing both the pageantry of armies riding into battle and the shocking, unchivalrous reality of actual combat, not to mention the comedy of the armoured Falstaff blundering about like a confused rhinoceros, the scene was, in 1965, one of the most realistic depictions of medieval warfare yet committed to film.

Outside this scene (in which he perhaps felt that the battle itself was sufficiently tragic without the antihero adding to the misery), Welles generally plays his part seriously, leaving the comedy to the exaggerated performances of Webb and Michael Aldridge (Pistol). This makes for an oddly subdued Falstaff, although undoubtedly it is realistic for a man of seventy-odd (which, thanks only partly to Francisco Puyol's excellent make-up work, the 49-year-old Welles certainly looks) to show little energy: Welles was perhaps over-preoccupied with the character's eventual fate. The result is that his weary Jack, though played beautifully in his more poignant scenes, lacks something when required to be boisterous, and is often not quite as alive as he needs to be.

The other performances – Rutherford's tired but trusting Nell; Keith Baxter's conflicted Hal, who becomes the cold and distant prince his father was even as Gielgud's King is rediscovering his humanity through deathbed guilt; Jeanne Moreau's devoted Doll Tearsheet; Norman Rodway's ferocious but quixotic Hotspur – are all at least equal to Welles', and in some cases arguably superior. Everybody involved displays an instinctive understanding of Shakespeare's text – although unfortunately the necessities of turning two and a half long plays (plus excerpts from *Richard II* and *The Merry Wives of Windsor*) into a single two hour film mean that much of this has been cut, with very occasional damage to the comprehensibility of the lines. The marvel is that Welles was still able to make such good sense out of a fraction of the text; and, while what has gone is sadly missed, the only alternative would have been to make a film some seven hours long.

Astonishingly, *Chimes at Midnight* was barely noticed in the English-speaking world on its release; in 1967, a Hollywood producer even wrote to Welles to ask if he had ever considered playing Falstaff on the big screen. For several decades afterwards it remained hard to come by outside Spain – a sad loss to film and Shakespeare buffs everywhere.

Nichts als Sünde (1965, East Germany, black and white)
Based on *Twelfth Night*
Directed by Hans Burger
Language: German
Runtime: 101 minutes
Believed lost

Deutsche Film's *Nichts als Sünde* was an occasionally surreal musical comedy loosely based on *Twelfth Night*; it is not thought to have survived.

Romeo and Juliet (1966, U.K., black and white)
Directed by Val Drumm and Paul Lee
Starring: Clive Francis, Angela Scoular, Veronica Clifford, Anthony Pedley, Richard Wilson
Runtime: 107 minutes

Romeo and Juliet started life as a production staged by faculty students of R.A.D.A., under the direction of Hugh Morrison; Drumm and Lee's recording of it, filmed by students from the London Polytechnic, was televised early in 1965, and received a limited theatrical release in the following year.

The film's theatrical and televisual origins are painfully obvious. The near constant use of close-up can do only so much to disguise the fact that it is all shot on a single set, and also enforces static blocking which, if it is the same as that used in the live production, must have made it tortuously slow. Costumes (mostly suggesting a period around 1530, which is roughly when the story was first written down by Luigi da Porto, although Romeo's doublet looks a few decades later) go unchanged throughout. Rather than recut the text to fit the television slot available, and therefore have to learn an effectively new script, the students have chosen simply to omit chunks of it so as to fit the time available, which is frustrating for the viewer who knows the play and possibly confusing for one who doesn't.

Nor is the acting, for the most part, anything special: although the beautiful enunciation for which R.A.D.A. is justly famous is much in evidence (albeit badly served by the flat sound recording), stars Clive Francis and Angela Scoular are simply too restrained to convince as passionate lovers. Damien Court-Thomas' Tybalt can sneer but lacks energy, and Hayward Morse's Mercutio is altogether shallow, while most of the older generation suffers from being portrayed by twenty-somethings. Two of these young actors do acquit themselves well in their middle-aged roles: Veronica Clifford brings an interesting touch of melancholy to the Nurse, and Richard Wilson (credited as Iain Wilson, his birth name) lends an unusual degree of depth to Juliet's father.

Ultimately, the principal value this film has lies in the glimpse it gives us of Francis, Clifford, Wilson, and Anthony Pedley (Friar Laurence), all much better known for later work, at the start of their careers.

Romeo and Juliet (1966, U.K., colour)
Directed by Paul Czinner
Starring: Margot Fonteyn, Rudolf Nureyev, Desmond Doyle, David Blair
Runtime: 124 minutes

The Royal Ballet's landmark production of Prokofiev's *Romeo and Juliet*, directed by Paul Czinner, choreographed by Kenneth MacMillan, conducted by Ashley Lawrence, and bringing together the two most celebrated dancers of the day, is a quite remarkable achievement. It is, of course, theatre-shot, and not to be judged as cinema: but the theatre in question is the Royal Opera House, whose towering, lavishly detailed sets succeed in carrying the viewer to early Renaissance Italy; and there is no question but that a profound visual sensibility informs Czinner's work. (The film would be a failure if it did not, since his principal task was to provide visuals to go with Prokofiev's music.)

The costumes, designed by Nicholas Georgiadis in bold primary colours, make inventive use of the styles of their era, the swirl of flowing sleeves lending itself to the movement of the ballet, while skirts are shortened to facilitate freer dancing (thus bringing a touch of the Sixties to proceedings). They are also tailored to character: Juliet (Margot Fonteyn) is the only Capulet to appear (even before meeting Romeo) in blue, a gentle colour established as belonging otherwise to the Montagues; Romeo (Rudolf Nureyev) and his friends wear light, tight, trapping-free costumes quite unlike those of the older generation; while Tybalt (Desmond Doyle) is clad in blood red.

Understanding that this was essentially a silent film, Czinner opted to move the plot forward by title cards taken from the production's programme notes. It would have helped if he had interspersed them between individual scenes rather than trying to explain whole acts in advance, but the conceit is effective – although, indeed, it is hardly necessary if the viewer has even a passing acquaintance with the play.

The dancing is uniformly superb. Even the fight scenes – difficult to render convincingly in dance form – succeed, as Mercutio (David Blair) turns the incorporation of ballet into an expression of his playfulness, while Doyle fences almost realistically, providing a neat contrast; the Veronese marketplace bustles authentically, while the three dancers credited as "Harlots" (Deanne Bergsma, Monica Mason, and Carole Needham) vigorously affirm their love of life; the bizarre sequence in which Romeo dances with Juliet's limp "corpse" successfully avoids the potential for unintentional comedy; and Fonteyn, like Ulanova before her, shows a quite astonishing affinity for her adolescent role despite being over forty.

I am not, I must confess, especially fond of ballet, and I nearly always find it frustrating to watch a Shakespearean film that lacks his language: but *Romeo and Juliet* is an expertly made and quite beautiful picture.

The Taming of the Shrew (1967, Italy / U.S.A., colour)

A.k.a. *La Bisbetica domata* (Italy)
Directed by Franco Zeffirelli
Starring: Elizabeth Taylor, Richard Burton, Michael Hordern, Natasha Pyne, Cyril Cusack
Runtime: 122 minutes
Academy Award nominations (1968): Best Art Direction (Lorenzo Mongiardino, John DeCuir, Elven Webb, Giuseppe Mariani, Dario Simoni, Luigi Gervasi); Best Costume Design (Irene Sharaff, Danilo Donati)

Franco Zeffirelli's first big-screen venture into Shakespearean territory[79] prefigures his later, more successful, *Romeo and Juliet* (1968) and *Hamlet* (1990) insofar as it is exquisitely designed and photographed: he has always been a very visual director, and here successfully immerses us in his pretty vision of mid-sixteenth century Italy, strongly influenced by paintings of the era. It is no coincidence that the two categories in which the film was nominated for Academy Awards were Art Direction and Costume Design. There, however, Zeffirelli's success ends.

It is not that his direction falters at the visionary level. From his trademark expertly handled crowd scenes down to the nicely observed details of the fairs, festivals and kitchens, it is uniformly fine: but the film suffers from three major flaws. The first is one that can dog productions of this particular play: instead of addressing the issues raised about misogyny, Zeffirelli seems to have chosen to embrace it. The tagline "In the war between the sexes, there always comes a time for unconditional surrender", not to mention the unspeakably crude theatrical trailer ("For every man who's ever given the back of his hand to his beloved, and for every woman who's deserved it"), invites the audience to applaud Kate's eventual defeat and submission (which are played quite seriously: this was reportedly Taylor's own decision, and a surprise to both Zeffirelli and Burton). The lack of irony in the face of Petruchio's behaviour is extremely distasteful.

The second flaw is the excision of much of the material relating to minor characters. Kate (Taylor in a series of low-cut

---

[79] His stage production of *Much Ado About Nothing*, starring Robert Stephens and Maggie Smith, was adapted for television by Alan Cooke in the same year: sadly, Zeffirelli's later efforts to develop a cinematic *Much Ado* came to nothing.

dresses) and Petruchio (Burton) are allowed a complete dominance of the film, which is not theirs in the play. (Admittedly Zeffirelli is less guilty in this respect than most previous screen directors of the *Shrew*, who often cut out secondary characters altogether.) Actors such as Michael York (Lucentio), Alan Webb (Gremio) and Cyril Cusack (Grumio), whose flair for comedy was considerably greater than Burton's, receive far too little screen time, and some two thirds of Shakespeare's text goes by the board in favour of extended sequences of what is presumably supposed to be slapstick. It is hard to escape the conclusion that Burton and Taylor's positions as producers of the film contributed to this situation.

The third and most serious flaw is closely linked to the second: the film is not funny. Burton's constant, infuriating laugh (effective in *Hamlet* (1964) but misplaced and overused here) serves only to remind the audience of this. He was a brilliant dramatic actor, and Zeffirelli a fine director of tragedy, but both should have left comedy well enough alone. One wonders what Zeffirelli's original choices for the leading roles, Sophia Loren and Marcello Mastroianni, might have done in place of Burton and Taylor, but it is doubtful if they would have been much more successful. *The Taming of the Shrew* is a delight to look at, but hard to watch.

A Midsummer Night's Dream (1967, U.S.A., colour)
Directed by George Balanchine and Dan Eriksen
Starring: Suzanne Farrell, Edward Villella, Arthur Mitchell, Mimi Paul
Runtime: 86 minutes

It had been a lifelong ambition of the great choreographer George Balanchine to base a ballet on *A Midsummer Night's Dream*, and he finally achieved it while working with the New York City Ballet in the 1960s. Using a score arranged from Mendelssohn's overture to the play, his Symphony No 9 for Strings, and four minor overtures (conducted for the film by Robert Irving), Balanchine created a work which he decided had to be enshrined for posterity.

The ballet is divided into two uneven acts: the first comprises Acts Two to Four of the play (the first act is cut, allowing this section to be set entirely in the forest); the second, half the length of the first, corresponds to Act Five. The problems of this structure will be addressed in a moment; but the film begins beautifully.

The opening credits go up over a panorama of glittering cobwebs lifted from Hal Mohr's design for Reinhardt's 1935 film of the play, before the eyes of Titania (Suzanne Farrell) appear in extreme close-up: which is, for obvious reasons, a very unusual shot in filmed ballet. The forest is exquisitely designed by Albert Brenner, a lush temperate woodland where summer reigns everywhere but in Oberon's wintry lair, and would look almost realistic if it were not for the perfectly flat ground. Barbara Karinska's costumes blend periods seamlessly: Greco-Roman for the fairies, with Oberon (Edward Villella) as a martial Caesar figure; late medieval for the mortals in the first act, possibly reflecting the strong influence of Chaucer and Boccaccio on Shakespeare's portrayal of Thesean Athens; while in the second act it conforms with Brenner's eighteenth century neo-classical design for Theseus' (Francisco Moncion) palace. The danger that the dragonfly wings worn by the younger fairies (children from Balanchine's School of American Ballet) will tip the portrayal of their world over into Victorian-style sentimentality is averted by the dark and dangerous performance of Arthur Mitchell[80] as a grinning, malicious Puck. Beautifully lit and perfectly danced, the film is never less than gorgeous to look at.

Whether it does justice to the play, however, is another matter. Balanchine lets the fairies dominate his ballet completely; the mechanicals – even Richard Rapp's touchingly innocent Bottom – are marginalised to the point of being barely noticeable. The play within the play, which would be very difficult to stage balletically (the aristocrats would be required to sit still for ten or twenty minutes, and stasis is fatal to dance), is cut altogether. Instead, Act Two consists of a wedding ball. Shakespeare rounded off his play with almost plotless comedy, but kept it to rather less than a fifth of the total running time: Balanchine's ballet gives over a third of its length to entirely plotless spectacle. Given that there is only one palace set, not very imaginatively photographed, as opposed to the four woodland sets used in the first act, this section of the film quickly becomes tedious.

This is an unfortunate end to what is a very fine ballet, and for two thirds of its length a delightful film.

---

[80] Founder of the Dance Theatre of Harlem.

Ithele na ginei vasilias (1967, Greece, black and white)
Based on *Hamlet*
A.k.a. *Meine konta mou, agapimeni* (Greece); *He Wanted to Become King* (international English title)
Directed by Angelos Theodoropoulos
Runtime: 88 minutes
Language: Greek
Believed lost

Angelos Theodoropoulos directed himself as the Hamlet-figure Alekos in Giannis V. Ioannidis' loose adaptation of Shakespeare's tragedy.

The Winter's Tale (1968, U.K., colour)
Directed by Frank Dunlop
Runtime: 151 minutes
Not seen by current writer

Dunlop's 1966 production of *The Winter's Tale* for the Edinburgh Festival was successful enough to be deemed worth televising, and the teleplay was subsequently released in cinemas. An interesting cast included Lawrence Harvey as Leontes, the young Jane Asher as Perdita, and Jim Dale of *Carry On* fame as Autolycus; Dale also composed the score together with Anthony Bowles. No attempt was made to adapt the play to the cinematic format; the critical response was and remains divided.

Do Dooni Chaar (1968, India, black and white)
Based on *The Comedy of Errors*
Directed by Debu Sen
Starring: Kishore Kumar, Asit Sen, Surekha Pandit, Sudha Rani, Tanuja Samarth
Language: Hindi
Runtime: 138 minutes

The legendary director Bimal Roy stepped back into the role of producer for this Indianised *Errors*. The story adapts easily to the Indian setting: although the Dromios (here named Sevak and played by Asit Sen) cannot be slaves as in the play, it is established that they have been brought up as servants because they are of a lower caste than their adoptive families; it is as natural for Anju (the Luciana character: Surekha Pandit) to live with her in-laws as in ancient Greece or Elizabethan England; there are near-exact equivalents for Angelo, the moneylender, the courtesan, and Dr Pinch.

The film, however, begins unpromisingly: the two pairs of twins line up on the screen and the narrator points out the differences between them. It is bad enough that the principal distinction between the two Sevaks is that one swings his arms and says "perhaps" a lot, without having this spelt out for us. Nor does the heavy-handedness end there, with woefully unfunny gurning, sped-up sequences, and even banana-skins, in evidence later. Kumar and Sen, though both very fine singers, are sadly given to overacting.

The female cast members are notably superior. The dynamic between Adriana (Suman: Sudha Rani) and Luciana has been reversed: here the tearful Suman is the hidebound sister and Anju the liberated one: but the actresses perform with exuberance and charm. It helps that they are both also very beautiful, whereas the men are chubby and distinctly unprepossessing. The actress playing the Sandeeps' mother (living in this version with the son equivalent to the Syracusan Antipholus) brings great poignancy to the final reunion.

Hemant Kumar's semi-Westernised score is jaunty, varied, and fun. Unfortunately, only about half the songs are related to the plot: others are linked to admittedly enjoyable digressions such as Sandeep's lone wandering in the jungle, and a marketplace festival scene. Both of these – particularly the latter, with its wildly flailing puppets, magnificently choreographed dances, and otherworldly conjuror-cum-fortune-teller – are beautifully composed and shot, and put the rest of the film in the shade if viewed as independent segments. But a film which is at least forty minutes too long and desperately slow-moving cannot afford to digress from its main storyline.

Do Dooni Chaar failed badly at the box office. Despite the impressiveness of some elements, in particular the score, the whole was deemed less than the sum of its parts.

Romeo and Juliet (1968, U.K. / Italy, colour)
A.k.a. *Romeo e Giulietta* (Italy)
Directed by Franco Zeffirelli

Starring: Leonard Whiting, Olivia Hussey, John McEnery, Milo O'Shea, Michael York
Runtime: 138 minutes
Academy Awards (1969): Best Cinematography (Pasqualino De Santis); Best Costume Design (Danilo Donati)
Academy Award nominations: Best Picture; Best Director (Franco Zeffirelli)

Hot on the heels of *The Taming of the Shrew* (1967) came Zeffirelli's second Shakespearean feature film, and he more than redeemed himself. Previous adaptations had tended to cast stars who were somewhat too old for the parts; even Zeffirelli, in his landmark 1960 stage production, cast a pair of twenty-somethings, John Stride and Judi Dench. For the film, however, he chose Leonard Whiting and Olivia Hussey, aged seventeen and fifteen respectively at the time of casting. (Romeo's age is unstated in the text, but Juliet is thirteen; it is doubtful if any actress quite that youthful could portray her convincingly). Both were reportedly second choices: if it is true, as Zeffirelli himself has claimed, that he asked Paul McCartney to play Romeo, we can be thankful that the Beatle refused. It is, however, not impossible that this is a joke. He then peopled his supporting cast with strong British and Italian character actors, and persuaded his idol Laurence Olivier to voice the Chorus and to dub the lines of Lord Montague (Antonio Pierfederici); the results are impressive.

Zeffirelli chose to set the play in the fifteenth century, in keeping with traditional Italian versions of the story – although the earliest account is set at the beginning of the fourteenth – and shot the film largely on location in Verona and other northern Italian towns. His stunningly photographed vision of Renaissance Italy is even more beautiful than in *The Taming of the Shrew*; but here, in contrast to the earlier film, he never allows it to overshadow the text. Shakespeare is well served, most of the cast achieving Olivier's trick of making classical diction sound natural: the inexperienced Hussey and Whiting were ill at ease with the language, but Zeffirelli's strong directorial hand guided them through it.

The stand-out performance is easily that of John McEnery as Mercutio: his initially comical, then increasingly wild, Queen Mab speech takes us deeper into the character's troubled soul than any other portrayal I have seen; his death scene brings tears to the eyes. He is also the first cinematic

Mercutio to hint that the character's affection for Romeo may be homosexual (picked up on by Baz Luhrmann in his 1996 version of the play): the influence of Zeffirelli's own sexuality on the interpretation has been guessed at, but nothing certain can be concluded about this.

The loveliness and youth of the two leads, coupled with the appeal of the play, made this the first original text Shakespearean film to achieve real popularity with teenage audiences – indeed, in that demographic only Luhrmann's version has surpassed it.[81] Both films were unfairly accused by critics of pandering to this audience ("drilling into the 'generation gap' as if it were an oil well" was how one reviewer described Zeffirelli's film) at the expense of the text, but in truth this is an excellent rendition of *Romeo and Juliet*, beautifully supported by Nino Rota's romantic score. The Luhrmann version may have shown greater inventiveness, but, as with the 1944 and 1989 renditions of *Henry V*, the two films should be seen as complementary, not opposed.

A Midsummer Night's Dream (1968, U.K., colour)
Directed by Peter Hall
Starring: Ian Holm, Diana Rigg, Helen Mirren, Judi Dench, Paul Rogers
Runtime: 124 minutes

The Royal Shakespeare Company's 1968 *Dream* (based on a 1962 stage production by the R.S.C.'s coming man, Peter Hall, who also directed the film) is an oddity. Ann Curtis' costumes mix styles and (apparently) periods, cod-Edwardian suits co-existing with eighteenth century collars and cloaks, more obviously Sixties boots and miniskirts, while Lysander (David Warner) wears a floral shirt straight from the King's Road, Starveling (Donald Eccles) appears to have borrowed his hat from Meg the Witch, and Hippolyta (Barbara Jefford) spends half the film looking like a dominatrix. There is an element here of satire against the absurd sartorial fads of the Carnabetian Army, in which the film's Lysander and Demetrius (Michael Jayston) would feel thoroughly at home: indeed, one could probably have seen every item in the film's wardrobe on the

---

[81] The stage production had had a similar effect in 1960, even anticipating the Beatles by making long hair fashionable in London..

streets of Swinging London. The green-skinned fairies, meanwhile – all of whom save the three principals (Ian Richardson, Judi Dench, and Ian Holm) are played by children – wear next to nothing. The result is surreal and disorientating.

The combination of Hall's psychedelic vision and the array of excellent acting talent assembled for the film boded very well, but against these militated Hall's inexperience with cinema ("I believe", he declared, "that Shakespeare's text only has film value in close-up" – a belief best debunked by watching this picture) and the paucity of his budget. The former results in an under-directed, static picture which fatally fails to transfer to the screen the zest of the play; the latter adds amateurish cinematography, ham-fisted editing, and atrocious sound quality to the debit side of the balance. The dubbed speeches sound identical in court or forest, and the recording equipment buzzes whenever anybody hits the letter S; the sun is often visible in scenes supposedly set at night. Hall was hardly the first or the last director to find that brilliance in the theatre was no guarantee of success in the cinema; but not even this cast – who could have made an excellent *Dream* given the chance – can rescue the film from its technical deficiencies.

Quella sporca storia nel West (1968, Italy, colour)
Based on *Hamlet*
A.k.a. *Johnny Hamlet* (U.S.A.); *That Dirty Story of the West* (international English title); *The Wild and the Dirty* (video title)
Directed by Enzo G. Castellari
Starring: Andrea Giordana, Horst Frank, Gilbert Roland, Françoise Prévost, Manuel Serrano
Language: Italian / English (released in two dubs)
Runtime: 91 minutes / 78 minutes (Germany)

The influences on this bizarre serving of spaghetti Shakespeare are not hard to spot. The juxtaposition of wide vistas with extreme close-ups, Francesco De Masi's guitar-jangling sub-Morricone score, and the laconic, unshaven, morally ambiguous hero himself (Andrea Giordana), cry out that Castellari was trying to be Sergio Leone. Unfortunately, neither he nor cinematographer Angelo Filippini possessed anything like Leone's mastery of the camera. Nor did his cast and crew measure up to the master's regular collaborators; and the clunking dialogue which replaces Shakespeare never once sounds remotely natural.

Westerns had been influenced by Shakespeare before – *Yellow Sky* (1949) appropriates themes from *The Tempest*; *Broken Lance* (1954) echoes *King Lear*; *Jubal* (1956) owes a certain amount to *Othello*, and *McLintock!* (1963) to *The Taming of the Shrew* – but *Johnny Hamlet* was the first direct adaptation into the horse-opera format since *A Sage Brush Hamlet* (1919). To date it remains the last on the big screen, although the 2002 TV movie *King of Texas* is based on *Lear*. Castellari's transference of the Hamlet story to Texas in the aftermath of the U.S. Civil War is at first none too forced. Scarred Confederate veteran Johnny Hamilton (Giordana) returns home to find his father dead, and his uncle Claud (a smooth, coolly villainous Horst Frank) married to his mother (Françoise Prévost) and master of the family ranch; he duly withdraws into himself, quarrelling with his former fiancée Ofelia (Gabriella Grimaldi) and confiding only in old friend Horace (Western veteran Gilbert Roland, famous for his many portrayals of the Cisco Kid: it is Horace, not Johnny, who wears the white hat to Claud's black, and who repeatedly has to rescue the out-of-his-depth Johnny from various assassins). Polonius (Giorgio Sammartino) is a corrupt sheriff, Rosencrantz and Guildenstern (Ennio Girolami and Ignazio Spalla) a pair of ex-Union soldiers turned hired bullies. A touch of metatheatre is added by the fact that the players – whose original function is quite lost from this version of the story – are performing *Hamlet*, and Johnny has a brief affair with their Ophelia (Stefania Careddu).

For some reason, however, Castellari allows the plot of the play to be derailed by some nonsense about missing gold and a Mexican bandit (Santana: Manuel Serrano) whom Claud has double-crossed. There is a confused message here about greed and the corrupting effects of war; Castellari's politics, like his film style, are lifted from the socialist Leone but markedly lack the latter's intelligence. These points had an undeniable pertinence in 1968, with hostilities in Vietnam at their height, but Castellari was not the man to make them. At one point Santana appears to be turning into Fortinbras, when his gang precipitates the final crisis by attacking the Hamilton ranch: but, in the final shootout – which overall lasts nearly half an hour, a good third of the film – the principals all manage to outlive the interloper. Johnny survives to ride off with Horace, while the uncredited Gravedigger cleans up the mess. In the midst of this

193

diversion there has been time for only one vague reference to the play: when Claud, here himself a former lover of Ofelia, murders her and frames Johnny, he does dump the body in a river. As there is no Laertes in the film, it is her father who comes after Johnny, and – in an extraordinarily heavy-handed example of the kind of religious allegory which frequently crops up in Italian and Spanish Westerns – tries to crucify him (allowing Gertrude briefly to become the Blessed Virgin in what is apparently supposed to be a pious reference but seems more like a parody of the Pietà), before being shot by Horace!

Clumsy and ill thought out from the beginning, *Quella sporca storia nel West* is, by the end, an irredeemable mess.

Ofelias blomster (1968, Denmark, colour)
Based on *Hamlet*
A.k.a. *Ophelia's Flowers* (international English title)
Directed by Jørgen Leth
Runtime: 7 minutes
Not seen by current writer

In 1965, Leth had directed an experimental *Hamlet*, in which he periodically interrupted the actors in well known speeches by beating on a drum, compelling them to begin again from the beginning. The whole was performed upon a set painted uniformly blue by Leth's collaborator Per Kirkeby. Three years later, he turned Ophelia's madness scene and subsequent death into a short film, starring Lene Adler Petersen, in the same costume of loose ribbons used in the stage version, against a blue backdrop set up on a peat bog in northern Zealand: once again, the beating drum repeatedly interrupted the monologue.

A print is held by the Danish Film Institute.

The Secret Sex Lives of Romeo and Juliet (1969, U.S.A., colour)
Based on *Romeo and Juliet*
A.k.a. *Juliet's Desire*; *The Sex Life of Romeo and Juliet* (U.S.A.)
Directed by Peter Perry
Starring: Deirdre Nelson, Forman Shane, James Brand, Mickey Jines, Vincene Wallace
Runtime: 92 minutes

A relic of the pre-VHS era, when the likes of Russ Meyer

dominated sexploitation cinema and there was a curious innocence about the whole business, *The Secret Sex Lives of Romeo and Juliet* is a softcore sex comedy affectionately spoofing Zeffirelli's film of the play and late Sixties pop culture in general (to a pseudo-Renaissance soundtrack, which manages to blend the "porn sax" typical of Meyer and his imitators with pastiche Nino Rota and the Willow Song from *Othello*).

Essentially, the plot of *Romeo and Juliet* is loosely adapted so as to cram in as many soft focus sex scenes and groan-worthy *Carry On*-style jokes as it can bear (and more – the plot and the sex are occasionally allowed to distract from one another, when they should be complementary). The word "lives", as opposed to "life", is well chosen: we never see the two principals (bright-eyed Deirdre Nelson, brimming with charm and contriving to look innocent in the most compromising of situations, and the somewhat nondescript Forman Shane) have sex with each other, but almost every other possible combination is achieved, particularly by Mickey Jines' lip-licking Lady Capulet. The whole farrago is played with tremendous enthusiasm by all concerned, and the actors clearly enjoyed themselves, but it is sufficiently repetitive to bore any but the most sweaty-palmed of viewers.

Today's sleazier adult video industry has, according to the Internet Movie Database, visited Shakespeare a few times, in *Hamlet: For the Love of Ophelia* (1995), *Othello 2000* (1997), and *A Midsummer Night's Cream* (2000). It is, however, no longer the norm for such pictures to be released in cinemas, and none of the above films has been. The "backstage" genre was appropriated for sex plots in *Romeo and Juliet* (1987) and *Romeo and Juliet II* (1988), but my understanding is that these have little to do with the play.

Hamlet (1969, U.K., colour)
A.k.a. *Shakespeare's Hamlet* (U.S.A.)
Directed by Tony Richardson
Starring: Nicol Williamson, Anthony Hopkins, Marianne Faithfull, Judy Parfitt, Gordon Jackson
Runtime: 117 minutes

Richardson adapted this slight *Hamlet* from his own stage production, and it shows. It is entirely shot in the Roundhouse theatre, with black backdrops and minimal sets: what is less obvious is how the original production was ever a success, let alone deemed fit for cinematic release.

The film is entirely flat. Williamson, frequently an annoying actor, is woefully inappropriate as Hamlet and looks far too old for the part (though in fact he was one of the youngest actors to play the Prince on the big screen); Horatio (the 46-year-old Gordon Jackson) seems practically in his dotage. Richardson was keen to focus on the Prince's relationship with Ophelia (Marianne Faithfull), and marginalises other characters to that end: but, beautiful as the young Faithfull was, she was not quite an actress of sufficient calibre to pull off this part – and the idea of Williamson in any kind of romantic role is laughable. Judy Parfitt makes a cold Gertrude: at her best, she seems to be implying complicity in her husband's murder; at her more frequent worst, she seems to be wishing herself elsewhere. It is hard to blame her. Only Anthony Hopkins as Claudius brings any kind of zest to his part, but he (just for a change) is far too young.

I had to remind myself at frequent intervals that Richardson directed the joyous *Tom Jones* (1963) and the drily sardonic *The Charge of the Light Brigade* (1968). None of those films' energy and invention is in evidence here. The only remarkable thing about the camera work is that actors are nearly always shot from the waist up, giving the disconcerting impression that they could not afford the bottom halves of the costumes; the closest the film comes to originality is in suggesting (logically enough) that the sailors who deliver Hamlet's letter to Horatio are the same pirates who captured the Prince on his way to England. It does occasionally veer into the bizarre – Claudius and Gertrude receive their court sitting up in bed; the poisoned pearl is the King's earring – but these touches are never made effective.

All in all, this is a waste of time and celluloid, and a low point in the careers of all concerned.

A Herança (1970, Brazil, black and white)
Based on *Hamlet*
Directed by Ozualdo Ribeiro Candeias
Language: Portuguese
Runtime: 90 minutes
Not seen by current writer

A Herança transferred the *Hamlet* story to rural Brazil, the Danish royals becoming a wealthy farming family.

Julius Caesar (1970, U.K., colour)
Directed by Stuart Burge
Starring: Jason Robards, Charlton Heston, John Gielgud, Richard Johnson, Diana Rigg
Runtime: 117 minutes

Burge, who had directed a television version of *Julius Caesar* in 1959, scarcely steps above the level of TV movies for four acts of this reprisal of the same play. John Gielgud, who played the title role, called the film "awfully bad" (adding "though I manage to be fairly effective in it"[82]). One gets the strong impression that Burge allocated the entire budget to the Battle of Philippi: but a carper might say that there is little point in having a strong battle scene if one has already bored half the audience out of the cinema before it happens.

This, however, would be an unfair judgement. It is true that the film looks cheap for most of the first ninety-odd minutes; it is also true that Jason Robards, a normally reliable character actor only slightly too old for the part, gives possibly the flattest performance of his career as Brutus (a role originally earmarked for Orson Welles): but it is difficult to suggest what else Burge might have done with his budget. He engaged the best actors available and gave the audience an impressive final showdown, if not one quite worthy of comparison with the epics that had gone so far out of fashion by 1970.

The costumes (designed by Robin Archer) are fantastical – Roman in style, but garishly coloured and cut of many cloths: metallic silk togas were hardly the rage in 44 B.C. – the sets (by Julia Trevelyan Oman) implausible, and Ken Higgins' photography hard on the eyes. The acting, however – with the single exception of Robards, of whom Charlton Heston remarked "I have never seen a good actor so bad in a good part"[83] – is by and large competent. Heston himself is deliciously devious reprising the role of Marc Antony, at perhaps a more appropriate age than when he first played it. One reservation I

---

[82] Gielgud, *Letters*, p. 358.
[83] Heston, Charlton, *In the arena: an autobiography* (New York, 1995), p. 419.

do have is over the casting of Christopher Lee in the eminently forgettable role of Artemidorus (a character described by Burge, on small evidence, as "quite, quite mad" – which observation, Lee later claimed, was the only direction he had received[84]): surely he would have been better employed as the Soothsayer.

The politics of the production are clear enough. Richard Johnson's Cassius, even at his most sinister, remains a man of honour; Gielgud's superficially benevolent Caesar is at base a despot ruled by vanity; Heston's Antony and Richard Chamberlain's Octavius, grinning to themselves after stirring up murderous mobs or casually condemning their closest relatives to death, are a pair of vicious politicians. Burge sets his film unequivocally in the Welles tradition, as a denunciation of tyranny: it is hardly an important one, but at least its heart is in the right place.

Faustão (1971, Brazil, colour)
Based on *The Merry Wives of Windsor*, *Henry IV, Part 1*, and *Henry IV, Part 2*
Directed by Eduardo Coutinho
Language: Portuguese
Runtime: 103 minutes
Believed lost
Saga Filmes' Falstaff movie, apparently set, like *A Herança*, in rural Brazil, starred Eliezer Gomes in the title role.

Korol Lir (1971, U.S.S.R., black and white)
Based on *King Lear*
A.k.a. *King Lear* (U.S.A.)
Directed by Grigori Kozintsev and Iosif Shapiro
Starring: Jüri Järvet, Valentina Shendrikova, Oleg Dal, Roman Gromadsky, Regimantas Adomaitis
Language: Russian
Runtime: 139 minutes
Kozintsev's last film before his death in 1973 was another Shakespeare adaptation, to complement his 1964 *Gamlet*. (When he died, he was reportedly planning to come out

---

[84] Lee, Christopher, *Tall, dark, and gruesome: an autobiography* (London, 1977), p. 272.

of retirement and adapt *The Tempest*.) Once again, state backing for his Leninfilm company meant that he was able to command a sizeable budget and work on an epic scale: and the text he chose to tackle was *King Lear*. This was the film Kozintsev saw as the crowning point of his career, and the fulfilment of "something that began its existence in childhood".[85]

Perhaps unsurprisingly given his politics, Kozintsev decided that the key to *Lear* was the King's realisation that he has "ta'en too little care" of the "poor naked wretches" who must regularly endure such hardships as his daughters visit upon him, and that his misrule of his family and misrule of the realm are intimately connected. In this *Lear*, the poor are with us always: at the very beginning the camera tracks crowds of people, mostly beggars and cripples, flocking to see the King (the Estonian actor Jüri Järvet, who learned Russian for the part). In the event, he shows himself to them for only an instant, shouting his rejection of Cordelia (Valentina Shendrikova) from the top of his highest tower; his subjects drop abjectly upon their faces as if before a wrathful god. Later, Edgar's (Leonhard Merzin) "Poor Tom" disguise is inspired by a band of wandering madmen to whom he attaches himself; the hovel in which Lear hides from the storm is their doss-house, and the "wretches" are before him in person when he has his epiphany. The propertied commons also suffer: the most arresting image of Cordelia's invasion is the sight of peasant farmers desperately fleeing what is about to become the field of battle with all they can carry.

The recreation of period is less sure-handed than in *Gamlet*: Kozintsev has set the play not in remote antiquity but in the fifteenth century (although it often looks more like late medieval Russia than the same era in England), and the clash between the eras – particularly between the play's pagan milieu and the Christianity of the Middle Ages – is not always perfectly resolved. This is a Christian world: Cordelia and the King of France (Juozas Budraitis), in an interpolated scene, are married according to the Roman rite, and Edgar plants a cross on Gloucester's grave: but woven into the film is the pagan notion of sacral kingship. The bleak, barren, forbidding landscape of the first part of the film displays the sickness of the realm; only when the French army arrives does the sun come out, and grass and flowers appear. This health, however, is an illusion, for though

---

[85] Quoted in the sleeve notes for the VHS, 1997.

decked in the fruits of his newly green kingdom Lear is still sick, and so too is Britain, about to suffer the ravages of war. The land is perhaps responding to the fact that, after a lifetime pent up in castles, the King is close to it once again, kissing the earth in symbolic marriage to his land.

The wild-haired Järvet, looking considerably older than his fifty years, brings to the role of the King an element of doubt that is often missing: this Lear is questioning his own sanity long before he entirely loses it, and it is never quite clear how mad he is; at times he could almost be taken for a bad-tempered geriatric Hamlet. Such an interpretation is by no means an easy one to render convincingly, but Järvet carries it off. The understatement of much of his performance – the "Reason not the need" speech is spoken quietly, to himself and the gods, after Goneril (Elze Radzinya) and Regan (Galina Volchek) have left him – lends power to the moments when he lets the dam burst.

Once again Kozintsev's direction and photography are for the most part superbly supported by the potent music of Dmitri Shostakovich: although the score does once or twice veer into melodramatic areas, most jarringly at the death of Edmund (Regimantas Adomaitis). The Christian-era setting of the film allows Shostakovich to set sacred music behind the scene in which, having buried his father, Edmund turns around and strides towards the smoke of the battlefield; as he enters the field of conflict, the music rises, combining with the groans of the wounded and the ubiquitous presence of fire to leave us in no doubt that this war is a near literal vision of Hell. The damnation of the realm is foreshadowed at the very beginning of the film, when Lear sits by a log-fire to announce his division of the kingdom, and the camera moves from this homely image to the same scene shot from the back of the fireplace, with flames licking the bottom of the screen and smoke blurring the picture.

At the very end of the film, as the Fool (Oleg Dal) plays a melancholy tune on his recorder before being thrust aside by the funeral procession, Edgar moves through the wreckage of Britain alone, his face inscrutable. He is become this play's Fortinbras: and, although he has given rather more evidence of a benevolent nature than the Prince of Norway, one is left with the same doubts that hang over the end of *Gamlet*: will the sick realm now be cured, or not? Once again, Kozintsev supplies no clear answer.

King Lear (1971, U.K. / Denmark, black and white)
Directed by Peter Brook
Starring: Paul Scofield, Alan Webb, Anne-Lise Gabold, Jack MacGowran, Robert Langdon Lloyd
Runtime: 137 minutes

In the same 2004 poll of the Royal Shakespeare Company's actors that declared *Kumonosu jô* (1957) to be the best Shakespearean film adaptation ever made, Paul Scofield's 1962 *Lear* (directed by Peter Brook, who had also directed Orson Welles in this part for television in 1953) was voted the best ever stage performance of a Shakespearean role. Nine years after their first collaboration on the play, Brook and Scofield returned to it for this quite extraordinary film.

Brook had made it clear that this was going to be a radical interpretation when he referred to *Lear* as "Shakespeare's *Endgame*" (following Jan Kott's essay on this theme). While Shakespeare's most proto-Beckettian work is surely *Timon of Athens*, and such a reading of *Lear* would be difficult to validate from an historical point of view, it is one to which the text does lend itself. Brook wears Beckett, and all his other influences – Brecht, whose alienation techniques are also evident in *The Tragedy of Macbeth* from the same year; Ingmar Bergman, whose starkly beautiful black-and-white photography may not be quite successfully replicated here, but whose films the atmosphere of *King Lear* repeatedly evokes; and the earliest origins of the Western theatre in Athenian tragedy, veteran Beckettian Jack MacGowran's Fool serving almost as a Chorus – on his sleeve.

Set in a bleak, snowbound and savage early medieval Anglo-Scandinavian world, the film creates an unremittingly freezing atmosphere in keeping with the pessimism of the play; to watch it is to endure the *Fimbulwinter* that in Nordic mythology precedes the end of the world. The Brechtian approach (evident in the camera work as well as in the direction, and the absence of music) may set us back from the characters, but does not prevent them from being powerfully drawn. Scofield's performance irresistibly reminds one of Kenneth Tynan's dictum on Lear, that one might as well try "to characterise an Alp"[86]: that is effectively what he has succeeded

---

[86] Tynan, Kenneth, *Curtains: selections from the drama criticism and related writings* (London, 1961), p. 18.

in doing here. The rest of the cast, particularly the acidic, semi-detached MacGowran, provide strong support; and the finale, with Goneril (Irene Worth) dashing out first Regan's brains and then her own against a rock on the seashore, and the mountain Lear finally crumbling (as this incarnation did not through his madness) when confronted with Cordelia's senseless death, is indescribably potent.

One could wish that the text had not been quite so substantially cut – more than half of the play has disappeared; however, a longer version would have been a different film. *Lear* can lend itself to epic: but Brook's vision (despite its use of similar broad, barren landscapes to those seen in Grigori Kozintsev's version, from whose shadow, in retrospect, Brook's film does not entirely succeed in escaping) is closed, anti-epic, almost claustrophobic. Only a close paring of the script could achieve this. There is no such thing as the definitive *Lear*; but Brook has made a major contribution to the history of the play. John Gielgud, when he wrote to congratulate Worth on her performance, declared that he doubted whether a better adaptation from Shakespeare had ever been brought to the screen.

The Tragedy of Macbeth (1971, U.K. / U.S.A., colour)
Directed by Roman Polanski
Starring: Jon Finch, Francesca Annis, Martin Shaw, Terence Bayler, John Stride
Runtime: 140 minutes

Polanski's gore-spattered *Macbeth* followed not long after the murder of his wife, Sharon Tate, by Charles Manson: critics understandably drew a connection, although Polanski himself said that the slaughter of Lady Macduff (Diane Fletcher) and her family was based on memories of his home in the Warsaw ghetto being sacked by the S.S. during World War Two. The film was partly funded by *Playboy*, which at that time made serious pictures as well as softcore pornography; the opening credits, as a result, tend to elicit sniggers in modern classrooms.

It is technically a period analogue, since Polanski moves the action from the eleventh century, when the historical Macbeth lived, to what looks like *circa* 1350. His rationale for this has never been explained, but perhaps he felt that audiences would be prepared for savagery in a film set in the so-called Dark

202

Ages but more shocked when it was set against the age of chivalry. (Some elements resulting from this grate: the historically aware Scottish viewer will wince on seeing Macduff (Terence Bayler) wearing the arms of the Douglases instead of his own clan.) This is a world with little elegance, where nobles eat like pigs and enjoy horrific bear-baitings, and with no honour – a point underscored by making Ross (John Stride) the Third Murderer of Banquo (Martin Shaw) and an accessory to the murders of the Macduffs, which he later reports as an innocent messenger.[87] Elements of the earlier period do intrude, however: the quasi-pagan coronation ceremony depicted in the film is accurate for early medieval Scotland, but had been more thoroughly Christianised by the fourteenth century.

Assisted by innovative camera lenses designed by Richard H. Vetter, Polanski creates a starkly realistic Middle Ages, shot in almost a documentary style. This is effective when watching lone warriors ride across a bleak Scottish landscape, and when Macbeth (Jon Finch) is butchering Duncan (an unusually robust and only just middle-aged Nicholas Selby) (the near-frenzied murder – whose violence is not gratuitous: it is the only way to account for the quantities of blood referred to in the text – is shown in full detail); but perhaps less so with the distinctly earthbound witches. These are no malign Fates, just three admittedly terrifying old women: and the downplaying of their supernatural nature affects the metaphysical side of the play. We seem to be closer to the godless world that some critics find in *King Lear* than to that of *Macbeth*.

The acting is understated, as suits Polanski's colour-drained vision: but, as the first cinematic Macbeths (at least in an original text version) to bring out the sexual side of the couple's relationship, Jon Finch and Francesca Annis certainly do not lack passion. Stride's calculating Ross, indeed, at times stands in contrast to the warmer-blooded King. Where ham is all too common, Finch and Annis present us with psychologically credible Macbeths.

The realism of the film is, however, most evident in the

---

[87] This is a conceit lifted from M. F. Libby's essay "Some Notes on Macbeth" (1893).

fight scenes. Choreographed by William Hobbs[88], they are dirty, brutal and exhausting; as Macbeth and Macduff wheeze and stumble and clang their swords off each other's heavy armour in the final scene, it is impossible not to feel the pain and fatigue they are suffering.

This bleak and pessimistic picture (which ends with Donalbain (Paul Shelley) limping towards the witches' lair to begin the whole cycle of violence again) is not without its flaws – human evil is strong, but the presence of the Devil is never really felt; though the sun is constantly overcast, too many scenes are set in daylight; the score, by The Third Ear Band, is occasionally inappropriate; and Annis' sleepwalking scene (distractingly performed nude) is not as effectively rendered as it might have been – but is, overall, a fascinating interpretation of *Macbeth* and a fine piece of film-making.

Antony and Cleopatra (1972, U.K / Spain / Switzerland, colour)
A.k.a. *Antoine et Cléopatre* (Switzerland); *Marco Antonio y Cleopatra* (Spain)
Directed by Charlton Heston
Starring: Charlton Heston, Hildegarde Neil, John Castle, Eric Porter, Roger Delgado
Runtime: 160 minutes / 138 minutes (cut version)

In his third and last cinematic outing as Marc Antony, Charlton Heston finally achieved his long-held ambition of starring in an epic adaptation of his favourite play, *Antony and Cleopatra*, directing himself after Orson Welles turned the project down. Unfortunately, neither his million-dollar budget – though put to inventive use – nor, it has to be said, his own skill behind the camera was equal to his ambition.

The film's faults and virtues alike are evident in the opening scene, in which Proculeius (Julian Glover) arrives in Alexandria, rides helter-skelter through the city without care for the Egyptians who get in his way (a foretaste of the destructive arrogance of Rome, displayed so bloodily later), and delivers Antony the news of Fulvia's death. The acting is strong and assured, Maurice Pelling's sets are spectacular, Heston's

---

[88] Hobbs, who also plays Young Seyward, would go on to direct the comic-realistic duels in Richard Lester's excellent *The Three Musketeers* (1974) and *The Four Musketeers* (1975).

204

direction is imaginative and fast-paced: but Rafael Pacheco's cinematography is mediocre at best, Johnny Scott's score overblown and sentimental, the set decoration by José María Alarcón and José Algueró displays a complete lack of visual sensibility, and the editing is abysmally inept. Throughout the film, Heston's imaginative touches of colour (such as a gladiatorial battle during Antony's first on-screen meeting with Caesar, enigmatically portrayed by John Castle) are turned into distractions from the scenes they adorn, partly because Heston pushes them too far, but largely by poor editing.[89]

The sterling Anglo-Spanish cast, among whom Heston's is the only American accent, perform for the most part excellently, although some minor characters sound a touch unnatural.[90] Unfortunately, however, Hildegarde Neil proves unequal to the part of Cleopatra. Neil was then in her early thirties, younger than the historical Cleopatra but not by any measure immature: but, although not altogether an inexperienced actress and certainly not a bad one, she had never taken on a part of such complexity. It would be interesting to see what she might have made of it ten years later; but here, while she occasionally touches the heights, she more often sounds like a spoilt schoolgirl, at one point even stamping her foot like Violet Elizabeth Bott. Carmen Sevilla, who plays Octavia in an unconvincing blonde wig, would have been a far more credible Cleopatra.

It was in the battle scenes that Heston's ambition defeated him. Actium in particular suffers the effects of budgetary constraints, smoke and gauze failing to conceal the use of model ships and footage lifted from *Ben-Hur* (1959) (although the gore of *Antony and Cleopatra*'s battles, with spurting blood and severed limbs much in evidence, would never have got past a 1950s censor). (Incidentally, like *Ben-Hur*, this film perpetuates the myth that Roman galleys were rowed by slaves like those of the Barbary corsairs. In fact, Roman oarsmen were

---

[89] Remarkably, this film's editor Eric Boyd-Perkins was also responsible for the sharply edited *The Wicker Man* (1973). The difference in quality is so marked that one can only conclude that he delegated much of the work on *Antony and Cleopatra*.

[90] Several of the Spanish actors were dubbed by Richard Johnson, who had played Cassius to Heston's Antony in *Julius Caesar* (1970), and who was in 1972 himself playing Antony for the R.S.C., in a much praised production which was televised two years later..

free men who rowed for pay.)

It is a problem for adaptors of this play that the pace slows down after Actium, which need not harm it in the theatre but is seldom good news in the cinema. Heston takes Antony's decline gently, with softer music and the lovers' camp filmed always in darkness after the battle while the sun shines bright on Caesar, but is unable to keep the film from flagging in the final act – a fault pointed up by the contrast to the frenetic energy it has shown hitherto. After Antony's suicide it struggles to hold the viewer's attention, reducing the death of the Queen to an anticlimax.

The director's own bitter verdict on the film is excessively harsh, but understandable: "The film I cared more about than any I've ever made", he later declared, "was a failure."[91]

Viola und Sebastian (1972, West Germany, colour)
Based on *Twelfth Night*
A.k.a. *Viola and Sebastian* (International English title)
Directed by Ottokar Runze
Starring: Karin Hübner, Michael J. Boyle, Inken Sommer, Heinz Theo Branding, Uwe Dallmeier
Language: German
Runtime: 93 minutes

Viola und Sebastian was avant-garde theatre director Ottokar Runze's first feature film as director. Made at the height of the psychedelic era, it sets *Twelfth Night* (the von Schlegel translation, heavily cut and occasionally tweaked to fit the modern surroundings) in the marshes of Schleswig-Holstein. Olivia (Inken Sommer) is the owner of a country inn managed by the oleaginous Malvolio (Heinz Theo Branding), while Orsino (Michael J. Boyle) is the kaftan-clad local landowner, who has turned his estate into a hippie colony called Illyria and surrounded himself with guitar-strumming flower children: an interpretation which suits the Duke's romanticism and self-absorption. The division between the houses is further marked by the difference in their music: Feste (Herbert Stass) sings in a traditional *lieder* style, while several songs that are his in the play

---

[91] Quoted by Rosenthal, Daniel, *100 Shakespeare Films* (London, 2007), p. 3.

are transferred to Viola (Karin Hübner) or Curio (uncredited), with tunes (by Hübner's then husband Frank Duval) which could come straight from Laurel Canyon.

The style of the film is remarkable. For the most part, with on-site sound recording, understated acting, and Horst Schier's documentary-style cinematography, it is plain and unadorned: but then we enter a musical sequence and the imagination of one or other of the characters (usually Orsino or Olivia), and what is on the screen becomes a sort of wild dream, full of tap-dancing wedding guests and country runs that continue Christ-like across the surface of a lake. This strange mix of realism with surrealism fits the setting perfectly, and helps cover up problems with the updating (such as the contrivance of separating the twins without a shipwreck, and Orsino's lack of his original's despotic power).

The casting, also, is impressive. The two couples imbue the piece with a bittersweet charm, the androgynous styles of the period making the resemblance of the twins credible (and Frank Glaubrecht as Sebastian *does* look extraordinarily similar to his "sister"); Uwe Dallmeier plays an unsympathetic Sir Toby, a charmless, cynical drunk, whose unlikeability helps the viewer to commiserate with Malvolio and Aguecheek (Gottfried Kramer). The latter's final fate is not glossed over – the film's closing images are of their loneliness, not the lovers' happiness. But the triumph of the picture is Duval's score, a minor classic of its kind and a perfect match with Runze's vision.

Jogo da Vida E da Morte (1972, Brazil, black and white)
Based on *Hamlet*
Directed by Mário Kuperman
Language: Portuguese
Runtime: 95 minutes
Believed lost

Hardly any details have survived concerning Futura Filmes' adaptation of *Hamlet*.

Mnogo shuma iz nichego (1973, U.S.S.R., colour)
Based on *Much Ado About Nothing*
A.k.a. *Much Ado About Nothing* (international English title)
Directed by Samson Samsonov

Starring: Galina Loginova, Konstantin Rajkin, Leonid Trushkin, Aleksei Samoilov, Tatyana Vedeneyeva
Language: Russian
Runtime: 77 minutes

Mosfilm's *Much Ado* is so drastically cut that the week between the betrothal and rejection of Hero (Tatyana Vedeneyeva) is collapsed into a single night, so that half the film takes place at the masked ball which occupies only one scene (II.1) of the play: its pace, however, remains at best moderate.

By 1973, the Soviet film industry was feeling the pinch; budgets were not what they had been, and this shows. Nevertheless, the film manages to look consistently interesting – and its locations convincingly Sicilian, through clever use of some of Russia's arid spaces and Greek-influenced buildings. The costumes range across the centuries: beginning *circa* the War of the Sicilian Vespers (1282), when Shakespeare's sources originally set the story, becoming Elizabethan for the ball, and thereafter hovering between the two, while Beatrice (Galina Loginova) looks strikingly modern throughout.

Loginova performs with charm and wit, but the same cannot be said of many others in the cast. Konstantin Rajkin, grinning inanely, makes a weirdly clownish Benedick: while this does help to make a contrast between his early frivolity and his seriousness in the latter part of the play, it never feels right for the character. Furthermore, the couple's sparring is marked from the beginning by too obvious affection: the bite is missing, and it is hard to imagine anybody being surprised that they end up together. Few other performances are memorable; Pavel Pavlenko and Erast Garin bring an unusual poignancy to the officers of the Watch, here portrayed as ancient soldiers who have seen better days, but they spend barely longer on screen than the plot absolutely demands.

Mnogo shuma iz nichego is a pretty film, and, despite Samsonov's problems with pacing, it does not drag too badly: but it is an indication that Soviet cinema was entering a more barren era.

Otello (1973, West Germany, colour)
Based on *Othello*
Directed by Roger Benamou and Herbert von Karajan
Starring: Jon Vickers, Peter Glossop, Mirella Freni, Stefania

Malagu, Aldo Bottion
Language: Italian
Runtime: 142 minutes

Opera and cinema are difficult art forms to bring together. Operatic performances appear absurdly exaggerated when seen in close-up; and while film can remove the artificiality of theatrical conventions whereby characters a few yards apart are supposedly unable to hear one another speak, it is hardly able to achieve this if they are singing at the tops of their voices. The Deutsche Oper von Berlin's 1973 film of Verdi's *Otello*[92] suffers from these problems, and from being entirely studio-shot – although it makes a virtue of the latter, with atmospheric lighting and Georges Wakhévitch's impressively realistic sets.

Verdi and Boito cut the whole first act of Shakespeare's play, loading the opera with even more back-story as it opens on the Cypriot coast (in a scene analogous with Act Two, Scene One of *Othello*) with the storm that scatters the Turkish fleet. The directors lead into this from an opening credit sequence played over the sound of howling wind and an image of the lion of St Mark, matching the tempestuous music with an unquiet sea on which Otello's ship is tossed like a cork, huge waves crashing into the shore and splashing the Chorus. The realism of the storm gives way to stylisation when Otello (Jon Vickers in surprisingly light make-up) reaches land: the sea calms behind him, only to rear high again whenever the music does.

The directors make considerable and inventive use of their godlike control of the weather: moonlight can seem as bright as day when Otello and Desdemona (Mirella Freni) sing their joyous "Già nella notte densa" (which in von Karajan's interpretation lacks the darkness that some directors impart to it); dawn can last the whole of Act Two (Act Three of the play) without the sun rising any higher. While the lighting revels in artificiality, however, the huge sets constitute an impressively authentic rendition of Venetian Cyprus in the early sixteenth century, emphasising the Byzantine influence on architecture, decoration and iconography: the East-West divide straddled by the occupation culture is expertly evoked.

---

[92] An opera premiered in 1887, with a libretto by Arrigo Boito that distilled Shakespeare's text to a quarter of its original length; it is here directed and conducted by the famously perfectionist Herbert von Karajan, arguably the world's most prestigious conductor at the time.

Nor is the cinematography (by Ernst Wild) made subservient to theatrical devices as is common in filmed theatre and opera: there are several memorable shots, from the ship in the first scene, to Otello's face reflected in a lily pond, Desdemona and Cassio (Aldo Bottion) framed by flowers, aerial shots of crowds and upward shots of the trumpeters during the ingenious "Come la ucciderò?" sequence (in which the singing of Iago (Peter Glossop) and Otello is shaped around the fanfare announcing Lodovico (José van Dam)), and the montage of tranquil waters, burning lamps, and religious icons that opens Act Four.

As for the cast: opera singers are not primarily actors, and cannot be judged by normal film or theatrical standards: but, whatever the yardstick, it is hard for Glossop not to emerge as the star of the production. Of course, it is true that the music itself constitutes a form of direction (especially since Verdi had to replace the characterisation lost in Boito's cutting of the text, and distract the audience from the implausibility of Otello succumbing quite so quickly to Iago's wiles), reducing the scope for interpretation. The cool, confident and commanding Iago of this film is therefore as much Verdi's as Glossop's or von Karajan's vision of the character: but he is at every turn more fully realised than Vickers' curiously innocent Otello. (Vickers is perhaps the stronger singer, but the edge is slight.) Freni, meanwhile, acts almost entirely *by* singing: her face is quite as beautiful as her voice, but not nearly so expressive.

One cannot help but wonder whether von Karajan had a point to make about Iago's role as an agent of Otello's own psyche when he cast two such physically similar singers as Glossop and Vickers, or whether it was purely coincidental. Intentional or not, it is certainly effective: Otello is corrupted by a colour-negative version of himself. Similar uses of visual symbolism abound: "Già nella notte densa" is performed in front of a mural of St George and the dragon, a simple vision of good triumphing over evil as Otello imagines he has already done in defeating the Turks and removing Cassio from his garrison: but the serpentine dragon may truly be Iago, the viper he still nurses in his bosom. Similar religio-military murals are all over the Venetian headquarters in Cyprus, looking down on the action that reflects their themes, until all is played out. Like the lion under the opening credits, the murals have already begun to crumble, but will outlast the human actors by generations. "Viva il Leon di San Marco" indeed.

Theatre of Blood (1973, U.K., colour)
Based on *The Tempest, King Lear* and other plays
A.k.a. *Much Ado About Murder*
Directed by Douglas Hickox
Starring: Vincent Price, Diana Rigg, Ian Hendry, Milo O'Shea, Robert Morley
Runtime: 104 minutes

To include here the gleefully vicious black comedy *Theatre of Blood* may seem heretical to the purist: but I believe it qualifies. Not so much for the extensive and numerous quotations from the plays on which the various murders, attempted murders and one attempted suicide are based (*Cymbeline, Hamlet, Henry VI, Part 1, Julius Caesar, King Lear, The Merchant of Venice, Othello, Richard III, Romeo and Juliet, Titus Andronicus,* and *Troilus and Cressida*), as because the structure and broad plotline (before the *Lear*-inspired ending) parody / pay homage to *The Tempest*. (The 2004 stage adaptation of the film emphasises this element, even renaming the antihero's daughter Miranda.)

Writer Anthony Greville-Bell crafted an exquisitely dark and witty screenplay for this tale of an under-appreciated tragedian (Edward Lionheart, played by Vincent Price) who takes his inspiration from the Shakespearean canon when slaughtering the Critics' Circle who slated his performances and denied him a coveted prize. (The conceit is a knowing nod to Price's earlier role as Dr Anton Phibes in *The Abominable Dr Phibes* (1971) and *Dr Phibes Rises Again* (1972), who used methods based on the Plagues of Egypt to dispose of the doctors he blamed for his wife's death.) The unashamed combination of high literacy and taboo humour has made *Theatre of Blood* a cult film, particularly popular among students.

Price, who later revealed that this was his favourite of his own films, hams his way with joyous abandon through the role, safe in the knowledge that Lionheart *is* a ham and never stops acting, so his performance can never be too over the top. (The film opens with an extended montage of excerpts from silent films of the plays, including many examples of egregious overacting from Frank R. Benson's *Richard III* (1911), E. Hay Plumb's *Hamlet* (1913), Dmitri Buchowetzki's *Othello* (1922), and

Peter Paul Felner's *Der Kaufmann von Venedig* (1923).) The cream of Britain's character actors lined up to be massacred: Michael Hordern is stabbed on the Ides of March; Dennis Price is speared and dragged behind a runaway horse; Arthur Lowe is decapitated in his sleep by assassins who emerge from a trunk; Jack Hawkins is tricked into smothering his wife (Diana Dors); Harry Andrews loses a pound of flesh ("It's Lionheart all right – only he would have the temerity to rewrite Shakespeare"); Robert Coote is drowned in a butt of Malmsey; Robert Morley (an unlikely Tamora in a pink suit) chokes on his beloved poodles (standing in for Chiron and Demetrius); and Coral Browne, who subsequently married Price, is electrocuted in a modern take on the burning of Joan of Arc. Milo O'Shea and Eric Sykes are the hapless policemen tracking the killers; Ian Hendry is the lone survivor. ("The cast was so good", Hickox remarked, "that all I had to do as director was open the dressing room doors and let the cameras roll!") At the end, Lionheart faces a despairing death in a burning theatre with the corpse of his beloved daughter (Diana Rigg, doubling as Ariel and Miranda before she becomes Cordelia[93]) in his arms.

A note is worth inserting here on Price's appearance and performance as Richard III in one segment of the film. This is clearly a parody of Laurence Olivier's 1955 turn as the hunchbacked King: but it is not Price's first connection with the part. In *Tower of London* (1939) – which, while not an adaptation of the play as such, owes a significant amount to both Shakespeare (also referencing *Macbeth* and *Julius Caesar*) and Colley Cibber – he had played Clarence to Basil Rathbone's Richard; and in its 1962 remake, directed by Price's regular partner in horror Roger Corman, Price himself had donned the hump.

The whole high-camp story is played out against a surreal alternative Seventies London where truly appalling dress sense holds sway, allowing Price and Rigg to assume some extraordinary disguises. Shakespearean references abound: Price hides out in the Burbage Theatre, uses a van marked "Avon Television", and lures Coote to his death in George Clarence's Wine Bar. The police in this version of the capital may not be able to find the lair of a villain whose principal accomplices are a

---

[93] In the stage adaptation, this part would be taken by Rigg's daughter Rachael Stirling.

gang of street-dwelling meths drinkers barely retaining the power of speech, but they can discover the vintage of wine found in a corpse's lungs. This is not a film for those with weak stomachs or a distaste for the sight of blood; but if you relish exaggerated performances and jet black humour, it can be recommended.

Un Amleto di meno (1973, Italy, black and white)
Based on *Hamlet*
A.k.a. *One Hamlet Less* (international English title)
Directed by Carmelo Bene
Starring: Carmelo Bene, Luciana Cante, Lydia Mancinelli, Giuseppe Tuminelli, Alfiero Vincenti
Language: Italian
Runtime: 70 minutes

"One Hamlet less," remarks Jules Laforgue after the Prince's death at the end of his 1887 story "*Hamlet* ou les suites de la piété filiale": "but the race is not lost." (The "race" consisted of the "Hamletist" French poets such as Baudelaire, Mallarmé, and Laforgue himself.) Carmelo Bene, giant of the Italian theatre and *Hamlet* obsessive, was strongly influenced by Laforgue in all five of his stage productions of the play: and he chose to bring down the curtain on his brief cinematic career with a tribute to Laforgue.

Laforgue's story centres on Hamlet's attempts to stage a play (*after* the deaths of Polonius and Ophelia), hampered by his desire for the Player Queen, Kate, and his tendency to drift off into soliloquy. Laforgue, however, was writing before Freud and Ernest Jones: what Bene serves up for us here is an extraordinary soup of Shakespeare, Laforgue, and Jones' *Hamlet and Oedipus* (1949). (He rejects a part of Laforgue's reading by restoring the characters' Shakespearean names: Laforgue had used the forms provided by Saxo Grammaticus.) Bene's Hamlet is a struggling and frustrated playwright-director who appears to be staging *Hamlet*: the boundaries between the play, offstage reality, and his fantasy life are so blurred as to be indistinguishable. Polonius (Giuseppe Tuminelli in cartoonish beard and tasselled nightcap) is both the play's Lord Chamberlain and an inept psychiatrist, who, in a scene shown repeatedly with small variations between those of the play within the play, whispers Freud's words on the Oedipus complex to a naked Gertrude (Luciana Cante). He is in fact speaking to the unseen Hamlet, as, elsewhere, both Gertrude and Ophelia (Isabella Russo) appear to be figments of Hamlet's fevered erotic imagination.

Beginning with the Ghost's longest speech under the opening credits, Bene uses considerably more of Shakespeare's text than Laforgue did, taking us on a rattling journey through *Hamlet* (in Italian translation, though when Laforgue's lines briefly replace Shakespeare, the former's original French is used): although it has been very heavily cut, and the style of filming holds the audience at arm's length emotionally, the narrative of the play remains intelligible.

Black backdrops break up and become glaring white, then change back to black; characters address the camera in extreme close-up when supposedly speaking to each other, Horatio (Franco Leo) in angrily emphatic tones somewhat at odds with his actual words; we now drift, now jump from one scene to the next; bags of money pass constantly from hand to hand; Fortinbras wanders through the play in spiked armour, only to remove his helmet and reveal that he has no head – or, rather, that it is invisible, an effect that falters slightly when he dons the crown in the final shot. Costumes get ever more overblown: they begin in Renaissance Europe, progressing through the Japanese and Egyptian stylings of the play within the play – possibly referring to the fashionable Orientalism of Laforgue's Paris – to surreal get-ups with giant cubes for sleeves. English Puritan garb of the seventeenth century is both referenced and mocked: Ophelia demurely covers her hair with a white coif while baring her breasts. The meaning of most of this is somewhat obscure.

"The rest is silence" is replaced with the last words of the Emperor Nero, "Qualis artifex pereat in me". Nero, of course, succeeded an uncle named Claudius, slept with his mother, and later murdered her; "Let not ever / The soul of Nero enter this firm bosom", prays the Prince; but Bene's principal target here is surely his Hamlet's artistic pretensions. It is a late original touch: but by this stage the early invention has long since drained out of the film, as Bene reuses his visual ideas again and again. Even in only seventy minutes, this at first fascinating film has time to bore.

Predstava "Hamleta" u selu Mrduši Donjoj (1973, Yugoslavia, colour)

Based on *Hamlet*
A.k.a. *Acting Hamlet in the Village of Mrdusa Donja* (international English title); *A Village Performance of Hamlet* (international English title)
Directed by Krsto Papić
Language: Serbo-Croat
Runtime: 96 minutes
Not seen by current writer

Acting Hamlet... began life in 1971 as a play by Ivo Brešan, which, like Kozintsev's 1964 film, played on the ambiguous status of *Hamlet* in Communist Eastern Europe (although Yugoslavia, unlike the Soviet Union, had never actually banned the play). A puffed-up local commissar (Bukara: Kresimir Zidaric) in rural Croatia in the late 1940s decides to stage an amateur *Hamlet* to increase the prestige of his village, ignoring the misgivings of the schoolmaster and casting himself as Claudius. The commissar has recently framed a local man for a theft committed by his treasurer: by a coincidence which stretches credibility, the victim's son Joco (Rade Serbedzija) is cast as the prince, and the treasurer as Laertes. Tensions mount through the rehearsals, until at last Joco's father commits suicide on the night of the performance, and Joco, having forced a confession from the treasurer, stabs Bukara for real. On the dying Bukara's insistence, the post-performance dance continues as if nothing has happened.

I have been unable to obtain a full recording of this film, and have seen only a few short clips, without subtitles. These were enough, however, to provide illustration of Vjenceslav Oreskovic's highly sophisticated cinematography, the use of Balkan pipes in Djelo Jusic's atmospheric score, and the earthy feel of Zeljko Senecic's design, which combine to create a brilliant realisation of the setting. When this was combined with the implicit denunciation of the regime which lies at the heart of the film, it must have made for a powerful viewing experience for Yugoslavs in 1973. However, despite a favourable reception at the Berlin Film Festival and a limited international release, the film was little noticed outside Yugoslavia.

Catch My Soul (1974, U.K. / U.S.A., colour)
Based on *Othello*
A.k.a. *Santa Fe Satan*

Directed by Patrick McGoohan
Runtime: 97 minutes
Not seen by current writer

> "Excellent wretch! Perdition catch my soul,
> But I do love thee: and when I love thee not,
> Chaos is come again." ~ *Othello*, Act III, Scene 3

> "Well, let me tell you a story
> 'Bout a blackamoor
> Written by an Anglo-Saxon
> Caucasian in 1604.
> *Othello*, he called it:
> We added rock 'n' roll
> And some Cajun blues,
> And called it *Catch My Soul*." ~ "Ballad of *Catch My Soul*"

Jack Good's 1968 musical *Catch My Soul, The Rock Othello* transferred the *Othello* story to a commune in New Mexico, with the Moor as a wandering evangelist who turns up and effectively usurps Iago's position as commune leader, setting in train a plot thereafter quite close to Shakespeare's; emphasising the racial theme, Cassio became a Civil Rights campaigner and Roderigo a Southern landowner. Good himself played Othello in the stage version, with Lance LeGault as Iago and Sharon Gurney as Desdemona: only LeGault would reprise his role on film, Richie Havens and Season Hubley taking over as the lead couple, while Good produced the film.

Good's ingenious lyrics make considerable use of lines from the play, with bluesy spoken interpolations by LeGault emphasising Iago's misogyny: songs such as "If Wives Do Fall," "Let Me the Cannikin Clink", "Very Well – Go To", "Put Out the Light", and "You Told a Lie", take their titles and much of their content from Shakespeare, but are perfectly suited to the music of Tony Joe White (who played Cassio in the film) and Emil Dean Zoghby. The music progresses slowly from a very bluesy style in early pieces such as the "Ballad" to something more like a conventional big show tune of the era in "You Told A Lie". *Catch My Soul* is a distinctive, powerful, and underrated rock opera: but Patrick McGoohan's film, by all accounts, did it no kind of justice.

For some reason, the screenplay was worked up from the

already adapted script of the British stage version, rather than the American one, meaning that it had to be *re*-adapted to an American setting. The low budget cannot have helped: but the chief problem, according to McGoohan in a 1995 interview, was Good himself, whose conversion to Catholicism inspired him to recut the film before release, to bring it into line with his newfound faith. The result was critical and commercial failure, a short-lived re-release marketed as an exploitation picture under the title *Santa Fe Satan*, followed by obscurity.

King Lear (1976, U.K., black and white)
Directed by Steve Rumbelow
Starring: Chris Auvache, Gengis Saner, Tim Jones, Stuart Cox, Monica Buford
Runtime: 43 minutes

Steve Rumbelow's 1973 deconstruction of *King Lear* for the Triple Action Theatre was brought to the screen in 1976 with the aid of the British Film Institute, ably photographed by Peter Harvey. (Considering that it was shot on video, a format barely out of its infancy in the 1970s, the picture looks remarkably good.) It is not the play: the plot is apparent only to the viewer who is already acquainted with it: but it manages to retain the original's spirit better than some straight adaptations.

The film opens in what looks like a medieval madhouse, fools gibbering and screaming, while, under a blanket in an exposed courtyard, a man (Chris Auvache as an unconventionally youthful King) apparently gives birth, first to two adult women (Monica Buford and Helena Paul, playing the elder daughters) and finally, like the dreaming Hecuba, to a burning torch. The sun disappears: from now until the end of the film, the action will be played out in the dark of night, entirely location shot, mostly outdoors, lit only by fire. (In a storm scene which must have absorbed much of the budget, the angry gods even hurl fire from the heavens upon Lear's heath.)

Lines are transposed, the Fool (Gengis Saner) cannibalising much of the absent Kent's part, while Edmund (Paul Mead) is pushed into the margins as Goneril (Buford) steals his words. Gloucester (Stuart Cox, who endows the Earl with a bizarre speech defect) is blindfolded from the beginning of the film, and has his eyes not removed but forcibly opened in Cornwall's (Mark Heron) assault – a literalisation of a critical

217

near-cliché. Edgar (Tim Jones, playing hauntingly on the recorder and occasionally bursting into snatches of "The Rain It Raineth Every Day" from *Twelfth Night*) not only remains in his "Poor Tom" persona throughout, but is even credited as "Tom", as if his sane self did not exist. There is no Cordelia. This is a *Lear* stripped of everything that might be found light or hopeful, until in the final shot the camera pulls back not only from the surviving characters but from Britain itself, retreating out to sea, abandoning a doomed country.

Hamlet (1976, U.K., colour)
Directed by Celestino Coronado
Starring: Tony Meyer, David Meyer, Helen Mirren, Quentin Crisp, Barry Stanton
Runtime: 65 minutes

Coronado's experimental picture, shot on video for a budget of only $5,000, is really more a filmed essay on aspects of *Hamlet* than an adaptation. The script is so heavily cut that it makes no sense unless the viewer is already thoroughly familiar with the play: even "To be or not to be" vanishes from its original place in the text, to be used instead as a voiceover at the beginning of the film.

The first of the two themes around which Coronado has structured his film is the divided nature of the Prince himself, visually represented by the breathtakingly simple conceit of casting identical twins (Tony and David Meyer) in the role. Thus Hamlet's soliloquies become debates, while his rejection of Ophelia (Helen Mirren) involves a physical fight between a tender Hamlet who still loves her and the cruel version who wins out. Even extraneous characters become symptoms of Hamlet's schizophrenia, with one twin as a Ghost from the Prince's subconscious, come to tell the other what Hamlet already knows; as the brothers also play Laertes, the two Hamlets end by destroying one another.

Coronado's second theme is incestuous desire. That much of what Hamlet says to Ophelia is directed in his mind at Gertrude – be it the misogynistic "I have heard of your paintings" outburst, or the bawdy banter before the play scene – has long been a critical commonplace: but here the vain, languid Queen and the doll-like Lolita-Ophelia are played by the same actress, Helen Mirren.[94] In the play scene, she even appears as Gertrude while speaking Ophelia's lines; the closet scene is murmured as if between lovers; and when the brothers split into Hamlet and Laertes, their rivalry is clearly sexual.

These confused royals share with Barry Stanton's corpulent, Neronian Claudius as bizarre a world as the budget could encompass. Their make-up is heavy and stylised; their costumes (by Natasha Korniloff and Mircea Marosin), scanty and fetishistic. The King expresses his remorse by driving nails through his hand in emulation of the Crucifixion; Quentin Crisp's sinister, sphinx-like Polonius (whose death occurs offscreen) peers at the world through an outsize monocle, giving us frequent extreme close-ups of his single bloodshot eye; the Player Queen (Vladek Sheybal) is a moustachioed drag queen in fright wig and silver breasts.

Fortunately, this farrago is just about held together by the strong central performances. They may have only a quarter of the text to work with, but the Meyer brothers prove as adept at speaking Shakespearean verse as the more experienced classical actors Mirren and Stanton. While Coronado's vision is indubitably interesting, and his achievement in bringing this film to the screen at all on his tiny budget considerable, it is hard to understand the critical acclaim *Hamlet* received in 1976: but his cast, at least, had earned it.

Intikam Melegi – Kadin Hamlet (1977, Turkey, colour)
Based on *Hamlet*
A.k.a. *The Angel of Vengeance – The Female Hamlet* (international English title)
Directed by Metin Erksan
Starring: Fatma Girik, Reha Yurdakul, Sevda Ferdag, Ahmet Sezerel, Orçun Sonat
Language: Turkish
Runtime: 80 minutes

Intikam Melegi gives us precisely what it promises: a female Hamlet (Fatma Girik), in modern Turkey. Hamlet Evren is a drama student from a family of powerful rural landowners, her boyfriend Orhan (Ahmet Sezerel in the Ophelia role) being

---

[94] Mirren was later to play Gertrude's original, Gerutha, in 1994's *Prince of Jutland*.

the son of their factor (Yüksel Gözen): and that is more or less it. Apart from allowing Rosencrantz and Guildenstern (Ayla Oranli and Senem Kayra) to live, and replacing the duel with a botched attempt to stage a hunting accident, director Metin Erksan's script sticks closely to *Hamlet*, many lines being directly translated (although much is cut, Act Four in particular being raced through at a gallop).

Erksan scatters the film with touches of bizarre imagination, some more effective than others. In her feigned madness (which rests largely on almost never blinking), Hamlet parades around in fancy dress, and conducts an imaginary orchestra with real instruments impaled on stakes in front of her. The Ghost (Ali Cagaloglu) appears like Dracula, through mist, lit from below, wearing an opera cape. The Evrens' house, crumbling but dignified without, is decorated indoors with the sort of sublime bad taste of which only the very rich of the Seventies and Eighties were capable.

Unfortunately the picture and sound quality are very poor, and Girik, though good at the more manic touches, lacks the versatility a Hamlet needs. Most other performances are on the flat side; and *Intikam Melegi* never comes close to matching up to its source material.

Eros Perversion (1979, Italy, colour)
Based on *Twelfth Night*
A.k.a *Twelfth Night*; *William Shakespeare's Twelfth Night* (U.S.A.)
Directed by Ron Wertheim
Not seen by current writer

Wertheim's porn version of *Twelfth Night* is now unavailable; I have been unable to uncover any details.

Falstaff (1979, West Germany, colour)
Based on *The Merry Wives of Windsor*
Directed by Götz Friedrich
Starring: Gabriel Bacquier, Márta Szirmai, Karan Armstrong, Jutta Renate Ihloff, Sylvia Lindenstrand
Language: Italian / German
Runtime: 126 minutes

Verdi's last opera, *Falstaff* (1893) was, like *Otello*, based on a libretto by Arrigo Boito. In adapting *The Merry Wives of*

Windsor, Boito took many liberties: most significantly, in the pursuit of economic casting, he cut out George Page and made his Anne figure, Nannetta, the daughter of the Fords instead. This, of course, is a serious alteration to the characters' relationships, especially since it is hard to believe that the Fords as Shakespeare wrote them can have been married nearly long enough to have a daughter of marriageable age herself. Slender, Shallow, and Evans have also disappeared, Dr Caius cannibalising many of their lines, while the Host is required to do little more than be long-suffering, and Nell Quickly's importance is much inflated. Indeed, it is she, rather than the Wives themselves, who plots and arranges Falstaff's downfall in the opera. (Interestingly, as well as making cuts, Boito incorporated into the first act the "What is honour?" speech from *Henry IV, Part 1*.)

These changes, and the reduction of Falstaff's assignations with Alice Ford from three to two, somewhat blunt the drama. Nannetta's marriage to Fenton has her mother's blessing from the start, her father favouring Caius; and Ford discovers his wife's fidelity immediately after the laundry-basket incident. It is easier to luxuriate in Verdi's music than to try to follow the hacked-about text: although this contains fewer than usual of his characteristic set pieces, it is nonetheless beautifully constructed.

Götz Friedrich's 1979 film, featuring the chorus of the Deutsche Oper von Berlin and the Vienna Philharmonic Orchestra conducted by Sir Georg Solti, does its best to rise above its origins, despite being entirely studio shot. The costumes (a hybrid of late Elizabethan and Regency styles, designed by Bernd Müller, with a few elements from different periods) do appear somewhat theatrical, insofar as the garb of characters living outside the Garter is unnaturally clean and new-looking: but this serves to point up the contrast between the citizens of Windsor and the shabby knight and his followers. The camera is almost constantly in motion; the picture is bright, clear and defined; Jörg Neumann's and Thomas Riccabona's sets – a battered and untidy Garter Inn, an implausibly exotic Thames-side garden, the homely dwelling of the Fords, and a fog-bound ruin that makes the Windsor Park scene appear straight out of a Hammer horror film – are elaborate and ambitious; few scenes are without background activity, including a washing-day sequence foreshadowing Falstaff's misfortune. A strong sexual charge and sense of bawdy runs through the film: the lovers (Max René Cossotti and Jutta Renate Ihloff), whose music is rather more lively and far less sickly-sweet than in Otto Nicolai's version, are barely able to keep their hands off each other; Nell (Márta Szirmai) plays her summoning of Falstaff (Gabriel Bacquier, playing the old knight as a great spoilt child in a 65-year-old's body and showing himself as accomplished an actor as he is a singer: his face in close-up is a treat to behold) as a seduction, flaunting her cleavage at him; both Wives (Karan Armstrong and Sylvia Lindenstrand) have a strong streak of the coquette in them.

The operatic form is better suited to tragedy than to comedy, and it is hard to deny that Boito's cuts damage the play: but for all that, as a musical celebration of fat Sir John, *Falstaff* can hardly be bettered, and this is a thoroughly enjoyable version.

The Tempest (1979, U.K., colour)
Directed by Derek Jarman
Starring: Heathcote Williams, Toyah Willcox, Jack Birkett, Karl Johnson
Runtime: 95 minutes

The Tempest might have been thought made for Jarman's offbeat style. The play can hardly be performed without a touch of the fantastic, but not many directors would people it with dancing sailors, dwarfs in ball gowns, and Elisabeth Welch singing "Stormy Weather" as Juno. Although it offers an interesting glimpse into Jarman's fertile mind, however, the bizarre end result does small service to the play.

The opening is intriguing, cutting between shots of the sea and the disturbed sleep of our unusually young Prospero (Heathcote Williams); what in the text is the dialogue of the sailors aboard the doomed ship is here whispered by the disembodied voice of Ariel (Karl Johnson), apparently in his master's troubled dreams. This is one way to cover for the fact that Jarman did not have a sufficient budget to film the shipwreck scene (the film was made on a shoestring, and it shows), but it is not a promising start. The bright, unnatural blue of the rolling sea at this point appears to be part of the dream, but as the film wears on, it becomes apparent that every outdoor scene has been shot through so thick a blue filter that all other colours have vanished and the picture has become badly blurred. The filter comes off only when we are within Prospero's "cell" – here, in defiance of the text, a well-appointed stately home, albeit one that seems to have run to seed in recent years.

A vague attempt at period analogue is made, with costumes (when there are any – most of the cast, as in Celestino Coronado's *Hamlet* (1976), appear naked at some point) suggestive of the Napoleonic era; but, appropriately with this text, there is more of fantasy than of history about them. Ariel's assorted modern outfits and the punkish hair ornaments of Miranda (Toyah Willcox) do not seem out of place in this world; Prospero's hairstyle has to be seen to be believed. Sebastian (Neil Cunningham), for no apparent reason beyond a vague and undirected anti-clericalism, has become a cardinal. This, however, is little more than window-dressing, seldom made relevant to the drastically cut text.

The performances are similarly inconsistent. Williams, in a role originally intended for comic actor Terry-Thomas (the mind boggles), is competent but underacts: the combination of understatement with Jarman's cold-blooded, arm's-length direction inevitably alienates the viewer. Jack "The Incredible Orlando" Birkett gives his usual camp turn as Caliban: Jarman almost makes this work – it is in keeping with his vision, insofar as he has one – but one is seldom in danger of mistaking Birkett for an actor. Two strong comic talents, Ken Campbell as Gonzalo and Christopher Biggins as Stephano, are criminally underused: the film is brighter whenever either of them is on screen. Willcox, meanwhile, proves a powerful and sensitive performer, bringing to life the first screen Miranda with a sexual identity: others had been little more than overgrown children. This has the disconcerting result that Miranda overshadows her father, and effectively dominates the play.

The sudden change of style with which the film ends, wheeling on the *South Pacific*-style sailors and Elisabeth Welch, is more puzzling than enlightening, and reduces the dismissal of Ariel and Prospero's crucial final speech to a postscript. One is left wondering whether, beyond perfunctorily tacking his favoured themes of homosexuality and punk-revolution onto the text, Jarman himself had much idea of what he was trying to do with *The Tempest* – although, if he did not, it would be strangely out of character. This is poor for filmed Shakespeare and poor for Jarman, and never once succeeds in engaging the viewer. To see what Jarman at his best could do with a theatrical classic of the late Renaissance, one is much better advised to watch his 1991 adaptation of Marlowe's *Edward II*.

Othello (1979, U.S.A., colour)
Directed by Liz White
Runtime: 115 minutes
Not seen by current writer

White's *Othello* began life as a summer production at her home in Martha's Vineyard in 1960. Studios and distributors alike proving cagey, she not only had to finance the film herself, but, when the long shoot (1962-66, working in summer only) was over, had to wait until 1980 to see its official premiere at Howard University – though it had in fact been shown a few months earlier at the Katherine Cornell Theatre. Despite the fact that her Othello, Yaphet Kotto – an unknown in the 1960s – had by 1979 become an international star, it never received a commercial release.

Act I was reportedly cut, as in Verdi's opera, although chunks of it appeared as flashbacks later in the film; a considerable amount of chopping and changing was needed to fit the play into 115 minutes. The film was chiefly noted, however, for its all black cast: the play's originally white characters spoke with American accents and wore modern dress, rendering the traditionally clad African Othello as much an outsider as ever. White herself played Bianca, with her son Richard Dixon as Iago and his wife Audrey Branker as Desdemona: it was very much a family-and-friends affair, but was praised for C. J. Dorkins' strong camera work and White's original directorial vision, an excoriating attack on domestic abuse and internalised racism (Othello is still darker skinned than the "white" characters) in the African-American community.

Othello, el comando negro (1982, Spain / France, colour)
Based on *Othello*
A.k.a. *Black Commando* (U.S.A.); *Othello* (U.S.A.); *Othello, the Black Commando* (U.S.A.); *Othello, le commando noir* (France)
Directed by Max H. Boulois
Starring: Max H. Boulois, Joanna Pettet, Tony Curtis, Nadiuska
Language: French

Runtime: 105 minutes

Boulois' updated Othello, with himself in the title role, is set among an elite mercenary corps (the Black Commando, with S.S.-style skulls on their cap badges) in a fictitious Caribbean country; Desdemona (Joanna Pettet) is a Red Cross doctor, and the Brabantio figure (Tom Hernández) a U.S. senator. The picture is largely scored to the better known works of Beethoven: a parachute attack is backed by the Fifth Symphony, the opening of Red Cross headquarters by the *Ode to Joy*, the courtship of the central couple by *Für Elise*, the Willow Song is replaced with the Last Sonata, and the Moonlight Sonata plays as Othello steels himself to murder his wife. Reaching the play after a half-hour lead-in, the film thereafter sticks pretty closely to Shakespeare's plot, though battle and training scenes are incorporated to emphasise the military setting. (As in *All Night Long* (1962), a doctored audio tape replaces the conversation in which Cassio – Ramiro Oliveros, equipped with unruly hair, tight jeans, and a motorbike – incriminates himself.)

The film is well acted, with Tony Curtis proving particularly impressive as a plausible, thuggish Iago. (It has been Curtis' misfortune to be remembered better for his early work, incongruously sporting an Elvis quiff and Brooklyn accent in 1950s historical epics, than for the character parts he took in more mature years. His once dubious acting had improved immeasurably by 1982.) The combination of arm's length direction, understated acting, the use made of music (almost entirely under non-dialogue scenes), and Domingo Solano's atmospheric, washed out cinematography, gives the film a strong feel of the *Nouvelle Vague*: it is hard to believe it was not made twenty years earlier. It is very much a curiosity; but it is also a well constructed and enjoyable film.

Angoor (1982, India, colour)
Based on *The Comedy of Errors*
Directed by Sampooran Singh Gulzar
Starring: Sanjeev Kumar, Deven Verma, Deepti Naval, Moushumi Chatterjee, Aruna Irani
Language: Hindi
Runtime: 129 minutes / 65 minutes (cut version)

"People want to remake superhits. Why remake a flop?" Thus Yash Johar to Sampooran Singh Gulzar, when the latter, disappointed with the way *Do Dooni Chaar* (1968) had turned out, announced his intention to have another stab at *The Comedy of Errors*, this time as director. Gulzar ignored his advice.

The voiceover with which *Angoor* is introduced does not raise the viewer's hopes. "This is William Shakespeare," we are told, as a sepia photograph appears of an Indian actor who resembles the playwright only in being bald and bearded. (This is used instead of a genuine portrait so that the "picture" can grin and give the film the thumbs-up at the end. Why the effect was not simply animated, as in the heavily *Monty Python*-influenced title sequence, is a mystery.)

After a prologue based on Egeon's scene-setting speech to Solinus, detailing how the two pairs of twins came to be separated, the action jumps forward a generation and we enter the story of the play, in modern small-town India. For simplicity's sake, the Egeon figure (Utpal Dutt) is killed off in the shipwreck, but before dying manages to communicate the names of his two babies to their rescuer. Thereafter, the adaptation follows *Do Dooni Chaar* fairly closely. The character standing in for Antipholus of Syracuse (Ashok: Sanjeev Kumar) is addicted to cheap detective novels; his fear of declaring his true identity is aroused not by a murderous Ephesian law, but by a paranoid terror of gangsters.

Angoor is, like *Do Dooni Chaar*, a musical in the old Bollywood style. As such, however, it is not the equal of the earlier film. The songs are repetitive and hard to distinguish from one another; they do not seem to fit in with the non-musical sequences; and, while Deven Verma as Bahadur (Dromio) performs his ganja-fuelled number with considerable panache, his voice is flat and monotonous. To these failings must be added the unimaginative direction and only intermittently witty script by Gulzar (operating well below par), which seldom provides the platform his stars deserve. Kumar and Verma give excellent comic turns in their respective dual roles, but considerably outshine their surroundings.

The film was a considerable success in India, easily compensating for the failure of *Do Dooni Chaar*. Some years later, it was re-released in a new cut, at barely half the length of the original film. It would be interesting to see whether the cuts improved the pace (which frequently flags in the longer version), or merely confused the plot: but as first cut, whatever the public may have thought in 1982, it is little more than a waste of talent.

Tempest (1982, U.S.A., colour)
Based on *The Tempest*
Directed by Paul Mazursky
Starring: John Cassavetes, Molly Ringwald, Raul Julia, Susan Sarandon, Gena Rowlands
Runtime: 140 minutes

Mazursky's odd little film turns *The Tempest* into a mid-life-crisis comedy about a Greek-American architect (Philip, played by the father of American independent cinema, John Cassavetes) who deserts his wife and runs away to a Mediterranean island. The wife (Cassavetes' off-screen wife Gena Rowlands) is a substitute for Antonio, whose intrigue with Alonzo (Vittorio Gassman) becomes an affair. Hardly any of the characters rises more than one step above stereotype. Antonia is a pretentious air-kisser hurting inside, Alonzo a sleazy Eurotrash tyrant boss, Ariel (Aretha, played with some gusto by Susan Sarandon but further from her Shakespearean original than any other character – even Gonzalo, who has become a harp-playing dippy hippy played by Lucianne Buchanan!) an irritating movie version of a "free spirit"; Miranda (Molly Ringwald) a bratty teen who is as much of the Eighties, and as annoying, as Stomu Yamashta's synth-heavy soundtrack; Caliban (Raul Julia, having enormous fun) a lecherous but forelock-tugging goatherd; while comedian Jackie Gayle plays Trinculo as himself.

Extended flashbacks to the separation of Philip and Antonia bear little resemblance to *The Tempest*, and take up well over half the film. Only in the last 45 minutes, at quite a rush, is Shakespeare's plot packed in – including a storm which, it is heavily implied, Philip really does raise by wizardry (although Kalibanos has predicted it – the writers' way of bottling out of full-blooded fantasy). The film ends with more reconciliations than even Shakespeare ever attempted – and certainly less plausible ones. The death of Philip and Antonia's marriage has been anatomised in some detail; Philip and Miranda are both apparently happy with Aretha, and neither has shown much interest in seeing Antonia again – but at the end of the film Philip and Antonia are back together, a situation apparently accepted uncomplainingly by Aretha and Miranda, while the entire cast waltzes around Kalibanos' cave exchanging requests for forgiveness as they pass.

Tempest is a bizarre mish-mash of ill-digested Shakespeare, bad special effects, two-dimensional dialogue, and enough impromptu renditions of Forties and Fifties show tunes almost to qualify it as a musical; apart from the luscious and lovingly filmed Greek scenery, it has very little to recommend it.

Lyubovyu za lyubov (1983, U.S.S.R., colour)
Based on *Much Ado About Nothing*
Directed by Tatyana Berezantseva
Language: Russian
Runtime: 84 minutes
Believed lost
This Mosfilm version of *Much Ado* seems to have sunk without trace.

Sogno di una notte d' estate (1983, Italy, colour)
Based on *A Midsummer Night's Dream*
Directed by Gabriele Salvatores
Language: Italian
Runtime: 104 minutes
Not seen by current writer
Salvatores' *Dream* turned the play into a rock opera, with music by Mauro Pagani and starring singer Gianna Nannini as Titania. It is notable for having anticipated the gay twist put on the play by Celestino Coronado in his 1985 film: apparently the potion makes Lysander (Luca Barbareschi) and Demetrius (Giuseppe Cederna) fall in love with each other.

A Midsummer Night's Dream (1985, U.K. / Spain, colour)
A.k.a. *Sueño de noche de verano* (Spain)
Directed by Celestino Coronado
Runtime: 80 minutes
Not seen by current writer
Originally made for Spanish television in 1984, Coronado's *Dream* was based on a British stage production, by the Lindsay Kemp Company: and, after a successful showing at the London Film Festival, it was released theatrically in the U.K. Shot in less than two weeks, on, as was Coronado's usual practice, a tiny budget, it was remarked on for its inventiveness

and daring.

Kemp and Coronado seem to have been highly compatible artistically. Kemp's alterations to the play, adding mime, dance, and musical numbers, and adapting the love-in-idleness plot so that Lysander (David Meyer) falls for Demetrius (David Brandon) and Hermia (Annie Huckle) for Helena (Cheryl Heazlewood), were very much in Coronado's style. The changeling boy (François Testory) spent much more time on screen than is usual, an androgynous figure, pitiably torn between the sinister Oberon (Michael Matou) and Titania (Jack Birkett); Kemp himself played Puck as a manipulative puppet-master, making full use of his dance training in a highly physical interpretation of the role.

Reviews and stills suggest that this was a bizarre and fascinating version of the play; sadly, it seems impossible to obtain.

The Angelic Conversation (1985, U.K., black and white / colour)
Based on the Sonnets
Directed by Derek Jarman
Starring: Paul Reynolds, Phillip Williamson
Runtime: 78 minutes

Possibly Jarman's most personal film, *The Angelic Conversation* is an experimental piece designed to accompany readings of fourteen of Shakespeare's sonnets by Judi Dench (all but one taken from those addressed to the Fair Youth). Produced by the British Film Institute, shot on video and often slowed to frame-by-frame, with no speech other than Dench's, it all but defines the limited-appeal art film. The picture is somewhat fuzzy, and the visual motifs – burning torches, a medallion reflecting sunlight, two men staggering around under the weight of a barrel and a beam respectively (an Atlas and a Christ), a seaside cave, clusters of blossom – are overused, their relevance to the text sometimes inapparent and sometimes excessively literal: but the stars perform well, Coil's remarkably varied score is strong and accomplished, and Dench's reading exquisite.

The worst fault of the film is that the gaps between the sonnets are too long; whenever Dench is not speaking, it begins to drag. It would have been more successful if Jarman had selected thirty or forty sonnets instead of fourteen. The number was chosen to match the number of lines in each, so that the film

229

itself is in a sense a sonnet, but this effect could surely have been sacrificed. As it is, *The Angelic Conversation* is tedious.

Ran (1985, Japan / France, colour)
Based on *King Lear*
A.k.a. *Chaos*
Directed by Akira Kurosawa
Starring: Tatsuya Nakadai, Mieko Harada, Yoshiko Miyazaki, Shinnosuke "Peter" Ikehata, Akira Terao
Language: Japanese
Runtime: 160 minutes
Academy Awards (1986): Best Costume Design (Emi Wada)
Academy Award nominations: Best Director (Akira Kurosawa); Best Art Direction (Yoshiro Muraki, Shinobu Muraki); Best Cinematography (Takao Saitô, Masaharu Ueda, Asakazu Nakai)

Kurosawa's last great epic, a rare venture into colour (and what colour!), frequently makes it onto critics' and directors' lists of the best films ever made. It had long been an ambition of the great director to give *King Lear* the same treatment he had given *Macbeth* in *Kumonosu jô* (1957), transferring the story to feudal era Japan:[95] indeed, he described his 1980 film *Kagemusha* as a "dress rehearsal" for *Ran*. (*Kagemusha* had broken Kurosawa's own record, set with *Shichinin no samurai* in 1954, for the most expensive Japanese film ever made: *Ran* smashed the bar again.) The end result, however, is not to be compared with the often lifeless *Kagemusha* (which is to me Kurosawa's most disappointing film). *Ran*, when it was finally made possible by an injection of foreign money,[96] was a stunning triumph.

The amount of work that went into this picture has become legendary. A team of costumiers spent two years stitching the brightly-coloured clothes; Kurosawa himself had been painting the detailed storyboards since the mid-1970s; there were not enough horses trained for film work in all Japan, so

---

[95] Specifically the late Warring States period, *circa* 1570 – *Kumonosu jô* takes place some decades earlier.
[96] Including personal contributions from Steven Spielberg – who has called Kurosawa "the pictorial Shakespeare of our time" – George Lucas, and Francis Ford Coppola.

more had to be imported from the U.S.A; the director's beloved wife died, and he broke filming for only one day.

Hidetora (Tatsuya Nakadai) is our Lear figure, a hard-bitten old warlord with just the bloodstained background one imagines Shakespeare's King to have had – and, like Peter Brook and Paul Scofield in 1971, Kurosawa and Nakadai let us see exactly why the King's elder children hate him. He compares himself to a scarred old boar too tough to eat, and jokes with his sons (replacing Lear's daughters in a reference to the legend of Motonari Mori) "Would you eat me?" The opening of the film, unlike *Kumonosu jô* which plunges us straight into the drama, is gently paced: one gets to enjoy Japan's gorgeous scenery and the bold primary colours of the costumes, while the viewer who knows the play is little exercised by the plot; by forty minutes in, one might begin to suspect that this is little more than a well-dressed *Lear* without the poetry – then, suddenly, we realise that we are in the dramatic territory that Kurosawa occupies best. From the moment the Third Castle (a full scale set, built to be destroyed, on the side of Mount Fuji) catches fire, there is no doubt that this is the equal of *Kumonosu jô*; and, when Nakadai steps slowly out, his burgeoning madness written on his face, we are in the presence of greatness.

The nature of feudal Japanese society, as well as Kurosawa's desire to make reference to Japan's own history and legends in addition to *King Lear*, necessitates considerably greater departures from Shakespeare's text than featured in *Kumonosu jô*. Not only does this Lear have sons instead of daughters: there is no Gloucester or Edgar, although there is a blind man (Mansai Nomura, blinded by Hidetora himself before his fall, and all the more significant given that Kurosawa's own eyesight was already failing him by 1985 and would be completely gone before he died). Edmund is replaced with Hidetora's scheming daughter-in-law, Lady Kaede (Mieko Harada). These differences are less surprising when one learns that Kurosawa's original plan was simply to invert the Motonari legend by giving the *daimyo* evil sons instead of good, and that he only later decided to base the film on *Lear*.

Kaede, a blend of Edmund with elements of Lady Macbeth but ultimately an original character, is one of the all-time great villains of the screen. She plots, bullies, seduces, and betrays without a shred of conscience, and with but one aim: to destroy Hidetora and all his family, in revenge for the deaths of

231

her own parents at his hands. Contrasted to her is the other daughter-in-law, Sué (Yoshiko Miyazaki), a passive, devoutly Buddhist Edgar / Cordelia (although her position in the plot is roughly analogous to Albany's), who has suffered similar loss but has forgiven Hidetora. Both represent major departures from Shakespeare's story, but they fit perfectly into a thoroughly Lear-like world.

For all the changes, and for all that he crafts the story perfectly to its Japanese setting, Kurosawa never lets us forget that we are watching *King Lear*. Still present are the storm, the Fool (a wonderful tragicomic performance by cabaret artiste Peter), and the utterly bleak conclusion on the cruelty of the gods. (Hidetora articulates this in words pretty much directly translated from Gloucester's, and the film ends with Sué's blind brother dropping his icon of the Buddha over a cliff.) Nor does it fail, however, to be thoroughly cinematic. The set-piece in which the castle is destroyed has already been mentioned: nobody who has seen it could forget Hidetora's appearance through the flames: there are also two brilliantly handled battle scenes, drawing on Sergei Eisenstein's work – the second also reminiscent of *The Chronicle History of King Henry the Fift with His Battell Fought at Agincourt in France* (1944) – yet both unmistakeably Kurosawa. They demonstrate exactly where that French and American money went.

Design, performances, direction, photography, all are flawless in the "Emperor"'s fitting swan-song.

Richard III (1986, France / Switzerland, colour)
Directed by Raoul Ruiz
Language: French
Runtime: 135 minutes
Not seen by current writer

Georges Lavaudant's stage production of *Richard III* for the Avignon Festival in 1984, starring Ariel García Valdés, was committed to film by Chilean director Raoul Ruiz, shooting mostly on location at Monteynard, high in the Alps. Stills show Elizabethan costumes, blurred images, and surreal touches such as Richard's impracticably long cloak forming a sort of tail for the serpentine king; critics speak of Ruiz' evocation of a disintegrating world in which Gloucester's deformity reflects the deformation of his environment. Jorge Arriagada's darkly potent score blends high, eerie whistles, choral work, and echoes of an angry sea.

After doing the festival circuit, the film vanished into the vaults.

Otello (1986, Italy / Netherlands, colour)
Based on *Othello*
Directed by Franco Zeffirelli
Starring: Plácido Domingo, Justino Díaz, Katia Ricciarelli, Urbano Barberini
Language: Italian
Runtime: 122 minutes
Academy Award nominations (1987): Best Costume Design (Anna Anni, Maurizio Millenotti)

Franco Zeffirelli's lavish *Otello*, conducted by Lorin Maazel, was and remained for twenty years the most expensive film of a classical opera ever made, and is still the most successful translation of opera into cinematic terms.[97] Overcoming the confinements of the form, the director uses every filmic device available: flashbacks (telling Otello's life story by means of a sequence reminiscent of Sergei Yutkevich's 1955 version), voiceovers, and multiple scene changes from one exquisitely designed set to another, allowing Zeffirelli – who assumed personal responsibility for production design – to create studies and armouries, orchards and battlement walks, and the deserted church in which Iago (Justino Díaz) sings his diabolic "Credo" and Otello (Plácido Domingo[98]) swears his vengeance. The characters stride as they sing, from one chamber to another, keeping the picture as fast-moving as the plot.

Where Herbert von Karajan in 1973 had given us a sunny, green, and living Cyprus, Zeffirelli's is as full of shadows as his hero's mind, creating an effect reminiscent of the films of F. W. Murnau. It is a closed, encircling world, turned in on itself and its inhabitants: more cannon are placed decoratively in the great hall and courtyard, where if fired they would destroy

---

[97] It has been surpassed in terms of expense only by the Kenneth Branagh / James Conlon film of *The Magic Flute* (2006).
[98] Perhaps the singer most associated with this part: he has played it in several live productions, and five times on television between 1976 and 2001.

Otello's own fortress, than aimed out at the surrounding sea; and as Iago's toils close round the Moor, Domingo's face appears more and more often framed, by spears, railings, latticed windows, even a magnifying lens, as if by the bars of a prison.

The director's dramatic focus is on the relationship between Domingo's majestic, passionate Otello and Díaz' earthy, superficially easygoing Iago. (Although it was no longer accepted in the 1980s for a white man to play Othello in original text versions,[99] the opera was a different matter. A black boy plays the young Otello in the flashback sequence, but Alfredo Marazzi's excellent makeup work makes it almost plausible that the youth could have grown into Domingo.) This results in slight marginalisation of other characters: Desdemona (Katia Ricciarelli) even loses her Willow Song, of which the Earl of Harewood wrote that "Nothing in Italian opera is so beautiful",[100] while Roderigo (Sergio Nicolai, sung by Constantin Zaharia), a part already heavily cut by the librettist Arrigo Boito, is still further reduced, leaving him barely more than a cameo. At the same time, Zeffirelli has used flashbacks to restore Shakespearean characters whom Boito cut out altogether, including Brabanzio (Remo Remotti) and the Doge (Antonio Pierfederici). This could easily have resulted in an imbalance between the threads of the story; it is fortunate that Zeffirelli was sufficiently skilled to avoid going too far.

While Domingo gives a "big" performance, it is by no means without subtlety; his physical performance as well as his voice movingly conveys his anguish as he is drawn into suspicion, of which he has interestingly displayed some early touches before Iago even begins to work on him. This interpretation could easily have led, as in Stuart Burge's *Othello* (1965), to the discredit of Otello's claim that he is "not easily jealous": but the momentary nature of the Moor's early jealousy, together with the obvious (harmless) flirtation between Ricciarelli and Urbano Barberini's handsome Cassio (cast for his looks, as several lingeringly homoerotic shots make clear; the part is sung by Ezio di Cesare), here renders it entirely plausible.

---

[99] One of the last to do so was Anthony Hopkins in 1981, for the B.B.C.'s *The Complete Dramatic Works of William Shakespeare*; the B.B.C. had also cast television's first black Othello, Gordon Heath, in 1955.

[100] Lascelles, George, Earl of Harewood, and Kobbé, Gustav, *Kobbé's Illustrated Opera Book* (London, 1989), p. 88.

The reduction of this noble figure to a man who throws his crucifix into the fire in an apparent Satanic pact, creeps about in a hooded cloak, and finally murders his wife in a sudden burst of shocking violence, for which the motion of the camera abruptly switches from stately smoothness to a wild whirling that would not be out of place in a battle scene, is played to perfection.

Despite understandable reservations about the cutting of the Willow Song, the majority of the critics adored *Otello*, and heaped it with praises. Shakespeare and Zeffirelli had scored another triumph, to rank alongside *Romeo and Juliet*.

Sen noci... (1986, Czechoslovakia, colour)
Based on *A Midsummer Night's Dream*
Directed by Vladimír Sís
Language: Czech
Runtime: 72 minutes
Believed lost

Sís' *Dream* began life as a ballet, using the music composed by Václav Trojan for Jiří Trnka's 1959 animated film version, at the Brno State Theatre in 1985. It was never released outside Czechoslovakia, and I can find no record of its survival.

Twelfth Night (1987, Australia, colour)
Directed by Neil Armfield
Runtime: 117 minutes
Not seen by current writer

Armfield's *Twelfth Night* is frequently confused with the 1988 TV adaptation of the same play by Kenneth Branagh and Paul Kafno; videos and DVDs of the Branagh / Kafno production are often wrongly described as Armfield's, which in fact has never been released for home viewing.

Based on Armfield's 1983 stage production for the Adelaide Arts Theatre, with a contemporary Caribbean setting, the film was entirely stage-bound. Gillian Jones played the twins.

Macbeth (1987, Finland, colour)
Directed by Pauli Pentti
Language: Finnish

Runtime: 70 minutes
Not seen by current writer

Pentti's film was a parody of American noir, with a plot based loosely on *Macbeth*. Mato Valtonen and Pirkka Hamalainen starred as the titular gangster and his moll, but the cast also included a character called Napoleon (Sakke Järvenpää). It was nominated for the Best Film prize at Italy's MystFest; and in the same year Pentti worked as assistant director on Aki Kaurismäki's *Hamlet liikemaailmassa*, a film with a similar conceit.

Macbeth (1987, France / Belgium, colour)
Directed by Claude d' Anna
Starring: Leo Nucci, Shirley Verrett, Philippe Volter, Johan Leysen
Language: Italian
Runtime: 133 minutes

Verdi's first Shakespearean opera, 1847's *Macbeth*, was the last to reach the silver screen. It is not hard to see why. The composer's immaturity in comparison with his later works is all too obvious; the music never attains the heights of an *Otello*, or complements Shakespeare's text in the same way – indeed, it is often downright inappropriate, veering into the almost Sullivanesque when it should be at its most sombre. (This is not to say that it is without touches of greatness. The chorus that greets the news of Duncan's murder, for instance, and Macduff's aria "La paterna mano", show signs of the Verdi to come.) Nor was he helped by the eccentric decision of the librettist, Francesco Maria Piave, to leave every murder apart from Banquo's off-stage, and even to omit Duncan and Lady Macduff from the cast altogether. What is a Macbeth whose victims go unseen?

Director Claude d' Anna brought to the opera, however, a striking visual imagination, which helped to turn it into a quite remarkable film. The bar for filmed opera had been raised by Zeffirelli's *Otello* (1986): and d' Anna rose to the challenge. Shooting on location in the Ardennes region, with the orchestra and chorus of the Teatro Comunale di Bologna conducted by Riccardo Chailly, he eschewed realism for a stylised medievalism that betrays strong Japanese influences – the appearance of Leo Nucci as Macbeth, in particular, appears to have been modelled on Toshirô Mifune's Washizu in *Kumonosu jô* (1957) – and conjured into being a grim, barbarous and decayed world. "The miasma of death", as he put it in his programme notes, "infects the kingdom."

D' Anna wears his influences on his sleeve. In addition to Kurosawa and Japanese theatrical tradition, they include the Universal horror movies of the 1930s: Lady Macbeth (Shirley Verrett) is introduced like Dracula, as the shadow of an unseen body moving slowly down a dimly lit stone staircase, while all is coloured in blacks, greys, blues and muted browns shot through a blue filter. Not until Macduff (Philippe Volter, sung by Veriano Luchetti) launches into "La paterna mano" does cinematographer Pierre Dupouey allow any red or green to appear, and only after Macbeth is slain does a splash of bright colour come to dominate the screen, in the form of Malcolm's (Antonio Barasonda) violent red battle flag.

A further motif springs from d' Anna's apparent conception of the Macbeth story as an obscene parody of the Arthur legend. Thus, Macduff's slaughtered family, in an elegiacally shot scene under the refugees' chorus "Patria oppressa", are brought to him by hooded figures on a barge, echoing the damsels who carry the dying Arthur to Avalon; Lady Macbeth is spotlighted lifting a gleaming claymore from Duncan's throne as if drawing the sword from the stone: and, in the "Is this a dagger?" scene, the floor turns to quicksand, and a witch's black arm rises up clutching the dagger like an unholy Excalibur.

The bleakness of d' Anna's vision is unremitting. The landscape of the film is dead; the witches (multiplied, like the assassins, far beyond their numbers in the play so as to provide employment for the chorus) are grimy, near-naked female Calibans, whose cave is an abandoned mine, where they scurry like rats across the slagheaps around its Hell-like maw. The action which d' Anna has invented to prevent the major arias from stemming the flow of the story is entirely devoted to emphasising the corruption of the Scottish realm. Banco (Johan Leysen, sung by the rich bass Samuel Ramey) sings his doom-laden "Come dal ciel precipita" in front of a forest of hanged men, while Macbeth's henchmen cut down and incinerate the corpses. Prostitutes entertain the nobles in the banquet scene, one of their clients wearing a grotesque leather nose, the original presumably lost to either violence or syphilis. In the overture to the sleepwalking scene, we see that the remains of the banquet are still rotting in the Macbeths' feast hall two acts later, picked over by the witches and the vermin they so resemble. During Macbeth's "Pietà, rispetto, amore", the opera's answer to the "Tomorrow" soliloquy, the tyrant breaks down the door he has had nailed shut, and bursts into Duncan's room to defy the Furies one last time. At the end, as Malcolm's men troop into the castle, the impression given by their marching feet and the triumphalist flag is distinctly fascistic, a feeling underscored when we see the leading assassin (Alain-Pascal Housiaux) butchering his former colleagues before pledging his allegiance to the new King.

Macbeth is one of Verdi's slightest works musically, and certainly unsatisfying: but Claude d' Anna has made probably the best possible film adaptation it could have received.

Hamlet liikemaailmassa (1987, Finland, black and white)
Based on Hamlet
A.k.a. Hamlet Gets Business; Hamlet Goes Business
Directed by Aki Kaurismäki
Starring: Pirkka-Pekka Petelius, Esko Salminen, Kati Outinen, Elina Salo, Esko Nikkari
Language: Finnish
Runtime: 86 minutes

Cult director Kaurismäki's decision to turn Hamlet into a comic film noir set in the Helsinki business world of the 1950s – a cut-throat realm of soulless offices and tasteless suits under an ever present pall of tobacco smoke – was characteristically eccentric. (Possibly Kurosawa's corporate thriller Warui yatsu hodo yoku nemuru (1960), which, while it was not an adaptation of Hamlet, did use a few elements of the play, was an influence.)

Hamlet liikemaailmassa is a strange beast. It utilises the plot of Shakespeare's play, but the characters are not the people they were. Hamlet (Pirkka-Pekka Petelius, fat and greasy and – though only 34 – looking too old for the part) may feel for family honour, but shows no respect, let alone even the pretence of love, to his father, alive or dead. He is a spoilt, over-grown child, who excites no comment by playing with crayons in the corner during a board meeting, and his mistreatment of Ofelia (Kati Outinen) is the product of casual lust and a nasty nature. Gertrud (Elina Salo) describes her first husband as "a tyrant who

238

never returned love", but it is hard to see how she can imagine that Klaus / Claudius (Esko Salminen) is any kind of improvement, when he does not even attempt to conceal his psychopathic contempt for her and for humankind in general; she greets her son's madness and the murder of Polonius (Esko Nikkari) alike, with apparent indifference. Rosencranz (Turo Pajala) and Gyldenstern (Aake Kalliala) are not Shakespeare's bewildered dupes, but Klaus' willing henchmen.

The acting does little to make up for the director / adaptor's reductive reading of the characters. With the exception of occasional poignancy from Outinen and an exaggerated performance from Nikkari, it is flat, emotionless, and dull. There is nothing human on display except cruelty, and that is portrayed woodenly.

Kaurismäki's occasional lurches into black comedy, which one suspects he was striving to achieve somewhat more consistently than he does, rather hinder the film than help it. The recurrent presence of rubber ducks (a gift from Ofelia to Hamlet; a business Klaus wants to move into; floating on the bath in which Ofelia drowns herself) is simply bemusing. The death of Lauri / Laertes (Kari Väänäen), staggering about with his head buried in Klaus' radio, is too late and misplaced a touch of humour to improve anything. Cinematography which resurrects every cliché of 1940s noir without a single inventive touch, an over-dramatic and incongruous soundtrack cobbled together from classical snippets, mid-century easy listening, and ugly Eighties rock, the clumsy mishandling of the anti-capitalist theme, and the uneasy impression that Kaurismäki believed he was being very clever, combine to drag the film down. It is not *Hamlet*; and, whether as parody, tribute, or reimagining, it makes a poor partner to *Hamlet*.

King Lear (1987, Bahamas / U.S.A., colour)
Directed by Jean-Luc Godard
Starring: Peter Sellars, Burgess Meredith, Molly Ringwald, Jean-Luc Godard
Runtime: 90 minutes

Jean-Luc Godard was at the forefront of the *Nouvelle Vague* and one of the leading lights of 1960s cinema. By 1987, however, he had long since retreated into self-absorbed and nigh impenetrable eccentricity – and, said his critics, into

239

masturbatory pretentiousness. His semiotic deconstruction of *King Lear* bitterly divided the critical fraternity, but is in truth neither as good nor as bad as it has been declared.

The film rests on an alternative-universe conceit: in the world of this *King Lear*, the Chernobyl disaster of 1986 has wiped out all art, and one of those attempting to recover it is a Shakespeare descendant (Peter Sellars) commissioned to piece together his ancestor's work. Meanwhile, a "Great Writer" (Norman Mailer) is trying to write an adaptation of *Lear* set in the surroundings of organised crime: and his Don Learo (Burgess Meredith) and Cordelia (Molly Ringwald) have come to life, and are overheard by Sellars in a restaurant, speaking a strange mixture of tough-guy reminiscences and the rejection scene. Into this mind-bending concept strays Godard himself as the dreadlocked Professor Pluggy, dropping profundities that are never quite as clever as they sound ("Never know, always see"; "Words are one thing, and reality, reality is another thing: and between them is no thing"; "Suppose we made a mistake, at the very, very beginning, and called red green: how would we know today?") in his slow-spoken Churchillian voice. He also provides an occasional director's commentary, anticipating the DVD revolution by many years.

The opening title cards, reading "King Lear: Fear and Loathing. King Lear: A Study. An Approach. King Lear: A Clearing. No Thing", flash up repeatedly throughout the film, whose effect is indeed comparable to that of the drugs ingested in *Fear and Loathing in Las Vegas*. Images of light (bonfires, sparklers, waving bulbs) constantly recur; previous interpreters of Shakespeare for the cinema are referenced (a photograph of Orson Welles sits incongruously in a book of Old Masters; Pluggy entertains a "Professor Kozintsev"); howling winds and screeching seagulls dominate the soundtrack, even indoors; at one point the script veers away from Shakespeare altogether, Cordelia becoming Joan of Arc and Sellars her inquisitor, speaking the dialogue of the trial records, before returning to the play for Pluggy to enjoy a death scene not unlike Gloucester's – a character to whom he has hitherto shown no resemblance whatsoever.

The Joan sequence is baffling at first viewing, but is in fact pivotal to the film. Godard is equating England's occupation of France during the Hundred Years' War with American dominance of world cinema – which, for good measure, he also wishes to compare with the gangsterism of Mailer's adaptation of the play, and the sexual abuse that he reads into Lear's relationship with his daughters. Under the surface of the film lies little more complex than crude anti-Americanism.

The result is a mess, all the more frustrating for the sense that Godard – or, more likely, Sellars, who was the real Shakespearean enthusiast on the project – has had some real insights into the play. The film is easily at its best when the gimmicks and interpolated dialogue are dropped, and Shakespeare's text is allowed to stand with Godard's visuals: especially since Meredith makes a fine Lear, one who should have been allowed to play the King as Shakespeare wrote him. The end, whose principal images – a white horse galloping along the beach, where Learo, with his back to the white-clad corpse of Cordelia, stares blankly out to sea – possess a stark beauty worthy of the text, is spoilt by the intrusion of a nonsensical sequence about the editing of the film by "Mr Alien" (Woody Allen in a split-second silent cameo). Somewhere within this film there may be a worthwhile essay on *King Lear*, struggling to get out: but it is buried very deep.

Interestingly, the film allegedly helped serve as a springboard for the career of a man who had nothing to do with it: Quentin Tarantino. Though a lifelong admirer of Godard, Tarantino has claimed that he fabricated an acting credit for *King Lear* to pad out his C.V. – proceeding on the justifiable assumption that very few people had seen it.

China Girl (1987, U.S.A., colour)
Based on *Romeo and Juliet*
Directed by Abel Ferrara
Starring: Richard Panebianco, Sari Chang, James Russo, Russell Wong
Runtime: 89 minutes

"A modern day Romeo & Juliet" ~ tagline to *China Girl*.

Abel Ferrara's inexplicable favourite of his own films does what it says on the tin, at least as far as plot is concerned. It is from first to last entirely derivative of *West Side Story* (1961), the Polish / Irish and Puerto Rican gangs merely having been replaced with Italians and Chinese, contesting a similar area of Manhattan: and it suffers throughout by comparison with the immeasurably superior musical. Joe Delia's score has a certain punch, but cannot stand up next to Bernstein; Nicholas St John's screenplay is unconvincing and forgettable; the leads are bland at best and wooden at worst. Whether paraphrasing Shakespeare badly in a fire escape balcony scene cribbed directly from the earlier film, or dying in each other's arms as the camera backs away upwards into a momentously clichéed crane shot, they never show one spark of believable passion.

Some of the superior talents in the supporting cast, notably James Russo as the Mercutio / Riff figure Alby, manage to breathe a little life into St John's flat dialogue, but they are fighting a losing battle; while unimaginative cinematography (admittedly well lit) married to absurd Eighties fashions leaves the film frankly ugly to look at. When at the end even Delia descends into sentimentalism, covering the closing credits with a maudlin ballad, one cannot help but be relieved that it is over.

Gamlet (1989, U.S.S.R., colour)
Based on *Hamlet*
A.k.a. *Hamlet* (international English title)
Directed by Gleb Panfilov
Language: Russian
Not seen by current writer

The last Soviet Shakespeare film was adapted by Gleb Panfilov from his own stage production at the LENKOM theatre, and starred his wife and regular collaborator Inna Churikova as Gertrude.

Hamlet: Prince of Denmark (1989, India, colour)
Directed by Sendhil Nathan
Runtime: 58 minutes
Not seen by current writer

Nathan's *Hamlet*, starring Kabir Ahamed, was released on 24th June 1989. I can find no further details concerning the picture.

Henry V (1989, U.K., colour)
Directed by Kenneth Branagh
Starring: Kenneth Branagh, Derek Jacobi, Brian Blessed, Ian Holm, Robert Stephens

Runtime: 137 minutes
Academy Awards (1990): Best Costume Design (Phyllis Dalton)
Academy Award nominations: Best Director (Kenneth Branagh); Best Actor in a Leading Role (Kenneth Branagh)

"[Despite] the genuine nature of Henry's humility and piety... [he is] a professional killer of chilling ruthlessness." ~ Kenneth Branagh.[101]

This was not Branagh's first Shakespearean screen adaptation – he had helmed a television production of *Twelfth Night* in 1988 – but it was his first feature film as director, and the first major original text adaptation of a Shakespeare play that had been attempted since Charlton Heston's *Antony and Cleopatra* in 1972. It was a very risky venture, and his backers were holding their breath: but the 28-year-old phenomenon ("looking all of twelve", as he himself later put it[102]) not only turned in his finished picture ahead of time and under budget, but proceeded to stun critics and audiences alike.

It was no coincidence that he was hailed as "the new Olivier": not only had he selected the same play to kick off the cinematic phase of his career as director-producer-star (like Olivier's version, starting a decade-long boom in Shakespearean cinema – and helping to revitalise the moribund British film industry in the process), but his film feels at times like a deliberate reply to Olivier's propagandistic version. No *Très Riches Heures* for Branagh: this is instead a grimly realistic look at mud-spattered medieval war. The contrasting appearances of the films are especially noteworthy, given that Angels & Bermans supplied the costumes for both: this time round, they won an Oscar.

Much was rightly made of the influence of Orson Welles' *Campanadas a medianoche,* and of the Vietnam War and the sub-genre of films it had spawned (not to mention the Falklands War, fresh in British memories when Branagh had first played the part in 1984), on the gritty, grimy vision realised here: but the northern French setting of the play, the Belfast background of the director, and the sense of damp and chill which this film possesses, combine to suggest that the horrific battles of the First

---

[101] Branagh, Kenneth, "Henry V" (1986), included in Jackson, Russell, and Smallwood, Robert (eds), *Players of Shakespeare 2* (Cambridge, 1988), p. 97.
[102] Branagh, *Beginning* (London, 1989), p. 149.

World War in the same region were also in Branagh's mind. It is impossible to hear Charles VI (played with fragile majesty by Paul Scofield) announce that "'Tis certain he hath passed the River Somme" without thinking of what befell there five hundred years later. (It is incidentally worth mentioning that Michael Bogdanov's biting, self-parodically jingoistic 1987 stage version of this play for the English Shakespeare Company, with its notorious "Fuck the Frogs" banner, was televised in 1989. Mixing eras as all the E.S.C.'s Histories did, it used much of the iconography of the Western Front.)

Every time there is a danger that the audience will be fooled, carried away by the rhetoric of the Chorus (the magnificent Derek Jacobi, as an actor in modern dress – a counterpoint to the Elizabethan Chorus of Olivier's version – wandering unscathed through the battlefields, and telling us to believe in the nobility of the human dregs hacking one another to pieces and robbing the corpses in front of us) or of the King (Branagh), or by Patrick Doyle's rousing score (which was criminally overlooked at the Oscars), Branagh as director undercuts it.

The Archbishop of Canterbury (Charles Kay), a figure of fun for Olivier, is here a repellent "chicken-hawk" poisoning the King's mind; Branagh enters not as nervous Burbage becoming the glorious monarch, but in sinister silhouette. He restores the treason of Scroop (Stephen Simms), Henry's near-psychopathic behaviour at Harfleur, and the execution of Bardolph (Richard Briers, extremely effective in a part well outside the range which might have been suggested by most of his previous work) – even showing us the latter, which Shakespeare could not do. He peppers his screenplay with flashbacks to scenes cut-and-pasted from various lines in the *Henry IV* plays, calculated to show Henry's rejection of Falstaff (Robbie Coltrane) in the most callous light. His Henry, like a modern veteran, suffers battle flashbacks during the peace talks in Act Five – by which time the character has grown in a way Olivier's never did, or needed to. His Agincourt is small-scale (partly for budgetary reasons), seen only at the low and vicious level of individual combats, as it would have been seen by participants; and when, in the post-battle scene, Doyle's beautiful voice rises singing *Non Nobis* as a tracking shot follows Henry across the battlefield carrying the body of Falstaff's page (a young Christian Bale), at the very climax of the music the French camp-followers rush forward to try to avenge their men-folk by lynching the invading king. At the very end, when all the Eastcheap characters except Robert Stephens' weary, near-tragic Pistol are dead, and the rulers are concluding their agreement, we are treated to the downbeat Chorus with which the play is meant to finish, reminding us that Hal died young and the reign of Henry VI was a blood-soaked fifty year disaster.

A cast of veteran British thespians, many of them to become regular Branagh collaborators, ably supports this vision; there is, indeed, hardly a complaint to make, except perhaps that Kenneth MacMillan's cinematography is not quite all it could be (though not unimpressive, it is a little flat compared to Branagh's later films). It is in many ways complementary to Olivier's version; certainly the cinema would be the poorer without either of them.

Resan till Melonia (1989, Sweden / Norway, colour animation)
Based on *The Tempest*
A.k.a. *Reisen til Melonia* (Norway); *The Journey to Melonia: Fantasies of Shakespeare's "The Tempest"*
Directed by Per Åhlin
Runtime: 104 minutes

Despite the title, this charming Swedish animated feature chiefly concerns a journey *from* Melonia (i.e. Prospero's island) to the neighbouring isle of Plutonia, which has no parallel in *The Tempest*. Until we leave Melonia, however, the play is quite closely adhered to, the script frequently echoing Shakespeare's text.

This Prospero is no exile: he chooses to live in Melonia, and, considering the beauty of the isle, one can hardly blame him. It is an unspoilt tropical paradise, which he and the very young Miranda share with an accident-prone Ariel in the form of a seagull, a mournful scarecrow of a Caliban (put together from vegetables – his head is a cabbage, with carrot nose and onion eyes), and a small, theatre-obsessed talking dog called William. (William later attempts to stage *The Tempest*, with several of the characters playing their Shakespearean equivalents, bringing a touch of postmodernism to proceedings.)

But opposite Melonia there stands Plutonia, a technocratic hell run on child slave labour and ruled over by the wine-bibbing capitalist tyrants Slagg and Slugg (who stand in not only for Antonio and Sebastian but for the more comical villainy of Stephano and Trinculo). The ship which Prospero's storm destroys is theirs, coming to colonise Melonia and steal the secrets of his magic; Ferdinand is a refugee from their armaments factory; it is they who promise Caliban his freedom, get him drunk – then kidnap him and return to Plutonia, leaving the plot of *The Tempest* behind as Prospero and his cohorts pursue them to rescue Caliban and all Ferdinand's fellow slaves.

The animation, though low-tech and with little complexity, is clever, cineliterate, and very pretty, effectively realising the worlds of both islands; it is supported by the pastiche Renaissance music of Björn Isfält, which despite the film's Victorian era setting is perfectly appropriate to Melonia, becoming more modern when the action moves from the forests to the smoky, steel-bound Plutonia. The ecological and anti-corporate messages are not overplayed, and – despite occasional longueurs for the adult or older child viewer – *Resan till Melonia* should enchant the very young without driving older members of the family away.

Romeo-Juliet (1990, Belgium, colour)
Based on *Romeo and Juliet*
Directed by Armando Acosta
Runtime: 120 minutes
Not seen by current writer

The only human being to appear in Acosta's film was John Hurt, in drag as a bag lady: all other parts were performed by cats. The framing plot was that Hurt's Dame aux Chats gathers up the feral felines of Venice to sail with them to New York; filming in both cities, plus Ghent, Acosta amassed some two hundred hours' footage of street cats, from which careful editing allowed him to put together a version of *Romeo and Juliet*, backed by Prokofiev's music and with a recorded script provided by a distinguished, mostly British cast. Robert Powell and Francesca Annis voiced the lovers. Online reviewers have remarked on the beauty of Acosta's cinematography; but, despite some demand, the film is pretty much impossible to obtain.

Rosencrantz & Guildenstern Are Dead (1990, U.K. / U.S.A., colour)
Based on *Hamlet*

Directed by Tom Stoppard
Starring: Gary Oldman, Tim Roth, Richard Dreyfuss, Iain Glen
Runtime: 117 minutes

Stoppard's famous 1967 play, expanding on the conceits of W. S. Gilbert's *Rosencrantz and Guildenstern* (1874) ("Hamlet is idiotically sane / With lucid intervals of lunacy" ~ Gilbert; "So there you are. Stark raving sane" ~ Stoppard) and turning *Hamlet*'s two most bewildered characters into ancestors of Vladimir and Estragon (connected by an ampersand in the title, emphasising their inseparability – they are less individuals than two halves of a single character), is a masterpiece of wit, erudition, and philosophical depth. What it is not, however, for all the inventiveness of Stoppard's direction and the talents of his leads (Gary Oldman and Tim Roth in the title roles; Richard Dreyfuss as the Player[103]), is cinematic.

Certainly the use of music and of theatrical devices help the film repay re-watching even if the viewer is sufficiently familiar with the play to need no reminder of the brilliance of the script. Debate has been spawned over the pieces of paper which blow in the wind whenever the plot and text intersect with those of *Hamlet*, helplessly buffeted as are Rosencrantz (Oldman) and Guildenstern (Roth) themselves, occasionally caught and fashioned into Leonardo-style inventions; over Stoppard's occasional tinkering with his own text (particularly his handling of the ending); and over the deliberate staginess of Iain Glen as the Prince and the other actors in the Shakespearean sections, which makes a pointed contrast to the naturalistic acting of Oldman and Roth. (Dreyfuss' acting is something else: a player playing a player playing a player, and inevitably stealing every scene.)

These occasionally contentious devices are to my mind effective, and certainly interesting. But they do not alter the fact that, for all its express-train dialogue, this is still a play. Having the two leads play their coin-tossing game on horseback (surely a difficult feat) does not a movie make; and, for all the deficiencies that are attendant on shooting in a theatre, one is left with the feeling that it would have been small loss if the makers had spent a fraction of the budget this film must have required simply

---

[103] Substituting for Sean Connery – Stoppard's original choice, who had dropped out, depending on whom one believes, either because of ill health or because another production offered him more money.

filming the play in performance.

Overall, the film never becomes much more than a curiosity. If one is already a fan of Stoppard's play, it is worth seeing at least once; but the newcomer to the text should see the play performed live before attempting the film.

Hamlet (1990, U.S.A. / U.K. / France, colour)
Directed by Franco Zeffirelli
Starring: Mel Gibson, Glenn Close, Alan Bates, Helena Bonham Carter, Ian Holm
Runtime: 130 minutes
Academy Award nominations (1991): Best Art Direction (Dante Ferretti, Francesca Lo Schiavo); Best Costume Design (Maurizio Millenotti)

It is said that, when Franco Zeffirelli saw Mel Gibson's portrayal of a character contemplating suicide in *Lethal Weapon* (1987), he jumped out of his seat shouting "To be or not to be!" Three years later, they produced this trimmed-down *Hamlet*. (Gibson had a Shakespearean background, having played Romeo at the Nimrod Theatre in Sydney in 1979.)

Always a stickler for historical authenticity, Zeffirelli chose to set the play in an early medieval context. The earliest surviving source, Saxo Grammaticus, writing at the end of the twelfth century, sets the Hamlet story in the sixth:[104] but that is far too early for the quite sophisticated and Christian world of the play. In fact, Shakespeare's Hamlet appears to be set at a Renaissance court where paganism and the Viking Age are still living memories;[105] but such an historical non-time would be difficult to portray on film: so Zeffirelli simply chose the earliest period in which the play's text would be remotely plausible – roughly, the eleventh century. Shot on location on the east coast of Scotland, the film captures early medieval Denmark beautifully (although some motifs, notably the Book of Kells-inspired tapestry in Gertrude's chamber, are more Irish than Scandinavian, while the doublet Hamlet wears in the play and

---

[104] *Vide* the 1994 film *Prince of Jutland*, starring Christian Bale, which brought Saxo's version – more or less – to the screen.
[105] Cf. John Updike's novel *Gertrude and Claudius* (2000), in whose thirty-year span five or six centuries seem to pass in the world outside Elsinore.

closet scenes is several centuries ahead of its time); the visuals are complemented by Ennio Morricone's haunting score.

The film's opening scene encapsulates most of its principal faults and virtues. It is the funeral of King Hamlet (Paul Scofield), an invented scene made up of snippets from later in the play, but existing more for reaction shots of the brooding Prince (Gibson), grieving Queen (Glenn Close), and calculating Claudius (Alan Bates). There, in barely more than a minute, we have on the debit side Zeffirelli's cavalier attitude to the text, and his two-tone approach to secondary characters such as the King; and on the credit side, his skill at close-ups and the histrionic strengths of these three leads. The first problem is one that casts a long shadow over the film: little may have been changed, but much has been chopped. The entire Fortinbras subplot has gone, and taken more than half the text with it; scenes are juggled about so that, for instance, "To be or not to be" happens *after* Hamlet's rejection of Ophelia (Helena Bonham Carter). Not for nothing was this *Hamlet* described as "the comic book version".[106] The second issue is less overarching, but still of importance. The film's morality may not be black and white, but Claudius is painted entirely black: Bates was a fine actor, but neither he nor Zeffirelli, nor the revised script, tries to give us any insight into the King's soul. He is simply evil – and Gertrude, while she has ambiguities of her own, is painted unequivocally as another of his victims. (Lines are even reapportioned to support these simplistic interpretations of character.)

The performances, however – including Bates', given the mangled script he was working with – are uniformly excellent. Gibson's apparently bipolar Prince (a condition which seems to fascinate Zeffirelli: it has been argued that he gave it to Mercutio in *Romeo and Juliet* (1968) as well) is one of the finest Hamlets ever to grace our screens; Close is an exquisite Gertrude. (Both, incidentally, employ note-perfect English accents.) Zeffirelli chose to concentrate on the Oedipal subtext to their relationship – too closely in some critics' view: he incorporates what looks like a simulated rape into the closet scene. This interpretation would be a challenge for any pair of actors; but both portray it sensitively. (As in much of the rest of the film, Zeffirelli was intent here on enlarging on Olivier's hints in his 1948 version,

---

[106] Quoted by Rosenthal, *100 Shakespearean films*, p. 42.

and generally complementing that picture: such was his reverence for it that he even obtained Olivier's bloodstained shirt from the duel scene and presented it to Gibson.)

It has been suggested that Zeffirelli's Shakespearean films should be viewed in isolation from the text, as if they were wholly original pieces. While I do not dispute that every film should stand up as a work of art in its own right, I find it impossible to separate adaptations from their originals: and this is an undeniably flawed *Hamlet*. It is, however, still a fine film, worthy to stand by Olivier's in the pantheon of Shakespearean cinema: but for a full realisation of the play in English, the world had to wait for 1996 and Kenneth Branagh.

Men of Respect (1991, U.S.A., colour)
Based on *Macbeth*
Directed by William Reilly
Starring: John Turturro, Katherine Borowitz, Dennis Farina, Peter Boyle, Rod Steiger
Runtime: 113 minutes

The idea of setting *Macbeth* in a gangland milieu was hardly new in 1991, but adaptor-director William Reilly's idea was a little more original than that: he wanted to use the play to paint a realistic picture of the New York Mafia. Such a conceit necessitated that the original text should be done away with; Reilly's script, however, sticks close to it, even incorporating occasional direct quotations. This is a risky strategy. Every echo of Shakespeare reminds the audience of what they are missing; there is hardly a scene or even a line that does not feel watered down. Furthermore, it makes departures from the original more glaring when they do occur. This Macbeth (Michael Battaglia, played by John Turturro) greets his wife's death not philosophically, but with floods of tears, only to be cold again directly afterwards; Birnam Wood is replaced with a prophecy about the stars falling, fulfilled – in a sign of desperation on Reilly's part – by a firework display.

This is not to say that the film is without its strengths. The basement-dwelling family of fortune-tellers (led by Lilia Skala) who stand in for the witches are suitably sinister; the consistent depiction of Mob life as unglamorous and undesirable is admirable, even if it is hard to imagine that successful major criminals would live in such poor conditions; the scene in which

250

Battaglia is "made", swearing to put the Mafia "before God, before country, and before family", is beautifully handled, and chillingly reflected at the end when the Fleance figure (David Thornton) takes the same oath, with the same brief venomous glance at Malcolm (Stanley Tucci) that Battaglia gave his father (Rod Steiger). Furthermore, the acting is uniformly impressive (though the material denies the actors the possibility of the excellence most of them have demonstrated elsewhere), and it is hard not to wonder what this cast might have done with an original text *Macbeth*.

Unfortunately, that is not what they had to work with. Instead they had Reilly's script and Reilly's direction, both of which are usually functional but seldom inspired. The result is a flat film, which struggles to maintain audience interest, and has rather less to say about American gangsterism than has already been said in several far superior pictures; it is also a career low for many of the cast.

My Own Private Idaho (1991, U.S.A., colour)
Based on *Henry IV, Part 1, Henry IV, Part 2* and *Henry V*
Directed by Gus Van Sant
Starring: River Phoenix, Keanu Reeves, William Richert, Udo Kier, James Russo
Runtime: 102 minutes

"Why, you wouldn't even look at a clock unless hours were lines of coke, dials looked like the signs of gay bars, or time itself was a fair hustler in black leather." ("Unless hours were cups of sack, and minutes capons, and clocks the tongues of bawds, and dials the signs of leaping-houses, and the blessed sun himself a fair hot wench in flame-coloured taffeta, I see no reason why thou shouldst be so superfluous as to demand the time of day.")

Cult director Gus Van Sant's decision to turn Prince Hal into a Midwestern rent boy was undeniably eccentric, even in the heyday of New Queer Cinema, but it is not entirely ineffective. Based largely on the Eastcheap scenes in the Second Henriad, the film takes its Hal figure, Scott (Keanu Reeves), on much the same journey as Shakespeare's Prince, through tutelage in debauchery at the hands of a gay Falstaff (Bob Pigeon, played by the superb William Richert), conflict with his ambitious but now weary father (Tom Troupe), to marriage with

251

a non-Anglophone standing in for Princess Catherine (Chiara Caselli), and a rejection of his former life and friends.

Into this story, however, Van Sant has intruded an extra character, Mike (River Phoenix), a narcoleptic fellow hustler who apparently falls in love with Scott; and Mike's story dominates the film. The result is that the two strands sit uneasily together. In the Eastcheap-inspired scenes, Mike takes the role of Ned Poins (notably in Van Sant's detailed recreation of the Gadshill robbery from *Henry IV, Part 1* and Hal's subsequent ribbing of Falstaff about his cowardice): but, while the character is exquisitely drawn and Phoenix plays him beautifully, he never seems to belong in the same film as the Shakespearean characters. The contrast between the modern, realistic dialogue in Mike's scenes and the paraphrases, pastiches, and straight lifts from Shakespeare in Bob's further underscores this. (It is no surprise to learn that it was a late decision to base the films on the *Henry* plays, based on Van Sant's admiration for *Campanadas a medianoche* (1965), several minor homages to which are detectable in this picture.)

Reeves' acting, as usual, tends towards the wooden, but this is not so out of place given Van Sant's cynical depiction of Scott / Hal: the director has seen to the cold heart of the character. By underlining the poverty of the Eastcheap crowd as strongly as he does, he also makes their eventual rejection all the more painful. At least this Hal will not be able to lead them all to war.

The folk-style soundtrack, use of half-imagined flashbacks during Mike's narcoleptic attacks, and presentation of some events (particularly sex scenes) by a succession of stills instead of action, all add to the surreal atmosphere which the use of Shakespearean poetry coming out of the mouths of down-and-outs and junkies helps to create; but the end result is a little too odd for its own good, especially since one can never quite lose the feeling that Van Sant was trying to make two different films. For all the talents of Phoenix and Richert, and the inventiveness of the updating, *My Own Private Idaho* is a patchy and uneven film.

Prospero's Books (1991, France / Italy / Netherlands / U.K. / Japan, colour)
Based on *The Tempest*

A.k.a. *L' Ultima tempesta* (Italy)
Directed by Peter Greenaway
Starring: John Gielgud, Michael Clark, Isabelle Pasco
Runtime: 124 minutes

"*Prospero's Books*", Roger Ebert remarked, "really exists outside criticism."[107] It is certainly not possible to treat Greenaway's extraordinary work as if it were a conventional adaptation. This is not a film of *The Tempest*: rather, it could be considered a film which uses the text of *The Tempest*, the play's source material, and almost every piece of arcana written in Shakespeare's lifetime as the foundation for a profound meditation on art, science, language, discovery, authorship and a myriad other subjects – as Kenneth S. Rothwell has called it, "a *Finnegans Wake* of visual art".[108] (Vincent Canby was less charitable: "a kind of obsessed collector's inventory of the Renaissance" was what he saw.)[109]

The inspirations for *The Tempest* were many: the *Essays* of Michel de Montaigne, the occult practices of Dr John Dee, the chequered fifteenth century career of Prospero Adorno, and the reports of Thomas Harriot from the New World, are among its strongest influences: and Greenaway's Prospero (John Gielgud, who had lobbied for decades to play this part on screen) is Dee, Harriot, and Shakespeare in one person as well as the play's magus. In the person of Shakespeare, he is in fact writing *The Tempest* as the film progresses: the twenty-fourth and last of the title's books is *35 Plays*, a First Folio with blank leaves where *The Tempest* should be; to this Prospero adds his manuscript, before hurling them both into the watery abyss after the rest of his library – but these books alone are rescued. (Several of the "lost" volumes are in fact genuine surviving works by Shakespeare's contemporaries, including Harriot's *A Brief and True Report of the New Found Land of Virginia*.) No other actor speaks until Prospero reveals himself to his shipwrecked victims: Gielgud, in an astonishing display of dramatic virtuosity, voices every part. (The single partial exception is Isabelle Pasco as Miranda, whose voice is combined with his for her lines.)

Visually, the film is quite stunning. Like Kurosawa,

---

[107] Ebert, Roger, *Roger Ebert's movie home companion* (New York, 1992), p. 519.
[108] Rothwell, *A history of Shakespeare on screen*, p. 200.
[109] Quoted by Morley, *John Gielgud*, p. 454.

Greenaway had been a painter before going into the cinema: and here he not only draws on his major influences Titian and Tintoretto, but references almost every master of the Renaissance from Leonardo to Rembrandt, throwing in what feels like a touch of Dalí for good measure – he has clearly been watching his Fellini too, and studying the masques of Inigo Jones – to create a surreally beautiful world which is at once the island of the play, Prospero's palace in Milan, and the kingdom of the imagination, exquisitely photographed by Sacha Vierny. Every word in the play is translated into image, often with the words themselves appearing on the screen simultaneously. There is not a shot in the entire film – even when grotesqueries such as the multiple Ariels urinating over a toy boat are depicted – that could not be framed and hung on a wall.

Through this world move human characters in exaggerated costumes of the early seventeenth century (designed by Ellen Lens and Emi Wada), with absurdly large hats and ruffs, and naked spirits like Greek statues come to life. Their motion is fluid and balletic: several, including Caliban (Michael Clark), were played by dancers: and it would be no exaggeration to describe the film as a ballet set to the words of Shakespeare. This element is exquisitely complemented by the music of Michael Nyman – substantially cut in the video release by Greenaway, who disliked the amount of singing Nyman had included. The resulting quarrel was so bitter that the two have not worked together since.

The entire work groans under the weight of Greenaway's enormous erudition, and defeats any attempt at absolute comprehension. It is perhaps wisest to attempt no analysis, but simply to absorb a wondrous piece of work by masters of their several arts. It is not *The Tempest*, and cannot honestly be recommended as an introduction to the play: but for the viewer who knows and loves Shakespeare's work already, *Prospero's Books* is a feast.

As You Like It (1992, U.K., colour)
Directed by Christine Edzard
Starring: Emma Croft, Andrew Tiernan, James Fox, Griff Rhys Jones
Runtime: 112 minutes

Christine Edzard's first film credit is as a set dresser on

Franco Zeffirelli's *Romeo and Juliet* (1968), whose associate producer, Richard B. Goodwin, became her husband. Unfortunately, she brings none of that picture's charm and warmth to her low-budget modern-dress *As You Like It*, which, while it has its imaginative touches, is ultimately a disservice to the text.

The importance of the film in one respect must be acknowledged: although period analogue productions had long been popular on stage and television, especially in the U.K., in 1992 they were still a rarity on the big screen. It is impossible to gauge how influential Edzard's decision to set the play in contemporary London was: but this film was certainly one of the first of the wave of inventive Shakespearean period analogues that were to be a significant feature of 1990s cinema. For that, at least, Edzard deserves credit.

Unfortunately, however, her bleak and chilly film completely fails to capture the delightful spirit of the play: which, while certainly not lacking in dark elements, should ultimately defeat them. By 1992 most directors had rediscovered this fact; but Edzard makes the quasi-Chekhovian interpretations of the 1970s look like Disney. This may be partly the fault of budgetary problems, but directorial decisions are also to blame: in addition to moving the pastoral and forest scenes to the depressed Docklands and turning the exiled court into homeless dossers, Edzard has turned the homes of Oliver and Frederick into what look like the foyers of disused offices. Seediness and cold pervade the film, and the actors never manage to convince us that their spirits are really bearing up under a degree of adversity that seems to have no sweet uses at all.

They do try. Emma Croft, playing Rosalind in a woolly hat, and Andrew Tiernan, doubling as Orlando and Oliver (like Superman, he takes off his glasses and becomes a different person – but Edzard apparently could not afford even the basic effects needed to bring the two brothers onto the screen at the same time), attack their parts gamely enough, while James Fox as an ennui-stricken upper class Jaques turns in a fine performance. The usually excellent Griff Rhys Jones, on the other hand, is badly miscast as Touchstone, draining the part of its humour – assisted in this by Edzard's direction at every turn.

Some of Edzard's ideas are simply bizarre. The wrestling match not only happens off-screen – the contestants fight without changing their clothes, Orlando in a hooded top and

Charles (Tony Armatrading) in a suit. Corin (Roger Hammond) is accompanied by a sheep, for no other reason than that he is a shepherd in the play. Songs are incongruously set to original Elizabethan tunes despite the modern surroundings.

Most damningly for an adaptation of a comedy, this production is quite devoid of laughs – indeed, one would be more likely to leave the cinema in the depths of depression. If Edzard wanted to make a point about the plight of the homeless, she could surely have found a more appropriate text: if she wanted to make a point about *As You Like It*, she failed.

Much Ado About Nothing (1993, U.K. / U.S.A., colour)
Directed by Kenneth Branagh
Starring: Emma Thompson, Kenneth Branagh, Denzel Washington, Richard Briers, Kate Beckinsale
Runtime: 111 minutes

The first English language feature film of one of Shakespeare's sharpest comedies, Branagh's *Much Ado* is among the most successful adaptation of any of the comic plays to the screen. Set in what appears to be the mid nineteenth century (a period to which he returned for *Hamlet* (1996), recreating it in much more detail than here), filmed against gorgeous Tuscan scenery (it may not look much like the supposedly Sicilian setting, but it certainly looks good), featuring such youth pin-ups as Kate Beckinsale (Hero), Keanu Reeves (Don John), and Robert Sean Leonard (Claudio), and photographed by the talented Roger Lanser, the film is undeniably handsome: but, over and above this, it boasts Branagh's instinctive understanding of Shakespeare's text.

The central performances, from a cast clearly having enormous fun, are excellent. Branagh and his then wife Emma Thompson inhabit the roles of the bickering Benedick and Beatrice as if born to play them; Denzel Washington holds his own alongside them as Don Pedro, equally at ease in comic and dramatic scenes. Nevertheless, it is in the acting that flaws are to be found. Reeves, although not by any means as bad as his shriller critics would have us believe, is essentially a one-note actor: the fact that the note he strikes is at least appropriate saves his portrayal of Don John from disaster, but one could still have wished for more subtlety. It is Michael Keaton, however, who is the weak point of the film. His decision to portray Dogberry with an impenetrable and not very convincing Irish accent was extremely misguided; and Branagh's direction of the Watch scenes, as rather heavy-handed slapstick, stands in sorry contrast to the lighter, defter comic touch that he brings to the rest of the film. It is all too easy for Shakespeare's clowns to become tiresome in the wrong hands; and here, despite Ben Elton's game mugging as the hapless Verges, it is hard not to be glad that the Watch scenes have been substantially cut.

These, however, are minor distractions from what is, overall, a delightful film, supported once again by a superb score from Patrick Doyle – who, as in *Henry V* (1989), takes a minor role so as to sing his own songs on screen. (Incredibly, none of the music had to be re-recorded.) From the opening shot of Thompson sitting in a tree reading the lyrics of "Sigh No More", through the energetic title sequence (the arrival of the princes was inspired by *The Magnificent Seven*), to the end – a spectacularly choreographed scene of the entire cast dancing through Leonato's gardens, filmed in a single extended shot – it never fails to charm.

William Shakespeare's Ill Met by Moonlight (1994, U.S.A., colour)
Based on *A Midsummer Night's Dream*
A.k.a. *A Midsummer Nights Dreame*
Directed by S. P. Somtow
Starring: Tim Sullivan, Heidi Blose, Judy Fei-Wing, Ron Ford, Rachel J. Sita Raine
Runtime: 128 minutes

The eccentric, aristocratic Thai composer and fantasy writer S. P. Somtow's occasional ventures into film are less celebrated than his other works, but bear his unmistakeable stamp. If nothing else, the music and the horror-veteran cast would mark out *Ill Met by Moonlight* – which, despite the interest it aroused at Cannes and the director's ongoing attempts to secure it a distributor, has not yet been released commercially – as a Somtow film.

He sets the play in East Los Angeles, with Oberon (Tim Sullivan) and Theseus (Robert Z'Dar) as vaguely gangsterish – though not rival – figures; the fairies are the local children of the night, the "forest" a shed used by Quince (Edward Bryant) as a studio plus the surrounding slum area. Incongruous references to trees, bushes, grassy banks, and the like are left intact. Some elements of this take on the play are very dark – Timothy Bottoms' scruffy, manic, violent Egeus is truly horrible. Others are quirkily effective – Flute (Fate Fatal, camp as Christmas and loving the role) discovers an identity as a transvestite after reluctantly taking the role of Thisbe. Others are unbelievably crass. In a clunking literalisation of a joke that is obvious enough in the text without needing to be put (rather disgustingly) on screen, Bottom's (Ron Ford) "ass-head" is not a donkey but an arse. Ha. Ha. Ha.

The quality of the performances varies. Sullivan is suitably menacing; Rachel J. S. Raine's oversexed Titania is always watchable; Bottoms does what can be done with an unconventional reading of an often thankless role: but many of the others are wooden or worse, the lovers in particular throwing away some beautiful lines and never conveying any stronger emotion than irritation – which the viewer is likely to share. Despite Somtow's facility in maintaining the look he has chosen for his film, uninteresting photography and the lack of relation between the look and the text mean that it hardly seems worth it; late nods to Thai culture seem forced; and only the score is a true success. Moving from Renaissance pastiche to rap, through quotes from Nino Rota, remixes of Grieg, and Thai music both traditional and pop, he displays and revels in an extraordinary versatility as a composer, and it is hard to avoid the conclusion that his talents are better employed in that medium than in film.

The Fifteen Minute Hamlet (1995, U.S.A., colour)
Directed by Todd Louiso
Runtime: 22 minutes
Not seen by current writer

Tom Stoppard's *Fifteen Minute Hamlet* (1978) is an expertly filleted dash through *Hamlet*, predating the work of the Reduced Shakespeare Company, whose first performance was a 25-minute *Hamlet* in 1981. Todd Louiso's film, starring himself as Ophelia and Austin Pendleton as the Prince, is slightly longer than the title promises, because of its viciously satirical framing device: here, the film industry exists in the Elizabethan era, and Shakespeare (Xander Berkeley) is a hapless writer-director, forced by a philistine producer (Michael Goldberg) to cut his masterpiece ever further, the finally approved version being only one minute long.

Richard III (1995, U.K. / U.S.A., colour)
Directed by Richard Loncraine
Starring: Ian McKellen, Annette Bening, Jim Broadbent, Maggie Smith, Kristin Scott Thomas
Runtime: 104 minutes
Academy Award nominations (1996): Best Art Direction (Tony Burrough); Best Costume Design (Shuna Harwood)

Richard III was inspired by Richard Eyre's 1990 stage production of the play, which had starred Ian McKellen and been set in the late 1930s: Shakespeare as alternative history. The film was very much a labour of love for McKellen, who produced it and wrote the screenplay as well as starring, and, when the money ran out during the filming of Bosworth Field, returned his fee so that the picture could be finished. In the process of adaptation, McKellen and director Richard Loncraine trimmed away over half the original text, to produce a lean, fast-paced political thriller – although it is hard not to feel that some of the excisions were unnecessary. (Unlike previous adaptations, they do not depend too heavily on Colley Cibber: the opening is indebted to *Henry VI, Part 3*, but uses very little text from the earlier play – although the film's tagline, "I can smile, and murder while I smile", is taken from that work and not *Richard III*.) The occasional modernisations of language – notably replacing "thou" with "you" – are not ineffective, although they can make a lover of the original text wince.

The alternative, quasi-fascist England created in the film is realised in impressive detail, with frequent references to real history – and slight distortions of geography: the royal palace has the exterior of St Pancras Station, but, unlike either the station or the real-life Palace, sits on the banks of the Thames; Bankside Power Station (now the Tate Modern art gallery) stands in for the Tower of London; the Royal Family's country retreat is Brighton Pavilion relocated to the seafront. (Olivier had similarly redrawn the map of London in 1955, locating Westminster Abbey next to the Tower.) The social-climbing Woodvilles become Simpsonesque Americans struggling to fit in with a thoroughly decadent British aristocracy; Marlowe's "The Passionate Shepherd" is sung to a tune reminiscent of the work of Glenn Miller; the Yorkist boar's head is displayed on a flag modelled on the swastika; military uniforms are, before

259

Richard's coup (when they become S.S. black), British in their cut, but German grey in colour. The effect is frightening: a vivid reminder of just how easily Britain could have suffered a similar fate to those of her European neighbours.

Comparisons between Richard and Adolf Hitler have a long history. Werner Krauss, himself a Nazi but with occasional differences of opinion with the party hierarchy, used the play as a thinly veiled satire against Goebbels in 1937 (to the delight of Göring); Laurence Olivier, who in his film version modelled the hunchbacked King on Jed Harris, had played a very Hitlerish Richard on stage in 1944; Bertolt Brecht, in his parable on Hitler's rise to power, *The Resistible Rise of Arturo Ui* (written in 1941, though it was not performed until the 1950s), had made frequent reference to *Richard III*. Brecht saw S.A. leader Ernst Röhm as a latter-day Hastings or Buckingham, and Richard's seduction of Anne as a metaphor for the *Anschluss* between Germany and Austria. *Arturo Ui*, with its American gangland setting, makes a particularly interesting point of comparison to this film, in view of the latter's frequent references to the *Godfather* trilogy, *White Heat* (1949), and other organised crime pictures. The objection of some critics, that royal and fascist politics do not mix, ignores the examples of Tsar Boris III of Bulgaria, King Carol II of Romania, and the Regent Paul of Yugoslavia, all of whom overturned constitutional settlements to rule dictatorially in the 1930s.

The look of the film changes subtly as it progresses: the replacement of the grey uniforms with the black garb of Richard's henchmen (the civilian Buckingham – a superbly slimy Jim Broadbent – appearing in the gaudiest uniform of all, a nice reference to the absurd military pretensions of some fascists) is one of the more obvious developments, but almost-recognisable British public buildings are also replaced with what increasingly resembles Nazi and early Soviet architecture. Film and photography are running motifs, creating a theme of imagery that cannot be trusted unless correctly interpreted: Clarence (Nigel Hawthorne) is an amateur photographer, who sees everything but observes nothing.

The cast is uniformly excellent. While, like Olivier's version, the film lacks a Queen Margaret, here many of her best lines have been transferred to Richard's mother (Maggie Smith – younger than two of her three "sons" and only a year older than McKellen, but convincing as the aged Duchess): and, in sharp contrast to the earlier film, it certainly does not lack powerful female presence. Women, indeed, are the mainstay of opposition to this Richard – led by Annette Bening as a formidable Queen Elizabeth, with Kate Steavenson-Payne always in tow as her daughter (who remains offstage in the play, but here is present at every major event). His mother's curse presages his downfall – and his mother is the one person for whose blessing McKellen's Richard really cares; and Elizabeth, by marrying her daughter to Richmond (Dominic West), seals his doom.

Over them all looms McKellen, one of the very few Crookbacks ever to be both convincingly disabled and genuinely threatening in combat – and, unlike Olivier, entirely credible as the plausible charmer the play requires him to be. "Richard III is an actor", as McKellen rightly observed: the audience must believe that he can fool those around him. For the first time in the cinema, we can. It is a great shame that this has been to date McKellen's only Shakespearean role on the big screen. He has played nearly all the great leads on stage, and fortunately television adaptations have preserved his performances as Richard II (1970), Macbeth (1979), Iago (1990), and Lear (2008) – though his *Hamlet* (1970) is currently missing, and *Richard II* has not yet been released on video or DVD.

It is hard not to wish for greater textual fidelity, and the restoration of the many characters missing from this adaptation: but it feels churlish to complain when what we have is such excellent cinema. With a larger budget, Loncraine and McKellen could perhaps have done more: but what they have produced is an important, and thrillingly watchable, anti-fascist statement – and one that oozes style – derived from a great work of drama.

Othello (1995, U.S.A. / U.K., colour)
Directed by Oliver Parker
Starring: Laurence Fishburne, Irène Jacob, Kenneth Branagh, Nathaniel Parker, Michael Maloney
Runtime: 123 minutes

Oliver Parker, who has since become one of British cinema's most energetic and imaginative interpreters of the classics (most notably in his coruscating version of *The Importance of Being Earnest* (2002)), shows little of his later style and sparkle in his rather flat directorial debut. It is well cast – Laurence Fishburne as Othello displays powerful intensity;

Kenneth Branagh, playing Iago as a sort of Elizabethan Flashman, and Michael Maloney, as an uncharacteristically sympathetic Roderigo, have an excellent feel for Shakespeare's language; and Irène Jacob makes a heart-rending Desdemona – but something is missing. Extensive location shooting in Italy, which should at least have made the picture look good, is somewhat undermined by mediocre cinematography and the fact that it largely takes place at night.

Some critics complained about the sex scenes which Parker inserted, but there is nothing offensive or unnecessary about them: he wished to show firstly that Othello and Desdemona had a passionate marriage, and secondly the power of jealousy. (Jacob spends more screen time in bed with Parker's brother Nathaniel as Cassio, in Othello's imagination, than with Fishburne.) Iago's brutal sex with Emilia (Anna Patrick) is similarly necessary to the story Parker wished to tell. Whether any of this is effective or not is another matter – Parker called *Othello* "an erotic thriller"[110]; his version struggles to justify either epithet – but it is easy to understand his motivation.

In fact, those hunting for offence to complain about were barking up the wrong tree: there is little ground here for any reaction stronger than disappointment. The talented cast is wasted; Charlie Mole's score is intrusive and inappropriate (like Parker, with whom he has continued in partnership, Mole has done immeasurably superior work since); and there is scarcely a memorable shot in the entire film.

Love Is All There Is (1996, U.S.A., colour)
Based on *Romeo and Juliet*
Directed by Joseph Bologna and Renée Taylor
Starring: Lainie Kazan, Joseph Bologna, Angelina Jolie, Nathaniel Marston, Renée Taylor
Runtime: 101 minutes / 120 minutes (Netherlands)

Love Is All There Is is a sentimental comic spin on *Romeo and Juliet* from husband-and-wife team Joseph Bologna and Renée Taylor. The feud is updated to the rivalry between two families of Italian caterers on City Island: loud, vulgar, third generation Sicilians, the Capomezzas (Bologna, Lainie Kazan, and Nathaniel Marston); and newly arrived Florentine

---

[110] Quoted by Rosenthal, *100 Shakespeare films*, p. 178.

aristocrats, the Malacicis (Paul Sorvino – who was to play an original text version of what is effectively the same part, Lord Capulet, later that year – Barbara Carrera, and Angelina Jolie). Gina (Jolie) and Rosario (Marston) play Shakespeare's lovers in a church hall production, all stiff costumes, wooden delivery, and fumbled lines: they become lovers for real, then spend the rest of the film quoting the play at each other, while the plot very loosely mirrors it, until the unhappy ending is avoided at the last minute and they get married. (Only one of the parallels has any neatness to it: the film's Paris is not a human rival but the city, to which Gina is to be sent to study ballet.)

There is some strong acting here, in the broad turns of Kazan and Taylor as well as in the somewhat subtler performances of Jolie and Sorvino, two actors who feel above the level of the material throughout: but the humour that the script manages to wring from what one would have thought would be the fertile sources of class conflict, superstition, maternal over-protection, and the antagonism (especially over food) between Northern and Southern Italians is, in the event, mostly feeble. Jeff Beal's confident and character-full Italianate score helps the film to pass, but it is hardly an experience worth repeating.

Tromeo and Juliet (1996, U.S.A., colour)
Based on *Romeo and Juliet*
Directed by Lloyd Kaufman
Starring: Jane Jensen, Will Keenan, Maximillian Shaun
Runtime: 102 minutes (U.S.A.) / 137 minutes (Australia) / 108 minutes (Argentina)

"Parting is such sweet sorrow." – "Yeah, it totally sucks." That's the level of wit in this infantile "comedy" from the downmarket outfit Troma Team. Troma fancy themselves as punk satirists, but in fact make the output of the Wayans Brothers look excessively intellectual. *Tromeo and Juliet* is made by and aimed at people who like to snigger at incest, severed appendages, and domestic abuse (not, I must emphasise, at witty treatments of these subjects – they are presumed to be funny in themselves), and think that setting *Romeo and Juliet* among New York street gangs ("in fair Manhattan, where we lay our scene") is an original idea. Its combination of "gross-out" "humour", gratuitous gore and soft-core pornography is so cack-handedly managed that every element undercuts the others, leaving the film a fetid mess unlikeable even by people who would enjoy its ingredients individually.

The closest it comes to a spark of originality is in including a range of porn titles punning on the plays of Shakespeare (*The Merchant of Penis*, *As You Lick It*); the intelligence of those involved can be judged from the reported fact that screenwriter James Gunn, asked to produce a script in iambic pentameter, simply told the director he had done so, and was believed. (Almost the only speeches to meet the request are those lifted straight from the play.)

I have a strong constitution, but *Tromeo and Juliet* came very close to making me throw up.

Looking For Richard (1996, U.S.A., colour)
Based on *Richard III*
Directed by Al Pacino
Starring: Al Pacino, Kevin Conway, Penelope Allen, Kevin Spacey
Runtime: 112 minutes

When screen legend Al Pacino stepped behind the camera for the first time, the film he had reportedly chosen to make was *Richard III*, starring himself. Whether the reports had been based on a misconception, or whether a straight adaptation really was planned and abandoned, what he eventually produced was something rather different – a curious hybrid between a film of the play and a film about the play, which also tries to explore the relationship of actors and the general public to Shakespeare, particularly in the United States.

Let us address first what we see of the adaptation. Pacino takes the unconventional decision to launch straight into the play, leaving even his cast bewildered about the background to the events. (Before modern productions with programme notes, it was a given that theatrical audiences would have seen the *Henry VI* plays, if indeed they were not being treated to the Colley Cibber version which incorporates large chunks of *Part 3*; most previous films had followed Cibber's lead to minimise confusion.) It seems that this would have been, if not a full text version, something very close to it; Pacino's reverence for Shakespeare could easily, had he made a complete *Richard*, have resulted in a film nearly four hours long.

The film's recreation of fifteenth century England – a dark, Gothic vision of the era – in New York on a micro-budget is impressive, and convinces right up to Bosworth Field (where an ill-advised wide shot lets us see how tiny the opposing armies are: it would have been better, in the absence of large numbers of extras, to have followed Kenneth Branagh's lead in *Henry V* (1989) and stuck to close-ups for the battle scene). The acting is another matter. Pacino had assembled a fine cast, but most show their inexperience with Shakespeare and their discomfort with English accents. A consistent policy on the latter would have helped the film considerably: instead we get some actors strangling their vowels, others managing competently enough, and still more simply not bothering. (An unexpected example of the last group is the otherwise excellent Kevin Spacey – who has elsewhere shown a facility for accents – as the Duke of Buckingham.)

Over Pacino's own performance looms the ghost of Laurence Olivier. The much parodied clipped intonation, exaggerated deformity and demonic characterisation are all in evidence. At times Pacino's native talent struggles out from under this dead weight, but all too seldom. Many of his fans shook their heads sadly and concluded that Shakespeare was a gap in his abilities: they would have to wait eight years for him to prove them spectacularly wrong in *The Merchant of Venice* (2004).

There is, however, no doubting his passion for Shakespeare and for the project, which come across most infectiously in the street scenes of the documentary portion of the film, in which he approaches random punters to discuss the Bard with them. He attempts to broaden the film's remit from Al's Notes on *Richard III* to a more general documentary about William Shakespeare – visiting Stratford, discussing the whole canon and how to act it with John Gielgud and Kenneth Branagh (both of whom make very pertinent points about the entirely unjustified inferiority complex with which American actors tend to approach Shakespeare: apparently it takes Britons to see this), topping and tailing the film with quotes from *The Tempest*. This, however, never quite takes off; part of the problem is the difficulty of tying them back in to the theme of *Richard III*, but more crucial is simple lack of time and space. Perhaps he should have been given a miniseries in which to develop these broader themes. He does, however, succeed in exploring the play as a play and not as a portrait of one character. That, together with the continuous thread of the adaptation, brings the film within the remit of this work, where other documentaries such as Pierre Lasry's *Shylock* (1999) do not belong.

Looking for Richard is undeniably a self-indulgent work, and one that can never quite decide what it is (which is understandable, given that it may not be what it set out to be): but for anybody with an interest in Shakespeare it makes fascinating viewing. Pacino here is on far from his finest form as an actor: but as an enthusiast he cannot be bettered.

Twelfth Night: Or What You Will (1996, U.K. / Republic of Ireland / U.S.A., colour)
A.k.a. *Twelfth Night*
Directed by Trevor Nunn
Starring: Imogen Stubbs, Helena Bonham Carter, Nigel Hawthorne, Ben Kingsley, Mel Smith
Runtime: 134 minutes

Sir Trevor Nunn is one of the U.K.'s most distinguished directors of Shakespeare. On the small screen, if one includes other directors' adaptations of his stage productions, he has given us *Antony and Cleopatra* (1974), *The Comedy of Errors* (1978), *Macbeth* (1979), *Othello* (1990), and *The Merchant of Venice* (2001), all of which rank among the best television adaptations the Bard has ever received. A *Twelfth Night* brought to the silver screen by such a luminary, with a star-studded cast led by his beautiful wife Imogen Stubbs, should have been a delight. The film is, indeed, very far from failure: but it is hard not to be disappointed.

Nunn sets the action in the Edwardian era, in what may be a Balkan Illyria or the Cornish coast where it was largely filmed. This affects the positions and relationships of the characters: Malvolio (Nigel Hawthorne) becomes a butler rather than a steward, a subtle but important downgrading of his status; while Feste (Ben Kingsley) seems to have wandered in from another world – though perhaps that is apt enough.

The strength of the performances varies. Stubbs' sparky Viola and Helena Bonham Carter's needy Olivia cannot be faulted (although the casting of Steven Mackintosh, who does not resemble Stubbs, as Sebastian was a rather eccentric decision: such dissimilarities are conventionally accepted on stage, but not on film); Kingsley's dark, sardonic, misanthropic turn is an unusual but interesting interpretation of the Fool; but Toby Stephens takes Orsino too far over the top, while Sir Toby (Mel Smith) and Sir Andrew (Richard E. Grant, doing his usual foppish thing) are never more than mildly amusing. The saddest surprise is Nigel Hawthorne, who surely had it in him to be a wonderful comic Malvolio: having huffed and spluttered his way in conventional style through the steward's earlier scenes, he is so restrained in the great set pieces that he ends by underplaying the part. One understands that Nunn would wish to keep his star back from the brink of ham, but he has reined him in too far, with the result that the viewer begins to yawn. The sense of boredom is exacerbated by the failure to maintain any evenness of pacing.

It is not hard to see Nunn's purpose: to expose the loneliness of characters who are too often played on the surface only. He and his talented cast achieve this, perhaps too well: one is left feeling that they have lost sight of the comedy along the way. Feste's haunting songs and the other characters' reactions should give us a glimpse into a world of sadness, not drop us there and fail to bring us back.

I first saw this film shortly after watching the Royal Shakespeare Company's touring production of the play, starring Edward Petherbridge. The contrast between the bright, slick stage version and the ponderous film could hardly have been more marked. Nunn and many of his actors were operating well below par when they made this one.

William Shakespeare's Romeo + Juliet (1996, U.S.A., colour)
Directed by Baz Luhrmann
Starring: Leonardo DiCaprio, Claire Danes, Pete Postlethwaite, Miriam Margolyes, Harold Perrineau
Runtime: 120 minutes
Academy Award nominations (1997): Best Art Direction (Catherine Martin, Brigitte Broch)

Luhrmann's dazzling dash through *Romeo and Juliet* was a considerable success at the box office, one of the very few Shakespearean film adaptations ever to break into the lucrative teenage market. (It was, indeed, the first Shakespeare film I saw at the cinema, aged fifteen; being something of a traditionalist at the time, I did not fully appreciate what Luhrmann had achieved.) Many middlebrow critics, however, were eager to dismiss it as M.T.V.-generation trash. They were very wrong.

Although it wears its intelligence lightly, the film is in fact as literate as it is stylish, referencing several of Shakespeare's other plays in billboard slogans or the costumes of guests at the Capulets' ball, and showing the influence at times (particularly in the famous scene in which the lovers, played by Leonardo DiCaprio and Claire Danes, first glimpse one another, through a fish tank: the use of water at critical moments in the plot runs through the film) of Arthur Brooke's 1562 poem from which Shakespeare took the story. (One wonders if the aquatic theme may have been further influenced by the fact that Brooke died by drowning shortly after completing the poem.) The strongest influences, however – openly acknowledged by Luhrmann – are the earlier adaptations *West Side Story* (1961) and Franco Zeffirelli's *Romeo and Juliet* (1968).

The action is moved to the fictional city of Verona Beach, in a lovingly created alternative version of 1990s Florida (all the sets were built specially, so as to keep the look of the movie consistent with Luhrmann's vision); the city is almost Miami, but with parts of Los Angeles, Mexico City, and Rio de Janeiro (whose famous statue of Christ the Redeemer stands above Verona Beach) thrown in, and a police chief who can pronounce sentences of banishment or summary execution – something the viewer never questions, having been by then drawn into Luhrmann's world. The city possesses not only Bardolatrous billboards but ranges of guns with the names of bladed weapons ("Longsword", "Rapier", "Dagger" etc.), and a postage company called Post Haste Dispatch – a witty way of retaining the relevance of archaisms in the text to the modern setting.

As in *West Side Story*, a racial element is introduced, with Anglo Montagues squaring off in Leone-inspired shootouts against Hispanic Capulets, and Mercutio (Harold Perrineau) as a black drug pusher. (Luhrmann's Queen Mab is Ecstasy, or something very similar, a reading that casts the speech in an intriguing new light). Hints dropped by Zeffirelli are enlarged upon – where Michael York and Natasha Parry flirted, the magnificently feline John Leguizamo and Diane Venora leave us in little doubt that Tybalt and Lady Capulet are lovers; where John McEnery implied Mercutio's homosexuality, Perrineau makes him screamingly gay (and all the better for being out: his

Mercutio may be less subtly drawn, but he seems to enjoy life far more than McEnery's version). Even the score lifts elements from Nino Rota's music for the Zeffirelli film.

Much of the cleverness, however, is hardly noticed at first viewing, because the film whips by so fast. Two hours' traffic it may be (it was reported that Luhrmann deliberately edited it to last exactly 120 minutes, so as to live up to the Chorus' promise), but the pace is unrelenting; by the end the viewer is left somewhat out of breath. Luhrmann began by directing television advertisements, a background which leaves many directors with an inability to sit still: but he turns it into a virtue, producing films that dazzle and excite and always repay repeat viewing.

Nor is it fair to allege, as some critics have done, that his direction leaves the actors struggling in its wake. In fact, they are well served, and return the compliment. The closest thing to a weak link in this film is Leonardo DiCaprio – though undeniably intense, he was not in 1996 the strong actor he later matured into, and his understanding of the verse seems limited – but his performance is still creditable enough, while Claire Danes makes a heartbreaking Juliet; an international assembly of veteran character actors gives them excellent support.

It is not without its flaws – some of the textual cuts, for instance, are unnecessary, and one or two word-image juxtapositions intended to make sense of the text verge on the patronising: but overall this is a stunning re-imagining of the story and a brilliantly inventive use of the text.

A Midsummer Night's Dream (1996, U.K., colour)
Directed by Adrian Noble
Starring: Lindsay Duncan, Alex Jennings, Desmond Barrit, Finbar Lynch, Osheen Jones
Runtime: 105 minutes

Adrian Noble's stage production of the *Dream* in the Royal Shakespeare Company's 1994-95 season had been a runaway success. His surreal world of flying umbrellas and randomly appearing doors, peopled by an extremely talented cast, brought alive for audiences the true magic of the play. It is understandable that he decided to create a record of it, and, if made for television as originally planned, this would be a moderately significant document of British theatrical history. But a cinematic release needs to be something more than a record of a stage performance: and this Noble fails to deliver.

He hangs the play on an original conceit: that it is literally a dream, taking place in the mind of a small boy (Osheen Jones) who has fallen into a Lewis Carroll-esque world. But this is all he adds to a film shot entirely in a theatre. The dreamlike (or trip-like) atmosphere is there, certainly, but not in the same measure as in a live performance, where one is accustomed to suspend disbelief and forgive unconvincing effects more readily than when watching a film: seeing the boards of the stage takes us out of Jones' dream and reminds us that we are in fact in Stratford.

That the magic is not quite satisfactory is a serious problem with a production that values the magic above the comedy, as Noble's does. There are smiles here, but few laughs, and the overall result is something not quite fish nor fowl. This is despite the sterling work of Noble's cast, most of them brought over from the stage version. All are strong classical actors from the best R.S.C. tradition, but their talent cannot save a film so unsure of what it wants to be.

This was Noble's first cinematic feature. One gets the strong impression that he had not fully grasped the differences between film and theatre as art forms when he made it. He never repeated the success of his stage *Dream*, and his regime at the R.S.C. ended in failure. Nevertheless, he is a talented theatrical director, and may yet conquer film as well: but at the first attempt he failed to do so.

Hamlet (1996, U.K. / U.S.A., colour)
A.k.a. *William Shakespeare's Hamlet*
Directed by Kenneth Branagh
Starring: Kenneth Branagh, Derek Jacobi, Kate Winslet, Julie Christie, Richard Briers
Runtime: 242 minutes / 150 minutes (cut version)
Academy Award nominations (1997): Best Art Direction (Tim Harvey); Best Costume Design (Alexandra Byrne); Best Original Dramatic Score (Patrick Doyle); Best Screenplay Based on Material Previously Produced or Published (Kenneth Branagh)

Branagh's third and most ambitious Shakespearean outing remains to date the longest film of any of the Bard's works, weighing in at a hefty four hours (with an intermission).

It is, in fact, probably longer than any version produced in the theatre either. There are three texts for *Hamlet*: the laughably corrupt First Quarto ("To be or not to be, aye there's the point"), the more authentic Second Quarto, and the slightly different version that made it to the First Folio. Each of the latter two is missing speeches that the other contains, although no serious scholar doubts that Shakespeare was the sole author of both. Branagh combined them in creating the script for his epic, and the end result earned him (and thus, indirectly, Shakespeare) an Oscar nomination. (At the same Oscars, Patrick Doyle's excellent work in scoring Branagh's films was at last recognised, though sadly not rewarded.)

Olivier (1948) and Zeffirelli (1990) had both, in their different styles, turned the play into a domestic tragedy: but the full text, embracing issues of politics, war, and practically every aspect of the human condition, is much more than that. Branagh became the first Anglophone film director to do full justice to *Hamlet*, and showed that a textually faithful Shakespeare adaptation could make just as great cinema as the pruning-shears approach of Olivier, Zeffirelli, and Welles.

To point up the neglected political aspects, he set the action in the mid nineteenth century, dressing all male characters apart from Hamlet (himself) and his university friends in gaudy Ruritanian military tunics, evoking such upheavals as the Year of Revolutions in 1848 and the Prusso-Danish war of 1864; the map of Northern Europe in this era was, as it is in the play, being redrawn. Fortinbras (Rufus Sewell), frequently cut out altogether in earlier versions, becomes a vitally important figure here – and we are shown the Norwegian assault on Elsinore beginning before Hamlet's duel with Laertes (Michael Maloney) even takes place, reminding us that, whatever happens, the invader will be the winner. (Fortinbras may praise Hamlet in death, but it is difficult to believe – especially given Sewell's cold-blooded characterisation – that he would ever have let him live.) The film ends where it began, at the foot of a statue of King Hamlet (Brian Blessed): but now, the Norwegians are destroying the monument. The obvious reference point in recent history here is the fall of the Soviet Union, but for the cineliterate viewer, this image would also evoke Eisenstein's masterful depiction of the *beginning* of the U.S.S.R. in *Oktyabr* (1928). One despotism is replaced by another, which will fall in its turn.

Many critics carped at Branagh's use of the extended text

271

and its demand for a huge cast to fill minor roles with celebrity cameos, but it is hard to see why. Jack Lemmon as the perturbed Marcellus, Gérard Depardieu as a suave Reynaldo, Richard Attenborough as the English Ambassador, John Mills in a non-speaking role as the spluttering King of Norway, Ken Dodd playing Yorick in a flashback to Hamlet's childhood, are all effective, thanks in large part to Branagh's direction, which never allows star egos to overpower the characters. (Dodd's appearance is especially useful in showing the viewer what Hamlet has lost in a dead man he truly loved – which is more, I have always suspected, than can be said about his father.) Perhaps it was going a little too far to have flashbacks to the fall of Troy while the Player King (Charlton Heston) delivers Aeneas' speech; certainly the feeling on first viewing is that Branagh got carried away, and wanted an excuse to insert John Gielgud (Priam) and Judi Dench (Hecuba) into his picture. Later, however, this vision of the horrors of war becomes chillingly relevant, as Hamlet praises Fortinbras' senseless conflict with Poland, and as the Norwegian despot turns his military might against unprepared Denmark.

The major roles are performed flawlessly. Derek Jacobi brings a deeper and subtler understanding to Claudius than any other interpretation I have seen.[111] This is a Claudius with a conscience, a Claudius who recognises something of himself in his nephew, a Claudius driven not only by ambition but by a genuine love for Gertrude (Julie Christie): when he says "My soul is full of discord and dismay", he means it, and he makes a refreshing change from the two-dimensionally villainous versions of the King we frequently have to endure. Christie herself, who came out of retirement to play the Queen, showed that she was not only still stunningly beautiful in her mid fifties, but still an excellent actress. It is a pity that Branagh's focus at times drove Gertrude into the background, and that his rejection of Oedipal readings reduced Christie's histrionic opportunities, but she nevertheless does more than justice to the part. Kate Winslet – who was cast as Ophelia without an audition, so

---

[111] Jacobi's own performance as Hamlet at the Oxford Playhouse in 1977 had been an inspiration to the young Branagh; he was to reprise the role for the B.B.C. in 1980, in one of the best of the corporation's *Complete Works* series, and to direct Branagh in his first professional appearance as the Prince, in Birmingham in 1988, recorded in the 1990 P.B.S. documentary *Discovering Hamlet*.

impressed had Branagh been by her reading for the part of Elizabeth in *Mary Shelley's Frankenstein* (1994) (which went, in the end, to Helena Bonham Carter) – displays the full range of her talents to astonishing effect. (The setting also allows Branagh to give her a brief death scene modelled on Millais' famous painting.)

Branagh's interpretation of the Prince's relationship with Ophelia was controversial: in what the viewer could interpret as her imagination but is by strong implication (later confirmed by Branagh) a flashback, he shows them in bed together. This recalls the old joke ("Drama student to elderly actor-manager: 'In your opinion, sir, does Hamlet sleep with Ophelia?' – 'Almost invariably'"), but also helps to give an insight into Ophelia's bawdy-filled madness; it is at the very least a valid reading. (It is interesting that the chorus of dispute was aimed only at this area of interpretation and not at the portrayal of the Ghost, who, as depicted by Brian Blessed and his makeup artist, is very possibly the Devil and not the dead King's spirit – which is just as controversial. One gets the feeling that these criticisms had more to do with prudery than with literary opinions.)

Added to these strengths and Doyle's score are Branagh's and cinematographer Alex Thomson's mastery of the camera, and the superb use they make of the exterior of Blenheim Palace (for the provision of which the Duke of Marlborough was rewarded with a minor role as a Norwegian general) and the exquisite interiors in red, black, and white created for the film. Shot entirely in 70mm film (to date the last feature film to use this expensive stock with no admixture of cheaper widths), with much use of the Kubrickian tracking shots of which Branagh is enamoured, the picture is captured in incredible detail. There is only one dud shot – in what has to be the most swashbuckling depiction yet of the final scene, Hamlet throws his rapier like a javelin at Claudius, and for slightly less than a second the camera unconvincingly follows it – in the entire four hours. That is an impressive record.

The distributors' uncertainty about the wisdom of releasing a Shakespearean feature with a four hour runtime persuaded Branagh to create an alternative 150-minute cut; but audiences by and large preferred the longer version. Nevertheless, *Hamlet* underperformed at the box office, and had to rely on video sales to make its money back, which says little for public taste. The sumptuous vision realised here is an achievement fit to rank alongside *Ran* (1985) as one of the best epic interpretations of Shakespeare, if not the best adaptations full stop.

A Thousand Acres (1997, U.S.A., colour)
Based on *King Lear*
Directed by Jocelyn Moorhouse
Starring: Jessica Lange, Michelle Pfeiffer, Jason Robards, Colin Firth, Jennifer Jason Leigh
Runtime: 105 minutes

Jane Smiley's Pulitzer-winning 1991 novel *A Thousand Acres* transferred the story of *King Lear* to modern Iowa to tell it from the elder daughters' point of view. Our narrator is Ginny (Jessica Lange), a childless but mumsy, optimistic, and thoroughly repressed Goneril; Lear (Larry: Jason Robards) is an unstable farmer who sexually abused Ginny and Rose (Michelle Pfeiffer, a bitter Regan figure) in their teens, but remains a pillar of their small community while his daughters are unfairly vilified after losing patience with him. In the novel, which allowed Smiley the freedom to ramble across the themes of *Lear* and to flesh out her alternative cast at her own pace, this conceit was reportedly effective, thought-provoking, and quite moving. On the journey to the screen, however, *A Thousand Acres* lost nearly all its depth and acquired buckets of cheap sentiment in its place.

Laura Jones' two-dimensional screenplay, dealing perfunctorily with key moments in its quest to cram the novel into a film too small to hold it, leaves every character looking selfish, dull, stupid, and utterly unlikeable. The talented cast, all performing better than the script deserves, fail to save the end product from coming across as a feature length soap opera, an effect only exacerbated by Richard Hartley's syrupy score. The film is a travesty of both play and novel.

Macbeth (1997, U.K., colour)
Directed by Jeremy Freeston
Starring: Jason Connery, Helen Baxendale, Graham McTavish, Hildegarde Neil
Runtime: 129 minutes

It is never a good sign when extras have to pay to appear in a film. It is still more ominous when the VHS appears before the picture reaches cinemas. In this case, one would have thought that, after viewing the film on video, somebody would have taken action to prevent its cinematic release; unfortunately, it somehow managed to find a distributor.

Made by the prolific but lacklustre outfit Cromwell Films, *Macbeth*'s publicity proclaimed it the first historically accurate version of the play, "authentically set in eleventh century Scotland". Apart from the fact that the play's plot is a travesty of history, if one is going to make such claims one should avoid opening with shots of the Sutton Hoo helmet (seventh century, and English) and the Lion Rampant banner (the royal arms of Scotland since the late twelfth century, but certainly not in the age of Macbeth). Both predictably became running motifs throughout the film.

These are forgivable faults: but, so far from being the only flaw, the depiction of history is actually one of the least appalling facets of the film. Freeston's direction is shoddy, and the scenes where he inexplicably let actors take over are even worse; the cinematography and sound recording are amateurish at best, more often disgracefully bad; Jason Connery in the title role – which his father had played very well on Canadian television in 1961 – is entirely out of his depth, and Baxendale as Lady Macbeth is little better. There is one single touch of originality in the film: the "is this a dagger" scene is set in a chapel, and the dagger at which Connery grasps is the shadow cast on the ground by a crucifix. If Freeston had displayed a similar level of invention throughout the picture, it would still be badly served Shakespeare and badly made cinema, but it would at least not bore. ·

Cromwell Films have attacked British history and literature in similar style in many other cheap, dull, badly put-together features. Their output (with the single exception of *King Lear* (1999)) is to be avoided.

Kaliyattam (1997, India, colour)
Based on *Othello*
A.k.a. *Play of the God* (U.S.A.)
Directed by Jayaraaj Rajasekharan Nair
Starring: Suresh Gopi, Lal, Manju Warrier
Language: Malayalam
Runtime: 130 minutes

The title of *Kaliyattam* declares its principal motif: the traditional southern Indian dance drama which was one of the precursors of modern *kathakali*. Set in Kerala in a vaguely defined distant past (as it happens, this form developed at precisely the period when Shakespeare was writing in England), the film turns Othello into Kannan Perumalayan (Suresh Gopi), an ageing *kaliyattam* troupe leader. The play is followed pretty much scene by scene, with only the smallest changes of detail necessary to accommodate cultural differences.

Gopi, and Manju Warrier as a sweet Thamara (Desdemona), perform strongly, but the film is dominated by Lal as Paniyan, the Iago figure. Able to switch instantaneously between stony-faced impassivity, hysterical self-pity, and childish glee at a plot gone right, Paniyan is terrifying in his unpredictability, and Lal's performance is breathtaking – all the more so considering that this was his first screen acting part; hitherto he had been known principally as a writer and director.

Even he, however, yields pride of place to the wondrously varied and beautiful scenery of Kerala – mountain, jungle, river, and dry plain alike are lovingly photographed by M. J. Radhakrishnan, so that the region itself is as much a character as any of the human players – and to the *kaliyattam* sequences. The insistent power of Gautam Mukherjee's music, the feverish atmosphere of the dances, entirely grips the viewer. At times the red-clad, masked dancers symbolise the state of Perumalayan's mind: in the scene corresponding to Act IV Scene 1, the maddened dancer rises from a collapse to see his colleagues looming threateningly over him, ranged along an outcrop of rock: and, in a neat reference to the long Western tradition of blackface Othellos, Perumalayan makes his first and last appearances with his face entirely painted. In one especially potent sequence, leading up to Thamara's murder, the film cuts back and forth between her singing a haunting Malayalam air substituted for the Willow Song, and Perumalayan lying on his back as an unseen assistant painstakingly applies his full, extraordinary, *kaliyattam* make-up in red, gold, and black.

Kaliyattam can move a little slowly at times, and has not quite the flair and imagination of Vishal Bharadwaj's *Omkara* (2006), but it remains a finely performed visual feast.

Shakespeare in Love (1998, U.S.A. / U.K., colour)

Based on *Romeo and Juliet* and *Twelfth Night*
Directed by John Madden
Starring: Joseph Fiennes, Gwyneth Paltrow, Geoffrey Rush, Colin Firth, Judi Dench
Runtime: 122 minutes
Academy Awards (1999): Best Picture; Best Actress in a Leading Role (Gwyneth Paltrow); Best Actress in a Supporting Role (Judi Dench); Best Art Direction (Martin Childs, Jill Quertier); Best Costume Design (Sandy Powell); Best Original Musical or Comedy Score (Stephen Warbeck); Best Screenplay Written Directly for the Screen (Marc Norman, Tom Stoppard)
Academy Award nominations: Best Director (John Madden); Best Actor in a Supporting Role (Geoffrey Rush); Best Cinematography (Richard Greatrex); Best Film Editing (David Gamble); Best Makeup (Lisa Westcott, Veronica Brebner); Best Sound (Robin O'Donoghue, Dominic Lester, Peter Glossop)

John Madden's delightfully erudite comedy (co-written by Tom Stoppard) became the surprise Oscar-sweeper of 1998/9. The story of a block-stricken Shakespeare attempting to write *Romeo and Ethel the Pirate's Daughter* had spent many years in pre-production, and at one point Julia Roberts had been cast as the female lead Viola de Lesseps (our Juliet / Viola figure in a plot which combines *Romeo and Juliet* with *Twelfth Night*, the conceit being that the events of the film inspired both plays – a satire on the so-called "biographical fallacy"). Given Roberts' frankly limited range and her poor record with accents, we can be glad that the part eventually went to Gwyneth Paltrow.

Original screenwriter Marc Norman had been working on the script for some years when Stoppard came on board, and noticed that Norman's plot (quite coincidentally) bore a resemblance to the whimsical 1944 novel *No Bed For Bacon*, by Caryl Brahms and S. J. Simon. Stoppard obtained a copy of *No Bed For Bacon*, and set about making sure that the film did not duplicate it too closely – while, at the same time, adding a number of knowing nods to moments in the novel. Later accusations of plagiarism were unjustified: Norman had evolved his plot independently. The publishers of *No Bed For Bacon* subsequently cashed in on the film's success by re-releasing it with the subtitle "A Story of Shakespeare and Lady Viola in Love". (It is true that Norman's heroine Belinda became Viola only when Stoppard joined the writing team, but this was because the latter pointed out that the name Belinda did not exist

277

before the Restoration period.)

Stoppard's erudition frightened the studio: would the relatively obscure references to the works of Marlowe (Rupert Everett) and Webster (Joe Roberts) with which he crowded the screenplay frighten off the punters? They need not have worried. The wit of the writers, charm and charisma of the cast, and detailed realisation of a semi-fantastical Elizabethan world, ensured that the film was a runaway hit, and it was well repaid for wearing its intelligence on its sleeve. It did not hurt it that more than half the dialogue is actually by Shakespeare, with much of the film taken up with rehearsals and performance of *Romeo and Juliet*, and frequent references to and quotations from other plays.

As a depiction of the workings of the London theatre in the 1590s, the film is far from accurate: but in its portraits of the principal personalities involved – badgered businessman Philip Henslowe (Geoffrey Rush), egotistical star Ned Alleyn (Ben Affleck), and the rest – it both rings true to any student of the era and accurately echoes characters of the modern film and theatrical worlds: no doubt part of the reason for its appeal to Academy voters.

At its centre are Fiennes and Paltrow, giving passionate performances as Shakespeare / Orsino / Romeo and Viola / Juliet, and trading Stoppardian witticisms with as fine a supporting cast as could be assembled. (The film was also the best possible reply to those still maintaining that Ben Affleck could not act: under Madden's direction he performs strongly, and his English accent, like Paltrow's, is flawless. Affleck has perhaps suffered from weaker writing and direction elsewhere.)

Whether it deserved to do quite so well at the Oscars when up against more heavyweight films such as *Elizabeth* and *Saving Private Ryan* is debateable: but there is no disputing that *Shakespeare in Love* is a triumph, and a loving tribute to the Bard.

King Lear (1999, U.K., colour)
Directed by Brian Blessed
Starring: Brian Blessed, Hildegarde Neil, Mark Burgess, Philippa Peak, Caroline Lennon
Runtime: 190 minutes

For this *Lear*, the usually unimpressive Cromwell Films worked together with LaMancha Productions, which may go some way to explaining why it is so much more watchable than *Macbeth* (1997) – or, indeed, any other Cromwell picture it has been my misfortune to see.

Brian Blessed, a veteran actor who had in recent years become a successful theatre director, took on (allegedly after quarrelling with the director originally assigned) the considerable challenge of directing himself in what is widely considered one of the most difficult parts ever written. His only previous experience behind the camera was in directing the Witches' scenes in *Macbeth*, which are static in the extreme: but that fault does not survive into *Lear*, whose direction may be slightly uncinematic but rests on strong theatrical foundations. Appropriately so, since it was largely from the theatre that Blessed drew his classically trained cast, probably the best a Cromwell film has ever had. Some directorial touches are especially neat: the "cliffs" scene, for instance, is shot in such a fashion that the audience does not see until Gloucester (Robert Whelan) actually jumps that he is *not* going to fall to his death. (A similar effect would, of course, have been achieved in the Jacobean theatre, whose lack of scenery would leave the audience as dependent as Gloucester on Edgar's false description of the scene.)

This is not to say that the film is without its faults. Chris Weaver's cinematography never rises above mediocrity; the editing (by Chris Gormlie) is incompetent, the continuity often wrecked by Gormlie's inability to remember whether it is supposed to be day or night; and period sense is thin on the ground. Blessed chose to return the play to its roots in pagan Celtic legend, referring to the celebrated epigram that calls *Lear* "the great Stonehenge of the mind":[112] but here, ancient costumes and war paint jostle with early medieval armour and late medieval castles, while Druidic sacrifices mix with crosses on shields and wall hangings. The farmland and Forestry Commission property used in the outdoor scenes is far too tame to belong to the ancient world (and tyre tracks are visible at one point); the French forces carry fleur-de-lys banners, and Goneril (Caroline Lennon) has tablecloths in her castle's dining hall.

Any *Lear*, however, stands or falls not by production design or editing, but by the central performance; and here

---

[112] Attributed to Samuel Johnson, but apparently a slight misquotation of G. K. Hunter in his 1972 edition.

Blessed delivers. His King is an extraordinary turn, strongly reminiscent of his portrayal of the last years of the Emperor Augustus in *I, Claudius* (TV, 1976) – albeit with rather more hair. By turns playful, forgetful, bullying, and hysterical, he shows from the first a man who has never been a good father but was once a great ruler, now in the grip of a mental decline which he himself recognises – his "let me not be mad" has a heart-breaking vulnerability to it. His early explosions follow a pattern: dangerous calm erupts into appalling violence, followed by icy cruelty, the collapse of a mind played out with the whole body: but this Lear also dances on the table like a happy child while his cheering knights chant his name. It must be plausible that the King is both hated by his family and loved by his followers, and Blessed is one of very few Lears to make it so. One of his boldest decisions was his handling of the "Blow, wind, and crack your cheeks" speech. Conventionally taken as the moment at which Lear finally loses his reason, this is usually played in a manner perfectly suited to Blessed's mode of acting – but he here rejects histrionics, and instead stands stock-still in the rain, delivering the speech slowly, in voiceover, with a terrible gentleness. It is an extraordinarily effective touch.

Supporting Blessed throughout is his wife Hildegarde Neil, as the wisest Fool in heathendom. It is not Neil but the Fool himself who seems to be forgetting that he is a jester: "Thou shouldst not have been old until thou hadst been wise" is delivered entirely seriously and with a deep tenderness. Instead of disappearing halfway through, Neil is present – reclothed, like Lear himself, in white – when the King awakens, and speaks several of the Doctor's lines, thus reinforcing her position as Lear's guardian angel: and, as the film ends with Lear's funeral, she speaks the Prophecy of Merlin from the Folio text, a speech which is almost invariably cut out of the play but which seems to fit here – better, perhaps, than where Shakespeare placed it. The effect is not only to banish the despair that usually accompanies the end of *Lear*, but to return to the pagan theme which was present in sinister form at the beginning of the film (when masked Druids slaughtered a goat during a lunar eclipse) and to render it curiously uplifting.

The whole is excellently supported by the haunting Celtic music of Paul Farrer (strongly influenced by James Horner's award-winning score for *Braveheart* (1995)): and the end result is a film which, while severely hampered by its small budget and dragged down by a Cromwell Films art team, is strongly directed and showcases some magnificent acting. It is unfortunate that Blessed has not continued as a director; but lovers of Shakespeare can still be thankful, despite William Houston's creditable efforts as the Prince in the former, that Cromwell's execrable *Hamlet* (2003) went straight to video, and their rumoured *Henry V* was never made.

Makibefo (1999, U.K., black and white)
Based on *Macbeth*
Directed by Alexander Abela
Starring: Martin Zia, Noeliny Dety, Gilbert Laumord, Jean-Noël
Language: Malagasy / English
Runtime: 73 minutes

Having failed to get any of his projects made in the U.K., Alexander Abela travelled in 1998 to Faux-Cap at the southern tip of Madagascar, with a crew of one (Jeppe Jungersen), to make a version of *Macbeth* set among the Antandroy people of the remote cape. With little experience and less money, and with a cast who not only lacked experience but had in some cases never seen a film, it was an extraordinarily ambitious plan: but, in the event, it paid off.

The life of the Antandroy is such that the scale of the story is easily contracted: the realm of Scotland becomes a small Malagasy fishing village, ruled by a chieftain with absolute power. In this context, the opening battle becomes the tracking down of a single fugitive standing in for Cawdor (Kidoure: Boniface); the Weird Sisters become a witch doctor (Victor Raobelina); the murder of Banquo-figure Bakoua (Randina Arthur) is intercut with the sacrifice of a zebu ox in celebration of Makibefo's (Martin Zia) coronation, the most spectacular of many recreations of traditional Malagasy rituals. At the climax, Makibefo brandishes the beast's severed head aloft, foreshadowing his own death. The sea, the livelihood of the tribe, is audible almost constantly in the background, mingling with Malagasy music; it is by sea that successful fugitives, unlike the hapless Kidoure who fled over the dunes, escape, Makidofy (Macduff: Jean-Noël) actually witnessing the murder of his family when he glances back from his boat; and it is by sea that Malikomy (an unusually violent Malcolm: Bien Rasoanan Tenaina) returns with his followers for a battle fought on the shore, dispensing with Birnam Wood.

The Malagasy dialogue, though occasionally reflecting the play, is largely spare and functional; Gilbert Laumord, the only professional actor in the cast, acts as narrator, introducing the piece and reading passages of Shakespeare's text as voiceovers in English. Every performance is naturalistic and understated; Abela's black and white cinematography superbly captures the stark beauty of Faux-Cap's gleaming white sands, and its crispness is complemented by that of Jungersen's sound recording. The film is an entire success, and deserves to be much more celebrated.

Macbeth-Sangrador (1999, Venezuela, black and white)
Based on *Macbeth*
A.k.a. *Sangrador, Bleeder*
Directed by Leonardo Henríquez
Language: Spanish
Runtime: 89 minutes / 86 minutes
Not seen by current writer

Macbeth-Sangrador sets the Macbeth story among bandits in Venezuela *circa* 1900, with the slight twist that Macbeth figure (Max: Daniel Alvarado) begins as an outsider drawn into the criminal world, so that Duran, the film's Duncan, is responsible for beginning the process of his corruption. Karina Gómez played Max's wife.

Macbeth in Manhattan (1999, U.S.A., colour)
Based on *Macbeth*
Directed by Greg Lombardo
Starring: Gloria Reuben, David Lansbury, Nick Gregory, John Glover, Harold Perrineau
Runtime: 97 minutes

Greg Lombardo reportedly based *Macbeth in Manhattan* on his own early experiences on the New York theatre scene. If this is so, then every lazy stereotype that infests films about actors is alive and well and living in New York City. The harassed, over-earnest director (John Glover), the self-pitying artistic martyr (David Lansbury), the egotistical star who can't act (Nick Gregory), and the predatory gay veteran (Christopher McCann), are here painted in strokes so broad as to go beyond even caricature.

The situation is simple enough: an ambitious actor cast as Macbeth (Max, played by Lansbury) is demoted to Macduff and replaced with a soap star (William: Gregory), whose subsequent affair with Max's girlfriend Claudia (Gloria Reuben, also playing Lady Macbeth) intensifies the jealousies in the cast until they spill into murder. The film's opening credits, in which bagpipes are played over footage of Manhattan street scenes, gives fair warning of how heavy-handed the attempts to link the plot of the play to the offstage sexual politics will be: thus, the affair becomes for Claudia / Lady Macbeth the murder of Duncan (Lombardo even intercuts a scene of Claudia showering after learning how little William cares for her with the sleepwalking scene), and for Max the equivalent to Macduff's bereavement. The end is heavily foreshadowed by much talk of the curse alleged to afflict the play, an example of its malevolence when William has a near-miss accident onstage, and a fantasy sequence in which Max becomes Macbeth and stabs the sleeping William: it is, therefore, no surprise at all when Max restages the accident, killing William and reclaiming both Claudia and the lead role, only to be confronted by William's ghost (in exactly the same makeup as Banquo (John Elsen)) on the opening night.

Throughout the picture, everybody constantly tells each other what great actors they all are. In fact, not one of them is up to *Macbeth*; William, at least, is supposed to be bad, but Gregory so overplays the soap star's lack of talent as to make it utterly implausible that he could ever have been cast. Harold Perrineau, as a *Henry V*-style Chorus filling in the story of the play for the audience in a strange mix of ghetto language and Shakespearean quotations, is operating on a plane so superior to the rest of the cast that he does not seem to belong in this film at all.

The production itself is of a standard that would disgrace a village hall, let alone the Cherry Lane Theatre (where it is set and was largely filmed): but its amateurishness is as nothing compared with the ill-advised sequences in which the actors imagine themselves inhabiting their roles for real in eleventh century Scotland. These resemble nothing so much as the cheapest fantasy serials; the costumes and sets are even cheesier than William's seduction technique. The comic elements are handled slightly better, but it is never possible to be entirely sure that the comedy is intentional.

The sadly wasted Perrineau is the only real attraction to this slight, unmeritable film.

10 Things I Hate About You (1999, U.S.A., colour)
Based on *The Taming of the Shrew*
Directed by Gil Junger
Starring: Julia Stiles, Heath Ledger, Larisa Oleynik, Joseph Gordon-Levitt, David Krumholtz
Runtime: 97 minutes

Around the end of the twentieth century, there briefly flourished a curious trend for turning literary classics into American high school movies. Thus *Emma* became *Clueless* (1995), *Les Liaisons Dangereuses* became *Cruel Intentions* (1999), and *The Taming of the Shrew* was loosely adapted into *10 Things I Hate About You* (1999).

The film's chief problem is that it is never quite sure whether it wants to be an ordinary teen comedy whose plot happens to have a good pedigree, or to satirise those comedies. The fact that so many of the characters are walking clichés of the genre – Kate (Kat Stratford, played by Julia Stiles) becomes the prickly alleged feminist; Petruchio (Patrick Verona: Heath Ledger) the bad boy with a good heart; Bianca (Larisa Oleynik) the spoilt princess; Gremio / Hortensio (Joey Donner: Andrew Keegan) the egomaniacal rich kid; Tranio (Michael: David Krumholtz) the fast-talking, nerdy guardian angel; Baptista (Walter: Larry Miller) the uptight father – would suggest the latter, if it were not for the fact that any sense of irony makes only sporadic appearances.

The film is not unintelligent: it is peppered with Shakespearean quotations, and it is a shared love of the Bard that lets Michael finally find a girlfriend; the screenplay's wit occasionally rises above the normal level of teen comedies; but the adaptors have had a hard time updating some parts of the story. Petruchio's mercenary motive becomes a bribe from Joey, which in turn becomes the guilty secret that teen movies demand the hero conceals from his girlfriend until ten minutes from the end, so that he can be dumped and then forgiven – yet another bow before the altar of cliché. The relationship between the leads is never that of Kate and Petruchio: instead it alternates between quick-fire insults and rather cloying sweetness. It also strains plausibility that Patrick, having been chosen to woo Kat because of his fearsome reputation, should so quickly be revealed to be such a thoroughly nice person.

In other words, this *is* a high school movie, and carries with it all that that implies – including a pop-driven soundtrack that mistakenly thinks itself cool. It may rise above the run-of-the-mill from time to time, but it never escapes the confines of its genre. More literate teenagers may enjoy it, but it is not really fare for adults.

A Midsummer Night's Dream (1999, Italy / U.K. / U.S.A., colour)
A.k.a. *Sogno di una notte di mezza estate* (Italy); *William Shakespeare's A Midsummer Night's Dream* (U.S.A.)
Directed by Michael Hoffman
Starring: Kevin Kline, Rupert Everett, Michelle Pfeiffer, Stanley Tucci, Calista Flockhart
Runtime: 116 minutes

Hoffman's star-studded *Dream*, set in Tuscany *circa* 1900, is a strange beast. Shakespearean veteran and regular Hoffman collaborator Kevin Kline shines as Bottom, but most of the rest of the cast feels out of place. Rupert Everett, as Oberon, plays Rupert Everett, and overplays him at that; Stanley Tucci, though an extremely talented actor, would never have been an appropriate Puck, and at nearly forty was perhaps a little too old for the part anyway; Calista Flockhart whines her way through Helena's lines, destroying the sympathy the character should receive. Even Anna Friel, for most of the film an excellent Hermia, lets her accent slip back to her native Lancashire once or twice.

This is not to say that it is all bad. The period analogue works, even if there are occasional anachronisms (the opera tunes that everybody walks around humming were several decades old by 1900, and hardly at the height of their popularity; while bicycles with lights and long-playing records were still in the future), and even if Hoffman fails to make any point about the relevance of the text to that particular era. The conceit of modelling the fairies on figures from Greco-Roman mythology is an effective one; the costumes and gorgeous Tuscan scenery are well served by rich photography; the play's sexual undertones are competently brought out; even the computer effects, though recognisable as such and a little primitive, are not embarrassingly bad. And, anachronistic or not, the running themes of opera and bicycles are certainly well handled. Little touches such as having the mechanicals' rivals apparently staging *Othello* also helped.

And yet... and yet. *A Midsummer Night's Dream* is a comedy, and, played well, can be hilarious. The movie, quite simply, lacks laughs – though it is clearly seeking them. Hoffman's direction drains the humour from practically every scene: even the play within the play, which has had audiences in stitches every time I have seen it live, falls flat. The end result is a film that is easy on the eye, but hollow.

Midsummer (1999, U.S.A., colour)
Based on *A Midsummer Night's Dream*
A.k.a. *A Midsummer Night's Dream* (working title)
Directed by James Kerwin
Starring: Domenica Cameron-Scorsese, Ashley Wood, Bruce DuBose, Renner St John, Arthur Morton
Runtime: 18 minutes

Midsummer is not *A Midsummer Night's Dream*. Set among the young and wealthy in modern Texas, it contains only snatches of the play's text – and, despite opening narration that outlines the backstory, little enough of its plot, the mechanicals in particular being sidelined to the point of invisibility. (Possibly they would have had a larger role, and the story would have been clearer, if the picture had been finished, instead of ending with a "To Be Continued" caption which was never fulfilled. But what there is contains so little dialogue, and that so chopped and shifted about, as to make this unlikely.) The film is best considered less as an adaptation than as a new work of art inspired by the *Dream*, in the manner of Fuseli's paintings or Mendelssohn's overture – which is put to effective use in the opening of the film, played under a busy and finely choreographed garden party scene.

Shot mostly on location in the Dallas area, the film is visually very fine, greens, blacks, whites, and creams predominating in a vision that drips mystery and magic; the concept of love-in-idleness as a designer drug (handled far more imaginatively here than in the DTV movie *Midsummer Night's Rave* (2002)) adds to the sense of disorientation and unreality. Astrological and tarot symbols crop up regularly, even in the configuration of lights in a nightclub toilet; gothic-looking fairies stalk the streets and woods in shimmering black; and a segue from Mendelssohn to Depeche Mode is carried off without seeming incongruous.

The actors are somewhat secondary to director Kerwin's conception, but Domenica Cameron-Scorsese nevertheless manages to deliver a moving performance as Hermia with only fragments of her dialogue intact, while Bruce DuBose makes a fearsome Oberon. The real stars, however, remain the art team. One can only wish that they could have afforded to make *Midsummer* at feature length.

Let the Devil Wear Black (1999, U.S.A., colour)
Based on *Hamlet*
Directed by Stacy Title
Starring: Jonathan Penner, Mary-Louise Parker, Jamey Sheridan, Jacqueline Bisset, Jonathan Banks
Runtime: 91 minutes

"So long? Nay then, let the devil wear black, for I'll have a suit of sables. O heavens! Die two months ago and not forgotten yet? Then there's hope a great man's memory may outlive his life half a year." ~ *Hamlet*, Act III, Scene 2

"Something is rotten in the City of Angels" ~ tagline to *Let the Devil Wear Black*

As both title and tagline display, this film wears its Bardic debts on its sleeve. However, although the plot is broadly that of *Hamlet* moved to the interface between the property business and the underworld in modern Los Angeles, and central character Jack could represent one (rather shallow) reading of the Prince, few of the other characters have much in common with their originals. Claudius (Carl: Jamey Sheridan) is now a grinning foolish-cunning spiv one step short of an *idiot savant*; Ophelia (Julia: Mary-Louise Parker) is a whiny student, far too similar to Jack / Hamlet himself; Horatio (Satch: Jonathan Banks) a gangster, motivated not by friendship, but by loyalty to the son of his slain capo. Only Polonius (Sol: Philip Baker Hall) remains something approximating to the Lord Chamberlain of the play: a mix of loving father, forgetful half-dotard, and corrupt, conspiratorial minister.

Penner, who wrote the screenplay, tried to remould the story in the light of *fin-de-siècle* nihilism. Unfortunately, what he produced was a largely flat and uninteresting mess, with gaping plot holes (Julia's death does not appear to be suicide, but is

287

never explained: the only people likely to murder her are the Rosencrantz and Guildenstern figures (Randall Batinkoff and Norman Reedus), who die before they have a chance) and only the occasional spark from the dialogue. The delivery, especially by Penner as the childish, self-obsessed Jack, is equally atonal. Jim Whitaker's cinematography, attempting to evoke urban gloom and isolation, succeeds merely in leaving the screen so black the action is often impossible to follow.

Overall, what strikes one most about *Let the Devil Wear Black* is that it is a singularly pointless film. It fails to say anything new about *Hamlet*, make any original use of the material, or even to entertain; and its departures from the play tie it in knots from which only incoherence emerges.

Titus (1999, Italy / U.S.A., colour)
Directed by Julie Taymor
Starring: Anthony Hopkins, Jessica Lange, Harry J. Lennix, Alan Cumming, Angus Macfadyen
Runtime: 162 minutes
Academy Award nominations (2000): Best Costume Design (Milena Canonero)

Titus Andronicus was all but written out of the canon between the Puritan closure of the theatres in 1642 and Peter Hall's famous 1955 production at the Shakespeare Memorial Theatre, starring Laurence Olivier.[113] It took until 1999 to reach cinemas: fortunately, Christopher Dunne's atrocious "video nasty" travesty, featuring some of the worst acting ever committed to film, failed to find a theatrical distributor, meaning that Julie Taymor's infinitely superior version was the first to hit the big screen. Taymor, like the play, was a relative stranger to the world of the cinema: but she brought to it as weird and wonderful a vision as this extraordinary work requires.

Taymor may have taken her cue from a contemporary illustration of an early performance of *Titus* in Shakespeare's day, which shows the characters in a mish-mash of Roman, Elizabethan, and fantasy costumes. Like *Hamlet*, the play has no

---

[113] The first great black classical actor, Ira Aldridge, created a heavily bowdlerised version in 1849 to allow himself to play Aaron, a part in which he enjoyed great success; but this was the only major production in 300 years.

identifiable historical setting: the Rome of this non-time combines elements of Republic, Principate, Dominate, and even the age of mythology: and so, logically enough, Taymor set her film (made in Italy and Croatia) outside historical time. The landscape is littered with ruins both Roman and modern; the Imperial dwelling is set in Mussolini's pseudo-classical headquarters; Titus and other military characters begin in third century Roman armour, civilians dress in vaguely modern suits with 1930s touches, while non-Romans are often clad as if for a science fiction film. (In-jokes abound too: the colours appropriated by the parties supporting Saturninus (Alan Cumming) and Bassianus (James Frain) are in fact those of modern Rome's two principal football teams.) Bizarrely, this mix – into which Taymor also stirs the surreal, partly computer-animated sequences which she dubbed "Penny Arcade Nightmares" – works, the disparate elements of costume and design being held together by a rigidly observed colour scheme: black, white, red, gold, and silver dominate the screen, while other colours are muted or excluded.

Like Adrian Noble in *A Midsummer Night's Dream* (1996), Taymor has set the play inside the fertile mind of a dreaming boy – even casting the same young actor, Osheen Jones, who played the boy in Noble's film. One cannot envy Jones his dreams, colourful though they undoubtedly are. Unlike Noble, however, Taymor brings Jones into the action as Titus' grandson (one of the few characters to survive the ultimate bloodbath). This is possibly the only approach to take with this play. Veering between high tragedy, preposterous melodrama, and surreal black comedy, it could never be plausible in an authentically realised historical setting, and Shakespeare has in any case avoided giving it one.

Taymor's direction and Felliniesque sensibilities are far from wasted on her talented cast: Anthony Hopkins, who found the experience so stressful that he nearly retired from acting as a result (but, fortunately, thought better of it), makes a strong and sympathetic Titus; Jessica Lange an at once regal, sexy and viperous Tamora; Harry J. Lennix, who had played Aaron on stage in New York and lobbied for the part, such a gleefully villainous Moor that one cannot help but enjoy his ingenious evil – and admire him when he rises to nobility in defence of his son. Cumming's Saturninus was found by some critics to be excessively camp, but I thought it a fine portrayal of a spoiled, insecure, mentally disturbed and sexually confused autocrat. Laura Fraser's lovely, tragic Lavinia and Colm Feore's rendition of Marcus as the only sane man in a world gone mad provide strong support; and over it all plays a memorably powerful score by Taymor's partner Elliot Goldenthal, whose themes range over as many styles and periods as the costumes, without ever once becoming incongruous.

At the end of the film, after the climactic bloodbath, we return to the Colosseum, where we began – in Taymor's words, "the original theatre of violence".[114] There, Lucius (Angus Macfadyen) proclaims his rule, and the picture closes with Jones walking into the sunset carrying Aaron and Tamora's infant son – a symbol at the last of hope for reconciliation. Shakespeare leaves the fate of Aaron's child open-ended: in many productions he is killed, and Taymor's 1994 stage version had kept the ambiguity of the text: but Macfadyen convinced her that Lucius, for all his capacity for cruelty, was a man of his word. Having sworn to do the child no harm, he would keep that oath: and that he does saves the film from despair.

Like any *Titus*, this is only for viewers with strong stomachs: but it will repay their tolerance. Taymor has turned one of Shakespeare's least performed plays into an inventive, original and beautiful film, and is to be applauded for it.

Hamlet (2000, U.S.A., colour)
Directed by Michael Almereyda
Starring: Ethan Hawke, Kyle MacLachlan, Diane Venora, Bill Murray, Julia Stiles
Runtime: 112 minutes

Almereyda's *Hamlet* transferred the action of the play to contemporary New York, setting it against the machinations of the Denmark and Norway Corporations in and around the Elsinore Hotel: effectively, attaching the conceit of *Hamlet liikemaailmassa* (1987) to the original text, just as *William Shakespeare's Romeo + Juliet* (1996) drew on *West Side Story* (1961). It is an interesting idea, approached with considerable inventiveness (though nods to – or, if one is feeling uncharitable, thefts from – *Hamlet* (1996) and *Romeo + Juliet* are in evidence): but ultimately he failed to carry it off.

---

[114] DVD commentary.

Ethan Hawke's woolly-hatted Generation X Hamlet is a film student, and the play to catch the conscience of the King is a silent video. Film and photographic images are running themes – the encounter with the Ghost is caught on a security camera; Ophelia's flowers are in fact Polaroid snaps (cf. the Zeffirelli and Branagh versions of the play – none of them uses real flowers). So far, so good, despite the necessary cuts to the dialogue: but from the beginning Almereyda must ask us to accept the implausible. A company director is "the King", his wife "the Queen" and his son "my lord"; the director's failure to explain this convincingly is ominous.

Sometimes, too, he overplays his motifs: having Ophelia (Julia Stiles) gaze into a swimming pool while Polonius (Bill Murray) is nattering, foreshadowing her death, was a good idea, but having her already imagine drowning herself was labouring the point – and then to drown her in a similar pool, thus unnecessarily losing Gertrude's beautiful speech, was surely a mistake. But this quibble pales beside the gaping holes in the re-plotting.

That Hamlet overhears Claudius (Kyle MacLachlan) at prayer by posing as his chauffeur is a nice touch: but then he leaves Claudius in the car and goes straight up to Gertrude's room. How he imagines his uncle could have got behind the arras is quite inexplicable: Claudius is the one person who clearly *cannot* be the eavesdropper. The letter which Claudius sends to his English subordinate is (unnecessarily incriminatingly) stored on disk. Hamlet is shown hacking into the file to change the text of the instructions – but then he brings the disk back to New York with him, because he brings the letter back in the play. How, then, do Rosencrantz and Guildenstern deliver the message that condemns them?

The most ham-fisted piece of updating in the whole film, however, is the fencing match. Disputes about who hit whom are rather pointless when the antagonists are rigged up to buzzers which keep an accurate tally; there is no unbated foil; and the plot so subtle "that even his mother shall encharge the practice / And call it accident" is to pull out a gun and blow Hamlet away in front of the whole court. Very convincing.

Does the acting, then, redeem the film? Sadly, the answer must be no. Hawke mooches around a video store, mumbling "To be or not to be" and generally failing to leave any clear impression on the viewer: this is Almereyda's fault and not

Hawke's. One gets the distinct impression that the director was so busy trying to be clever that he completely forgot about actually directing: all the actors involved have displayed considerable talent elsewhere, but here are like puppets with cut strings.

To attempt another Hamlet so soon after Zeffirelli and Branagh was always going to be a risk: and in this case it backfired badly on Almereyda. The film is intermittently interesting, but ultimately a severe disappointment.

Love's Labour's Lost (2000, France / U.K. / Canada, colour)
A.k.a. *Peines d'amour perdues* (Canada: French title / France)
Directed by Kenneth Branagh
Starring: Alessandro Nivola, Alicia Silverstone, Kenneth Branagh, Natascha McElhone, Nathan Lane
Runtime: 93 minutes

In 1998, with three excellent Bardic adaptations under his belt, Kenneth Branagh formed the Shakespeare Film Company to make three more. In the event, however, the critical and commercial failure of the first, *Love's Labour's Lost*, scuppered the company, meaning that his *As You Like It* (2006) and *Macbeth* (t.b.a.) had to be postponed.

Taking his cue from Harley Granville Barker's remark that the play is "never very far from the formalities of song and dance"[115], Branagh took the audacious decision to turn it into a musical in the vein of Hollywood toe-tappers of the Thirties and Forties, and accordingly moved the action to the eve of World War Two – which not only suits the style of the adaptation and brings out the play's Wodehousean elements, but is also the most recent period in which its premises can be easily made credible in a Western European setting. Taking precisely the opposite approach to that he had with his gargantuan (but excellent) *Hamlet* (1996), he filleted the text until only a small fraction of the actual play was left, leaving room for the songs and filling in plot (such as it is) with jocular faux-newsreel footage narrated by himself in an uncannily accurate take-off of genuine British newsreels of the period. (One can hardly bring this particular play to a broad audience without major cuts; it

---

[115] Granville Barker, Harley, *Prefaces to Shakespeare: Volume 2* (London, 1958), p. 442.

has been argued that it was never performed for the groundlings in Shakespeare's own day, and this is the only feature film yet made of it, although an American production is reportedly planned in 2011.)

The idea is not a bad one: but the result, while by no means as terrible as many critics would have their readers believe, is certainly a disappointment from Branagh – by some distance the weakest of his adaptations to date. One must ask: what went wrong? Those who do not slate the entire production indiscriminately are inclined to pick on former teen-queen Alicia Silverstone, who plays the Princess. It is fair to say that classical theatre is not her forte, but it is not, in this slimmed-down version, a particularly demanding part, and in fact she copes with it well enough. Like most of the Americans in the cast, however (except Nathan Lane as a vivacious Costard), she never really rises higher than competence.

It is a little odd to see teen-movie stars like Silverstone and Matthew Lillard (Longaville) share the screen with both comic performers like Lane and Timothy Spall (a preposterous – and often very funny – Armado) and heavyweight classical actors like Branagh and Adrian Lester (Dumaine); and, although Branagh and Lester can be amusing when called upon, and strong direction keeps Lillard and Silverstone from faltering, there is a talent gap. (Branagh was also, at 39, surely a little old to be playing the student Berowne.) Overall, the cast is decent, but not particularly impressive; and Emily Mortimer is cruelly wasted as Katherine. She seems to be one of the weaker singers in the cast, but has shown herself elsewhere to be an excellent actress: yet nearly all of her already small role has been cut.

There are, indeed, no real show-singers here apart from Lane (who gives a stirring rendition of "There's No Business Like Show Business") and Lester. All are in tune, but better than this is required for a musical. Nor is the dancing much better than patchy: Lester and most of the ladies impress, but many of the supporting cast prove rather clumsy; and Branagh's usually sure-footed direction becomes depressingly literal-minded in his attempts to wring humour from the musical numbers. (Spall's delivery of "I Get A Kick Out of You" is giggle-worthy, but principally for his facial contortions.) But the film does have one great advantage over other musicals, including those it steals from: having lifted all the best songs from all the best shows from the dawn of the talkies until well into the 1950s, it has a soundtrack to be proud of. There's not a dud song in it.

Slight, certainly, and not without many flaws: but still an enjoyable enough movie for all that, if one simply lets the bright colours, classic tunes, and delightful Oxford locations wash over oneself. Twice, also, Branagh does remind us of the planes on which he more usually operates: in his beautiful delivery of (both versions of) the "From women's eyes" speech; and in his handling of the ending, which can be anticlimactic but which he ties in to his 1939 setting with a bold *Casablanca* reference, to poignant effect. Unfortunately, however, he overplays his hand here, going on into a misjudged silent montage depicting the characters' war records (even killing off Boyet (Richard Clifford)) and V.E. Day reunion. It remains hard for a fan not to feel let down: fortunately, *As You Like It* was to mark a brilliant return to form.

I et hjørne av verden (2000, Norway, colour animation)
Based on Sonnet XVIII
A.k.a. *In a Corner of the World* (international English title)
Directed by Pjotr Sapegin
Runtime: 8 minutes
Not seen by current writer

Amorous claymation frogs declaim the eighteenth sonnet ("Shall I compare thee to a summer's day?"). The frogs were animated against a real location background on the coast of northern Norway.

Jiyuan qiaohe (2000, Singapore, colour)
Based on *Romeo and Juliet*
A.k.a. *Chicken Rice War* (International English title)
Directed by Chee Kong Cheah
Starring: Pierre Png, May Lee Lum, Gary Yuen, Su Ching Teh
Runtime: 100 minutes

Why on earth anybody would wish to remake *Love Is All There Is* (1996) is utterly bewildering: but that is what Chee Kong Cheah (better known as "CheeK") has done here.

No debt to the American film is acknowledged, but the similarities appear too close to be coincidental. The young offspring of rival catering families (Pierre Png as Fenson Wong and May Lee Lum as Audrey Chan) appear together in a college production of *Romeo and Juliet*, become a couple for real, and spark a series of supposedly comical events which vaguely resemble those of the play, with frequent cookery references.

The script of *Jiyuan qiaohe* includes probably more direct and near quotations from the play than that of *Love Is All There Is* (plus a lot of talking to camera), but this does not make up for the banality of the non-Shakespearean dialogue and the monotony of the acting, next to which *Love Is All There Is* looks like a masterpiece – to say nothing of the shallowness of a plotline in which a girl who originally looks more like a Rosaline than a Juliet is won round with diamonds (crude product placement courtesy of Tiffany). The few jokes recognisable as such fall flat, and a mournful soundtrack dominated by Dido with occasional incongruous bursts of Chinese opera can hardly be said to help, while a bizarre subplot about a friend of Fenson's (Kevin Murphy) stalking a DJ is simply pointless. Nor does tragedy come nearly as close as in the earlier film, in which the lovers do nearly die before a happy ending is imposed: that things will end well here is never in doubt, which is hardly appropriate to an adaptation of *Romeo and Juliet*.

Titus Andronicus (2000, U.S.A., colour)
Directed by Richard Griffin
Runtime: 167 minutes
Not seen by current writer

Titus Andronicus was the first and, as it turned out, last film from independent outfit South Main Street Productions. Filmed largely on location in Bristol, Rhode Island, it transferred the story to a modern corporate setting. It was well reviewed, director Richard Griffin's visual originality and star Nigel Gore's verse speaking in particular being much praised. In an interesting touch, the Goths were, in keeping with their name, black-clad and white-faced; to judge from stills, the photography was excellent.

Among the projects suspended when South Main Street Productions foundered were versions of *Macbeth* and *A Midsummer Night's Dream*; a possible *Romeo and Juliet* had also been mentioned. Instead, Griffin went on to make mostly zombie splatter films. If *Titus* was as good as the critics claimed, this is to be much regretted. I have been unable to trace a copy of the film.

Scotland, Pa. (2001, U.S.A., colour)
Based on *Macbeth*
Directed by Billy Morrissette
Starring: James LeGros, Maura Tierney, Christopher Walken, Kevin Corrigan, Tom Guiry
Runtime: 104 minutes

In the mid 1970s, the then teenaged Billy Morrissette, dividing his time between flipping burgers and studying English literature, noticed parallels between his work and his reading that had gone unobserved by everybody else. He determined to create a *Macbeth* set in a burger bar in small-town Seventies Pennsylvania; and, some decades later, *Scotland, Pa.* (named for and set in a real town) came into being, the first of a slew of loose adaptations from Shakespeare that became more popular on the big screen than original text versions in the early 2000s.

This bizarre mix of black comedy and nostalgia-fest begins with three stoned hippies (Amy Smart, Timothy "Speed" Levitch, and Andy Dick) discussing fried chicken in an abandoned funfair: "The fowl is foul. The fair is fair." There they will meet with Joe McBeth, from whose subconscious, Morrissette heavily hints, they sprang in the first place. Joe is played by James LeGros, who forms with Maura Tierney a finely observed double act as a thirty-something boy-and-girl-next-door stuck in dead end jobs at Duncan's Café, the domain of the self-satisfied bully Norm Duncan (James Rebhorn). Scotland, at the beginning of the film, is a town so dull that when a brawl at Duncan's is broken up it merits slow motion and heroic chords: but things are about to liven up.

Duncan is duly dropped into the deep-fat frier, long-haired rocker Malcolm (Tom Guiry) and sulky gay teen Donald (Geoff Dunsworth) sell the restaurant to the McBeths for a song, and we witness the birth of drive-thru as the weird hippies foretold, complete with McDonald's jokes (McBeth's even uses a big M as a logo). But all is not well in Scotland – vegetarian detective McDuff (Christopher Walken) is in town, hunting for Norm's murderers (not to mention a site for the restaurant *he* plans to run on retiring from the force); and Pat McBeth can't accept that the burn she sustained during the murder has healed, so buys ever larger jars of ointment, conceals it in a Macbeth tartan oven glove, and finally, fatally, cuts off her hand while her husband wrestles with the detective on the rooftop. Joe is poetically punished for his crimes against taste as well as his slayings, ending impaled on the steer-horns he has affixed to the front of his car; and the final shot is of the now retired lieutenant, in a chef's hat, standing in front of the deserted McDuff's Café. The people of Scotland, it seems, have very little use for vegetarian food.

The whole bizarre concoction celebrates the clothes, cars, music, and hair of the Seventies, the exaggerated recreation of the decade adding to the film's decidedly trippy atmosphere. Holding it all together is Morrissette's snappy, literate script, referencing the play, the gangster adaptation *Joe MacBeth* (1955), and the pop culture of its era, and treating all with savage humour which the talented cast expertly bring out. (The bubbly Tierney and the deadpan Walken are particularly impressive.) There is no other film quite like *Scotland, Pa.*; it will not be to all tastes, but I thoroughly enjoyed it.

O (2001, U.S.A., colour)
Based on *Othello*
A.k.a. *The One* (Europe: English title)
Directed by Tim Blake Nelson
Starring: Mekhi Phifer, Josh Hartnett, Julia Stiles, Andrew Keegan, Martin Sheen
Runtime: 95 minutes

O was completed in 1999, but the Columbine shootings made it impolitic to distribute a film dealing with murder in a high school setting, and its release was delayed by nearly two years. By the time it came out, the Nineties craze for transferring the classics to American high school milieux (see *10 Things I Hate About You* (1999), which shares two lead actors with *O*) had passed, and the Shakespeare boom had effectively ended with the failure of *Love's Labour's Lost* (2000). These factors hit the film hard; it performed poorly in the U.S., and did not receive a release in many other countries. This fate was not deserved by what is, for the "teen" genre, an unusually intelligent and well-crafted film.

Taking a tragedy as its source material saved it, of course, from the stereotypes of high school comedy that ensnared *10 Things I Hate About You*; but it also shows considerably greater fidelity to the original. Where the earlier

297

film merely lifted its major plot elements from *The Taming of the Shrew* and added a few references to other plays (a look-at-me tactic which *O* largely avoids, although in one scene a lesson on *Macbeth* is being given), this is an ingenious, almost scene-for-scene recreation of *Othello* in the context of a private school in North Carolina, with a basketball team standing in for the Venetian army. The one new element is that the coach, Duke Goulding (Martin Sheen, standing in not only for the Doge but for authority in general, often including that wielded in the play by Othello himself), is the father of the Iago figure (Hugo, played with understated menace by Josh Hartnett). This provides Hugo with a stronger motive for his actions than his original had, which is not necessarily a positive point: it reduces the power of the "Demand me nothing" speech, and lessens the chill of Iago's malice, although Hartnett's fine performance provides chills aplenty.

The tagline given to the film, "Everything Comes Full Circle", is a near-quotation from *King Lear* ("the wheel is come full circle"): but it also represents a genuine running theme. Like Orson Welles' 1952 version of the play, *O* begins and ends with the same scene: here, we are shown doves and a hawk, the team's mascot, under a glass dome which forms a letter "O", while Hugo speaks in voiceover of his envy of the hawk and desire to fly; the "O" will reappear, as a broken-off basket brandished by the Othello figure (Odin: Mekhi Phifer), and the "full circle" theme be raised again.

The notion that these students would resort to murder is a hard one to swallow, but is made more plausible both by the strength of the acting – with the exception of the slightly stilted Andrew Keegan[116] as an unsympathetic Cassio, the leads all give powerful performances – and by the introduction of a drug-related subplot (cf. *All Night Long* (1962)), which also symbolises Odin's corruption at Hugo's hands, the latter drawing his victim back into the cocaine habit he had earlier shaken off; both are probably high in the final scene, and the "not wisely but too well" speech is delivered in the language of the ghetto, in contrast to Odin's earlier more well-spoken habits. The rap-driven soundtrack fits in well with the basketball scenes and the

---

[116] Keegan seems to make a habit of starring in modernised Shakespeare, beginning with *10 Things I Hate About You*, and progressing through *O* to the very poor straight-to-DVD film *A Midsummer Night's Rave* (2002).

racial theme; at the very end, as the impassive Hugo is led away in handcuffs and Duke appears about to go mad with grief, it gives place to the *Ave Maria* from Verdi's *Otello*.

Attempts to tell Shakespeare's stories without his original text invariably struggle to replace what they have lost, and *O* is no *Othello*: but it is a better effort than most in this line, and a worthwhile film in its own right. It deserved greater success than it met with at the box office.

The Children's Midsummer Night's Dream (2001, U.K., colour)
Based on *A Midsummer Night's Dream*
Directed by Christine Edzard
Starring: Dominic Haywood-Benge, Rajouana Zalal, Leane Lyson, Oliver Szczypka, Jamie Peachey
Runtime: 115 minutes

At first glance, the wonder of *The Children's Midsummer Night's Dream* is that nobody thought of it before: to film the first play most British schoolchildren study, with a cast composed of eleven-year-olds. That Christine Edzard, responsible for the cold and gloomy *As You Like It* (1992), could bring such warmth to this picture compounds the surprise: but, for all the charm it intermittently musters, it is far from an unqualified success.

The film begins as a simple school production of the play: the audience files into the assembly room where it is being staged as the opening credits go up: but when the curtain opens, we see not children but life-size puppets, voiced by adult actors – an effect reminiscent of the wonderful *Animated Tales* of the early 1990s. (At the end, the mechanicals' play will be performed in the hall, with the puppets watching from the stage.) Only when Hermia comes to speak does the focus suddenly shift: a girl (Jamie Peachey) jumps up in the audience and bursts out "I would my father looked but with my eyes!" Demetrius (John Heyfron) and Lysander (Danny Bishop) likewise stand forth to converse with the puppets of Theseus and Egeus; when the latter depart, the curtain closes and the audience shuffle off, leaving the lovers together.

From this point the film proceeds for a while as if it is indeed the story of these twenty-first century South London schoolchildren, chatting in the playground or over the telephone. This is perhaps its weakest segment. The problem is that these *are* children, untrained in classical acting and with only a limited understanding of their lines: and they are for the most part unable to do justice to Shakespeare's verse or, crucially in a production presumably aimed at children of similar age, to render it intelligible to an audience inexperienced in Shakespeare. The film drags badly until it reaches the wood.

Here begins such magic as there is, as costumes revert to the early modern era (*circa* 1640, long after Shakespeare's death but satisfactorily archaic and pretty, in strong greens and reds) and a forest springs up in the assembly hall. The effect, while counter-realistic, is quite charming: and Edzard's device of distributing the longer speeches among the ten fairies who constantly watch the action both relieves the strain on her young leads and helps keep the pace from flagging too badly.

It is not enough, however, to compensate for the self-consciousness and inexperience of the juvenile cast. This is such that several critics walked out of the film's British premiere; those who stayed to the end, to see the caption "This film was made without the support of the Arts Council of England", were for the most part hard pressed to blame the Council's decision. To the question of why no similar project had been attempted before, *The Children's Midsummer Night's Dream* provides a depressingly obvious answer.

Richard II (2001, U.S.A., colour)
A.k.a. *William Shakespeare's Richard the Second* (U.S.A.: DVD title)
Directed by John Farrell
Starring: Matte Osian, Barry Smith, Kadina de Elejalde, Robert F. McCafferty, Ellen Zachos
Runtime: 93 minutes

The first (and to date only) feature film of *Richard II*, a play which director Farrell unpromisingly described as "flawed", is a strange beast. (A little known one, too: it had only a brief run in selected cinemas in New York before being relegated to DVD. Many television versions of the same play have had higher production values and attracted larger audiences.) The tagline "In a world outside time, anything is possible" seems to suggest that the audience is in for another era-jumping *Titus* (1999): as it turns out, however, its purpose is to prepare us for the fact that the film's modern costumes do not mean that any attempt has been made to set it in a credible version of the twenty-first or any other century.[117] The imagination shown in *Titus* is sadly lacking here.

Farrell's minuscule budget is partly to blame. It compelled him to shoot on cheap video, and the sound and picture quality suffer as a result. The picture was made in the space of two weeks, shot entirely on location at the abandoned Army base Fort Strong, near Boston; but while this is not an unsuitable site for military and prison locations, and the occasional interpolated battle scenes, it can never convince as Richard's palace. The King's downfall is meaningless without a sense of what he has lost: but this Richard (Matte Osian) is hardly better dressed or accommodated at the height of his power than when he is a wretched prisoner. He and his courtiers dress in Army camouflage; his "crown" is a West Point cap without braid (although it makes a crack like a gunshot when dropped in the deposition scene); never once, at the Palace, the house of John of Gaunt (Frank O'Donnell), or anywhere else, do we see a building that looks habitable. All sense of royalty is missing.

This is not to say that the picture is without strengths. The acting, if often stilted, is intermittently good; the intricate flashbacks-within-flashbacks structure of Farrell's screenplay is effective and never confusing (although it might have been had I not been familiar with the play); the oddly bloodless battle scenes (the taking of Bristol Castle is dramatised, as are several other events that occur offstage in the play) are well choreographed; and the score, by Liz Ficalora and Andrew Frazier, provides sturdy support. (It plays only under non-dialogue scenes. The combination of the absence of music and the use of echo in the dialogue enhances the alienation effect, which it would be easier to applaud if one could be sure it was deliberate.)

Farrell has taken considerable liberties with Shakespeare's script – and cutting nearly half of it is only the start. Aumerle (Ellen Zachos) and Scroop (Lisa Beth Kovetz) are now women; Aumerle's plot against Bolingbroke (Barry Smith) is excised; and, in the biggest departure, a different conspiracy by Queen Isabel (Kadina de Elejalde) is inserted in its place, so that the groom who appears in the scene preceding Richard's death is

---

[117] Cf. Trevor Nunn's brilliantly inventive Old Vic production in 2005, starring Kevin Spacey, which did succeed in rooting *Richard II* in the modern world.

in fact the Queen in disguise, having killed Northumberland (a strong performance by Robert F. McCafferty) on her way in. (This would surprise their historical originals.) During the confusion of Exton's attack, Isabel is killed; a long silent shot of Richard weeping over her body completely changes the focus of the ending, which is hardly that of the play at all. Richard escapes, and Exton has to hunt him down in a *Rambo*-style chase through the woods (the climax of a series of Vietnam-movie references in earlier battle and forest scenes); at the very end, he is shot running towards the sea, whose sound has played under most of the film and on whose shore the "Let's talk of graves" speech was spoken. And over Richard's surf-washed corpse, without a word of the final scene or Bolingbroke's remorse, the credits go up.

My Kingdom (2001, Italy / U.K., colour)
Based on *King Lear*
Directed by Don Boyd
Starring: Richard Harris, Emma Catherwood, Tom Bell, Reece Noi, Jimi Mistry
Runtime: 117 minutes

Transferring the story of *King Lear* to the criminal underworld of modern-day Liverpool and casting the legendary Richard Harris in the Lear role must have seemed a brilliant idea; but Don Boyd failed to make the film the concept deserved. Harris, in one of his last roles as Sandeman, an aged lion among gangsters, is indeed excellent – a Scouse Hidetora; but it is hard not to wish that he was speaking Shakespeare's lines instead of the rather lacklustre screenplay he had to work with, in which there is hardly a memorable moment.

He is not the only actor to be wasted. Lynn Redgrave as his wife is written as wholesomely dull, and dies in the first few minutes; Emma Catherwood as the colourless Cordelia figure is given practically no dramatic material, her role in the plot substantially diminished and her death being given to Sandeman's grandson (Reece Noi, credited only as "The Boy" and also filling the roles of both the Fool and the audience's surrogate when plot points need explained); Jimi Mistry, as an expanded and more intelligent counterpart to Cornwall in the play, taking on some of Edmund's attributes, hams away with gleeful villainy but is not well served by his lines.

Nor is the gangster element ever made credible. In spite of some major deviations from Shakespeare's plot, one cannot easily escape the conclusion that the screenwriters (principal among whom was Boyd himself) were more concerned with putting the play into a modern context than with developing that context. There are holes in it a mile wide, not least the complete failure to explain what any of the featured mobsters actually does to earn a dishonest living, or why nobody finds it suspicious when Sandeman's bodyguards are absent at crucial moments.

Boyd's direction shows some flair but little consistency, veering between gritty realism and occasional stylisation and never quite fulfilling its promise in either sphere; but it is ultimately the script which makes this a deeply disappointing film and a waste of the wealth of acting talent it contains. For some reason, many sources wrongly list this as a TV movie; it probably should have been.

Macbeth: The Comedy (2001, U.S.A., colour)
Based on *Macbeth*
Directed by Allison L. LiCalsi
Runtime: 91 minutes
Not seen by current writer

Macbeth: The Comedy was the only film of director Allison L. LiCalsi and production outfit Tristan Films; after a couple of festival appearances in New York, it disappeared. However, although Tristan Films cannot now be contacted, their website remains, complete with quite full information on the film.

Crediting only "story and additional dialogue" to William Shakespeare, the film cast the Macbeths (Erika Burke and Juliet Furness) as a lesbian couple, with three extremely camp, male Witches (Phillip Christian, Christopher Briggs, and Michael Colby Jones), in a fantasy Scotland where Renaissance and modern costumes mingle, and the favoured décor is wall-to-wall tartan. Shakespeare's words elicit banal replies ("I feel now the future in the instant" – "I thought you might"), and have to be translated for the dim-witted Duncan (John Little). LiCalsi cited *Monty Python* and *Blackadder* as influences, aiming high. The trailer, and mixed online reviews, suggest that she was somewhat over-ambitious: there is small evidence that LiCalsi and her team possessed enough imagination to carry off the conceit.

303

Rave Macbeth (2001, Germany, colour)
Based on *Macbeth*
A.k.a. *Rave Macbeth – Nacht der Entscheidung* (Germany, DVD title)
Directed by Klaus Knoesel
Starring: Michael Rosenbaum, Nicki Lynn Aycox, Jeffrey Vanderbyl, Jamie Elman, Marguerite Moreau
Runtime: 87 minutes

In adapting *Macbeth* to a clubland setting (supposedly somewhere in America but filmed in a real dance club in Munich), screenwriter Harry Ki reached the unorthodox conclusion that the key to the play was Hecate – whose scenes are conventionally cut from modern productions, and are in any case believed to have been written by Thomas Middleton, not Shakespeare. The goddess of the witches, though retaining her name, becomes male and apparently mortal. As played by the suavely sinister Jeffrey Vanderbyl, he is a trilby-wearing drug baron in a swivel chair, prone to gnomic comments and quotes from the play: the entire gang that has replaced the Scottish realm, even Duncan-figure Dean (Kirk Baltz), "the King of the Rave", take their orders from him. Yet his motives remain those of his original – to damn his subjects' souls. He and his three disciples are still witches.

Although the structure of Dean's realm at first matches that of the play – loyal doorman MacDuff (Mathias Schullan), recently promoted lieutenants Marcus (Michael Rosenbaum, somewhat wooden in the Macbeth role; but then, the part is written that way) and Troy (Banquo: Jamie Elman), and Marcus' ambitious, manipulative girlfriend Lidia (Nicki Lynn Aycox), plus an extratextual girlfriend for Troy (Helena: Marguerite Moreau) – the play is only very loosely adhered to. Lidia is willing to lie outright to Marcus in the course of propelling him to power, and to kill Helena with her own hands: most unlike Lady Macbeth. Troy is killed before Dean; Marcus is "king" for only a few minutes (in real time – the film takes place across one night) before MacDuff (who, here, is avenging only Dean – there is no slaughtered family) puts paid to his and Lidia's dreams. While Dean and Hecate get one or two memorable lines, the rest of the dialogue is mostly as banal as the conversation of real ravers.

Arturo Smith's cinematography certainly captures the experience of narcotic over-indulgence, and in fact runs a serious danger of making viewers feel sick. The camera sways and staggers like a drunkard on a ship, while disco lights flash in a manner dangerous to epileptics, and the background swims in and out of focus. Though it does possess genuine energy and invention, *Rave Macbeth* is not an experience I can honestly recommend, except possibly as a form of aversion therapy for drug abusers.

Though in English, and featuring a largely American cast, the film never received a theatrical release outside Germany.

Kannaki (2002, India, colour)
Based on *Antony and Cleopatra*
A.k.a. *Kannagi*
Directed by Jayaraaj Rajasekharan Nair
Starring: Lal, Nandita Das, Siddique, Geethu Mohandas
Language: Malayalam
Runtime: 127 minutes

Having turned *Othello* into the remarkable *Kaliyattam* (1997), Jayaraaj returned to Shakespeare a few years later. Once again, he transferred the setting of one of the great tragedies to a remote village in southern India (the Palakkadan mountains, exquisitely photographed by M. J. Radhakrishnan), at an unspecified period. (Sabitha Jayaraaj's award-winning costumes, in bold primary colours – red predominates, approaching ever closer to the hue of blood as the film wears on – look much more modern than those in *Kaliyattam*, and most characters smoke cigarettes, but the village is as technologically backward and isolated from the outside world as that in the previous film.) Manikyan (Lal as the Antony figure) is a cockfighting champion who represents his friend Choman (Octavian, played by Siddique) against all comers. Nandita Das plays the local beauty of suspect reputation, with a name almost as evocative in southern India as Cleopatra's in the West: Kannaki, the Malayalam form of Kannagi, heroine of the Tamil epic *Silappadikaram*. Choman hopes to marry off his sister Kumudam (Octavia: Geethu Mohandas) to Manikyan, but the cockfighter falls in love with Kannaki, setting the stage for conflict.

But *Antony and Cleopatra*, far more than *Othello*, is a

political tragedy. Jayaraaj's protagonists command no armies; their quarrels shake no empires, and the villagers who take sides have chosen to do so. Nor is the suspicion of witchcraft raised against Kannaki any substitute for the cultural enmity between Egypt and Rome depicted in the play. Shorn of its political elements, the story is inevitably reduced to soap opera. As such, it is too slight to justify *Kannaki*'s running time, and the film frequently drags. This is in spite of the undoubted talents of most of those involved. The film never looks less than beautiful, and Kaithapram Vishwanathan's music, weightier in feel than most Indian film scores, supports the visuals perfectly. Even the song sequences, though less naturalistically integrated than in *Kaliyattam*, work, because they are well tailored to character and circumstances. Particularly impressive is an ecstatic communal dance at a religious festival, Lal leading scarlet-clad devotees who brandish gleaming sickles hung with bells. Even the cockfighting scenes, though hard to watch – one cannot altogether dismiss the suspicion that the birds were genuinely suffering – undeniably display excellent photography and editing. Lal, though perhaps a little too prone to brooding, makes a fine, noble Manikyan; and, if Kannaki lacks some of Cleopatra's spirit and much of her complexity, it is the script's fault and not Das'.

For all its strengths, *Kannaki* makes a disappointing follow-up to *Kaliyattam*, not because of any actual failing in Jayaraaj's execution, but because he chose the wrong play for this kind of treatment. An Indianised *Antony and Cleopatra* is perfectly conceivable, but it would need to be painted on a larger canvas than the village setting allows.

It was rumoured in 2009 that Jayaraaj intended to make a film based on *Macbeth*, but as yet no further information is available.

La tragédie de Gonzague (2002, France, black and white)
Based on *Hamlet*
Directed by Jérôme Bouyer
Language: French
Runtime: 12 minutes
Not seen by current writer

La tragédie de Gonzague transferred the story of *Hamlet* to a circus, whose popular clown (Philippe Ponty) is poisoned by his jealous brother (Cyril Bosc). The Gertrude figure was played by a man, David Ayala, and the avenging son by a woman, Clémentine Yelnik; no other characters are credited.

The Maori Merchant of Venice (2002, New Zealand, colour)
Based on *The Merchant of Venice*
A.k.a. *Te Tangata Whai Rawa o Weniti* (New Zealand); *The Merchant of Venice* (New Zealand)
Directed by Don Selwyn
Starring: Ngarimu Daniels, Waihoroi Shortland, Te Rangihau Gilbert, Scott Morrison, Reikura Morgan
Language: Maori
Runtime: 158 minutes

Since first meeting Maori language scholar Dr Pei Te Hurinui Jones in the 1950s, Don Selwyn had fostered the ambition to stage Jones' Shakespeare translations: and when he was invited to mount a production of a Maori play at the Koanga Festival in 1990, he chose Jones' 1945 rendition of *The Merchant of Venice*, casting distinguished stage star Waihoroi Shortland as Shylock, a role he would reprise for this version. The production was a considerable success, and Jones determined to commit it to film: but in 1990 there had never been a feature film entirely in the Maori language (this would in fact be the first), and it took him ten years to raise the money.

The world of the film is at once a vaguely seventeenth century Venice (costumes tending to the post-Shakespearean, Aragon (Samson Pehi) in particular smacking more of the other end of the century in his curled wig and long-aproned waistcoat: though, in an interesting contrast with the usual foppish portrayals of the Prince, Pehi makes him a loud boor beneath his finery), and a timeless New Zealand. Canals and Italianate buildings are used as well as the costumes, but the set decoration is very much Maori (traditional statues and weaves litter Belmont, while the more modern paintings in Shylock's house are also native in inspiration), while straw houses and the encroaching tropical forest are always in evidence. In the powerful, wordless opening sequence, Morocco (Lawrence Makoare) is guided through the trees to Belmont by both African torchbearers and local dancers, while spirits derived from the islands' mythology flit about at the edge of sight – a possible tribute to the fact that Jones also translated *A Midsummer Night's*

Dream. When he finally arrives, Maori and Moroccan musical styles are intertwined, perfectly capturing the film's "edge of two worlds" feel at its best. (The score, by Clive Cockburn and Hirini Melbourne, and played by the New Zealand Symphony Orchestra, is always at its best when Melbourne's atmospheric Maori stylings are allowed to dominate over the often rather pompous pseudo-Italian style preferred by Cockburn.) Only the court scene is of entirely Western design: it is set in a church, Antonio (Scott Morrison) wearing a jerkin emblazoned with a large orange cross. This attempt to emphasise Shylock's outsider status falls somewhat flat, owing to the inclusion in the court scene of a large crowd of Jews who yell their support for the moneylender, and abandon him only when he agrees to convert to Christianity[118]: but at least this final touch lends great power to Shortland's exit. As Shylock stumbles out of court with Gratiano's (Sonny Kirikiri) taunts ringing in his ears, he is utterly friendless.

The acting is of variable standard. Shortland at his bitter best is impressive, though he often seems rather understated, a fault he shares with many of the cast; Morrison (who had not acted before) is decidedly wooden, though Ngarimu Daniels' cool, self-possessed Portia is a treat to watch. Reikura Morgan as an excessively romantic but inwardly conflicted Jessica has many of the film's finest moments, including a conclusion in which, like many modern Jessicas, she appears to suffer doubt over her decision – but, unlike some, defiantly rejects these feelings and goes into Belmont with Lorenzo (Te Arepa Kahi). It is questionable whether this Jessica is capable of happiness. However, the inexperience of the supporting cast shows: added to this is the fact that Maori is not an economical language, and it has taken heavy cuts to the translated script to keep the film within a length not far short of the full English text. This inevitably results in a slow pace, stately at its best, as in Morocco's entry, but patience-stretching at other times. Bella Erikson's somewhat plodding editing does nothing to correct this fault.

For all its flaws, however, *The Maori Merchant of Venice* is a very handsome film, a fascinating glimpse into modern Maori theatre, and – as both the world's first Maori-only feature and

---

[118] Cf. Michael Radford's 2004 film, in which there are indeed Jews in the court, but they turn on Shylock out of disgust at his bloodthirstiness.

New Zealand's first Shakespeare adaptation – an important piece of cinema history.

King Rikki (2002, U.S.A., colour)
Based on *Richard III*
A.k.a. *The Street King* (U.S.A., video and DVD title)
Directed by James Gavin Bedford
Starring: Jon Seda, Tonantzin Carmelo, Timothy Paul Perrez, Laura Cerón, Mario López
Runtime: 91 minutes

Richard III was in 2002 arguably overdue for the gangster treatment which other plays (particularly *Macbeth*) had repeatedly undergone; and a backdrop of urban warfare between Mexican-American street toughs in East Los Angeles is eminently suited to the story. James Gavin Bedford's movie, however, can hardly be said to live up to this concept. Given that his previous (and indeed subsequent) track record was largely as an editor, his few ventures into directing consisting mostly of softcore pornography, this is not especially surprising: if anything, the wonder is that the film is no worse.

The opening of the picture, in which an image of Shakespeare on a wall is sprayed over with cap, shades, and earrings, is possibly its most imaginative moment, but unfortunately comes to symbolise the desecration of the play. The disappointment is not immediate: it begins promisingly, with Rikki the Pig (Jon Seda) talking conspiratorially to camera, characters' criminal records flashing onto the screen as they are introduced, some neat camerawork that manages to convey the squalor of the world the hoodlums inhabit without making the film ugly, all over pulsing Mexican music.

The rot sets in only after the first battle (a raid on a rival gang's drugs lab, standing in for Tewkesbury). Seda's monologues begin to fill up with clunking exposition: writer Jesse Graham feels the need to explain in unnecessary detail the backdrop of the cross-border drugs trade, and has resorted to this lazy device to do it. He then begins to introduce characters and plot elements with no parallels in the play: a distant family who control the trade and issue orders to both the Ortegas (House of York) and the Rojas (House of Lancaster); and one of their men, a corrupt cop and childhood friend of Rikki, Juan Vallejo (Mario López). Vallejo will eventually become Richmond, killing Rikki in an all but accidental encounter and walking away with his ill-gotten loot, but before that time he has little more place in the film than in the play. Attempts to make his character enigmatic just make him look inconsistent, and it has been suggested that he was written in purely to create a part for López, who was by some distance the project's biggest name.

Seda's performance, at least, is fun. Shorn of his deformities, this "carefree" Richard, as the actor called him, can fully enjoy his own villainy and the power it briefly brings him, and clearly does, bringing the audience along with him as he cheerfully seduces not only the character equivalent to the Lady Anne (Tonantzin Carmelo) but his brother Jorge's girlfriend (Isabella Donato) (the fifteenth century originals of these ladies were in fact sisters); uses his mother to carry the message that seals Jorge's (Clarence – Manny Perez) doom; and murders Eduardo (Edward IV – Timothy Paul Perez) with contaminated cocaine, finished off with a syringe full of air. (Like the real Edward IV but unlike Shakespeare's, Eduardo fails to die of sorrow when he hears of Jorge's death.) Seda is cool, casual and smiling from first to last: we never get to see whether he could have played Richard's eve-of-battle attack of conscience, but what he is given he does with relish.

Unfortunately, he is not supported by Graham's ponderous and meandering script. The dialogue is forgettable, and the departures from the original have not been thought through. A version which stuck more closely to Shakespeare's plot might have produced a better film; but it would have required a writer with a sense of logic and an ear for speech, and a director not unduly preoccupied with breasts. This is not that picture.

The Seasons Alter (2002, U.K., colour)
Based on *A Midsummer Night's Dream*
Directed by Roger Lunn
Starring: Keira Knightley, Cherie Lunghi, Lloyd Owen
Runtime: 4 minutes

"400 years ago, William Shakespeare wrote about climate change. Just poetry?" This question gets Futerra's well-intentioned short campaign film off to a poor start; the use of Keira Knightley, possibly the most overrated actress of the 2000s, risked taking it downhill from there.

Futerra is essentially an environmentalist lobby group masquerading as a film company; its aims are laudable, but its pictures less so. *The Seasons Alter* takes Titania's beautiful speech about the damage wrought to the natural world by the fairies' dissension, cannibalises a few lines from other scenes in the *Dream*, and applies them to what humanity has done to the planet: an effective enough conceit, if it had been managed better. The three actors bicker in a dimly-lit conference room while images of environmental destruction play on a projector screen behind them; although credited as Helena, Knightley in fact speaks the bulk of Titania's lines. As usual, she leads with her chin and brings too little variation to her delivery; she is certainly out of her depth next to her impressive (and underused) co-stars; but she does pass the vital test and convey the meaning of her lines to the audience. Unfortunately, the camerawork – an extreme example of the energetic style fashionable in the early 2000s – will probably have left them feeling too seasick to notice.

As Alegres Comadres (2003, Brazil, colour)
Based on *The Merry Wives of Windsor*
Directed by Leila Hipólito
Starring: Elisa Lucinda, Zezé Polessa, Guilherme Karan, Ernani Moraes, Bel García
Language: Portuguese
Runtime: 109 minutes

Apart from transferring the setting to Tiradentes in the 1850s, Hipólito's film is in effect a straight rendition of *Merry Wives*, with most of the dialogue either paraphrased or directly translated, and barely a scene out of place.

The shift in setting works very well. Hipólito has not had to look hard for cultural parallels: the characters and situations work essentially unchanged in their new surroundings, with such mild tweaks as Evans-figure Padre Arnaldo (Milton Gonçalves) being Portuguese instead of Welsh, and the folk traditions of Brazil provide a striking carnivalesque version of the Windsor Park scene. It is also well realised in design, particularly in Yamê Reis' beautiful costumes.

Slightly less impressive, in some quarters, is character interpretation. The unsympathetic Falstaff figure (Fausto: Guilherme Karan), first seen robbing a widow (Maria Sá) on a train, is somewhat crudely drawn, and while Karan's

311

exaggerated facial expressions raise a smile, he has not quite the charisma the part requires; I could not help feeling that Antônio Petrin, on impish form as the Host, would have made a better knight. Most of the cast acquit themselves with competence, Gonçalves droning, Caius (Chico Díaz) ranting, Rocha (Frank Ford: Ernani Moraes) swivelling his eyes, while the Wives (Elisa Lucinda and Zezé Polessa) and Nell (Maria: Bel García) stay in mischievous control of their situations: but somehow, neither they nor Eduardo Souto Neto's lively Latin score ever manage to generate the energy this play should have. The reading of Slender (Silva: Raphael Primo) as a gay dandy is crassly overplayed to not very funny effect – though it does come with a pay-off at the end of the film, when he is actually quite happy to find he has married a boy.[119]

As Alegres Comadres is handsomely made and undeniably entertaining: but not more than mildly so. Uneven pacing and one or two slightly lacklustre performances mean that a film which could have dazzled sadly fails to do so.

Macbeth (2003, U.S.A., colour / black and white)
Directed by Bryan Enk
Starring: Peter B. Brown, Moira Stone, Bob Brader, Britt Lafield, Yuri Lowenthal
Runtime: 75 minutes

Third Lows Productions' anarchic metatheatrical fantasy *Macbeth*, made on a minuscule budget, is an extraordinary experience. It manages to turn its own indecision as to what it wants to be – anti-corporate satire rubs shoulders with distanced quasi-Brechtianism and commentary on the nature of theatre and film, while all collide with a surreal drugged-up sensibility – into a virtue, as the constant shifts of style and focus refuse to let the audience stop thinking.

In the foreground of the update is the notion of the Scottish kingdom as a modern American corporation whose hatchet-men are literal killers, a blackly comic exaggeration of capitalist ruthlessness: office geek Ross (Dan Maccarone) chats cheerfully into his mobile telephone while blasting industrial spy

---

[119] This is not the first production of *Merry Wives* to treat Slender this way: Primo is strongly reminiscent of Eugene Brezany in the Shakespeare Society of America's 1970 teleplay.

Cawdor's (Matthew Gray) brains all over his desk. Interestingly, after the murder of Duncan (a thuggish Tom Reid), the office sets disappear until Malcolm (Britt Lafield, playing a calculating and unsympathetic incarnation of the prince) and Macduff (Bob Brader) meet in their English exile to plot a restoration. During the reign of Macbeth (Peter B. Brown), nightclub and rooftop scenes that fit with this world are interspersed with deliberately artificial sequences set in an empty theatre. "Is this a dagger" is played to a camera held by Lady Macbeth (Moira Stone), who circles her husband, filming him with one hand and holding out the dagger with the other, while we cut back and forth between her point of view and a long shot from the auditorium; the Porter (Frank Cwiklik) is a stand-up comedian, whose laugh track (coming from an invisible audience!) continues throughout the deliberately wildly overplayed scene of Macduff's arrival and the body's discovery; Banquo's (Yuri Lowenthal) ghost is made up almost like a clown, and plays up the absurdity of his appearance to mock Macbeth; the murderers (Amy Caitlin Carr and Tom Mazur) come down the aisle of the theatre to slay Lady Macduff (Michele Schlossberg) on stage. Exit signs abound, but Brown's back is always turned to them. The film ends back in this theatre space, with the surviving thanes in the audience as Malcolm makes his oleaginously ingratiating final speech.

Some visual flourishes – the witches (Christiaan Koop, Carrie Johnson, Jennifer Clark) as disembodied faces floating in the darkness; Duncan and Banquo paying off a Charon-like ferryman (Gerald Owen Koop) as they arrive at Inverness; a sinisterly lit Seyton (Trav S. D.) looming over Macbeth in top hat and tails – have nothing to do with either of these visions: but, perhaps because little could clash with so varied a realisation, they remain oddly effective.

The deliberate distortion of sound and picture, mid-scene jumps from one setting to another, use of black and white for soliloquies, and unashamed artificiality, not to mention the cutting of half the text, could easily have scuppered the film: and, indeed, there are moments that make little sense in their new context, while the mispronunciation of place names will grate with the viewer acquainted with Scottish geography: but it is never less than watchable, even when one is unsure of what Enk wishes to say. Although Brader's hamming lets down Macduff's scenes, most of the cast is impressive, and Brown's strong central performance carries the film. His speed-addled broker / king is a never less than fascinating interpretation of the role.

Hamlet_X (2003, Germany, colour / black and white)
Based on *Hamlet*
Directed by Herbert Fritsch
Language: German
Runtime: 238 minutes total

Hamlet_X, partly shot in Berlin's Volksbühne and using its company in the cast, is a series of 33 short films inspired by *Hamlet*. Some of these are scenes or extracts from the play, though not in order: it takes us until the ninth film, "Die Soldaten" ("The Soldiers"), to reach Act One, Scene One: others depart at tangents of varying oddity. A series of talking heads (an insurance agent, the captain whose ship took Hamlet to England, Ophelia's gynaecologist, an elderly pilgrim in a lift which goes round in an eternal loop instead of up and down, and many others) address the camera about the events of the play as if being interviewed as witnesses; often, latching onto the mental state of Hamlet or Ophelia, these characters themselves go progressively madder over the course of their scenes.

Most of these non-Shakespearean vignettes seem rather pointless: none more so than the longest film in the series, "HellSehnOhr", in which a restaurateur natters for twenty minutes to his uninterested daughters about the outdated petty gossip of the Danish court: but the scenes from the play are not without interest, though treated eccentrically. Lines are repeated *ad nauseam*, and no character is played by the same actor in any two of the films; but some of the modern twists are effective. The very first short, "Bentley", references the 1921 *Hamlet* of Asta Nielsen (q.v.) with a female "Prince" and a Horatio who is obviously her lover: sexual confusion will become a theme much harped upon, with various heavily sexualised Ophelias (one pregnant, one a man in drag, one rollerblading in a long translucent dress and glowing green underwear, and so forth) and a male Player Queen who is raped by Lucianus and appears to enjoy the experience. Other updates are more light-hearted: in "Tatort" ("Crime Scene"), Rosencrantz and Guildenstern become inept policemen; in "Die Krone" ("The Crown") an exasperated Gertrude tries to coach the childish Claudius in his opening speech (I.2). Yet others, such as "Die Soldaten" and the starkly atmospheric black-and-white rendition of Claudius' penitence scene as "Zweifel" ("Doubt"), are simply played "straight": these tend to be the most effective.

Critical clichés satirised in "Forensik" ("Forensic Psychology"), where they are over-analysed by a pretentious academic, are served up straight-faced in other "talking head" films; characters repeatedly ignore what is going on around them, whether it involves murder, the growth of plants at a supernatural rate, or the unexplained opening of luminescent portals; half-hearted references intended to compare Claudius with Hitler ("Arbeit macht frei") are made but never followed through; and all the while the incessant repetition drums the audience over the head. Herbert Fritsch could have packed everything he manages to say about *Hamlet* into one of these short films; to make 33 was sheer self-indulgence.

Gedebe (2003, Malaysia, colour)
Based on *Julius Caesar*
Directed by Namron
Language: Malay (Kelantan dialect)
Runtime: 65 minutes
Not seen by current writer

Gedebe, an independent film which began life as a theatrical project in the Experimental Theatre of Kuala Lumpur, sets its loose reworking of *Julius Caesar* in the city's underground music scene. Caesar is the charismatic leader of a skinhead gang (the title could be translated as "Kingpin"), and Brutus (Zul Huzaimy Marzuki) an undercover policeman who has become his target's friend, but gets involved with internecine plots within the gang.

The film's trailer consists of one unbroken fight scene under red disco lights, backed by thumping, angry music. It reveals Namron's rough-and-ready way of filming (and also cannot help betraying the low budget that partly enforced this style), but it has tremendous energy.

Maqbool (2003, India, colour)
Based on *Macbeth*
Directed by Vishal Bharadwaj

315

Starring: Irfan Khan, Tabu, Pankaj Kapur, Piyush Mishra, Naseeruddin Shah
Language: Urdu / Hindi
Runtime: 132 minutes

Maqbool is a colourful translation of *Macbeth* into the terms of Indian cinema (complete with songs, although these are incorporated realistically rather than simply burst into in the normal Bollywood style) and the Mumbai underworld. Many of its influences, however, are as Western as the play: the keening human voices in Bharadwaj's epic score owe a lot to Hans Zimmer's music for *Gladiator* (2000), while over the depiction of gangsterism looms the shadow of *The Godfather* (1972) – Pankaj Kapur as the Duncan figure (Jahangir, known as "Abbaji" or "Father") in particular modelling his performance closely on Marlon Brando's Vito Corleone.

Although, as in Kurosawa's *Kumonosu jô* (1957), the Macduff plotline is excised for simplicity's sake, the screenplay sticks fairly closely to the play. The witches and murderers are combined into two corrupt policemen (Om Puri and Naseeruddin Shah, the grand old men of Indian films) who moonlight as astrologers: Puri is the "straight" one and Shah the comic relief. Banquo is metamorphosed into Kaka (Piyush Mishra), who becomes a symbol of the divide between old and new, East and West, in modern India, when his robed and turbaned henchmen square off against Maqbool's (Irfan Khan) in their Tarantinoesque suits and shades. His son Guddu (Ajay Gehi) combines the roles of Fleance and Malcolm, marrying Abbaji's daughter (Masumi Makhija).

The film's Lady Macbeth, Nimmi (Tabu), is Abbaji's mistress before she is Maqbool's: an interesting twist to the story which brings their relationship into sharp focus. Khan and Tabu portray beautifully a deeply loving couple drawn as much by their affection as by ambition into a destructive path: they share a tenderly erotic seduction scene, very daring by the puritanical standards of the Indian cinema, and a painful parting when complications following a miscarriage bear Nimmi to insanity and death. Maqbool, unlike his original, is still able to be touched at this point, though his mind too is slowly slipping away as his enemies close in. (His reign shrinks to occupy only a few minutes of the movie between Abbaji's murder, 78 minutes in, and the closing of the net.)

The drama is played out against exquisite sets, and

gorgeously photographed by Hemant Chaturvedi, who knows exactly how to put India's sunshine to its best cinematic uses. The result is one of the most successful of the many gangland Macbeths.

Shakespeare's Merchant (2003, U.S.A., colour)
Based on *The Merchant of Venice*
Directed by Paul Wagar
Runtime: 86 minutes
Not seen by current writer

For independent feature *Shakespeare's Merchant*, Paul Wagar moved Venice to a grotesque near-future California, in which (for no explained reason) violent anti-Semitism runs riot. The brief clips that I have seen reveal an interesting take on the play, effectively updated, in which Antonio (Donald Robert Stewart) and Bassanio (John D. Haggerty) are very explicitly made lovers. This interpretation (a rare one on film), of course makes Bassanio's pursuit of Portia still more obviously mercenary, and Antonio's loss and loneliness greater, than in adaptations which do not pursue this angle. Michael Kaulkin's neoclassical score seems slightly overused, but certainly makes enjoyable listening.

The language is much altered: it is understandable that ducats are changed to dollars, but within one speech "rheum" becomes "phlegm", "gaberdine" becomes "means of dress", "stranger cur" becomes "mangy dog", "spurn" becomes "strike", and so forth – there is hardly a line exactly as Shakespeare wrote it. If this was the case throughout the film, it would make frustrating viewing for any lover of the play.

The acting appears competent, and the camerawork is strong, but it is difficult to make any judgement on the basis of five minutes of a feature film.

Richard: Memories from the Scrapbook (2004, Denmark, colour)
Based on *Henry VI, Part 3* and *Richard III*
Directed by Anna Neye Poulsen
Runtime: 11 minutes
Not seen by current writer

Poulsen's short starred Lars Henning as Gloucester and herself as Lady Anne, and was set in a modern milieu; more

317

than this I have been unable to find out.

The Merchant of Venice (2004, U.S.A. / Italy / Luxembourg / U.K., colour)
A.k.a. *Il Mercante di Venezia* (Italy); *William Shakespeare's The Merchant of Venice* (U.S.A.)
Directed by Michael Radford
Starring: Al Pacino, Lynn Collins, Jeremy Irons, Joseph Fiennes, Kris Marshall
Runtime: 138 minutes

Radford's *Merchant*, the first major Shakespearean film to use the original text since Kenneth Branagh's *Love's Labour's Lost* (2000), underwent several cast changes before reaching the silver screen: Cate Blanchett (cast as Portia) and Ian McKellen (cast as Antonio) dropped out, while the rumoured Shylock Dustin Hoffman – who had played the part on stage to great acclaim – discovered that Al Pacino had already been given the role. To the disconcertion of many, including myself, the near-unknown Lynn Collins replaced Blanchett, while Jeremy Irons, who had made some questionable choices recently, took over from McKellen. We were wrong to worry. Every performance in the finished film was well nigh flawless; Irons gave his finest turn in years. Antonio is often a thankless role, and it is far from easy to portray both sides of his character: his deep unspoken love for Bassanio seems to sit uneasily with his bigotry: but Irons conveyed both perfectly.

Radford also struggled with budgetary problems. His decision to go for an authentic Venetian setting in 1596 would have made the film costly even with unknown actors: as it was, he had to ask his established stars (in particular the hugely expensive Pacino) to take a considerable pay cut. It is a tribute to their love of Shakespeare and their confidence in Radford that they agreed.

After the long run of period analogue adaptations in the 1990s, it was a bold decision on Radford's part to return to an Elizabethan-era setting: but he had an excellent purpose, which was to set the often problematic play firmly in its correct historical context – the only way, it might be argued, in which the text could be fully understood as a study, not a statement, of anti-Semitism. The caption at the opening, describing the historical background, which many critics saw as an attempt to get Shakespeare off the hook, was in fact necessary to explain to a modern audience the society into which they were about to be drawn. Whereas previous "dress" productions suffered from a tendency to use the period simply as a pretty backdrop, Radford went to great pains to give the viewer a realistic slice of sixteenth century life, in which Venice herself is a major character. There are one or two minor historical slip-ups (Portia's portrait is in a fifteenth century style; an Australian black swan makes a picturesque but anachronistic appearance, and so forth), but one never loses the sense of authenticity. Populated by torch-wielding preachers, red-capped Jews, blood-spattered butchers, and prostitutes with rouged nipples, this is a living, bustling Venice, a Venice one can practically smell.

Radford was criticised for concentrating too heavily on the darker side of the play, but in fact the comedic elements are still present: all he did was to avoid the trap, into which some directors fall, of turning *The Merchant* into two different plays. The often tiresome Launcelot Gobbo (Mackenzie Crook) may have been drastically cut, but the scenes with Portia's suitors, and the business with the rings in Act Five, still raise the viewers' smiles.

There were, however, some distinctly odd decisions taken concerning the script. Radford was hardly the first adaptor to feel the need to modernise some of Shakespeare's archaisms: but if he believed an audience would understand "hath" and "doth", why not "thou"? If references to Phoebus are too obscure, why does Erebus remain? Was it really necessary for "a bondman's key" to become "a slavish voice" when the context made the meaning perfectly clear?

Radford began and ended his film with scenes he had invented. At the opening, a friar standing in a gondola preaches against usury, rousing the crowd to attack Jews and throw them into the canals; Shylock greets Antonio warmly, only to be spat upon. At the end, Jessica (Zuleikha Robinson) sits alone at sunrise watching the fishermen outside Belmont, and looking wistfully at the turquoise ring that her father thinks she has exchanged for a monkey. This was a risky undertaking, but in the event the interpolated scenes – assisted by Benoît Delhomme's exquisite cinematography – complement the play beautifully.

Brilliantly conceived, masterfully acted (especially by Pacino as a truly tragic Shylock), this film can readily be forgiven for occasional wobbles in the screenplay. The first major original text Shakespearean adaptation of the twenty-first century was a remarkable success, and hopefully prefigures many more.

Huapango (2004, Mexico, colour)
Based on *Othello*
Directed by Ivan Lipkies
Starring: Manuel Landeta, Lisset, Alejandro Tommasi, Alfredo Castillo
Language: Spanish
Runtime: 101 minutes

The title of this adaptation is a fair indication of its real subject: *huapango* dancing, specifically in the context of the competitive dance festivals of the Huasteca region of Mexico. Like *All Night Long* (1962), it appropriates the plot of *Othello* to give structure to what is not really a dramatic film at all; but, even more than *All Night Long*, it struggles to keep its two strands convincingly together, especially since most of the cast were chosen for their dancing rather than acting abilities. The camp, bald, goateed Iago figure (Santiago: Manuel Landeta) in particular is badly overplayed, although he is not assisted by a soap-opera script which simplifies and spells out his motivations (reduced to lust for Julia / Desdemona (Lisset)) and makes him far more openly emotional than the original.

Othello (Otilio: Alejandro Tommasi) has also suffered in the adaptation. He is no longer black, nor an outsider in any sense other than being a little older than the other characters: on the contrary, he is a wealthy rancher and the Governor's cousin, and, so far from defying prejudice, his marriage with Julia is celebrated by the whole community. This makes a nonsense of Othello's isolation, and the character comes across as little more than a gullible brute – an especial shame considering that Tommasi is possibly the best actor in the picture. (This may not be unconnected with the fact that Tommasi is not a dancer.)

The flat dialogue, the relentless sameness of Alberto Lee's sun-drenched cinematography, the lack of cohesion between dramatic, comic and dance-based scenes, the dilution of Emilia's part by dividing it among several characters, and above all the two-dimensional performances of almost everybody but Tommasi, hurt *Huapango* badly: but it has its good points too. A

320

well realised, if slightly sentimental, picture of small-town Mexico is strongly sketched; Sigfrido Barjau's editing is skilled and effective, especially in the final scene, where we cut back and forth between the dance festival and Julia walking to her doom; and the dancing itself is brilliantly performed. The conceit that the diversion of electricity to light the festival has created a power-cut in the town allows not only for some much more inventive lighting than has appeared earlier in the film, but for a beautiful shot of the dead Julia surrounded by candles as if lying in state; one can only wish that Lipkies and Lee had provided some comparable images earlier in the film. The ending, which is in any case undermined by Landeta's overacting, is not enough to redeem *Huapango*.

Kate – La bisbetica domata (2004, Italy, colour animation)
Based on *The Taming of the Shrew*
A.k.a. *Kate – The Taming of the Shrew* (international English title)
Directed by Roberto Lione
Language: Italian
Runtime: 77 minutes
Not seen by current writer

The first stop-motion animated feature ever made in Italy was a version of *The Taming of the Shrew*. It toured a few festivals of children's films, winning a jury prize in Chicago, before dropping off the radar, and has not been heard of since.

Souli (2004, France / Madagascar / U.K., colour)
Based on *Othello*
Directed by Alexander Abela
Language: French / Malagasy
Runtime: 94 minutes
Not seen by current writer

Where *Makibefo* simply told the *Macbeth* story in the context of traditional Malagasy life, *Souli* had a rather more complicated take on *Othello*, examining it in the light of the West's exploitative relationship with Africa, and the complicity of some Africans in that exploitation. The story is seen through the eyes of Carlos (Eduardo Noriega), an ambitious Spanish student who comes to Madagascar in search of "the Thiossan tale": a legend now known only to one man, a Senegalese writer named Souli (Makena Diop), living among the French expatriate community in Ambola. Carlos thus becomes embroiled in the triangle between Othello-figure Souli, his white French lover Mona (Desdemona: Jeanne Antebi), and her ex, Yann (Iago: Aurélien Recoing).

Unfortunately, the rental service of the African Film Library is still awaiting its delayed launch at the time of writing, and hence I have seen only a trailer for *Souli*.

Macbeth (2004, Sweden, colour)
Directed by Bo Landin and Alex Scherpf
Language: Saami / Swedish
Not seen by current writer

The first feature film in the Saami language, *Macbeth* was made by Scandinature, a company previously known for nature documentaries. It is set among the Saami people of the far north in a heavily stylised non-time: swords whose shape looks medieval coexist with belts of bullets: but otherwise it follows the play closely. Unfortunately I have been unable to obtain the whole film, seeing instead only a ten minute trailer: but that was enough to show how ably the beauty and strangeness of the Lapp setting was used. The crown of Scotland is an iron band studded with reindeer antlers, spiky as a crown of thorns and of a piece with the harsh landscape; Inverness, meanwhile, is a shimmering, translucent ice palace. Even swords and daggers are carved from ice, at once rock-hard and ephemeral, light diffracting through the blood that stains them. The witches are often glimpsed distortedly *through* sheets of ice; the furs in which almost every character is swathed emphasise their animalistic nature, while the occasional use of other styles of clothing forges connections between characters – Lady Macbeth's (Anitta Suikkari) lacy black sleeves mirroring the ghostly white draperies of the witches. Banquo's murderers, in a breathtaking sequence, chase him down across the snow in a dog sled.

Macbeth is brilliantly conceived, hauntingly scored, and gorgeously shot. Its unavailability is a sad loss.

Richard III (2005, U.K., colour)
Directed by Max Day
Starring: Jamie Martin, Caroline Burns Cooke, Max Day, Judy

Carey, Jason Wing
Runtime: 54 minutes

In 2001, a feature in a local paper compared the gang lords of Brighton's notorious Whitehawk estate to the ruthless princes of Renaissance Europe. A young independent film-maker called Max Day read the article, and was inspired to set *Richard III* on the estate. Struggling with an almost non-existent budget, the dangers of shooting in Whitehawk itself, and the difficulty of getting permission to use other, safer locations, he ended up spending more than three years on the project: but in 2005 it finally received a local release in selected Brighton cinemas.

Day's script brutally cut the text to less than a quarter of the play, partly for budgetary reasons and partly to remove anything which did not chime with the new setting. In this he was successful: the incongruities that plague some period analogues such as Michael Almereyda's *Hamlet* (2000) are entirely absent from *Richard III*. Here Edward IV (John Rackham) is a shaven-headed thug lording it over Whitehawk until struck down with cancer; the outsider status of the Woodvilles (Caroline Burns Cooke and Dominic McChesney) is, in a clever reversal of the original, marked by their middle class accents; Margaret (Judy Carey) is a malign Tarot-reading bag lady, never seen to interact with the other characters, who becomes Nemesis as she spits out her curses in voiceover before each fresh murder. Clarence (Jason Wing) is imprisoned in a pub and drowned in a beer barrel; Hastings' (Richard Hawley) severed head is tossed into a skip; Bosworth Field is fought under the stands at Brighton Races, to the strains of "House of the Rising Sun". Every one of these reinterpretations works.

Unfortunately, the shortage of money is obvious. Wobbly, fuzzy camera work and distinctly unconvincing effects, especially in fight and death scenes, undermine Day's vision, while the overall look of the film (despite some occasionally effective noirish touches in the lighting) bears an unfortunate resemblance to an episode of *EastEnders*. Jamie Martin as Richard does his best to salvage things with a stonily psychopathic performance, but his lack of joy in his own crimes transmits itself to the audience, and the crooked king's charm is never felt. He is supported well enough – Hawley's Hastings and Lorraine Woodley's Lady Anne are particularly impressive – but Day's reading places all secondary characters firmly in Richard's shadow, even Elizabeth and his mother (Janet May) appearing pallid and pathetic when they have to share the screen with him.

Leo Carey, Kan Lailey, and Raphaela Reilly-Szostak provide an effortlessly stylish and appropriate score, incorporating several songs from the E.M.I. label (including "Richard III", by Supergrass): the concept is, overall, well realised, and the achievement of making the film on so small a budget cannot fail to impress: but not much of it lingers long in the mind.

West Bank Story (2005, U.S.A., colour)
Based on *Romeo and Juliet*
Directed by Ari Sandel
Starring: Noureen DeWulf, Ben Newmark, Joey Naber, A. J. Tannen
Runtime: 20 minutes
Academy Awards (2007): Best Short Film (Live Action) (Ari Sandel)

As a second-hand copy (via *West Side Story* (1961), although the use of competing restaurants as a backdrop is reminiscent of *Love Is All There Is* (1996) and *Jiyuan qiaohe* (2000)), *West Bank Story* is far removed from *Romeo and Juliet*: but the inclusion of a parody balcony scene qualifies it for inclusion here.

The use of cross-cultural love affairs as a metaphor for the Israeli-Palestinian conflict is not new (see *Torn Apart* (1990)): but where previous attempts at such a treatment had tended towards the heavy-handed and the worthy, this engaging little musical spoof has a much lighter touch. All possible clichés are not only used but acknowledged as such, while Yuval Ron's deliberately overblown and overtly stereotypical score exploits the similarities between Jewish and Arabic musical styles; the rhymes are bad and the dialogue corny, but once again this is done knowingly, and pointed up in a deliberate parody of the musical genre. ("May I come to your balcony tonight and annoy your family with an over-dramatic song about love and feelings?") The choreography (by Raymond Del Barrio) pastiches that of *West Side Story* very effectively.

Before the contrived happy ending (a fire destroys the rival restaurants and forces cooperation to get the businesses back on their feet), the film manages to make some surprisingly

324

daring jokes. A customer orders "Death by Chocolate Suicide Bomber"; a gay Palestinian militant (Del Barrio) is seen adding miniature umbrellas to Molotov cocktails. These lend an edge to what nevertheless manages to remain a sweet film, whose cast and crew's obvious enjoyment is irresistibly infectious. Lacking the substance to fill any greater length, it is ideally suited to its twenty minute runtime, and injects a much needed sense of humour into the dangerous situation it depicts.

El Sueño de una noche de San Juan (2005, Spain / Portugal, colour animation)
Based on *A Midsummer Night's Dream* and *Macbeth*
A.k.a. *Midsummer Dream* (international English title)
Directed by Ángel de la Cruz and Manolo Gómez
Runtime: 85 minutes

The creators of *El Sueño de una noche de San Juan* said that it should be considered not as an adaptation of *A Midsummer Night's Dream* but as a sequel, dealing with the fairies' doings in the modern world (to be precise, the fictional Duchy of Oniria, where casually dressed modern teenagers mingle with adults in distinctly Victorian stylings, and futuristic technology exists side by side with a forelock-tugging feudal attitude). However, writers Ángel de la Cruz and Beatriz Iso appropriated names from the play for the human Onirian characters, among whom only Philostrate truly resembles his Shakespearean namesake.

Into a brew which owes little enough to the *Dream* are stirred *Macbeth* (with the film's Demetrius, a grasping financier, as a potential Macbeth of the fairy and Onirian worlds, complete with witches) and *The NeverEnding Story* (1984), of which this picture is essentially a poor pastiche: the existence of the fairies and their world is threatened by humanity's lack of imagination, and it is up to spoilt teen Helena to save them. Occasional references (love potions, supernatural fog, an amatory triangle, and some marginalised mechanicals) and quotations aside, this scenario has little to do with *A Midsummer Night's Dream*: and the film's own poverty of invention and wit bears sad testament to the very fault it denounces. The animation is of Nineties video game standard, Arturo Kress' score is bland and forgettable, and it is hard not to conclude that the many distinguished actors in the Anglophone cast (the English language dub, contrary to usual practice, was recorded at the same time as the Spanish and

Catalan tracks for simultaneous release) either signed onto the project without reading the script, or did it to pay the bills.

Macbeth 3000: This Time, It's Personal (2005, Canada, colour)
Based on *Macbeth*
Directed by Geoff Warren Meech
Starring: Bill Stepec, Kate Hortop, Denis Logan, Ryan Gilhooly
Runtime: 114 minutes / 120 minutes

SuperGun Cinema's "guerilla film" (meaning that it was largely filmed in public spaces without permission) combines the story of *Macbeth* with a James Bond spoof. Macbeth (Bill Stepec) is a U.S. special operative, appointed to succeed the traitorous Vice-President Cawdor on the whim of the dim-witted President Duncan (Jaime Cobban); Macduff (Denis Logan) is his British counterpart "Agent 69", a barely disguised Bond parody, complete with characters named "Nicklepenny" (Shona Athey, trading sexual puns almost bad enough for a real Bond film) and "Q-Ball" (Trevor Matthews in the world's least convincing bald wig).

The opening battle, staged as a raid on an Iraqi chemical weapons factory, is technically impressive considering the project's minuscule budget: but even here the amateurish acting and pitiable humour that characterise the film are already in evidence. Occasional touches of genuine atmosphere, such as the witches looming out of the darkness in front of Macbeth's car and sending him careering off the road, are overshadowed by all-round woodenness, terrible English and Scottish accents, and desperately unfunny gags about Banquo's (Ryan Gilhooly) sexuality and the incompetence of Macduff's hidebound, bureaucratic sidekicks the Agents Steve (Ben Davis and Chad Holmes). Since the latter could be read as belittling the role of British forces in Iraq – the Steves sit around making tea while a mostly American team does all the work – it is also potentially highly offensive, and very surprising in a Canadian production. For its ambition, its inventive premise, and its underdog status, *Macbeth 3000* garners a lot of goodwill: but this is squandered within ten minutes.

Following a limited release in Canada, the film disappeared. Its imminent release on DVD was promised for several years, before it was finally placed online for free viewing in 2009.

Stredoletní noci sen (2005, Czech Republic, colour)
Based on *A Midsummer Night's Dream*
A.k.a. *A Midsommer Nights Dreame* (international English title); *A Deepsummer Night's Dream*; *Imago Patri*
Directed by Radek Tuma
Language: Czech
Runtime: 65 minutes
Not seen by current writer

Tuma's version of the *Dream* seems to have been a little unconventional: some actors are credited as playing themselves, and it went by a bewildering array of different titles. I have, however, been unable to discover any detailed information about it. It has never been shown outside a handful of festivals in the Czech Republic.

She's the Man (2006, U.S.A., colour)
Based on *Twelfth Night*
Directed by Andy Fickman
Starring: Amanda Bynes, Channing Tatum, Laura Ramsey, Alex Breckenridge, James Snyder
Runtime: 105 minutes

By 2006, the 1990s fad for adapting the classics into teen comedies was long dead, and nobody showed much interest in reviving it – except screenwriter Karen McCullah Lutz, who had had a success with *10 Things I Hate About You* (1999) and was not willing to let Shakespeare rest. From *The Taming of the Shrew* she turned her attentions to *Twelfth Night*, metamorphosing Orsino's court into a high school soccer team.

The difficulty is that what worked with a mostly light-hearted early comedy such as *Shrew* is not so easily transferred to a middle comedy like *Twelfth Night*. Without bereavement or any worse danger than embarrassment, *She's the Man* lacks the play's dark side: Sebastian (James Kirk) and Viola (Amanda Bynes) do not think each other dead, Olivia (Laura Ramsey) has no lost brother, and the marginalised Malvolio figure (James Snyder, with touches of Aguecheek about him and an out of place reference to Feste in his name) attracts no sympathy whatsoever. (Oddly, he has a pet tarantula called Malvolio, while a character utterly unlike Aguecheek (Clifton MacCabe Murray) is named

Andrew.) Lutz and her co-writers even add two extra ciphers for the audience to hate: the exes of both twins, played by Alex Breckenridge and Robert Hoffman.

The film has none of the charm that redeemed *10 Things*, depending instead on bursts of hyperactivity from the camera and cliché-ridden characters, of whom only Viola – thanks to the combination of Bynes' feisty performance and dim echoes of Shakespeare – achieves a third dimension. It is merely a bog-standard high school romantic comedy with a loosely attached sporting theme, which happens to follow (more or less) the Viola / Orsino plotline of *Twelfth Night*: and, even while emphasising the theme of sexual ambiguity, Lutz cannot bear to have any character utter the word "gay". Only one scene works as comedy: an interpolated sequence in which Bynes, pursued round a carnival by various characters, has to perform multiple quick-changes between her male and female guises. There is no scene which works as romance.

10 Things was an interesting if not entirely satisfying engagement with original material; *She's the Man* is a travesty.

Omkara (2006, India, colour)
Based on *Othello*
A.k.a. *Issak* (proposed title rejected in public vote); *O Saathi Re* (proposed title rejected in public vote); *Othello* (working title)
Directed by Vishal Bharadwaj
Starring: Ajay Devgan, Saif Ali Khan, Kareena Kapoor, Vivek Oberoi, Konkona Sen Sharma
Language: Hindi
Runtime: 152 minutes

The gangland setting of *Maqbool* was a fairly conventional one for *Macbeth*: a gangster *Othello*, however, was a much more original notion. Vishal Bharadwaj, long regarded as an arthouse director, was finally by 2006 able to command the necessary finances for a step into the mainstream, and took the bold decision to return to Shakespeare for his first really big film, set not in the urban underworld of *Maqbool* but against the stunning scenery of Uttar Pradesh and Maharashtra.

The Venetian Senate and army become a gang attempting to break into legitimate provincial politics, led by Omi Shukla (Ajay Devgan, the Othello figure); Brabantio (Bhaisaab: Naseeruddin Shah) is a hypocritical politician quite willing to do business with the low-caste criminal he rejects as a son-in-law. Apart from the ubiquitous presence of mobile phones and the replacement of the handkerchief with a jewelled waist-bracelet (like that which stands in for Angelo's chain in *Do Dooni Chaar* (1968)), the text of *Othello* is barely strayed from: many stretches of dialogue are almost direct translations. While English paraphrases tend to draw attention to their own poverty of language by comparison when they approach too near the original script, this problem is less acute with foreign language adaptations – even, in my experience, when one is ignorant of the language and reliant on subtitles – and the script of *Omkara* is sharp and potent.

The acting is strong all round. Vivek Oberoi stands out as a troubled Kesu (Cassio), frustrated by his own hot temper and the knowledge that, as an educated man, he could do better than the gangster's life; Kareena Kapoor makes a sweetly innocent Dolly (Desdemona) whose final fate is suitably horrifying; Bipasha Basu is an alluring Billo (Bianca) – but Saif Ali Khan's cold, coarse, psychopathic Langda (Iago) towers over the film. Having little chance to appear without Khan, Devgan, despite a highly effective performance, remains in his shadow. As in *Maqbool*, the cast are supported superbly by Bharadwaj's score, which moves from exuberance through pomp to unearthliness, perfectly mingling its Indian and Western elements; and the visuals can hardly be bettered.

A carper could assert that Tassaduq Hussain's cinematography, while highly accomplished, is too Hollywoodised and lacks individuality; or that the criminal setting does slightly remove from Omi the sympathy that Othello should receive – although it adds to Dolly's, as she never fully understands the violence of the men among whom she has landed. This, however, would be to split hairs. *Omkara* is a worthy successor to *Maqbool*, and deservedly established Bharadwaj as a major film-maker not only in India, but on the international stage.

Ye yan (2006, China, colour)
Based on *Hamlet*
A.k.a. *Night Banquet* (working title); *The Banquet* (international English title)
Directed by Xiaogang Feng

Starring: Ziyi Zhang, Daniel Wu, You Ge, Xun Zhou, Jingwu Ma
Language: Mandarin
Runtime: 131 minutes

In the wake of *Wo hu cang long* (*Anglice*: *Crouching Tiger, Hidden Dragon* (2000)), Chinese martial arts epics enjoyed a global summer, and were able to muster bigger budgets than ever before. Towards the more ambitious end of the scale was *The Banquet*, announced as "a loose adaptation" of *Hamlet*, for which was constructed what was at the time the largest set ever built in China – hardly a country noted for the modesty of its cinematic production values.

As a matter of fact, the film (set during the Five Dynasties and Ten Kingdoms period that followed the fall of Tang in the tenth century) sticks quite close to Shakespeare until the play within the play. The sole major exception is the fact that the Gertrude figure (Wan: Ziyi Zhang) is the Prince's (Wu Luan: Daniel Wu) stepmother – allowing the film to make more explicit the attraction between them without touching the edge of biological incest. (It also allowed them to cast the young and extraordinarily beautiful Zhang – four years younger than Wu – in the part, but this was not the primary consideration: it had originally been written for an older actress.) After the play scene, the Prince's banishment follows immediately, without the murder of Polonius, and a plot not much like the original is required to bring the characters back together at the eponymous banquet, where a slaughter not dissimilar to that at the end of the play disposes of most of the cast. (Wan, however, survives, and the Polonius figure – Minister Yin (Jingwu Ma) – is the last to die.)

Although Wu's enigmatic Prince, tinged with self-pity and hiding behind an actor's mask, is interesting, and Xun Zhou's Ophelia figure (Qing Nu) pitiable, the film's focus is squarely on the Empress – the most complex role Zhang had yet been asked to play, and one she incontestably rises to. Wan is calculating, manipulative, and cruel, but at the same time playful, emotional, and endued with a genuine love for her stepson and perhaps even her husband (Emperor Li: You Ge in the Claudius role). The Emperor, meanwhile, is massively charismatic, and, though even more ruthless than his original, ultimately remembers his honour and commits suicide in a scene that leaves one wondering that You Ge has not become better known than he is outside China. (The actor's fear of flying, which makes overseas work difficult, may have something to do with this.) No character is allowed to sit within the simplistic divisions into good and evil that the genre sometimes lends itself to – instead they have all the moral complexity of Shakespeare's versions.

The film is, as we have come to expect, beautiful to look at, spectacular sets (by Timmy Yip) augmented by lavish computer effects, exquisitely designed colour-coded costumes, flawless choreography (dances by Yuanyuan Wang, fights by the great Wo-Ping Yuen). They can hardly be blamed for the fact that the styles they put together in *Wo hu cang long* and subsequent films had by 2006 become perhaps a little over familiar. There are new elements here: the ubiquitous presence of masks, whether the theatrical ones favoured by Wu Luan or the face-modelled visors of the Imperial guard; more blood than is usually seen in mainland Chinese cinema, reflecting a growing influence from Hong Kong and Japan. But there is not enough to distract from the sense of having seen it – and, well done though it is here, seen it done better – before. Tan Dun's score, meanwhile, is his most Westernised work to date, and hardly seems to belong in a Chinese period film.

The film's many deliberate references to traditions of Chinese theatre do mark something new in Chinese cinema – not only a reference to the play's own metatheatrical tricks, but another sign of Japanese influence, inspired at least in part by Kurosawa's use of *Noh* traditions. Unfortunately, however, outside the play scene itself, they are not blended well into the film, instead interrupting the flow of the plot. The result is to render the film, in spite of all the strong acting and visual splendour, awkward and lurchingly paced: a fault compounded by inconsistent editing. This is a sad failing in what is so nearly an excellent film.

As You Like It (2006, U.S.A. / U.K., colour)
Directed by Kenneth Branagh
Starring: Bryce Dallas Howard, David Oyelowo, Romola Garai, Kevin Kline, Brian Blessed
Runtime: 122 minutes

Following the commercial failure of *Love's Labour's Lost* (2000), Kenneth Branagh was compelled to shelve the

Shakespeare Film Company and his projected adaptations of *Macbeth* and *As You Like It*. Eventually, however, he was able to talk H.B.O. into a deal to make the latter (complete with a credit to the long dormant S.F.C.), although the gap between production (which wrapped in July 2005) and premiere was a long and tortuous fourteen months.

Branagh had announced that he intended, not to retire from acting, but to scale back his commitments in that area in order to concentrate on directing: and *As You Like It* was the first of his Shakespearean features in which he retreated behind the camera – aptly so, as there was no obvious part for him in the play. Since his first visit to Japan some twenty years previously, he had harboured the desire to set this particular piece there in the early Meiji era, *circa* 1880: and this, despite attracting some opprobrium for his use of a largely non-Asian cast, he did, to quite beautiful effect.

The film's most obvious strength lies in the design, an area in which Branagh and his regular collaborators consistently shine. Tim Harvey's sets and Susannah Buxton's style-blending costumes (mingling European elements into the Japanese look in true Meiji fashion) are utterly exquisite. The cast, also, is perfect. Bryce Dallas Howard reminds us why Johnson wrote that the man not delighted by Rosalind was incapable of delight, while Romola Garai is easily her equal as Celia; David Oyelowo makes a more forceful and intelligent Orlando than audiences are perhaps used to, and Adrian Lester a devilishly sexy Oliver. Brian Blessed excels in the double role of the Dukes, touching his white-haired and stooping Senior with a melancholy almost comparable with that of Jaques (Kevin Kline), and making the much younger, armour-clad Frederick a paranoiac, perpetually on the edge of complete mental collapse.

The mood of the film is very different from Branagh's earlier big screen attempts at the comedies. Where *Much Ado About Nothing* (1993) and *Love's Labour's Lost* rattled by like express trains, punching up their jokes, *As You Like It* – despite heavy textual cuts – is a considerably slower beast, closer in feel to Branagh's televised *Twelfth Night* (1988): and, like the latter, it emphasises the melancholic strain over the comedy. (For partly budgetary reasons, it is also shot in a more intimate style than any Branagh picture since *Henry V* (1989).) The film opens with a dramatisation of Frederick's violent coup; until Rosalind reaches the forest, the sun is not seen, nor any line played for laughs (and some of the funniest are deliberately excised). Even when the film does enter more light-hearted regions, Branagh restrains his bad habit of backing up verbal byplay with unsubtle sight gags, instead simply luxuriating in the complementary beauty of language and image.

The main supports of this Kurosawa- and Yamada-influenced vision are not the characters around whom the plot revolves, but its aloof philosophers. In the foreground is Jaques, often portrayed either as bitter or as unattractively self-satisfied in his wit, or a grotesque combination of the two, but here played by Kline as something much simpler and more sympathetic – a man of high intelligence who reacts to the world and its follies with unaffected sadness. More self-effacing but no less important is the eternally patient Corin (Jimmy Yuill), whom Branagh gives an entire new back-story as a Christian missionary turned shepherd, allowing him to appropriate the lines of Martext and Hymen, and conduct the quadruple wedding at the end of the play. He has a counterpoint in the hermit (uncredited) who converts Frederick, here made a Buddhist holy man.

The film looks set to finish with a song-and-dance finale transplanted directly from *Much Ado*: but in the midst of their skipping through the forest, the revellers pass the stricken Frederick. Celia stops to kiss her father – then leaves him. The now ex-duke remains catatonic until, after all others have departed, Jaques approaches and sits by him, striking up an unheard conversation: a reminder, even while the music (by the ever reliable Patrick Doyle, less obtrusive than usual, but pastiching Japanese styles with his habitual facility) dances on, of the dark side of the play. The true close is a clever piece of metatheatre: Howard delivers the epilogue while wandering (in male costume) amid the film crew, picking up a cup of coffee, and finally retreating to her trailer, the last words of the film – spoken by Branagh in voiceover – being "And... cut". (Howard is not exactly playing herself here: the epilogue's persona remains male, she retains the English accent she adopted for the part, and the trailer is marked as belonging not to "Miss Howard" but to "Rosalind". Fantasy and reality thus coexist.) In marked contrast to the peculiar pointlessness of the epilogue in the Paul Czinner film (1936), this fits nicely with the extreme stylisation of what has gone before: more than usually, Branagh is intent on reminding us that we are watching a work of art.

As You Like It was initially released to theatres in only two countries, Italy and Greece. Outside these, it did a brief round of festivals before being consigned to DVD – a victim of the timidity and ignorance of distributors, who had become once more as scared of the name "Shakespeare" as they had been in the 1980s – and finally limping into British cinemas in August 2007, only to be savaged by a largely philistine critical fraternity. (It was not helped by coinciding with the release of Branagh's genuinely disappointing remake of the 1972 classic *Sleuth*, which helped to sour the critics against him.) In the United States, as part of the H.B.O. deal, it went straight to television around the same time. American critics were considerably more appreciative than their British counterparts: but it is still hard not to feel that this film deserved much better treatment all round.

Romeo & Juliet: Sealed with a Kiss (2006, U.S.A., colour animation)
Based on *Romeo and Juliet*
Directed by Phil Nibbelink
Runtime: 76 minutes

Sealed with a Kiss (which debuted on DVD, before inexplicably receiving a limited theatrical release in Los Angeles) is a quite dreadful pun, warning the prospective viewer that Shakespeare's star-crossed lovers have been transformed into anthropomorphised seals in a cartoon possessing all the sickly sweetness of Disney and none of the imagination or humour. In a ham-fisted allegory of racism – a subject addressed much better in earlier adaptations of the same play – the Montagues are brown seals and the Capulets white, and colour is repeatedly referred to. (Before gate-crashing the Capulet party, here held on a wrecked pirate ship, the Montagues paint themselves white.)

Paris, Tybalt, and Escalus are combined in the person of Prince, a monstrous and despotic elephant seal who woos Juliet, throws Mercutio (non-fatally) off a cliff, and banishes Romeo out of jealousy rather than stern justice; the Nurse becomes Kissy the Kissing Fish, squeaky-voiced, bubbly, and painfully annoying, while the Friar is a grumpy sea otter whose experiments appear strongly tinged with the supernatural. Shakespeare is quoted, misquoted, and riffed on at every turn, complete with the old (and never challenged) schoolboy error of assuming that "wherefore" means "where". Nobody is permitted an unhappy ending. One can at least be thankful that some of the little invention the film contains is lavished on the problem of how the lovers can survive: Romeo, in a reversal of Juliet's declaration that "I will kiss thy lips; / Haply some poison yet doth hang on them, / To make me die with a restorative", kisses his "dead" love, ingests some of the Friar's potion, and falls apparently dead himself, allowing the families to be reconciled in grief before both their children recover.

Forgettable songs disappoint compared to the stylishly jazzy incidental music; hoary old jokes fall flat (one *Titanic* parody did make me laugh: but, like the Shakespearean references, it will undoubtedly go over the heads of anyone young enough to enjoy this film – I would put the optimum viewing age at about three). The animation – traditional cel for the characters, digital for their environment – is unimpressive; and the whole idea of the obviously juvenile Romeo and Juliet as romantic leads, let alone of Juliet as the object of the gargantuan Prince's affection, feels faintly inappropriate. But the main question remains this: why did anybody imagine that this film needed to be made?

Measure for Measure (2006, U.K., colour)
A.k.a. *William Shakespeare's Measure for Measure*
Directed by Bob Komar
Starring: Daniel Roberts, Josephine Rogers, Simon Phillips, Simon Nuckley
Runtime: 72 minutes

The first English language version of the so-called "Problem Play" *Measure for Measure* to reach the big screen was an ultra-low-budget film set in the British Army in the frighteningly near future. All non-clerical characters, even the pimps and whores, have here been transformed into soldiers, bringing the whole of Vienna within one barracks and providing a not *too* implausible modern context for the plot. The despotic power wielded by Duke Vincentio (Simon Phillips) and Angelo (Daniel Roberts) may not be matched by any real general in the Western world, but it is credible in a military context: and the breakdown in discipline caused by Vincentio's licence explains Angelo's crackdown adequately enough. This indiscipline is illustrated in the opening sequence: these soldiers take cocaine and fondle each other in public, and burn their own flag while footage from Iraq plays in the background; even the Duke takes part in the debauchery.

The Iraq War is directly referred to only in that fleeting shot, but is clearly the intended backdrop for this adaptation, replacing the vaguely described Central European conflict of the play. Claudio (Simon Nuckley) is viciously abused in his cell by a female guard in scenes reminiscent of Abu Ghraib; when Angelo, implored to show pity, replies that "I show it most of all when I show justice, / For then I pity those I do not know", he could be a Blairite minister defending detention without trial. When Claudio's survival is finally revealed, he is brought out of prison in a hood like the "unlawful combatants" of the 2000s.

The screenplay is by and large a serviceable abridgement of the play, though using less than a third of the text (and here and there inexplicably eking it out with odd lines from *Romeo and Juliet*): but there are some sad losses. Barnardine disappears altogether, while Lucio (Luke Leeves) is present only when the plot absolutely requires him, draining much of the colour from the play. Act Four Scene One vanishes, so that we never see Isabella (Josephine Rogers) and Mariana (Emma Ager) together until after the supposed execution of Claudio – which makes Isabella's plea for Angelo's life still less plausible, coming at the request of an apparent stranger.

There are a few interesting directorial decisions, some more effective than others. The Duke, in his clerical disguise, affects blindness: convenient both for disguise (smoked glasses) and spying, but also symbolic – he was indeed blind as a monarch, but as a priest becomes all-seeing. (References to his return are pointedly juxtaposed with religious statuary, hinting at the critical theory that Vincentio is in fact God – though as this is a clearly fallible Duke, it is unlikely that Komar meant to endorse this position.) The priest replacing Friar Peter (Roberto Argenti), when he questions the Duke's plan, is allowed to show serious spirit and opposition, the lines "It rested in Your Grace / T' unloose this tied-up justice when you pleased" becoming a denunciation of Vincentio's rule: but minutes later he prostitutes his office by knowingly allowing the impostor to hear Angelo's confession. A sign of how far Vienna's corruption has reached, or directorial sloppiness? Angelo's first importunities to Isabella are overheard by two soldiers, though the matter is never mentioned again – a misstep, as the fact that they could come forward at any time undercuts the audience's fear for the heroine. And at the end, following the lead set by Estelle Kohler in John Barton's landmark 1970 production for the R.S.C., Isabella refuses Vincentio's hand. (Shakespeare, of course, intriguingly left her response unstated, which puts it at the discretion of the director.)

The modern setting seldom feels incongruous, and the verse-speaking is strong and assured: but Rogers fails to fill the role of Isabella. It is true that everybody seems cold-blooded in this *Measure for Measure* – Phillips' Vincentio shows a detachment which verges on the sociopathic as he toys with other characters' lives – but a passionless and unvarying Isabella is fatal to the play. Even Roberts, whose half-restrained, dangerous, tortured Angelo is quite excellent, cannot make up for Rogers' shortcomings: and, in the end, her monotonous performance undermines the picture.

Macbeth (2006, Australia, colour)
A.k.a. *M.* (working title)
Directed by Geoffrey Wright
Starring: Sam Worthington, Victoria Hill, Lachy Hulme, Gary Sweet, Steve Bastoni
Runtime: 105 minutes

By 2006 the field was becoming distinctly crowded for gangland Macbeths, but none on the big screen – unless one counts Bryan Enk's 2003 version (q.v.), which is hardly a gangster film as conventionally understood, and is in any case somewhat obscure – had yet used the original text. Geoffrey *"Romper Stomper"* Wright's transposition of the play to the present day Melbourne docklands was, therefore, a more original idea than it might appear at first glance.

Unfortunately, it was not one to which Wright was equipped to do justice. The film is lacklustre from the start, largely unimaginative in design, photography, and updating: but worst of all is the handling of the script. The adaptation, largely the work of Victoria Hill (who played Lady Macbeth), cuts, tweaks, transposes and reapportions lines, frequently spoiling the scansion and even the sense for no good reason. Shakespeare can stand a lot of this sort of thing: most of his greatest filmic adaptors, in particular Orson Welles (though he treated *Macbeth* with more respect than other texts), have similarly played around with the script: but here it is done pointlessly and ineptly, and the result is confusion.

This is exacerbated by the fact that most of the secondary players show little sign of having known what the lines meant before they were mangled, let alone what (if anything) they may mean in the forms rendered. Star Sam Worthington is, at least, not guilty of this – only of a crippling lack of presence. Hill herself, and Gary Sweet's charismatic Duncan, go some way to making up for this, but the heart of the film remains blank.

One area whose treatment is at least interesting in conception is the portrayal of the Witches by Chloe Armstrong, Kate Bell, and Miranda Nation. These are no rigwoody hags, but attractive teenagers who first appear vandalising a graveyard and later cavort naked in the Macbeths' kitchen, always unnaturally lit in reds or purples, and actually having sex with the King in the second prophecy scene. Banquo (Steve Bastoni) does not see them, and it is strongly hinted that Macbeth's first glimpse of them as he visits the grave of his infant son is their only occurrence outside his imagination – which completely changes their significance. The discrepancy between their appearance and the text is hard to swallow, and the actresses' inexperience combines with Worthington's dullness to scupper their scenes.

Macbeth succeeds in being simultaneously flashy and boring, never half as daring or clever as it imagines, and seldom making any kind of sense.

Rockin' Romeo & Juliet (2006, U.S.A. / Germany, colour)
Based on *Romeo and Juliet*
Directed by David McGaw
Starring: David McGaw, Virtic Emil Brown, Michael Haboush, Ginger Wade
Runtime: 93 minutes

Rockin' Romeo & Juliet is a rock musical by Anglo-American band OGGI – essentially a vanity project by their frontman David McGaw. It began as an outdoor stage show in Los Angeles in the summer of 2001; five years later, despite having virtually no budget, McGaw decided to turn the show into a film, casting himself as a somewhat middle-aged Romeo.

There are attempts at an inventive realisation of the fantastical setting: Japanese stylings meant to evoke kabuki theatre on the Capulet side, and European Renaissance costumes for the Montagues, mingle with modern elements: but every part of this mixture is cheap and unconvincing. The acting, furthermore, is uniformly atrocious. Most of the cast act as if reading their lines from a teleprompter, while McGaw himself speaks every word as if it is of life-or-death consequence; there is small sign that anybody understood what they were saying. The band's other vocalist, Ginger Wade, in male drag as Benvolio, adopts a strangled and unconvincing English accent, apparently in imitation of McGaw's Liverpudlian tones.

The best that can be said is that the band's music does benefit by default, being the only element of the film which is not a complete artistic failure. Even so, those of the songs which are used to advance the plot, rather than as mere accompaniment, suffer from desperately trite lyrics: and even the best utterly fail to justify McGaw's frequent citation of such distinguished influences as the Rolling Stones and Led Zeppelin. A severe delusion of grandeur appears to have been the main driving force behind this film.

Prince of the Himalayas (2006, China, colour)
A.k.a. *Ximalaya wangzi* (China: Mandarin title)
Directed by Sherwood Hu
Language: Tibetan
Runtime: 108 minutes
Not seen by current writer

Sherwood Hu's *Prince of the Himalayas* transferred a by all accounts quite faithful rendition of the *Hamlet* story to the stunning mountain backdrop of medieval Tibet. The trailer reveals a lavishly designed, beautifully shot film, apparently fast-paced and bloody: but it is too short to reveal much.

Hamlet (2007, Serbia, colour)
A.k.a. *Hamlet, ciganski princ* (working title)
Directed by Aleksandar Rajkovic
Language: Serbo-Croat / Roma
Runtime: 105 minutes
Not seen by current writer

Rajkovic's *Hamlet*, starring Igor Djordjevic, was set among Roma rubbish collectors on the outskirts of modern Belgrade, and used a mostly non-professional supporting cast. It attempted to comment on the religious and ethnic tensions in the Balkans – the "Danish" gang are Orthodox Christians, while Muslims take the place of the Norwegians – and the harshness of post-Communist life: but the film received mixed reviews and disappeared after doing the festival circuit.

The available trailer shows that Rajkovic stuck closely to the play's plot, though the poetry is sadly missed. Silvia Strozzi's scenography ably captures the brutality and squalor of the setting, while Dragan Kresic's haunting Roma-style music saves it from becoming merely depressing.

Hamlet (2007, U.K., colour)
A.k.a. *Fodor's Hamlet* (DVD)
Directed by Alexander Fodor
Starring: William Belchambers, Di Sherlock, Alan Hanson, Lydia Piechowiak, Tallulah Sheffield
Runtime: 131 minutes

The director's description of his film as "set in a surrealistic, nightmarish, Kafkaesque no man's land... not so much a modern version... as a lateral concept"[120] suggests something similar to Bryan Enk's *Macbeth* (2003). The viewer who expects this will, however, be sadly disappointed. The impression one gets is that it was merely lack of budget which compelled Fodor to eschew realism: unfortunately, to realise a surreal vision requires rather more imagination than is on display here. Occasionally having Gertrude (Di Sherlock) and the Players speak their lines in German, and cutting away to Hamlet's childhood self (uncredited) running around a bright white room and laughing, does not make a film "Kafkaesque". Essentially, contrary to Fodor's claims, his *Hamlet* is indeed set in the modern world – Elsinore appears to be a not very well frequented seaside hotel – and his "surrealism" is merely a thin excuse for the lack of conviction with which that world, empty apart from the speaking characters, is presented.

The attempts at original readings fall rather flat. A female Horatio (Katie Reddin-Clancy) is not particularly surprising, nor is she the first Horatio to show an attraction to the Prince: they actually share three kisses as Hamlet (William Belchambers) lies dying. A Polonius (Lydia Piechowiak) who is

---

[120] Quoted in the sleeve notes for the DVD, 2008.

not only female but young, the *sister* of Laertes (Jason Wing) and Ophelia (Tallulah Sheffield), is indeed startling – because the concept is so much at odds with the text that it makes no sense. The text itself is heavily cut, with many lines transposed – and many lines fluffed: Belchambers stumbles twice in the "To be or not to be" speech alone. When this is taken together with the flatness of virtually all the performances – James Frail's exuberantly sinister Ghost is a lone exception – the impression is of an early rehearsal rather than a production ready to be seen. On the other hand, given the one-dimensional readings of key characters which Fodor's sleeve notes for the DVD revealed, it is unlikely that the actors would ever have become much more impressive under his direction. His Ophelia is a bimbo, his Laertes a chippy yob, and he sees nothing more to them. Fodor must bear much more blame than the cast for the result.

After its premiere, *Hamlet* disappeared from cinemas, and reappeared on DVD as *Fodor's Hamlet*, with notes and blurb by the writer-actor-director himself. Modesty, it appears, is not among Alexander Fodor's virtues: but on the evidence of this film, he has much to be modest about.

The Tempest (2007, U.S.A., colour)
Directed by Carmella Cardina
Starring: J. Karen Thomas, Heather Fox, Katrina Gourley, John Bader, Michael LeBlanc
Runtime: 118 minutes

Cardina's low-budget independent *Tempest* transfers the story to modern Los Angeles, with a squat (whose timbered interior, especially as shot with a hand-held camera, vaguely resembles a tall ship's hold) as Prospero's (J. Karen Thomas) cell, and the run-down estate surrounding it as the island. The titular storm is an attack by a gang of crusties (the spirits) on the cars of C.E.O. Alonso (James DiStefano) and his people as they pass through the rough area. The logic of this update is slightly shaky. The estate lacks the isolation of an island; it is not plausible that Miranda (Heather Fox) has seen no mortal men but Caliban (John Bader) and her father; the business world of the film appears to rely on succession by primogeniture.

The slightly surreal tone of the piece makes it easier to accept these anomalies. This is aided by the casting, which is deliberately counter-realistic: Prospero and Antonio (Laura

Bradley) are both still supposed to be male, though played by women; Prospero is black, his brother and daughter white. (Of course, casting a black Prospero turns the proto-colonial themes often seen in this play on their head.) Meanwhile, in the dance of the goddesses, Iris is played by a man, drag artist Miss Amanda. The casting of Bradley, albeit as a male Antonio, brings out an intriguing element of eroticism in his/her relationship with Sebastian (Will Wallace): the incitement scene, though poorly blocked – the predatory Bradley circles Wallace at least twice too often – is clearly played as a seduction.

Magic steals slowly into the picture: the "tempest" could be entirely natural, as could the hyperactive Ariel's (Katrina Gourley) early spying activities, but it gradually becomes apparent that Ariel really is invisible, and that Prospero's powers are as real as in the play. By the time Ariel reveals herself to the wizard's enemies, in a glittering purple gown with wings spread behind her, we are back in the realm of full blown fantasy: yet Caliban is still nothing more than a deranged tramp wrapped in a blanket.

The quality of both acting and filming varies. Thomas' commanding and charismatic Prospero easily dominates the film, well supported by Gourley and Bader; but the whiny Fox makes an unlikeable Miranda, and Michael LeBlanc as Ferdinand is distinctly flat. There are several blips in the filming, surely not all deliberate and hardly any well advised, while the editing (by Cardina herself) is poorly handled, often destroying any consistency of pacing. The film's greatest strength, after Thomas' performance, is the score, by Bradley and Michael Wallace, which displays an almost infinite variety of moods and styles. For all its unevenness, *The Tempest* always displays enough inventiveness to keep the viewer's interest.

It has not as yet received a commercial release.

Othello (2007, South Africa, colour)
Directed by Eubulus Timothy
Not seen by current writer

Eubulus Timothy's *Othello* began as a stage production for The Other Theatre Company, set in modern day South Africa and filmed as *Othello: A South African Tale* in 2005, but not apparently released in cinemas. Two years later, Timothy turned it into a feature film; the central role, originally played by Sello

Maake Kaa Ncube, was taken by Royston Stoffels. It was shot in and around Cape Town, with a mostly volunteer cast and crew, their families helping out and cooking meals for them, and rushed to a limited release; Laurence Chetty, as in the original, provided a score evocative of the new setting. The tiny budget is far from apparent in the slickly made trailer, which makes the film look almost opulent.

The racial theme was made more complex by the casting of a black Iago, Hakeem Kae-Kazim. This Iago, much darker than Stoffels and with his strong Nigerian accent marking him out from the South African actors, is still more of an outsider than Othello, but knows exactly how to play the aristocratic whites. The trailer gives far more time to the ferociously intense Kae-Kazim than to the barely visible Stoffels: it appears that, once again, Iago has stolen the show.

Richard III (2008, U.S.A., colour)
Directed by Scott M. Anderson
Not seen by current writer
"William Shakespeare's greatest villain is about to visit... Hollywood."[121]

After a long and troubled attempt to get his screenplay for a modern American *Richard III* made, Scott M. Anderson decided to direct, produce, and star in it himself. He managed to persuade a few rather better known actors to take roles in it, ceding top billing to David Carradine as Buckingham, probably thanks to Carradine's recent comeback in *Kill Bill: Vol. 2* (2004).

The trailer suggests a slick, stylish gangland thriller, combining a much more opulent L.A. setting than 2002's *King Rikki* with Shakespeare's unmodernised dialogue, with a touch of racial conflict thrown in (the Plantagenets are white, the despised Woodvilles Hispanic). Unfortunately, however, despite success on the festival circuit, the film has not to date received a theatrical or D.V.D. release.

Were The World Mine (2008, U.S.A., colour)
Based on *A Midsummer Night's Dream*
A.k.a. *Fairies: A Musical Dream Come True* (working title)

---

[121] From the trailer.

Directed by Tom Gustafson
Starring: Tanner Cohen, Wendy Robie, Judy McLane, Zelda Williams, Nathaniel David Becker
Runtime: 92 minutes

Tom Gustafson's *Were The World Mine* is a feature length remake of his own 25 minute short *Fairies* (2003): but, while *Fairies* merely takes the love-in-idleness conceit from *A Midsummer Night's Dream* and runs (though not very far) with it, *Were The World Mine* actually owes the bones of its plot to the play. The set-up of the two films is the same. Timothy (Tanner Cohen) is the only openly gay pupil at an all male private school; encouraged by his English teacher, Ms Tebbit (Wendy Robie, who played the same role in *Fairies*), he discovers a secret formula for a love philtre in the text of *A Midsummer Night's Dream* while rehearsing the role of Puck, and uses it to win his fantasy object Jonathon (Nathaniel David Becker) and to awaken gay feelings in many of his former tormentors.

The difference is that *Fairies* ends here. The fact that Timothy is exactly imitating Puck's behaviour, which causes such chaos in the play, is ignored, as is any doubt over the morality of compelling love by magic: we end with a joyfully gay rugby team composed entirely of happy couples, and all possible complications brushed aside. Thus *Fairies* sacrifices both drama, and its connection to the play which inspired it, for a swift canter to a trite conclusion. In expanding it, Gustafson decided to follow Shakespeare more closely. Here, Timothy is truly Puck, and Ms Tebbit Oberon, with the whole town taking over the roles of the capricious fairies' victims: and, although the film still *ends* with Timothy and Jonathon together and the locals' homophobia banished, the bigoted and the blameless alike have suffered much on the journey.

Interspersed with this are a number of breathtakingly camp musical sequences, the lyrics mostly lifted straight from the play. There are other, smaller references to Shakespeare: Flute's objection to playing a woman is paraphrased, and placed in the mouth, not of one of the boys given actual female parts, but of the boy playing Flute (and therefore Thisbe). Too often, it crosses the line into the obvious and the downright cheesy: but Gustafson is not concerned with subtlety, but with exposing prejudice and telling a feel-good fairy tale at the same time. It takes too long to get to the love-in-idleness sequence, but thereafter is often very funny: and the end, however far it stretches credulity that Jonathon remains with Timothy after the spell is lifted, is genuinely uplifting.

The Hamlet Adventure (2008, Bulgaria / U.S.A. / Germany, colour)
Based on *Hamlet*
A.k.a. *Avantyurata Hamlet* (Bulgaria)
Directed by Greg Roach and Ivaylo Dikanski
Language: English / Bulgarian / Spanish / German
Runtime: 81 minutes / 108 minutes (extended version)
Not seen by current writer

In 1999, Greg Roach attempted to turn *Hamlet* into an all-singing, all-dancing musical, entitled *I, Hamlet* and starring Assen Pavlov. The project foundered; but he later returned to Bulgaria, where *I, Hamlet* had had its abortive existence, and, with his producer and fellow *Hamlet*-obsessive Stanislav Semerdijev, turned what footage had been shot in 1999 into a *Looking for Richard* style documentary about the film that never was, interspersing it with interviews with cast and crew. The film was not a success: variety.com slammed its "hollow concept" and "spectacular pretentiousness"[122], and it has not had a theatrical release outside Bulgaria.

Manatsu no yo no yume (2009, Japan, colour)
Based on *A Midsummer Night's Dream*
A.k.a. *Manatsu no yoru no yume* (Japan); *A Midsummer Night's Dream* (international English title); *A Midsummer's Okinawan Dream* (international English title)
Directed by Yuji Nakae
Runtime: 105 minutes
Not seen by current writer

Nakae's take on the *Dream* moved the setting to modern Japan, with Yuki Shibamoto playing a Tokyo office worker (Yuriko) very loosely based on Hermia. When she relocates to her ancestral Okinawa, pursued by Demetrius-figure Atsushi (Toshihiro Wada), the familiar complications follow, involving

---

122

http://www.variety.com/review/VE1117936640.html?categoryid=31&cs=1
.

attempted stagings of traditional drama, a love potion, and the interventions of Puck-like spirit Majiru (Honami Kurashita).

The trailer – sadly lacking subtitles – reveals a bombastic, loud, and colourful film with slightly unconvincing special effects. It has not yet been released outside Japan.

Iago (2009, Italy, colour)
Based on *Othello*
Directed by Volfango De Biasi
Starring: Nicolas Vaporidis, Laura Chiatti, Aurelien Gaya, Fabio Ghidoni
Language: Italian
Runtime: 101 minutes

The conceit on which this alleged comedy hangs is that it turns *Othello* on its head: here, Otello (Aurelien Gaya) is manipulative and selfish, and our sympathy is supposed to lie with Iago (Nicolas Vaporidis). The characters are mostly architecture students at the University of Venice: Otello, string-pulled in by his father, a corrupt African politician (Mamadou Dioumé), proceeds to steal Iago's designs and his girlfriend Desdemona (Laura Chiatti). Having asked us to accept a borderline racist premise, the film then expects us to side with Iago as he takes a revenge much like that in the play, albeit without its bloody conclusion: at the end, Iago and Desdemona bewilderingly get back together.

The film is handsomely shot by Enrico Lucidi, the young cast attractive and not untalented, and the notion of inverting *Othello*'s moral universe is certainly an inventive one. Monica Celeste's costumes, incorporating Jacobean elements into convincingly modern fashions, are very cleverly designed. Ultimately, however, *Iago* founders on its script, which executes the central idea so poorly that the result is distasteful wherever it is not merely boring.

Romeo & Juliet vs. The Living Dead (2009, U.S.A., colour)
Based on *Romeo and Juliet*
Directed by Ryan Denmark
Runtime: 84 minutes
Not seen by current writer

Third Star Films' *Romeo & Juliet vs. The Living Dead* rests on the same conceit as Seth Grahame-Smith's novel *Pride and Prejudice and Zombies* (also 2009): a canonised literary classic is reworked, with zombies. (The title is misleading: Romeo (Jason Witter) is in fact one of the living dead. Third Star had already given Shakespeare similar treatment in *Hamlet the Vampire Slayer* (2008), directed by Witter; but *Hamlet* disappeared after being shown at one small festival in New Mexico.) To judge from the trailer, they clearly had fun with the possibilities: when a Capulet servant bites his thumb at a Montague zombie, it gets bitten off; "Oh happy dagger" becomes, with a tip of the hat to the *Evil Dead* series, "Oh happy chainsaw"; "Wherefore art thou Romeo?", yet again mistaken as meaning "where", is answered by an apparently disembodied hand falling on Juliet's (Hannah Kauffmann) shoulder from behind, pulling her backwards: cue scream.

The tiny budget – most obvious in the makeup (by Maeve Brandau) – and the implausibility of combining stock shots of Verona with footage clearly shot in much more modern surroundings (most of the movie was filmed in Albuquerque), can hardly be helped. A script which sprinkles "thous" and "haths" across anachronistic and often banal dialogue, actors who sound much less at ease with the language than with the concept, and apparent major departures from the story, are more serious flaws: but it is difficult to judge the film on the basis of two minutes of footage. Online reviews are enthusiastic, and it was obviously enjoyable to make.

All's Well That Ends Well (2009, U.K., colour)
Directed by Marianne Elliott
Not seen by current writer
In June 2009, the National Theatre revived an old practice, described above in the piece on the Gielgud / Burton *Hamlet* (1964): a live performance was filmed and broadcast to cinemas as it was performed, allowing it to be viewed by a much wider audience than could come to the theatre. The play, Racine's *Phèdre*, proved such a success in this format that it became the National's regular practice: and, on 1st October, Shakespeare's *All's Well That Ends Well* – directed by Marianne Elliott and starring Michelle Terry – was broadcast to an audience of 26,000.

Unfortunately, it has to date been the National's policy

not to release these recordings on DVD, for fear of losing the immediacy of a live broadcast; hence, all that is available of *All's Well* is a short trailer and a not much longer documentary about the production. These emphasise its dark fairytale atmosphere: gloom-shrouded forests, magic lantern animation, lavish nineteenth century costumes, and direct references to Perrault and the Grimms, are much in evidence. It is visually gorgeous; reviews suggest that it was also extremely well acted.

As of July 2010, no new Shakespeare films have, so far as I can discover, been released this year. Several exciting projects are in the pipeline: Julie Taymor's *The Tempest*, starring Helen Mirren as a cross-gendered Prospera, has been delayed by the folding of Miramax, but is due out in December; Ralph Fiennes' modern day *Coriolanus*, the first feature film of that play, is in post-production; *Hamlet A.D.D.*, a surreal time-hopping look at the easily distracted Prince's ability to procrastinate, awaits a release date; animated comedy *Gnomeo and Juliet*, in which the feuding families are replaced with indoor and outdoor garden gnomes, is due next year; Michael Radford and Al Pacino are rumoured to have teamed up again to make *King Lear*. The long and fascinating story of cinema's love affair with William Shakespeare shows no sign of ending.

INDEX

All artists mentioned in the text are indexed for every big screen Shakespearean film adaptation with which they were associated. Surnames including "de", "von", etc., are listed by their first capitalised word: thus Herbert von Karajan appears under K, but Gus Van Sant under V. Screenwriting credits are included only when the text is substantially original to the writer in question. Shakespeare's sources are credited only where text from their works not incorporated into the original plays has been added to the film scripts.

Abbott, George	book, *The Boys from Syracuse* (1940)
Abela, Alexander	director, producer, cinematographer, screenwriter, *Makibefo* (1999) director, screenwriter, *Souli* (2004)
Abramov, A.	director, *Dvenadtsataya noch* (1955)
Acosta, Armando	director, screenwriter, cinematographer, *Romeo-Juliet* (1990)
Adler, Allen	story, *Forbidden Planet* (1956)
Adomaitis, Regimantas	Edmund, *Korol Lir* (1971)
Affleck, Ben	Ned Alleyn / Mercutio, *Shakespeare in Love* (1998)
Ager, Emma	Mariana, *Measure for Measure* (2006)
Ahamed, Kabir	Hamlet, *Hamlet: Prince of Denmark* (1989)
Åhlin, Per	director, editor, screenwriter, *Resan till Melonia* (1989)
Ahsan, Mehdi	screenwriter, *Khoon Ka Khoon* (1935)
Aimée, Anouk	Georgia Maglia / Juliet Capulet, *Les Amants de Vérone* (1949)
Alarcón, José María	set decorator, *Antony and Cleopatra* (1972)
Aldridge, Michael	Ancient Pistol, *Campanadas a medianoche* (1965)
Algueró, José	set decorator, *Antony and Cleopatra* (1972)
Allen, Penelope	herself / Queen Elizabeth, *Looking for Richard* (1996)
Allen, Woody	Mr Alien, *King Lear* (1987)
Almereyda, Michael	director, pixillography, *Hamlet* (2000)
von Alten, Ferdinand	Rodrigo, *Othello* (1922) Prince of Aragon, *Der*

351

352

	artistic advisor, director of Witches' scenes, & Edward the Confessor, *Macbeth* (1997)
	director & Lear, *King Lear* (1999)
	Oberon (voice: English version), *El Sueño de una noche de San Juan* (2005)
	Frederick / Senior, *As You Like It* (2006)
Block, Irving	story, production designer, *Forbidden Planet* (1956)
Blom, August	director, *Hamlet* (1910)
	director, *For Åbent Tæppe* (1911)
Bloom, Claire	Lady Anne, *Richard III* (1955)
Blore, Eric	Pinch, *The Boys from Syracuse* (1940)
Blose, Heidi	Hermia, *William Shakespeare's Ill Met by Moonlight* (1994)
Bodenstein, Christel	Beatrice, *Viel Lärm um nichts* (1964)
Boggs, Francis	director, *The Merry Wives of Windsor* (1910)
Boito, Arrigo	librettist, *Bianco contro negro* (1913)
	librettist, *Otello* (1932)
	librettist, *Otello* (1973)
	librettist, *Falstaff* (1979)
	librettist, *Otello* (1986)
Boky, Colette	Alice Ford, *Die Lustigen Weiber von Windsor* (1965)
Bologna, Joseph	director, screenwriter & Mike Capomezza, *Love Is All There Is* (1996)
Bonafé, Pepa	Portia, *Shylock* (1913)
Bondarchuk, Sergei	Othello, *Otello* (1955)
Bonham Carter, Helena	Ophelia, *Hamlet* (1990)
	Olivia, *Twelfth Night: Or What You Will* (1996)
Boniface	Kidoure, *Makibefo* (1999)
Borowitz, Katherine	Ruthie Battaglia, *Men of Respect* (1991)
Bosc, Cyril	The brother, *La tragédie de Gonzague* (2002)
Bottion, Aldo	Michael Cassio, *Otello* (1973)
Bouchier, Chili	Simonetta Steno / Desdemona, *Carnival* (1931)
Boulois, Max H.	director, producer, screenwriter ,& General Othello, *Othello, el comando negro* (1982)
Bourchier, Arthur	Henry VIII, *Henry VIII* (1911)

355

director & Macbeth, *Macbeth* (1913)

Bourne, Adeleine — Gertrude, *Hamlet* (1913)

Bouyer, Jérôme — director, co-producer, screenwriter, editor, *La tragédie de Gonzague* (2002)

Bowles, Anthony — composer, musical director, *The Winter's Tale* (1968)

Boyd, Don — executive producer, *The Tempest* (1979)

director, screenwriter, *My Kingdom* (2001)

Boyd-Perkins, Eric — editor, *Julius Caesar* (1970)
editor, *Antony and Cleopatra* (1972)

Boyle, Michael J. — Orsino, *Viola und Sebastian* (1972)

Boyle, Peter — Matt Duffy, *Men of Respect* (1991)

Bradley, David — producer, designer, cinematographer, editor & Macbeth, *Macbeth* (1946)
director, producer & Marcus Junius Brutus, *Julius Caesar* (1950)

Brader, Bob — Macduff, *Macbeth* (2003)

Bradley, Laura — composer, music supervisor, & Antonio, *The Tempest* (2007)

Braithwaite, Lilian — Italia Steno, *Carnival* (1931)

Branagh, Kenneth — director & Henry V, *Henry V* (1989)
director, producer, & Benedick, *Much Ado About Nothing* (1993)
Iago, *Othello* (1995)
himself, *Looking for Richard* (1996)
director & Hamlet, *Hamlet* (1996)
director, producer, & Berowne / Narrator (voice), *Love's Labour's Lost* (2000)
director, producer, executive producer, *As You Like It* (2006)

Brand, James — Ye Storyteller, *The Secret Sex Lives of Romeo and Juliet* (1969)

Brandau, Maeve — special effects makeup, *Romeo & Juliet vs. The Living Dead* (2009)

Branding, Heinz Theo — Malvolio, *Viola und Sebastian* (1972)

Brando, Marlon — Marc Antony, *Julius Caesar* (1953)

356

Brandon, David	screenwriter & Demetrius, *A Midsummer Night's Dream* (1985)
Brandt, Mathilde	Gertrude, *Hamlet* (1921)
Branker, Audrey	Desdemona, *Othello* (1979)
Brasseur, Pierre	Raffaele, *Les Amants de Vérone* (1949)
Brebner, Veronica	senior makeup artist, senior hair stylist, *Shakespeare in Love* (1998)
Breckenridge, Alex	Monique, *She's The Man* (2006)
Brenner, Albert	art director, *A Midsummer Night's Dream* (1967)
Brešan, Ivo	writer (play), screenwriter, *Predstava "Hamleta" u selu Mrduši Donjoj* (1973)
Briers, Richard	Lieutenant Bardolph, *Henry V* (1989)
	Leonato, *Much Ado About Nothing* (1993)
	Polonius, *Hamlet* (1996)
	Nathaniel, *Love's Labour's Lost* (2000)
	Adam, *As You Like It* (2006)
Briggs, Christopher	Southern Sister, *Macbeth: The Comedy* (2001)
Brignone, Mercedes	Gertrude, *Amleto* (1917)
Britton, Nellie Hutin	Portia, *The Merchant of Venice* (1916)
Broadbent, Jim	Duke of Buckingham, *Richard III* (1995)
Broch, Brigitte	set decorator, *William Shakespeare's Romeo + Juliet* (1996)
Brook, Peter	director, *King Lear* (1971)
	himself, *Looking for Richard* (1996)
Brown, Bernard B.	sound department, *The Boys from Syracuse* (1940)
Brown, Joe E.	Francis Flute, *A Midsummer Night's Dream* (1935)
Brown, Peter B.	Macbeth, *Macbeth* (2003)
Brown, Virtic Emil	Juliet Capulet, *Rockin' Romeo & Juliet* (2006)
Browne, Coral	Chloe Moon, *Theatre of Blood* (1973)
Brubeck, Dave	himself, *All Night Long* (1962)
Bryant, Edward	Peter Quince, *William Shakespeare's Ill Met by Moonlight* (1994)
Brydone, Alfred	Edward IV, *Richard III* (1911)
Buchanan, Lucianne	Dolores, *Tempest* (1982)

Buchel, Brian — Lelio, *Carnival* (1931)
Buchowetzki, Dmitri — director, *Othello* (1922)
Budraitis, Juozas — King of France, *Korol Lir* (1971)
Buel, Kenean — director, *As You Like It* (1908)
producer, *As You Like It* (1912)
Buford, Monica — Goneril, *King Lear* (1976)
Burge, Stuart — director, *Othello* (1965)
director, *Julius Caesar* (1970)
Burger, Hans — director, screenwriter, *Nichts als Sünde* (1965)
Burgess, Mark — Edgar, *King Lear* (1999)
Burke, Erika — Macbeth, *Macbeth: The Comedy* (2001)
Burrough, Tony — production designer, *Richard III* (1995)
Burton, Richard — Narrator (voice: English version), *Sen noci svatojanske* (1959)
Hamlet, *Hamlet* (1964)
producer & Petruchio, *The Taming of the Shrew* (1967)
Bushman, Francis X. — director & Romeo Montague, *Romeo and Juliet* (1916)
Butterworth, Charles — Solinus, *The Boys from Syracuse* (1940)
Buxton, Susannah — costume designer, *As You Like It* (2006)
Byford, Roy — Sir John Falstaff, *Falstaff the Tavern Knight* (1923)
Bynes, Amanda — Viola Hastings, *She's the Man* (2006)
Byrne, Alexandra — costume designer, *Hamlet* (1996)
Cabot, Sebastian — Iago, *Othello* (1946)
Lord Capulet, *Romeo and Juliet* (1954)
Cagaloglu, Ali — Ghost, *Intikam Melegi – Kadin Hamlet* (1977)
Cagney, James — Nick Bottom, *A Midsummer Night's Dream* (1935)
Calhern, Louis — Gaius Julius Caesar, *Julius Caesar* (1953)
Calmettes, André — director, *Macbeth* (1909)
director, *Richard III* (1912)
Cameron-Scorsese, Domenica — Hermia, *Midsummer* (1999)
Campbell, Ken — Gonzalo, *The Tempest* (1979)
Candeias, Ozualdo Ribeiro — director, producer, screenwriter, production designer, costume designer, cinematographer, *A Herança* (1970)
Caninenberg, Hans — Claudius, *Hamlet, Prinz von*

359

Catherwood, Emma	Jo, *My Kingdom* (2001)
Cavanova, Mary	Juliet Capulet, *Romeo e Giulietta* (1927)
Cayatte, André	director, screenwriter, *Les Amants de Vérone* (1949)
Cederna, Giuseppe	Demetrius, *Sogno di una notte d' estate* (1983)
Celeste, Monica	costume designer, *Iago* (2009)
Cerón, Laura	Emalita Ortega, *King Rikki* (2002)
Cerval, Claude	Adrien Lesurf, *Ophélia* (1963)
Cesare, Ezio di	Michael Cassio (voice), *Otello* (1986)
Chabrol, Claude	director, screenwriter, *Ophélia* (1963)
Chabukiani, Vakhtang	director & Othello, *Otelo* (1960)
Chailly, Riccardo	conductor, *Macbeth* (1987)
Chakiris, George	Bernardo, *West Side Story* (1961)
Chamberlain, Richard	Gaius Octavius Thurinus, *Julius Caesar* (1970)
Chang, Sari	Tye, *China Girl* (1987)
Chaplin, Saul	composer, musical director, *Kiss Me Kate* (1953)
	composer, music supervisor, associate producer, *West Side Story* (1961)
Chatterjee, Moushumi	Sudha Tilak, *Angoor* (1982)
Chaturvedi, Hemant	cinematographer, *Maqbool* (2003)
Chee Kong Cheah	director, screenwriter, associate producer, *Jiyuan qiaohe* (2000)
Chetty, Laurence	composer, *Othello* (2007)
Chiaki, Minoru	Yoshiaki Miki, *Kumonosu jô* (1957)
Chiatti, Laura	Desdemona, *Iago* (2009)
Childs, Martin	art director, *Henry V* (1989)
	art director, *Much Ado About Nothing* (1993)
	production designer, *Shakespeare in Love* (1998)
Ching Teh, Su	Penelope Chan, *Jiyuan qiaohe* (2000)
Christian, Phillip	Scary Sister, *Macbeth: The Comedy* (2001)
Christie, Julie	Gertrude, *Hamlet* (1996)
Churikova, Inna	Gertrude, *Gamlet* (1989)
Cinthio, Giovambattista Giraldi	story elements, *Othello* (1922)
Clark, Jennifer	Third Witch, *Macbeth* (2003)
Clark, Michael	choreographer & Caliban, *Prospero's Books* (1991)
Clemens, Brian	screenwriter, *An Honourable*

	Murder (1960)
Clifford, Richard	Duke of Orléans, *Henry V* (1989)
	Conrade, *Much Ado About Nothing* (1993)
	Boyet, *Love's Labour's Lost* (2000)
	Le Beau, *As You Like It* (2006)
Closas, Alberto	Don Beltrán de Lara, *La Fierecilla domada* (1956)
Close, Glenn	Gertrude, *Hamlet* (1990)
Cloutier, Suzanne	Desdemona, *The Tragedy of Othello: The Moor of Venice* (1952)
Cobban, Jaime	President Duncan, *Macbeth 3000: This Time, It's Personal* (2005)
Cocchi, V.	Leontes, *Una Tragedia alla corte di Sicilia* (1914)
Cockburn, Clive	composer, *The Maori Merchant of Venice* (2002)
Coghlan, Rose	Rosalind, *As You Like It* (1912)
Cohen, Tanner	Timothy, *Were The World Mine* (2008)
Colaci, Paolo	Othello, *Otello* (1914)
Colby Jones, Michael	Sassy Sister, *Macbeth: The Comedy* (2001)
Colleano, Bonar	Lennie, *Joe MacBeth* (1955)
Colleran, Bill	director, cinematographer, *Hamlet* (1964)
Collier, Constance	Lady Macbeth, *Macbeth* (1916)
	vocal coach, *The Taming of the Shrew* (1929)
Collins, Edwin J.	director, *The Taming of the Shrew* (1923)
Collins, Lynn	Portia, *The Merchant of Venice* (2004)
Colman, Ronald	Anthony John / Othello, *A Double Life* (1947)
Coltrane, Robbie	Sir John Falstaff, *Henry V* (1989)
Comerio, Luca	director, *Amleto* (1908)
Compton, Fay	Emilia, *The Tragedy of Othello: The Moor of Venice* (1952)
Connery, Jason	Macbeth, *Macbeth* (1997)
Conway, Kevin	himself / Lord Hastings, *Looking for Richard* (1996)
Cooke, Caroline Burns	Queen Elizabeth, *Richard III* (2005)
Cookson, S. A.	Earl of Salisbury [not in surviving footage], *King John*

(1899)

Alonzo, *The Tempest* (1905)

Cardinal Campeius, *Henry VIII* (1911)

Horatio, *Hamlet* (1913)

Cooper, George A. — director, *Julius Caesar* (1926)

Coote, Robert — Roderigo, *The Tragedy of Othello: The Moor of Venice* (1952)

Oliver Larding, *Theatre of Blood* (1973)

Cordy, Raymond — Bautista de Martos y Ribera, *La Fierecilla domada* (1956)

Coronado, Celestino — director, producer, set decorator, *Hamlet* (1976)

director, producer, *A Midsummer Night's Dream* (1985)

Corrigan, Kevin — Anthony "Banko" Banconi, *Scotland, Pa.* (2001)

Cortes, Erlinda — unknown role, *Romeo at Julieta* (1951)

Cossira, Emilio — Roméo Montague, *Roméo et Juliette* (1900)

Cossotti, Max René — Fenton, *Falstaff* (1979)

Costello, Maurice — unknown role, *Richard III* (1908)

Marc Antony, *Antony and Cleopatra* (1908)

unknown role, *Julius Caesar* (1908)

unknown role, *The Merchant of Venice* (1908)

unknown role, *King Lear* (1909)

Lysander, *A Midsummer Night's Dream* (1909)

Orlando, *As You Like It* (1912)

Courant, Curt — cinematographer, *Hamlet* (1921)

Coutinho, Eduardo — director, screenwriter, composer, *Faustão* (1971)

Cowie, Laura — Anne Boleyn, *Henry VIII* (1911)

Cox, Stuart — Earl of Gloucester, *King Lear* (1976)

Crane, Frank Hall — Polixenes, *The Winter's Tale* (1910)

Crisham, Walter — Angus, *Joe MacBeth* (1955)

Crisp, Quentin — Polonius, *Hamlet* (1976)

Croft, Emma — Rosalind, *As You Like It* (1992)

Cronyn, Hume — Polonius, *Hamlet* (1964)

Crook, Mackenzie — Launcelot Gobbo, *The Merchant of Venice* (2004)

de la Cruz, Ángel — director, screenwriter, *El Sueño de una noche de San Juan* (2005)

Cruze, James	Posthumus Leonatus, *Cymbeline* (1913)
Cukor, George	director, *Romeo and Juliet* (1936)
	director, *A Double Life* (1947)
Culkin, Kit	extra, *West Side Story* (1961)
	Player Queen, *Hamlet* (1964)
Cumming, Alan	Saturninus, *Titus* (1999)
	Sebastian, *The Tempest* (2009)
Cunningham, Neil	Sebastian, *The Tempest* (1979)
Curtis, Ann	costume designer, *A Midsummer Night's Dream* (1968)
Curtis, Tony	Colonel Iago, *Othello, el comando negro* (1982)
Cusack, Cyril	Grumio, *The Taming of the Shrew* (1967)
	Duke of Albany, *King Lear* (1971)
	Adam, *As You Like It* (1992)
Cushing, Peter	Osric, *Hamlet* (1948)
Cwiklik, Frank	Porter, *Macbeth* (2003)
Czinner, Paul	director, producer, *As You Like It* (1936)
	director, producer, *Romeo and Juliet* (1966)
Dal, Oleg	Fool, *Korol Lir* (1971)
Dale, Jim	composer & Autolycus, *The Winter's Tale* (1968)
Dallmeier, Uwe	Tobias Rülp, *Viola und Sebastian* (1972)
Dalton, Phyllis	costume designer, *Henry V* (1989)
	costume designer, *Much Ado About Nothing* (1993)
Dam, José van	Lodovico, *Otello* (1973)
Dando, Walter Pfeffer	director, *King John* (1899)
Danes, Claire	Juliet Capulet, *William Shakespeare's Romeo + Juliet* (1996)
Daniels, Ngarimu	Portia, *The Maori Merchant of Venice* (2002)
Daniels, William H.	cinematographer, *Romeo and Juliet* (1936)
Dankworth, John	himself, *All Night Long* (1962)
Das, Nandita	Kannaki, *Kannaki* (2002)
Davis, Ben	Agent Steve, *Macbeth 3000: This Time, It's Personal* (2005)
Dawson, Ralph	editor, *A Midsummer Night's Dream* (1935)
Day, Max	director, producer, editor, & Duke of Buckingham, *Richard III* (2005)

De Biasi, Volfango — director, screenwriter, *Iago* (2009)

DeCuir, John — art director, production designer, *The Taming of the Shrew* (1967)

DeForest, Lee — producer, *Julius Caesar* (1926)

De Masi, Francesco — composer, *Quella sporca storia nel West* (1968)

De Putti, Lya — Emilia, *Othello* (1922)

De Riso, Camillo — director & unknown role, *Otello* (1920)

De Santis, Pasqualino — cinematographer, *Romeo and Juliet* (1968)

Deane, Dacia — Katherine Minola, *The Taming of the Shrew* (1923)

Dearden, Basil — director, producer, *All Night Long* (1962)

Debar, Andrée — Portia, *Le Marchand de Venise* (1953)

Degeorge — Sir John Falstaff, *Falstaff* (1911)

Del Barrio, Raymond — choreographer & Bruce, *West Bank Story* (2005)

Delgado, Miguel M. — director, *Romeo y Julieta* (1943)

Delgado, Roger — Soothsayer, *Antony and Cleopatra* (1972)

Delhomme, Benoît — cinematographer, *The Merchant of Venice* (2004)

Delia, Joe — composer, *China Girl* (1987)

Delvair, Jeanne — Lady Macbeth, *Macbeth* (1909)

Dench, Judi — Titania, *A Midsummer Night's Dream* (1968)
Narrator (voice), *The Angelic Conversation* (1985)
Nell Quickly, *Henry V* (1989)
Hecuba, *Hamlet* (1996)
Elizabeth I, *Shakespeare In Love* (1998)

Denmark, Ryan — director, producer, screenwriter, cinematographer, editor, *Romeo & Juliet vs. The Living Dead* (2009)

Depardieu, Gérard — Reynaldo, *Hamlet* (1996)

Desfontaines, Henri — director & unknown role, *Hamlet* (1908)
director, *La Mégère apprivoisée* (1911)
director, *Falstaff* (1911)
director, *Shylock* (1913)

Desmond, William — Larry Lang, *A Sage Brush Hamlet* (1919)

Dety, Noeliny — Valy Makibefo, *Makibefo* (1999)

Devgan, Ajay — Omkara "Omi" Shukla, *Omkara* (2006)

DeWulf, Noureen — Fatima, *West Bank Story* (2005)

Dexter, John — director, *Othello* (1965)

Dexter, Rosemary — Juliet Capulet, *Giulietta e Romeo* (1964)

Díaz, Chico — Dr Caius, *As Alegres Comadres* (2003)

Díaz, Justino — Iago, *Otello* (1986)

DiCaprio, Leonardo — Romeo Montague, *William Shakespeare's Romeo + Juliet* (1996)

Dick, Andy — Jesse, *Scotland, Pa.* (2001)

Dickson, William K. L. — director, cinematographer, *King John* (1899)

Diestel, Edith — Regan, *King Lear* (1916)

Dieterle, William — director, *A Midsummer Night's Dream* (1935)

Dillon, Carmen — production designer, *The Chronicle History of King Henry the Fift with His Battell Fought at Agincourt in France* (1944)
art director, *Hamlet* (1948)
art director, *Richard III* (1955)

Dion, Hector — Iago, *Othello* (1908)
Edmund, *King Lear* (1916)

Dioumé, Mamadou — Otello's father, *Iago* (2009)

DiStefano, James — Alonso, *The Tempest* (2007)

Dixon, Richard — Iago, *Othello* (1979)

Djordjevic, Igor — Hamlet, *Hamlet* (2007)

Dmitriyev, Igor — Rosencrantz, *Gamlet* (1964)

Dodd, Ken — Yorick, *Hamlet* (1996)

Domingo, Plácido — Otello, *Otello* (1986)
singer (theme *In Pace*), *Hamlet* (1996)

Donati, Danilo — costume designer, *The Taming of the Shrew* (1967)
costume designer, *Romeo and Juliet* (1968)

Donato, Isabella — Lupe, *King Rikki* (2002)

Dorkins, C. J. — cinematographer, editor, *Othello* (1979)

Dors, Diana — Maisie Psaltery, *Theatre of Blood* (1973)

Douglas, Paul — Joe "Mac" MacBeth, *Joe MacBeth* (1955)

Doyle, Desmond — Tybalt Capulet, *Romeo and Juliet* (1966)

Doyle, Patrick — composer & Alexander Court, *Henry V* (1989)
composer & Balthazar, *Much*

	Ado About Nothing (1993)
	composer, music producer, *Hamlet* (1996)
	composer, *Love's Labour's Lost* (2000)
	composer & Amiens, *As You Like It* (2006)
Drake, Alfred	Claudius, *Hamlet* (1964)
Dreyfuss, Richard	Player, *Rosencrantz & Guildenstern Are Dead* (1990)
Drumm, Val	director, *Romeo and Juliet* (1966)
DuBose, Bruce	Theseus / Oberon, *Midsummer* (1999)
Dun, Tan	composer, *Ye yan* (2006)
Duncan, Lindsay	Hippolyta / Titania, *A Midsummer Night's Dream* (1996)
Dunlop, Frank	director, *The Winter's Tale* (1968)
Dunsworth, Geoff	Donald Duncan, *Scotland, Pa.* (2001)
Dupouey, Pierre	cinematographer, *Macbeth* (1987)
Dupuis, Claudine	Blanca de Martos y Ribera, *La Fierecilla domada* (1956)
Dutt, Utpal	Raj Tilak, *Angoor* (1982)
Duval, Frank	composer, *Viola und Sebastian* (1972)
Dux, Eckart	Fenton, *Die Lustigen Weiber von Windsor* (1950)
	Rosencrantz, *Hamlet, Prinz von Dänemark* (1961)
Dyer, Anson	director, screenwriter, animator, *'Amlet* (1919)
	director, screenwriter, animator, *Oh'phelia* (1919)
	director, screenwriter, animator, *The Merchant of Venice* (1919)
	director, screenwriter, animator, *Othello* (1920)
	director, screenwriter, animator, *Romeo and Juliet* (1920)
	director, screenwriter, animator, *The Taming of the Shrew* (1920)
Dynam, Jacques	Florindo, *La Fierecilla domada* (1956)
Ebert, Carl	Antonio, *Der Kaufmann von Venedig* (1923)
Eccles, Donald	Robin Starveling, *A Midsummer*

	Night's Dream (1968)
Edwards, J. Gordon	director, *Romeo and Juliet* (1916)
Edzard, Christine	set dresser, *Romeo and Juliet* (1968)
	director, *As You Like It* (1992)
	director, *The Children's Midsummer Night's Dream* (2001)
Eibenschütz, Lia	Jessica, *Der Kaufmann von Venedig* (1923)
Elejalde, Kadina de	Queen Isabel, *Richard II* (2001)
Elliot, Gertrude	Ophelia, *Hamlet* (1913)
Elliott, Marianne	director, *All's Well That Ends Well* (2009)
Elman, Jamie	Troy, *Rave Macbeth* (2001)
Elsen, John	Joe / Banquo, *Macbeth in Manhattan* (1999)
Elter, Marco	director, editor, *Dente per dente* (1943)
Elton, Ben	Headborough Verges, *Much Ado About Nothing* (1993)
Elvey, Maurice	director, *Love in a Wood* (1915)
Emerson, John	director, *Macbeth* (1916)
Engel, Alexander	Herr Reich, *Die Lustigen Weiber von Windsor* (1950)
	Ghost, *Hamlet, Prinz von Dänemark* (1961)
Enk, Bryan	director, producer, *Macbeth* (2003)
Eriksen, Dan	director, *A Midsummer Night's Dream* (1967)
Erikson, Bella	editor, *The Maori Merchant of Venice* (2002)
Erksan, Metin	director, screenwriter, *Intikam Melegi – Kadin Hamlet* (1977)
Esser, Paul	Sir Johannes Spenser, *Die Lustigen Weiber von Windsor* (1950)
Evans, Maurice	Macbeth, *Macbeth* (1961)
Everett, Rupert	Kit Marlowe, *Shakespeare in Love* (1998)
	Oberon, *A Midsummer Night's Dream* (1999)
Ewers, Hanns Heinz	screenwriter, *Ein Sommernachtstraum in unserer Zeit* (1913)
van Eyck, Peter	Paul Claudius, *Der Rest ist Schweigen* (1959)
Fabbri, Pina	Paulina, *Una Tragedia alla corte di Sicilia* (1914)
Fairbanks, Douglas	Petruchio, *The Taming of the Shrew* (1929)

367

Garin, Erast	Verges, *Mnogo shuma iz nichego* (1973)
Garrick, David	additional dialogue, *The Taming of the Shrew* (1929)
	additional dialogue, *Richard III* (1955)
Garson, Greer	Calpurnia, *Julius Caesar* (1953)
Garwood, William	Friar Laurence, *Romeo and Juliet* (1911)
	unknown role, *The Merchant of Venice* (1912)
	Iachimo, *Cymbeline* (1913)
Gassman, Vittorio	Alberto Alonzo, *Tempest* (1982)
Gauntier, Gene	scenarist & unknown role, *As You Like It* (1908)
Gaya, Aurelien	Otello, *Iago* (2009)
Gayle, Jackie	Trinc, *Tempest* (1982)
Gazzolo, Lauro	Battista Minola, *La Bisbetica domata* (1942)
Ge, You	Emperor Li, *Ye yan* (2006)
Gehi, Ajay	Guddu, *Maqbool* (2003)
Gemp, Robert	Edward IV, *Richard III* (1912)
Genn, Leo	Constable of France, *The Chronicle History of King Henry the Fift with His Battell Fought at Agincourt in France* (1944)
Georgiadis, Nicholas	production designer, costume designer, *Romeo and Juliet* (1966)
Gerrard, Douglas	Bassanio, *The Merchant of Venice* (1914)
Gert, Valeska	Puck, *Ein Sommernachtstraum: ein heiteres Fastnachtsspiel* (1925)
Gervasi, Luigi	set decorator, *The Taming of the Shrew* (1967)
Geva, Tamara	Oberon, *Ein Sommernachtstraum: ein heiteres Fastnachtsspiel* (1925)
Ghidoni, Fabio	Cassio, *Iago* (2009)
Gibbons, Cedric	art director, settings, *Romeo and Juliet* (1936)
	art director, *Julius Caesar* (1953)
	art director, *Kiss Me Kate* (1953)
	art director, *Forbidden Planet* (1956)
Gibson, Mel	Hamlet, *Hamlet* (1990)
Gielgud, John	Gaius Cassius Longinus, *Julius Caesar* (1953)
	Chorus, *Romeo and Juliet* (1954)
	Duke of Clarence, *Richard III* (1955)

director & Ghost (voice), *Hamlet* (1964)

Henry IV, *Campanadas a medianoche* (1965)

Gaius Julius Caesar, *Julius Caesar* (1970)

Prospero / everybody else (voices), *Prospero's Books* (1991)

himself, *Looking for Richard* (1996)

Priam, *Hamlet* (1996)

Gilbert, Te Rangihau — Bassanio, *The Maori Merchant of Venice* (2002)

Gilhooly, Ryan — Banquo, *Macbeth 3000: This Time, It's Personal* (2005)

Gill, Basil — Ferdinand, *The Tempest* (1905)

Duke of Buckingham, *Henry VIII* (1911)

Marcus Junius Brutus, *Julius Caesar* (1926)

Gillespie, A. Arnold — special effects, *Forbidden Planet* (1956)

Giordana, Andrea — Johnny Hamilton, *Quella sporca storia nel West* (1968)

Girik, Fatma — Hamlet Evren, *Intikam Melegi – Kadin Hamlet* (1977)

Girolami, Ennio — Ross, *Quella sporca storia nel West* (1968)

Glaubrecht, Frank — Sebastian, *Viola und Sebastian* (1972)

Glen, Iain — Hamlet, *Rosencrantz & Guildenstern Are Dead* (1990)

Glenn, Grosvenor — Second murderer, *Macbeth* (1946)

Gaius Cassius Longinus, *Julius Caesar* (1950)

Glossop, Peter (I) — Iago, *Otello* (1973)

Glossop, Peter (II) — production sound mixer, *Othello* (1995)

production sound mixer, *Hamlet* (1996)

production sound mixer, *Shakespeare in Love* (1998)

sound, *Love's Labour's Lost* (2000)

sound mixer, *As You Like It* (2006)

Glover, John — Richard, *Macbeth in Manhattan* (1999)

Glover, Julian — Gaius Proculeius, *Antony and*

	Cleopatra (1972)
Godard, Jean-Luc	director, editor, & Professor Pluggy, *King Lear* (1987)
Goldberg, Michael	screenwriter, executive producer, & Producer, *The Fifteen Minute Hamlet* (1995)
Goldenthal, Elliot	composer, orchestrator, *Titus* (1999)
Golubentsev, Aleksandr	composer, *Ukroshchenie stroptivoy* (1961)
Gomes, Eliezer	Faustão, *Faustão* (1971)
Gómez, Karina	Max's wife, *Macbeth-Sangrador* (1999)
Gómez, Manolo	director, producer, *El Sueño de una noche de San Juan* (2005)
Gonçalves, Milton	Padre Arnaldo, *As Alegres Comadres* (2003)
Good, Jack	screenwriter, lyricist, producer, *Catch My Soul* (1974)
Goodwin, Richard B.	associate producer, *Romeo and Juliet* (1968)
Gopi, Suresh	Kannan Perumalayan, *Kaliyattam* (1997)
Gordin, Jacob	writer (play *The Yiddish King Lear*), *The Jewish King Lear* (1912)
	writer (play), *The Yiddish King Lear* (1934)
Gordon, Julia Swayne	Desdemona, *Othello* (1908)
	unknown role, *Richard III* (1908)
	Portia, *The Merchant of Venice* (1908)
	Cordelia, *King Lear* (1909)
	Helena, *A Midsummer Night's Dream* (1909)
	Olivia, *Twelfth Night* (1910)
	Queen Catherine, *Cardinal Wolsey* (1912)
Gordon, Ruth	screenwriter, *A Double Life* (1947)
Gordon-Levitt, Joseph	Cameron James, *10 Things I Hate About You* (1999)
Gore, Nigel	Titus Andronicus, *Titus Andronicus* (2000)
Gorin, Charles Igor	Frank Ford, *Die Lustigen Weiber von Windsor* (1965)
Gormlie, Chris	editor & MacDonwald, *Macbeth* (1997)
	editor, fight organiser, *King Lear* (1999)

Gounod, Charles	composer, *Romeo and Juliet* (1900)
	composer, *Romeo and Juliet* (1916)
	composer, *Romeo e Giulietta* (1927)
Gourley, Katrina	Ariel, *The Tempest* (2007)
Gözen, Yüksel	Orhan's father, *Intikam Melegi – Kadin Hamlet* (1977)
Graatkjaer, Axel	cinematographer, *Hamlet* (1921)
	cinematographer, *Der Kaufmann von Venedig* (1923)
Graham, Jesse	screenwriter, *King Rikki* (2002)
Grammaticus, Saxo	story elements, *Hamlet* (1921)
Grant, Richard E.	Sir Andrew Aguecheek, *Twelfth Night: Or What You Will* (1996)
Gray, Matthew	Thane of Cawdor, *Macbeth* (2003)
Grayson, Godfrey	director, *An Honourable Murder* (1960)
Grayson, Kathryn	Lilli Vanessi / Katherine Minola, *Kiss Me Kate* (1953)
Greatrex, Richard	cinematographer, *Shakespeare in Love* (1998)
Green, Harry	Big Dutch, *Joe MacBeth* (1955)
Green, Johnny	conductor, music supervisor, *West Side Story* (1961)
Greenaway, Peter	director, art department, *Prospero's Books* (1991)
Greenwood, Edwin	director, *Falstaff the Tavern Knight* (1923)
Gregory, Nick	William Reeves / Macbeth, *Macbeth in Manhattan* (1999)
Grétillat, Jacques	Hamlet, *Hamlet* (1908)
Greville-Bell, Anthony	screenwriter, *Theatre of Blood* (1973)
Grey, Clifford	Lelio, *Carnival* (1921)
Griffin, Richard	director, producer, *Titus Andronicus* (2000)
Griffith, D. W.	director, *The Taming of the Shrew* (1908)
	producer, *Macbeth* (1916)
Grimaldi, Gabriella	Ofelia Polomo, *Quella sporca storia nel West* (1968)
Grossman, Miriam	Toibelle Mosheles, *The Yiddish King Lear* (1934)
Grothe, Franz	composer, *Die Lustigen Weiber* (1936)
Gruebner, Russell	Gaius Cinna "the Poet", *Julius Caesar* (1950)
Guazzoni, Enrico	director, *Bruto* (1911)

Guiry, Tom	Malcolm Duncan, *Scotland, Pa.* (2001)
Gulzar, Sampooran Singh	lyricist, additional dialogue, *Do Dooni Chaar* (1968)
	director, screenwriter, *Angoor* (1982)
	lyricist, *Maqbool* (2003)
	lyricist, *Omkara* (2006)
Gunn, James	screenwriter, associate director, executive producer & Found-a-Peanut Father, *Tromeo and Juliet* (1996)
Gustafson, Tom	director, producer, screenwriter, *Were The World Mine* (2008)
Gwenn, Edmund	Rupert K. Thunder / Macbeth, *The Real Thing at Last* (1916)
Haboush, Michael	Mercutio, *Rockin' Romeo & Juliet* (2006)
Haggerty, John D.	Bassanio, *Shakespeare's Merchant* (2003)
Hall, Peter	director, *A Midsummer Night's Dream* (1968)
Halley, Ina	Anna Reich, *Die Lustigen Weiber von Windsor* (1950)
Hämäläinen, Pirkko	Lady, *Macbeth* (1987)
Hammer, Ina	Goneril, *King Lear* (1916)
Hammond, Roger	Corin / Lebeau, *As You Like It* (1992)
	Archbishop, *Richard III* (1995)
Hammooda, Ibrahim	Romeo Montague, *Shuhaddaa el gharam* (1942)
Haniff, Hussain	director, *Istana berdarah* (1964)
Hannen, Nicholas	Duke of Exeter, *The Chronicle History of King Henry the Fift with His Battell Fought at Agincourt in France* (1944)
	Archbishop, *Richard III* (1955)
Hanson, Alan	Claudius, *Hamlet* (2007)
Harada, Mieko	Lady Kaede, *Ran* (1985)
Hardinge, H. C. M.	writer (play *Sirocco*), *Carnival* (1921)
	writer (play *Sirocco*), *Carnival* (1931)
Hardwicke, Cedric	Edward IV, *Richard III* (1955)
Harris, Paul	Aurelius Rex, *All Night Long* (1962)
Harris, Richard	Sandeman, *My Kingdom* (2001)
Hart, Lorenz	lyricist, *The Boys from Syracuse* (1940)
Hartley, Richard	composer, *A Thousand Acres* (1997)

376

	Memories from the Scrapbook (2004)
Henríquez, Leonardo	director, screenwriter, editor, *Macbeth-Sangrador* (1999)
Henschke, Alfred	writer (intertitles), *Ein Sommernachtstraum: ein heiteres Fastnachtsspiel* (1925)
Henson, Leslie	William Shakespeare / Page / Charlie Chaplin / Duncan I, *The Real Thing at Last* (1916)
Herlie, Eileen	Gertrude, *Hamlet* (1948)
	Gertrude, *Hamlet* (1964)
Hernández, Tom	Senator Fergusson, *Othello, el comando negro* (1982)
Heron, Mark	Duke of Cornwall, *King Lear* (1976)
Hervé, Jean	Bassanio, *Shylock* (1913)
Hervey, Irene	Adriana, *The Boys from Syracuse* (1940)
Heston, Charlton	costume designer, *Macbeth* (1946)
	Marc Antony, *Julius Caesar* (1950)
	Marc Antony, *Julius Caesar* (1970)
	director & Marc Antony, *Antony and Cleopatra* (1972)
	Player King, *Hamlet* (1996)
Heyfron, John	Demetrius, *The Children's Midsummer Night's Dream* (2001)
Hickox, Douglas	director, *Theatre of Blood* (1973)
Higgins, Ken	cinematographer, *Julius Caesar* (1970)
Hill, Victoria	producer & Lady Macbeth, *Macbeth* (2006)
Hilliard, Harry	Romeo Montague, *Romeo and Juliet* (1916)
Hipólito, Leila	director, producer, screenwriter, *As Alegres Comadres* (2003)
Hobbs, William	Cypriot officer, *Othello* (1965)
	fight director & Young Seyward, *The Tragedy of Macbeth* (1971)
	duel arranger, *Hamlet* (1990)
	fight arranger, *Shakespeare in Love* (1998)
Hoffman, Michael	director, producer, *A Midsummer Night's Dream* (1999)
Hoffman, Robert	Justin, *She's the Man* (2006)
Hoffmann, Carl	director, *Die Lustigen Weiber* (1936)

379

Jarrico, Paul	screenwriter, *All Night Long* (1962)
Järvenpää, Sakke	Napoleon, *Macbeth* (1987)
Järvet, Jüri	Lear, *Korol Lir* (1971)
Jayaraaj Rajasekharan Nair	director, *Kaliyattam* (1997) director, *Kannaki* (2002)
Jayaraaj, Sabitha	costume designer, *Kannaki* (2002)
Jayston, Michael	Demetrius, *A Midsummer Night's Dream* (1968)
Jean-Noël	Makidofy, *Makibefo* (1999)
Jefford, Barbara	Titania (voice: English version), *Sen noci svatojanske* (1959) Hippolyta, *A Midsummer Night's Dream* (1968)
Jenks, George Elwood	screenwriter, *A Sage Brush Hamlet* (1919)
Jennings, Alex	Theseus / Oberon, *A Midsummer Night's Dream* (1996)
Jensen, Jane	Juliet Capulet, *Tromeo and Juliet* (1996)
Jines, Mickey	Lady Capulet, *The Secret Sex Lives of Romeo and Juliet* (1969)
Jocelyn, André	Yvan Lesurf, *Ophélia* (1963)
Johns, Mervyn	Friar Laurence, *Romeo and Juliet* (1954)
Johnson, Arthur V.	Petruchio, *The Taming of the Shrew* (1908)
Johnson, Carrie	Second Witch, *Macbeth* (2003)
Johnson, Karl	Ariel, *The Tempest* (1979)
Johnson, Richard	Gaius Cassius Longinus, *Julius Caesar* (1970) Marcus Aemilius Lepidus (voice) / Alexas (voice) / Publius Ventidius Bassus (voice), *Antony and Cleopatra* (1972)
Johnson, Tefft	Orsino, *Twelfth Night* (1910) Henry VIII, *Cardinal Wolsey* (1912) Senior, *As You Like It* (1912)
Jolie, Angelina	Gina Malacici / Juliet Capulet, *Love Is All There Is* (1996)
Jones, Allan	Antipholus of Ephesus / Antipholus of Syracuse, *The Boys from Syracuse* (1940)
Jones, Gillian	Viola / Sebastian, *Twelfth Night* (1987)
Jones, Griff Rhys	Touchstone, *As You Like It* (1992)
Jones, Kathleen Hazel	Jessica, *The Merchant of Venice*

Jones, Laura	(1916) screenwriter, *A Thousand Acres* (1997)
Jones, Osheen	Boy, *A Midsummer Night's Dream* (1996) Young Lucius, *Titus* (1999)
Jones, Pei Te Hurinui	translator, *The Maori Merchant of Venice* (2002)
Jones, Tim	Tom, *King Lear* (1976)
Jordan, Dorothy	Bianca Minola, *The Taming of the Shrew* (1929)
Jory, Victor	Oberon, *A Midsummer Night's Dream* (1935)
Joubé, Romuald	unknown role, *La Mégère apprivoisée* (1911) Antonio, *Shylock* (1913)
Julia, Raul	Kalibanos, *Tempest* (1982)
Junger, Gil	director & Teacher, *10 Things I Hate About You* (1999)
Jungersen, Jeppe	sound, *Makibefo* (1999) sound, *Souli* (2004)
Junkermann, Hans	Polonius, *Hamlet* (1921)
Jusic, Djelo	composer, *Predstava "Hamleta" u selu Mrduši Donjoj* (1973)
Kaddatz, Gerhard	costume designer, *Viel Lärm um nichts* (1964)
Kae-Kazim, Hakeem	Iago, *Othello* (2007)
Kalliala, Aake	Gyldenstern, *Hamlet liikemaailmassa* (1987)
Kanin, Garson	screenwriter, *A Double Life* (1947)
Kapoor, Kareena	Dolly Mishra, *Omkara* (2006)
Kapur, Pankaj	Jahangir "Abbaji" Khan, *Maqbool* (2003)
von Karajan, Herbert	director, musical director, conductor, artistic supervisor, *Otello* (1973)
Karan, Guilherme	João Fausto, *As Alegres Comadres* (2003)
Karger, Maxwell	director, *Romeo and Juliet* (1916)
Karinska, Barbara	costume designer, *A Midsummer Night's Dream* (1967)
Kasatkina, Lyudmila	Katharina Minola, *Ukroshchenie stroptivoy* (1961)
Kauffmann, Hannah	Juliet Capulet, *Romeo & Juliet vs. The Living Dead* (2009)
Kaufman, Lloyd	director, producer, screenwriter, & Shocked Onlooker, *Tromeo and Juliet* (1996)
Kaulkin, Michael	composer, *Shakespeare's Merchant* (2003)

Kaurismäki, Aki	producer, *Macbeth* (1987)
	director, producer, screenwriter, *Hamlet liikemaailmassa* (1987)
Käutner, Helmut	director, producer, screenwriter & Betrunkener Kneipengast, *Der Rest ist Schweigen* (1959)
Kay, Charles	Archbishop of Canterbury, *Henry V* (1989)
Kayra, Senem	Gul, *Intikam Melegi – Kadin Hamlet* (1977)
Kazan, Lainie	Sadie Capomezza, *Love Is All There Is* (1996)
Keane, James	director & Earl of Richmond, *Richard III* (1912)
Keaton, Michael	Constable Dogberry, *Much Ado About Nothing* (1993)
Keegan, Andrew	Joey Donner, *10 Things I Hate About You* (1999)
	Michael Cassio, *O* (2001)
Keel, Howard	Fred Graham / Petruchio, *Kiss Me Kate* (1953)
Keen, Malcolm	Gaius Cassius Longinus, *Julius Caesar* (1926)
	Duncan I, *Macbeth* (1961)
Keenan, Will	Tromeo Que, *Tromeo and Juliet* (1996)
Kemp, Lindsay	screenwriter, costume designer, production designer, & Puck, *A Midsummer Night's Dream* (1985)
Kent, Charles	Duncan I, *Macbeth* (1908)
	Old Capulet, *Romeo and Juliet* (1908)
	director, *Antony and Cleopatra* (1908)
	Gaius Julius Caesar, *Julius Caesar* (1908)
	director, *A Midsummer Night's Dream* (1909)
	director & Malvolio, *Twelfth Night* (1910)
	director, producer, & Jacques, *As You Like It* (1912)
Kerr, Deborah	Portia, *Julius Caesar* (1953)
Kerridge, Mary	Queen Elizabeth, *Richard III* (1955)
Kerwin, James	director, producer, *Midsummer* (1999)
Keys, Nelson	Lady Macbeth, *The Real Thing at Last* (1916)
Khachaturyan, Aram	composer, *Otello* (1955)
Khan, Irfan	Miyan Maqbool, *Maqbool*

	(2003)
Khan, Saif Ali	Langda Tyagi, *Omkara* (2006)
Khodursky, Antoni	Gremio, *Ukroshchenie stroptivoy* (1961)
Ki, Harry	screenwriter, *Rave Macbeth* (2001)
Kier, Udo	Hans, *My Own Private Idaho* (1991)
Kikaleishvili, Zura	Iago, *Otelo* (1960)
King, Nel	screenwriter, *All Night Long* (1962)
Kingsley, Ben	Old Capulet (voice), *Romeo-Juliet* (1990)
	Feste, *Twelfth Night: Or What You Will* (1996)
Kirikiri, Sonny	Gratiano, *The Maori Merchant of Venice* (2002)
Kirk, James	Sebastian Hastings, *She's the Man* (2006)
Kirkeby, Per	set designer, set decorator, costume designer, *Ofelias blomster* (1968)
Kirvalishvili, A.	makeup supervisor, *Otelo* (1960)
Kline, Kevin	himself, *Looking for Richard* (1996)
	Nick Bottom, *A Midsummer Night's Dream* (1999)
	Jaques, *As You Like It* (2006)
Knightley, Keira	Helena, *The Seasons Alter* (2002)
Knoesel, Klaus	director, *Rave Macbeth* (2001)
Knoles, Harley	director, *Carnival* (1921)
	producer, *Carnival* (1931)
Kolosov, Sergei	director, translator & himself, *Ukroshchenie stroptivoy* (1961)
Komar, Bob	director, cinematographer, *Measure for Measure* (2006)
Koop, Christiaan	First Witch, *Macbeth* (2003)
Koop, Gerald Owen	Ferryman, *Macbeth* (2003)
Koren, Sergei	Mercutio, *Romeo i Zhulietta* (1955)
Korngold, Erich Wolfgang	composer, music arranger, *A Midsummer Night's Dream* (1935)
Korniloff, Natasha	costume designer, *Hamlet* (1976)
Korth, Ellen	Princess Lieselotte / Desdemona, *Othello* (1918)
Kosma, Joseph	composer, *Les Amants de Vérone* (1949)
Kostal, Irwin	music supervisor, orchestrator, *West Side Story* (1961)
Kotto, Yaphet	Othello, *Othello* (1979)

Kovetz, Lisa Beth — Stephen Scroop, *Richard II* (2001)

Kozintsev, Grigori — director, *Gamlet* (1964)
director, *Korol Lir* (1971)

Kramer, Gottfried — Andreas Bleichenwang, *Viola und Sebastian* (1972)

Kramer, Hans — Sir Johannes Spenser (voice), *Die Lustigen Weiber von Windsor* (1950)

Krasina, Olga — Bianca Minola, *Ukroshchenie stroptivoy* (1961)

Krasker, Robert — cinematographer, *The Chronicle History of King Henry the Fift with His Battell Fought at Agincourt in France* (1944)
cinematographer, *Romeo and Juliet* (1954)

Krauss, Werner — Iago, *Othello* (1922)
Shylock, *Der Kaufmann von Venedig* (1923)
Nick Bottom, *Ein Sommernachtstraum* (1925)

Krebs, Helmut — Fenton (voice), *Die Lustigen Weiber von Windsor* (1950)

Kresic, Dragan — composer, *Hamlet* (2007)

Kress, Arturo B. — composer, *El Sueño de una noche de San Juan* (2005)

Krevalid, A. — Fortinbras, *Gamlet* (1964)

Kroner, Maurice — David Mosheles, *The Yiddish King Lear* (1934)

Krüger, Hardy — John H. Claudius, *Der Rest ist Schweigen* (1959)

Krumholtz, David — Michael Eckman, *10 Things I Hate About You* (1999)

Kühne, Friedrich — Brabantio, *Othello* (1922)

Kulagin, Sergei — Grumio, *Ukroshchenie stroptivoy* (1961)

Kumar, Hemant — composer, *Do Dooni Chaar* (1968)

Kumar, Kishore — Sandeep (double role), *Do Dooni Chaar* (1968)

Kuperman, Mário — director, screenwriter, *Jogo da Vida E da Morte* (1972)

Kumar, Sanjeev — Ashok Tilak (double role), *Angoor* (1982)

Kurashita, Honami — Majiru, *Manatsu no yo no yume* (2009)

Kurosawa, Akira — director, producer, screenwriter, editor, *Kumonosu jô* (1957)
director, screenwriter, editor, *Ran* (1985)

La Badie, Florence — Miranda, *The Tempest* (1911)
Portia, *The Merchant of Venice* (1912)
Imogen, *Cymbeline* (1913)

Lafield, Britt — Malcolm III, *Macbeth* (2003)

Laforgue, Jules — writer (story), *Un Amleto di meno* (1973)

Lailey, Kan — composer, *Richard III* (2005)

Lal — Paniyan, *Kaliyattam* (1997)
Manikyan, *Kannaki* (2002)

Landeta, Manuel — Santiago, *Huapango* (2004)

Landin, Bo — director, producer, screenwriter, *Macbeth* (2004)

Lane, Nathan — Costard, *Love's Labour's Lost* (2000)

Lane, Rosemary — Phyllis, *The Boys from Syracuse* (1940)

Lang, Matheson — Shylock, *The Merchant of Venice* (1916)
co-writer (play *Sirocco*) & Silvio Steno / Othello, *Carnival* (1921)
co-writer (play *Sirocco*) & Silvio Steno / Othello, *Carnival* (1931)

Lange, Jessica — Ginny Cook Smith, *A Thousand Acres* (1997)
Tamora, *Titus* (1999)

Lansbury, David — Max / Macduff / Macbeth, *Macbeth in Manhattan* (1999)

Lanser, Roger — cinematographer, *Much Ado About Nothing* (1993)
cinematographer, *As You Like It* (2006)

Lapis, Joe — sound department, *The Boys from Syracuse* (1940)
sound, *A Double Life* (1947)

Larionova, Alla — Olivia, *Dvenadtsataya noch* (1955)

Laumord, Gilbert — Narrator, *Makibefo* (1999)

Laurie, John — Oliver de Boys, *As You Like It* (1936)
Captain Jamie, *The Chronicle History of King Henry the Fift with His Battell Fought at Agincourt in France* (1944)
Francisco, *Hamlet* (1948)
Sir Francis Lovel, *Richard III* (1955)

Lavagnino, Angelo Francesco — composer, *The Tragedy of Othello: The Moor of Venice* (1952)
composer, *Campanadas a*

medianoche (1965)

Lavaudant, Georges	stage director, *Richard III* (1986)
Lavrovsky, Leonid	director, screenwriter, choreographer, *Romeo i Zhulietta* (1955)
Lawrence, Ashley	conductor, *Romeo and Juliet* (1966)
Lawrence, Florence	Banquet guest, *Macbeth* (1908)
	Juliet Capulet, *Romeo and Juliet* (1908)
	unknown role, *Richard III* (1908)
	Cleopatra VII, *Antony and Cleopatra* (1908)
	Katharina Minola, *The Taming of the Shrew* (1908)
	Calpurnia, *Julius Caesar* (1908)
Lean, David	editor, *As You Like It* (1936)
Leblanc, Georgette	Lady Macbeth, *Macbeth* (1915)
LeBlanc, Michael	Ferdinand, *The Tempest* (2007)
Ledger, Heath	Patrick Verona, *10 Things I Hate About You* (1999)
Lee, Alberto	cinematographer, *Huapango* (2004)
Lee, Carey	Queen Elizabeth, *Richard III* (1912)
Lee, Christopher	Spear carrier, *Hamlet* (1948)
	Artemidorus, *Julius Caesar* (1970)
Lee, Paul	director, *Romeo and Juliet* (1966)
Leela	singer, *Gunasundari Katha* (1949)
	singer, *Gunsundari* (1955)
Leeves, Luke	Lucio, *Measure for Measure* (2006)
LeGault, Lance	Iago, *Catch My Soul* (1974)
LeGros, James	Joe "Mac" McBeth, *Scotland, Pa.* (2001)
Leguizamo, John	Tybalt Capulet, *William Shakespeare's Romeo + Juliet* (1996)
Lehman, Ernest	screenwriter, *West Side Story* (1961)
Leigh, Jennifer Jason	Caroline Cook, *A Thousand Acres* (1997)
Lemmon, Jack	Marcellus, *Hamlet* (1996)
Lenard, Cesira	Desdemona, *Otello* (1914)
von Lenkeffy, Ica	Desdemona, *Othello* (1922)
Lennix, Harry J.	Aaron, *Titus* (1999)
Lennon, Caroline	Goneril, *King Lear* (1999)
Lens, Ellen	costume designer, *Prospero's*

	Books (1991)
Leo, Franco	unknown role, *Quella sporca storia nel West* (1968)
	Horatio, *Un Amleto di meno* (1973)
Leonard, Robert Sean	Count Claudio, *Much Ado About Nothing* (1993)
Lepanto, Vittoria	Desdemona, *Otello* (1909)
Lessey, George	Romeo Montague, *Romeo and Juliet* (1911)
Lester, Adrian	Dumaine, *Love's Labour's Lost* (2000)
	Oliver de Boys, *As You Like It* (2006)
Lester, Dominic	assistant dubbing mixer, *Henry V* (1989)
	sound re-recording mixer, *Othello* (1995)
	sound re-recording mixer, *Twelfth Night: Or What You Will* (1996)
	sound re-recording mixer, *Hamlet* (1996)
	sound re-recording mixer, *Shakespeare in Love* (1998)
Leth, Jørgen	director, *Ofelias blomster* (1968)
Letts, Pauline	Cleopatra VII, *Antony and Cleopatra* (1951)
Leven, Boris	production designer, *West Side Story* (1961)
Levenstein, Fannie	Hanneloere Mosheles, *The Yiddish King Lear* (1934)
Levitch, Timothy	Hector, *Scotland, Pa.* (2001)
Leysen, Johan	Banco, *Macbeth* (1987)
LiCalsi, Allison	director, co-producer, screenwriter, *Macbeth: The Comedy* (2001)
Liedtke, Harry	Bassanio, *Der Kaufmann von Venedig* (1923)
de Liguoro, Giuseppe	producer, *Amleto* (1908)
	director & Lear, *Re Lear* (1910)
Lillard, Matthew	Longaville, *Love's Labour's Lost* (2000)
Lindenstrand, Sylvia	Meg Page, *Falstaff* (1979)
Linder, Max	Romeo, *Romeo se fait bandit* (1910)
Lione, Roberto	director, producer, screenwriter, *Kate – La bisbetica domata* (2004)
Lipkies, Ivan	director, screenwriter, *Huapango* (2004)
Lisset	Julia, *Huapango* (2004)

387

Little, John	Duncan I, *Macbeth: The Comedy* (2001)
Lloyd, Robert Langdon	Edgar, *King Lear* (1971)
Lo Savio, Gerolamo	second unit director, *Otello* (1909)
	director, *Re Lear* (1910)
	director, *Il Mercante di Venezia* (1910)
Lo Schiavo, Francesca	set decorator, *Hamlet* (1990)
Lobe, Friedrich	Elias, *Der Kaufmann von Venedig* (1923)
Logan, Denis	assistant director & Macduff, *Macbeth 3000: This Time, It's Personal* (2005)
Loginova, Galina	Beatrice, *Mnogo shuma iz nichego* (1973)
Lombardo, Greg	director, screenwriter, *Macbeth in Manhattan* (1999)
Loncraine, Richard	director, *Richard III* (1995)
Longden, John	Julian Caesar, *An Honourable Murder* (1960)
Loos, Theodor	Michael Cassio, *Othello* (1922)
López, Manuel Villegas	screenwriter, *La Fierecilla domada* (1956)
López, Mario	Juan Vallejo, *King Rikki* (2002)
Louise, Anita	Titania, *A Midsummer Night's Dream* (1935)
Louiso, Todd	director, producer, screenwriter, & Ophelia, *The Fifteen Minute Hamlet* (1995)
Lowe, Arthur	Horace Sprout, *Theatre of Blood* (1973)
Lowenthal, Yuri	Banquo, *Macbeth* (2003)
Lubitsch, Ernst	director, screenwriter, *Romeo und Julia im Schnee* (1920)
Luchetti, Veriano	Macduff (voice), *Macbeth* (1987)
Luchko, Klara	Viola / Sebastian, *Dvenadtsataya noch* (1955)
Lucidi, Enrico	camera operator, *Titus* (1999)
	cinematographer, *Iago* (2009)
Lucinda, Elisa	Sra Rocha, *As Alegres Comadres* (2003)
Ludwig, Rolf	Benedick, *Viel Lärm um nichts* (1964)
Luhrmann, Baz	director, producer, *William Shakespeare's Romeo + Juliet* (1996)
Lum, May Yee	Audrey Chan / Juliet Capulet, *Jiyuan qiaohe* (2000)
Lunghi, Cherie	Titania, *The Seasons Alter* (2002)
Lunn, Roger	director, *The Seasons Alter*

388

Lutz, Karen McCullah

(2002)

screenwriter, *10 Things I Hate About You* (1999)

screenwriter, *She's the Man* (2006)

Lynch, Finbar

Philostrate / Puck, *A Midsummer Night's Dream* (1996)

Lyson, Leane

Puck, *The Children's Midsummer Night's Dream* (2001)

Matthews, Trevor

Q-Ball, *Macbeth 3000: This Time, It's Personal* (2005)

MacBean, L. C.

director, *The Real Thing at Last* (1916)

McCafferty, Robert F.

Earl of Northumberland, *Richard II* (2001)

McCann, Christopher

Derek / Duncan I, *Macbeth in Manhattan* (1999)

McChesney, Dominic

Earl Rivers, *Richard III* (2005)

McDowall, Roddy

Malcolm III, *Macbeth* (1948)

McElhone, Natascha

Rosaline, *Love's Labour's Lost* (2000)

McEnery, John

Company, *Othello* (1965)

Mercutio, *Romeo and Juliet* (1968)

Osric, *Hamlet* (1990)

Macfadyen, Angus

Lucius Andronicus, *Titus* (1999)

McGaw, David

director & Rockin' Romeo Montague, *Rockin' Romeo & Juliet* (2006)

McGoohan, Patrick

Johnnie Cousin, *All Night Long* (1962)

director, *Catch My Soul* (1974)

MacGowran, Jack

Fool, *King Lear* (1971)

McHugh, Frank

Peter Quince, *A Midsummer Night's Dream* (1935)

McKellen, Ian

executive producer & Richard III, *Richard III* (1995)

Mackintosh, Steven

Sebastian, *Twelfth Night: Or What You Will* (1996)

MacLachlan, Kyle

Claudius, *Hamlet* (2000)

McLane, Judy

Donna, *Were The World Mine* (2008)

McLeay, Franklyn

Hubert de Burgh [not in surviving footage], *King John* (1899)

MacLiammóir, Micheál

Iago, *The Tragedy of Othello: The Moor of Venice* (1952)

MacMillan, Kenneth (I)

screenwriter, choreographer, *Romeo and Juliet* (1966)

MacMillan, Kenneth (II)

cinematographer, *Henry V*

	(1989)
McTavish, Graham	Banquo, *Macbeth* (1997)
	Duke of Albany, *King Lear* (1999)
Ma, Jingwu	Minister Yin, *Ye yan* (2006)
Maazel, Lorin	conductor, music producer, *Otello* (1986)
Macario, Erminio	producer, screenwriter & Amleto, *Io, Amleto* (1952)
Maccarone, Dan	Thane of Ross, *Macbeth* (2003)
Machavariani, Aleqsi	composer, *Otelo* (1960)
Mack, Max	director, *Othello* (1918)
Madan, J. J.	director, *Zalim Saudagar* (1941)
Madden, John	director, *Shakespeare in Love* (1998)
Madhok, D. N.	director, *Dil Farosh* (1937)
Magnier, Pierre	Laertes, *Le Duel d' Hamlet* (1900)
Mailer, Norman	The Great Writer, *King Lear* (1987)
Maitland, Lauderdale	Petruchio, *The Taming of the Shrew* (1923)
Makhija, Masumi	Sameera Khan, *Maqbool* (2003)
Makoare, Lawrence	Prince of Morocco, *The Maori Merchant of Venice* (2002)
Makowska, Helena	Ophelia, *Amleto* (1917)
Maksimova, Antonina	Emilia, *Otello* (1955)
Malagu, Stefania	Emilia, *Otello* (1973)
Malone, Mary	Juliet Capulet, *Romeo and Juliet* (1908)
Maloney, Michael	Dauphin Louis, *Henry V* (1989)
	Rosencrantz, *Hamlet* (1990)
	Roderigo, *Othello* (1995)
	Laertes, *Hamlet* (1996)
Mancinelli, Lydia	Kate, *Un Amleto di meno* (1973)
Mankiewicz, Joseph L.	director, *Julius Caesar* (1953)
Marak, Otakar	Romeo Montague, *Romeo e Giulietta* (1927)
Marazzi, Alfredo	key makeup artist, *Otello* (1986)
Margolyes, Miriam	Audrey, *As You Like It* (1992)
	Nurse, *William Shakespeare's Romeo + Juliet* (1996)
Marian, Edwin	Borachio, *Viel Lärm um nichts* (1964)
Mariani, Giuseppe	art director, production designer, *The Taming of the Shrew* (1967)
Marlowe, Christopher	lyricist ("The Passionate Shepherd"), *Richard III* (1995)
	writer (excerpt from *Dr Faustus*), *Shakespeare in Love*

	(1998)
Marosin, Mircea	costume designer, *Hamlet* (1976)
Marqués, María Elena	Juliet Capulet, *Romeo y Julieta* (1943)
Marsh, Linda	Ophelia, *Hamlet* (1964)
Marshall, Kris	Gratiano, *The Merchant of Venice* (2004)
Marston, Nathaniel	Rosario Capomezza / Romeo Montague, *Love Is All There Is* (1996)
Marston, Theodore	director, *The Winter's Tale* (1910)
Martelli	Claudius, *Amleto* (1917)
Martin, Catherine	production designer, title designer, associate producer, *William Shakespeare's Romeo + Juliet* (1996)
Martin, Jamie	producer & Richard III, *Richard III* (2005)
Marzuki, Zul Huzaimy	Brutus, *Gedebe* (2003)
Mason, James	Marcus Junius Brutus, *Julius Caesar* (1953)
Mason, Monica	Harlot, *Romeo and Juliet* (1966)
Maté, Rudolph	cinematographer, *Der Kaufmann von Venedig* (1923)
Mathie, Marion	Portia Smith, *An Honourable Murder* (1960)
Matou, Michael	Oberon, *A Midsummer Night's Dream* (1985)
Matthews, A. E.	Not Worth Murdering But Murdered, *The Real Thing at Last* (1916)
Maurice, Clément	director, *Roméo et Juliette* (1900) director, producer, *Le Duel d' Hamlet* (1900)
Maxwell, Edwin	Baptista Minola, *The Taming of the Shrew* (1929)
May, Janet	Duchess of York, *Richard III* (2005)
Mayniel, Juliette	Lucie, *Ophélia* (1963)
Mazur, Tom	Second Murderer, *Macbeth* (2003)
Mazursky, Paul	director, producer, screenwriter & Producer, *Tempest* (1982)
Mead, Paul	Edmund, *King Lear* (1976)
Medvedev, Vadim	Orsino, *Dvenadtsataya noch* (1955) Guildenstern, *Gamlet* (1964)
Meech, Geoff Warren	director, cinematographer, editor & Fleance, *Macbeth*

	Measure (2006)
Mifune, Toshirô	Taketori Washizu, *Kumonosu jô* (1957)
Miler, Mildred	Meg Page, *Die Lustigen Weiber von Windsor* (1965)
Millenotti, Maurizio	costume designer, *Otello* (1986)
	costume designer, *Hamlet* (1990)
Miller, Ann	Lois Lane / Bianca Minola, *Kiss Me Kate* (1953)
Miller, Frank	screenwriter, *Juliet and Her Romeo* (1923)
Miller, Larry	Walter Stratford, *10 Things I Hate About You* (1999)
Miller, Marvin	Robby the Robot (voice), *Forbidden Planet* (1956)
Miller, Sonny	lyricist, *All Night Long* (1962)
Miller, Wesley C.	recording supervisor, *Forbidden Planet* (1956)
Mills, J. Royal	Malcolm III, *Macbeth* (1946)
Mills, John	King of Norway, *Hamlet* (1996)
Mingus, Charles	himself, *All Night Long* (1962)
Mirren, Helen	Hermia, *A Midsummer Night's Dream* (1968)
	Gertrude / Ophelia, *Hamlet* (1976)
	Prospera, *The Tempest* (2010)
Mishra, Piyush	Kaka, *Maqbool* (2003)
Miss Amanda	Iris, *The Tempest* (2007)
Mistry, Jimi	Second Sailor, *Hamlet* (1996)
	Jug, *My Kingdom* (2001)
Mitchell, Arthur	Puck, *A Midsummer Night's Dream* (1967)
Miyazaki, Yoshiko	Lady Sué, *Ran* (1985)
Modi, Sohrab	director & Hamlet, *Khoon Ka Khoon* (1935)
Mohandas, Geethu	Kumudam, *Kannaki* (2002)
Mohr, Hal	cinematographer, *A Midsummer Night's Dream* (1935)
Mole, Charlie	composer, *Othello* (1995)
Moncion, Francisco	Theseus, *A Midsummer Night's Dream* (1967)
Mongiardino, Lorenzo	production designer, *The Taming of the Shrew* (1967)
	production designer, *Romeo and Juliet* (1968)
Montagnini, Felice	composer, *La Bisbetica domata* (1942)
Montalban, Ricardo	Claudius (voice: English version), *Hamlet, Prinz von Dänemark* (1961)

Montano, Beni	Georg V. Hartung / Othello, *Othello* (1918)
Montesi, Rossana	Bianca Minola, *La Bisbetica domata* (1942)
Moore, Marshall	director, *Brutus and Cassius* (1918)
Moorhouse, Jocelyn	director, *A Thousand Acres* (1997)
Moraes, Ernani	Sr Rocha, *As Alegres Comadres* (2003)
Morano, Gigetta	Katherina Minola, *La Bisbetica domata* (1913)
Moreau, Jeanne	Doll Tearsheet, *Campanadas a medianoche* (1965)
Moreau, Marguerite	Helena, *Rave Macbeth* (2001)
Moreno, Mario ("Cantinflas")	Romeo Montague, *Romeo y Julieta* (1943)
Moreno, Rita	Anita, *West Side Story* (1961)
Morgan, Reikura	Jessica, *The Maori Merchant of Venice* (2002)
Morley, Robert	Meredith Merridew, *Theatre of Blood* (1973)
Morricone, Ennio	composer (DVD), *Richard III* (1912) composer, *Hamlet* (1990)
Morrison, Scott	Antonio, *The Maori Merchant of Venice* (2002)
Morrissette, Billy	director, screenwriter & Man Walking Dog, *Scotland, Pa.* (2001)
Mortimer, Emily	Katherine d' Alençon, *Love's Labour's Lost* (2000)
Morton, Arthur	Puck, *Midsummer* (1999)
Mounet, Paul	Macbeth, *Macbeth* (1909)
Mounet-Sully	Hamlet, *Hamlet* (1909)
Mourad, Laila	Juliet Capulet, *Shuhaddaa el gharam* (1942)
Movar, Dunja	Ophelia, *Hamlet, Prinz von Dänemark* (1961)
Mowbray, Alan	Angelo, *The Boys from Syracuse* (1940)
Mukherjee, Gautam	composer, *Kaliyattam* (1997)
Müller, Bernd	costume designer, *Falstaff* (1979)
Mullin, Eugene	director, *Twelfth Night* (1910)
Muraki, Shinobu	production designer, *Ran* (1985)
Muraki, Yoshiro	production designer, costume designer, *Kumonosu jô* (1957) production designer, *Ran* (1985)
Murphy, Kevin	Leon Deli, *Jiyuan qiaohe* (2000)
Murray, Bill	Polonius, *Hamlet* (2000)

	Merchant of Venice (1927)
Newmark, Ben	David, *West Bank Story* (2005)
Newton, Robert	Ancient Pistol, *The Chronicle History of King Henry the Fift with His Battell Fought at Agincourt in France* (1944)
Nibbelink, Phil	director, editor, screenwriter & Prince (voice), *Romeo & Juliet: Sealed with a Kiss* (2006)
Nicolai, Otto	composer, *Die Lustigen Weiber von Windsor* (1917)
	composer, *Die Lustigen Weiber von Windsor* (1950)
	composer, *Die Lustigen Weiber von Windsor* (1965)
Nicolai, Sergio	Sailor, *Tempest* (1982)
	Roderigo, *Otello* (1986)
Nielsen, Asta	producer & Hamlet, *Hamlet* (1921)
Nielsen, Leslie	Commander John J. Adams, *Forbidden Planet* (1956)
Nikkari, Esko	Einari, *Macbeth* (1987)
	Polonius, *Hamlet liikemaailmassa* (1987)
Nivola, Alessandro	King Ferdinand, *Love's Labour's Lost* (2000)
Noble, Adrian	director, *A Midsummer Night's Dream* (1996)
Noble, John W.	director, *Romeo and Juliet* (1916)
Noi, Reece	Boy, *My Kingdom* (2001)
Nolan, Jeanette	Lady Macbeth, *Macbeth* (1948)
Nomura, Mansai	Tsurumaru, *Ran* (1985)
Norman, Marc	producer, screenwriter, *Shakespeare in Love* (1998)
Novelli, Amleto	Hamlet, *Amleto* (1910)
	unknown role, *Brutus* (1910)
Novelli, Ermete	Lear, *Re Lear* (1910)
	Shylock, *Il Mercante di Venezia* (1910)
Novelli, Olga Giannini	Goneril, *Re Lear* (1910)
	Portia, *Il Mercante di Venezia* (1910)
Novello, Ivor	Count Andrea Scipione, *Carnival* (1921)
Nucci, Leo	Macbeth, *Macbeth* (1987)
Nuckley, Simon	Claudio, *Measure for Measure* (2006)
Nunn, Trevor	director, *Twelfth Night: Or What You Will* (1996)
Nureyev, Rudolf	Romeo Montague, *Romeo and Juliet* (1966)

Nyman, Michael	composer, musical director, pianist, *Prospero's Books* (1991)
O'Brien, Edmond	Bill Friend, *A Double Life* (1947) Publius Servilius Casca, *Julius Caesar* (1953)
O'Brien, Terence	Tubal, *The Merchant of Venice* (1916)
O'Donnell, Frank	John of Gaunt, *Richard II* (2001)
O'Donoghue, Robin	sound re-recording mixer, *Henry V* (1989) sound re-recording mixer, *Much Ado About Nothing* (1993) sound re-recording mixer, *Othello* (1995) sound re-recording mixer, *Twelfth Night: Or What You Will* (1996) sound re-recording mixer, *Hamlet* (1996) sound re-recording mixer, *Shakespeare in Love* (1998)
O'Herlihy, Dan	set designer & Macduff, *Macbeth* (1948)
O'Neil, Barry	director, *The Winter's Tale* (1910) director, *Romeo and Juliet* (1911)
O'Shea, Milo	Friar Laurence, *Romeo and Juliet* (1968) Inspector Boot, *Theatre of Blood* (1973)
Oberoi, Vivek	Keshav "Kesu Firangi" Upadhyay, *Omkara* (2006)
Oldman, Gary	Rosencrantz, *Rosencrantz & Guildenstern Are Dead* (1990)
Oleksenko, Stepan	Laertes, *Gamlet* (1964)
Oleynik, Larisa	Bianca Stratford, *10 Things I Hate About You* (1999)
Oliver, Edna May	Nurse, *Romeo and Juliet* (1936)
Oliveros, Ramiro	Major Michael Cassius, *Othello, el comando negro* (1982)
Olivier, Laurence	Orlando de Boys, *As You Like It* (1936) director, producer, & Henry V, *The Chronicle History of King Henry the Fift with His Battell Fought at Agincourt in France* (1944) director, executive producer, & Hamlet / Ghost (voice), *Hamlet* (1948)

397

	director, producer, & Richard III, *Richard III* (1955)
	Othello, *Othello* (1965)
	Chorus (voice) / Lord Montague (voice), *Romeo and Juliet* (1968)
Oman, Julia Trevelyan	production designer, *Julius Caesar* (1970)
Oranli, Ayla	Rezzan, *Intikam Melegi – Kadin Hamlet* (1977)
Oreskovic, Vjenceslav	cinematographer, *Predstava "Hamleta" u selu Mrduši Donjoj* (1973)
Ortmann, Wilfried	Don Pedro, *Viel Lärm um nichts* (1964)
Osian, Matte	Richard II, *Richard II* (2001)
Oswald, Marianne	Laetitia, *Les Amants de Vérone* (1949)
Otterson, John	production designer, *The Boys from Syracuse* (1940)
Outinen, Kati	Ofelia Polonius, *Hamlet liikemaailmassa* (1987)
Owen, Lloyd	Oberon, *The Seasons Alter* (2002)
Oyelowo, David	Orlando de Boys, *As You Like It* (2006)
Pacheco, Rafael	cinematographer, *Antony and Cleopatra* (1972)
Pacino, Al	director, producer, screenwriter & himself / Richard III, *Looking for Richard* (1996)
	Shylock, *The Merchant of Venice* (2004)
Pagani, Mauro	composer, *Sogno di una notte d' estate* (1983)
Pajala, Turo	Malcolm III, *Macbeth* (1987)
	Rosencranz, *Hamlet liikemaailmassa* (1987)
Paltrow, Gwyneth	Viola de Lesseps / Romeo Montague / Juliet Capulet, *Shakespeare in Love* (1998)
Pandit, Surekha	Anju, *Do Dooni Chaar* (1968)
Panebianco, Richard	Tony, *China Girl* (1987)
Panfilov, Gleb	director, *Gamlet* (1989)
Panzer, Paul	Macduff, *Macbeth* (1908)
	Romeo Montague, *Romeo and Juliet* (1908)
	unknown role, *Richard III* (1908)
	Michael Cassio, *Othello* (1908)
	unknown role, *The Merchant of Venice* (1908)

	unknown role, *Julius Caesar* (1908)
	Lieutenant to Octavius, *Antony and Cleopatra* (1908)
Papic, Krsto	director, screenwriter, *Predstava "Hamleta" u selu Mrduši Donjoj* (1973)
Parfitt, Judy	Gertrude, *Hamlet* (1969)
Parker, Mary-Louise	Julia Hirsch, *Let the Devil Wear Black* (1999)
Parker, Nathaniel	Laertes, *Hamlet* (1990)
	Michael Cassio, *Othello* (1995)
Parker, Oliver	director, *Othello* (1995)
Parkhomenko, Aleksei	production designer, *Romeo i Zhulietta* (1955)
Parkinson, Harry B.	director, producer, *Macbeth* (1922)
	producer, *The Merchant of Venice* (1922)
Parry, Natasha	Lady Capulet, *Romeo and Juliet* (1968)
Pasco, Isabelle	Miranda, *Prospero's Books* (1991)
Pasquali, Ernesto Maria	director, *Bianco contro negro* (1913)
Pasternak, Boris	translator, *Otello* (1955)
	translator, *Gamlet* (1964)
	translator, *Korol Lir* (1971)
Pastrone, Giovanni	director & Gaius Julius Caesar, *Giulio Cesare* (1909)
Patrick, Anna	Emilia, *Othello* (1995)
Paul, Helena	Regan, *King Lear* (1976)
Paul, Mimi	Helena, *A Midsummer Night's Dream* (1967)
Pavlenko, Pavel	Dogberry, *Mnogo shuma iz nichego* (1973)
Pavlov, Assen	Hamlet / himself, *The Hamlet Adventure* (2008)
Peachey, Jamie	Hermia, *The Children's Midsummer Night's Dream* (2001)
Peak, Philippa	Third Witch, *Macbeth* (1997)
	Cordelia, *King Lear* (1999)
Pedley, Anthony	Friar Laurence, *Romeo and Juliet* (1966)
Peele, George	co-writer (play), *Titus* (1999)
	co-writer (play), *Titus Andronicus* (2000)
Pehi, Samson	Prince of Aragon, *The Maori Merchant of Venice* (2002)
Peil, Edward	Claude Dutton, *A Sage Brush Hamlet* (1919)
Pelar, R.	Narrator (voice: Czech

Pierfederici, Antonio	Lord Montague, *Romeo and Juliet* (1968)
	Doge of Venice, *Otello* (1986)
Pineschi, Azeglio	director, producer, *La Bisbetica domata* (1908)
Pineschi, Lamberto	director, producer, *La Bisbetica domata* (1908)
Pious, Minerva	Rosie, *Joe MacBeth* (1955)
Plumb, E. Hay	director, *Hamlet* (1913)
Png, Pierre	Fenson Wong / Romeo Montague, *Jiyian qiaohe* (2000)
Poggioli, Ferdinando Maria	director, adaptor & unknown role, *La Bisbetica domata* (1942)
Polanski, Roman	director, *The Tragedy of Macbeth* (1971)
Polessa, Zezé	Sra Lima, *As Alegres Comadres* (2003)
Ponty, Philippe	composer & The clown, *La tragédie de Gonzague* (2002)
Popov, Andrei	Iago, *Otello* (1955)
	Petruchio, *Ukroshchenie stroptivoy* (1961)
Popp, Lucia	Anne Page, *Die Lustigen Weiber von Windsor* (1965)
Porten, Franz	director & Othello, *Othello* (1909)
Porten, Henny	Desdemona, *Othello* (1909)
	Portia, *Der Kaufmann von Venedig* (1923)
Porten, Rosa	Emilia, *Othello* (1909)
Porter, Cole	composer, lyricist, *Kiss Me Kate* (1953)
	composer, *Love's Labour's Lost* (2000)
Porter, Eric	Gnaeus Domitius Enobarbus, *Antony and Cleopatra* (1972)
Postlethwaite, Pete	Player King, *Hamlet* (1990)
	Father Laurence, *William Shakespeare's Romeo + Juliet* (1996)
Pouget, Armand	Ghost, *Amleto* (1917)
Pouget, Fernanda Negri	unknown role, *Otello* (1906)
	unknown role, *Amleto* (1908)
	unknown role, *Romeo e Giulietta* (1908)
	Ophelia, *Amleto* (1910)
Poulsen, Anna Neye	director, executive producer & Lady Anne, *Richard: Memories from the Scrapbook* (2004)
Powell, Dick	Lysander, *A Midsummer Night's Dream* (1935)

Powell, Robert	Romeo Montague, *Romeo-Juliet* (1990)
Powell, Sandy	costume designer, *Shakespeare in Love* (1998)
Prévert, Jacques	screenwriter, *Les Amants de Vérone* (1949)
Prévost, Françoise	Gertrude Hamilton, *Quella sporca storia nel West* (1968)
Previn, André	musical director, *Kiss Me Kate* (1953)
Price, Dennis	Hector Snipe, *Theatre of Blood* (1973)
Price, Vincent	Edward Lionheart, *Theatre of Blood* (1973)
Primo, Raphael	Abraão Silva, *As Alegres Comadres* (2003)
Prokofiev, Sergei	composer, *Romeo i Zhulietta* (1955)
	composer, *Romeo and Juliet* (1966)
	composer, *Romeo-Juliet* (1990)
Psilander, Valdemar	Einar Lowe / Othello, *For Åbent Tæppe* (1911)
Puri, Om	Inspector Pandit, *Maqbool* (2003)
Puyol, Francisco	make-up artist, *Campanadas a medianoche* (1965)
Pyne, Natasha	Bianca Minola, *The Taming of the Shrew* (1967)
Quertier, Jill	set decorator, *Shakespeare in Love* (1998)
Rachold, Gerhard	Don Juan, *Viel Lärm um nichts* (1964)
Rackham, John	Edward IV, *Richard III* (2005)
Radford, Michael	director, *The Merchant of Venice* (2004)
Radhakrishnan, M. J.	cinematographer, *Kaliyattam* (1997)
	cinematographer, *Kannaki* (2002)
Radzinya, Elze	Gertrude, *Gamlet* (1964)
	Goneril, *Korol Lir* (1971)
Raine, Rachel J. Sita	Titania, *William Shakespeare's Ill Met by Moonlight* (1994)
Rajkin, Konstantin	Benedick, *Mnogo shuma iz nichego* (1973)
Rajkovic, Aleksandar	director, screenwriter, *Hamlet* (2007)
Ramey, Samuel	Banco (voice), *Macbeth* (1987)
Ramin, Sid	music supervisor, orchestrator, *West Side Story* (1961)

Ramsey, Allen	director, *Julius Caesar* (1913)
Ramsey, Laura	Olivia, *She's the Man* (2006)
Randell, Ron	Cole Porter, *Kiss Me Kate* (1953)
Rani, Sudha	Suman, *Do Dooni Chaar* (1968)
Rankin, Virginia	Duke of York, *Richard III* (1912)
Ranous, William V.	Macbeth, *Macbeth* (1908)
	director & Othello, *Othello* (1908)
	Friar Lawrence, *Romeo and Juliet* (1908)
	director & Richard III, *Richard III* (1908)
	Gaius Julius Caesar Octavian, *Antony and Cleopatra* (1908)
	director, producer & Gaius Cassius Longinus, *Julius Caesar* (1908)
	Shylock, *The Merchant of Venice* (1908)
	director & Lear, *King Lear* (1909)
	Nick Bottom, *A Midsummer Night's Dream* (1909)
Rao, Govindrajulu Subba	King, *Gunasundari Katha* (1949)
Rao, Kamalakara Kameshwara	screenwriter, *Gunasundari Katha* (1949)
	director, screenwriter, *Gunsundari* (1955)
Rao, Kasturi Siva	backing singer & Boy, *Gunasundari Katha* (1949)
Raobelina, Victor	Witch doctor, *Makibefo* (1999)
Rapoport, Iosif	director, production designer, *Mnogo shuma iz nichego* (1956)
Rapp, Richard	Nick Bottom, *A Midsummer Night's Dream* (1967)
Rathbone, Basil	Tybalt Capulet, *Romeo and Juliet* (1936)
Raye, Martha	Luce, *The Boys from Syracuse* (1940)
Raymond, Charles	Hamlet, *Hamlet* (1910)
	director & Hamlet, *Hamlet* (1912)
Rebhorn, James	Norm Duncan, *Scotland, Pa.* (2001)
Reddin-Clancy, Katie	Horatio, *Hamlet* (2007)
Reddy, Kadri Venkata	director, *Gunasundari Katha* (1949)
Redgrave, Lynn	Mandy Sandeman, *My Kingdom* (2001)
Redman, Joyce	Emilia, *Othello* (1965)

Rée, Max — costume designer, *A Midsummer Night's Dream* (1935)

Reedus, Norman — Jesse Brautigan, *Let the Devil Wear Black* (1999)

Reeves, Keanu — Scott Favor, *My Own Private Idaho* (1991)

Don John, *Much Ado About Nothing* (1993)

Reggiani, Serge — Angelo / Romeo Montague, *Les Amants de Vérone* (1949)

Reid, Hal — screenwriter & Rohowaneh, *Indian Romeo and Juliet* (1912)

Cardinal Wolsey, *Cardinal Wolsey* (1912)

Reid, Tom — Duncan I, *Macbeth* (2003)

Reid, Wallace — Oniatare, *Indian Romeo and Juliet* (1912)

Reilly, William — director, screenwriter, *Men of Respect* (1991)

Reilly-Szostak, Raphaela — composer, *Richard III* (2005)

Reimann, Thyra — Maria Lowe / Desdemona, *For Åbent Tæppe* (1911)

Reinhardt, Max — director, producer, *A Midsummer Night's Dream* (1935)

Reis, Yamê — costume designer, *As Alegres Comadres* (2003)

Remotti, Remo — Brabanzio, *Otello* (1986)

Reuben, Gloria — Claudia / Lady Macbeth, *Macbeth in Manhattan* (1999)

Revelle, Hamilton — Hamlet, *Amleto* (1914)

Reynolds, Paul — Lover, *The Angelic Conversation* (1985)

Riccabona, Thomas — production designer, *Falstaff* (1979)

Ricciarelli, Katia — Desdemona, *Otello* (1986)

Richard, Frida — Leah, *Der Kaufmann von Venedig* (1923)

Richardson, Ian — Oberon, *A Midsummer Night's Dream* (1968)

Polonius, *Rosencrantz & Guildenstern Are Dead* (1990)

Richardson, Ralph — Duke of Buckingham, *Richard III* (1955)

Narrator (voice), *Campanadas a medianoche* (1965)

Richardson, Tony — director, *Hamlet* (1969)

Richert, William — Bob Pigeon, *My Own Private Idaho* (1991)

Richter, Gerd — costume designer, set designer, *Hamlet, Prinz von Dänemark* (1961)

404

Ries, Irving G.　　　　　　　　special effects, *Forbidden Planet* (1956)

Rigg, Diana　　　　　　　　　Helena, *A Midsummer Night's Dream* (1968)
Portia, *Julius Caesar* (1970)
Edwina Lionheart, *Theatre of Blood* (1973)

Ringham, Walter　　　　　　　Claudius, *Hamlet* (1913)

Ringwald, Molly　　　　　　　Miranda Dimitrius, *Tempest* (1982)
Cordelia Learo, *King Lear* (1987)

Risdon, Elisabeth　　　　　　　Rosalind Duke, *Love in a Wood* (1915)

Rivera, Lelane　　　　　　　　Desdemona, *Otello* (1932)

Roach, Greg　　　　　　　　　director & himself, *The Hamlet Adventure* (2008)

Robards, Jason　　　　　　　　Marcus Junius Brutus, *Julius Caesar* (1970)
Larry Cook, *A Thousand Acres* (1997)

Robbins, Jerome　　　　　　　director, choreographer, *West Side Story* (1961)

Roberts, Daniel　　　　　　　Angelo, *Measure for Measure* (2006)

Roberts, Joe　　　　　　　　　John Webster, *Shakespeare in Love* (1998)

Robey, George　　　　　　　　Sir John Falstaff, *The Chronicle History of King Henry the Fift with His Battell Fought at Agincourt in France* (1944)

Robie, Wendy　　　　　　　　Ms Tebbit, *Were The World Mine* (2008)

Robinson, Zuleikha　　　　　　Jessica, *The Merchant of Venice* (2004)

Robson, Flora　　　　　　　　Nurse, *Romeo and Juliet* (1954)

Rodgers, Richard　　　　　　　composer, *The Boys from Syracuse* (1940)

Rodolfi, Eleuterio　　　　　　Petruchio, *La Bisbetica domata* (1913)
director, *Amleto* (1917)

Rodway, Norman　　　　　　　Henry "Hotspur" Percy, *Campanadas a medianoche* (1965)

Rogers, Josephine　　　　　　　Isabelle, *Measure for Measure* (2006)

Rogers, Paul　　　　　　　　　Nick Bottom, *A Midsummer Night's Dream* (1968)

Roland, Gilbert　　　　　　　Horace, *Quella sporca storia nel West* (1968)

Román, Antonio　　　　　　　director, *La Fierecilla domada* (1956)

Sá, Maria	Widow, *As Alegres Comadres* (2003)
Sahu, Kishore	director, producer & Hamlet, *Hamlet* (1954)
St John, Nicholas	screenwriter, *China Girl* (1987)
St John, Renner	Titania / Hippolyta, *Midsummer* (1999)
Sais, Marin	Maria, *Twelfth Night* (1910)
Saitô, Takao	assistant camera, *Kumonosu jô* (1957)
	cinematographer, *Ran* (1985)
Salazár, Manuel	Otello, *Otello* (1932)
Salminen, Esko	Klaus, *Hamlet liikemaailmassa* (1987)
Salo, Elina	Gertrud, *Hamlet liikemaailmassa* (1987)
Salou, Louis	Ettore Maglia, *Les Amants de Vérone* (1949)
Salvatores, Gabriele	director, screenwriter, *Sogno di una notte d' estate* (1983)
Samarth, Tanuja	Pyari, *Do Dooni Chaar* (1968)
Sammartino, Giorgio	Sheriff Polomo, *Quella sporca storia nel West* (1968)
Samoilov, Aleksei	Don Pedro, *Mnogo shuma iz nichego* (1973)
Samsonov, Samson	director, *Mnogo shuma iz nichego* (1973)
Sandel, Ari	director, producer, screenwriter, *West Bank Story* (2005)
Sanderson, Challis	director, *The Merchant of Venice* (1922)
Saner, Gengis	composer & Fool, *King Lear* (1976)
Sarandon, Susan	Aretha Tomalin, *Tempest* (1982)
Saville, Phillip	Mark Anthony, *An Honourable Murder* (1960)
Sawyer, Gordon E.	sound supervisor, *West Side Story* (1961)
Scaife, Edward	cinematographer, *All Night Long* (1962)
Schaefer, George	director, producer, *Macbeth* (1961)
Schafheitlin, Franz	Polonius, *Hamlet, Prinz von Dänemark* (1961)
Schall, Heinz	director, *Hamlet* (1921)
	director, *Macbeth* (1922)
Schell, Maximilian	Hamlet, *Hamlet, Prinz von Dänemark* (1961)
Scherpf, Alex	director, screenwriter, & Murderer 2, *Macbeth* (2004)
Schier, Horst	cinematographer, *Viola und*

Sherlock, Di	Gertrude, *Hamlet* (2007)
Sheybal, Vladek	Player Queen, *Hamlet* (1976)
Shibamoto, Yuki	Yuriko, *Manatsu no yo no yume* (2009)
Shimura, Takashi	Noriyasu Odagura, *Kumonosu jô* (1957)
Shortland, Waihoroi	Shylock, *The Maori Merchant of Venice* (2002)
Shostakovich, Dmitri	composer, *Gamlet* (1964)
	composer, *Korol Lir* (1971)
	composer, *Intikam Melegi – Kadin Hamlet* (1977)
	composer, *Hamlet liikemaailmassa* (1987)
Shourds, Sherry	assistant director, *A Midsummer Night's Dream* (1935)
Siddique	Choman, *Kannaki* (2002)
Sidney, George	director, *Kiss Me Kate* (1953)
Silverstone, Alicia	Princess of France, *Love's Labour's Lost* (2000)
Silvi, Lilia	Catina, *La Bisbetica domata* (1942)
Simm, Ray	art director, *All Night Long* (1962)
Simmons, Jean	Ophelia, *Hamlet* (1948)
Simms, Stephen	Lord Scroop, *Henry V* (1989)
Simon, Michel	Shylock, *Le Marchand de Venise* (1953)
Simonelli, Giorgio	director, *Io, Amleto* (1952)
Simoni, Dario	set decorator, *The Taming of the Shrew* (1967)
Sís, Vladímir	director, choreographer, *Sen noci...* (1986)
Skala, Lilia	Lucia, *Men of Respect* (1991)
Skobtseva, Irina	Desdemona, *Otello* (1955)
Slater, John	Othello, *Othello* (1946)
Slezak, Leo	Sir John Falstaff, *Die Lustigen Weiber* (1936)
Smalley, Phillips	director & Shylock, *The Merchant of Venice* (1914)
Smart, Amy	Stacy, *Scotland, Pa.* (2001)
Smiley, Jane	writer (novel), *A Thousand Acres* (1997)
Smith, Arturo	cinematographer, *Rave Macbeth* (2001)
Smith, Barry	Henry IV, *Richard II* (2001)
Smith, Maggie	Desdemona, *Othello* (1965)
	Rosaline Capulet (voice), *Romeo-Juliet* (1990)
	Duchess of York, *Richard III* (1995)

Smith, Mel	Sir Toby Belch, *Twelfth Night: Or What You Will* (1996)
Smoktunovsky, Innokenti	Hamlet, *Gamlet* (1964)
Snyder, James	Malcolm Festes, *She's the Man* (2006)
Solano, Domingo	cinematographer, *Othello, el comando negro* (1982)
Solter, Harry	unknown role, *Romeo and Juliet* (1908)
	unknown role, *Richard III* (1908)
	Baptista Minola, *The Taming of the Shrew* (1908)
Solti, Georg	conductor, *Falstaff* (1979)
Sommer, Inken	Olivia, *Viola und Sebastian* (1972)
Somtow, S. P.	director, producer, composer, *William Shakespeare's Ill Met By Moonlight* (1994)
Sonat, Orçun	Osman, *Intikam Melegi – Kadin Hamlet* (1977)
Sorvino, Paul	creative consultant & Count Piero Malacici, *Love Is All There Is* (1996)
	Fulgencio Capulet, *William Shakespeare's Romeo + Juliet* (1996)
Soshalsky, Vladimir	Michael Cassio, *Otello* (1955)
	Tranio, *Ukroshchenie stroptivoy* (1961)
Spacey, Kevin	himself / Duke of Buckingham, *Looking for Richard* (1996)
Spall, Timothy	Rosencrantz, *Hamlet* (1996)
	Don Adriano de Armado, *Love's Labour's Lost* (2000)
Spalla, Ignazio	Guild, *Quella sporca storia nel West* (1968)
Speaight, Robert	Marc Antony, *Antony and Cleopatra* (1951)
Spira, Camilla	Gretchen Reich, *Die Lustigen Weiber von Windsor* (1950)
Sriranjani	Gunasundari, *Gunasundari Katha* (1949)
Stanford, Thomas	editor, *West Side Story* (1961)
Stanton, Barry	Oswald, *King Lear* (1971)
	Claudius, *Hamlet* (1976)
Stass, Herbert	Feste, *Viola und Sebastian* (1972)
Steavenson-Payne, Kate	Princess Elizabeth, *Richard III* (1995)
Steiger, Rod	Charlie d'Amico, *Men of Respect* (1991)

Steinrück, Albert	Tubal, *Der Kaufmann von Venedig* (1923)
Stepec, Bill	Macbeth, *Macbeth 3000: This Time, It's Personal* (2005)
Stephens, Robert	Prince Escalus, *Romeo and Juliet* (1968)
	Ancient Pistol, *Henry V* (1989)
Stephens, Toby	Orsino, *Twelfth Night: Or What You Will* (1996)
	Demetrius (voice: English version), *El Sueño de una noche de San Juan* (2005)
Stevens, Marti	Delia Lane, *All Night Long* (1962)
Stevens, Warren	Lieutenant "Doc" Ostrow, *Forbidden Planet* (1956)
Stewart, Donald Robert	Antonio, *Shakespeare's Merchant* (2003)
Stewart, Sophie	Celia, *As You Like It* (1936)
Stieda, Heinz	Horatio, *Hamlet* (1921)
Stiles, Julia	Kat Stratford, *10 Things I Hate About You* (1999)
	Ophelia, *Hamlet* (2000)
	Desi Brable, *O* (2001)
Stoffels, Royston	Othello, *Othello* (2007)
Stone, Moira	Lady Macbeth, *Macbeth* (2003)
Stoppard, Tom	director, screenwriter, *Rosencrantz & Guildenstern Are Dead* (1990)
	writer (play), *The Fifteen Minute Hamlet* (1995)
	screenwriter, *Shakespeare in Love* (1998)
Stow, Percy	director, *The Tempest* (1908)
Strassner, Joe	costume designer, *As You Like It* (1936)
Streich, Rita	Alice Fluth (voice), *Die Lustigen Weiber von Windsor* (1950)
Stride, John	Thane of Ross, *The Tragedy of Macbeth* (1971)
Strozzi, Silvia	scenographer, *Hamlet* (2007)
Stuart, Howard	Edward V, *Richard III* (1912)
Stuart, Violet	Lady Anne, *Richard III* (1912)
Stubbs, Imogen	Viola, *Twelfth Night: Or What You Will* (1996)
Suikkari, Anitta	Lady Macbeth, *Macbeth* (2004)
Sullivan, Tim	Oberon, *William Shakespeare's Ill Met by Moonlight* (1994)
Sutherland, A. Edward	director, *The Boys from Syracuse* (1940)
Sweeney, William	Porter / Doctor, *Macbeth* (1946)

Trnka, Jiří	director, art director, *Sen noci svatojanske* (1959)
Trojan, Václav	composer, *Sen noci svatojanske* (1959)
	composer, *Sen noci...* (1986)
Troupe, Tom	Jack Favor, *My Own Private Idaho* (1991)
Truman, Ralph	Mountjoy, *The Chronicle History of King Henry the Fift with His Battell Fought at Agincourt in France* (1944)
Trushkin, Leonid	Count Claudio, *Mnogo shuma iz nichego* (1973)
Tsignadze, Vera	Desdemona, *Otelo* (1960)
Tucci, Stanley	Mal d'Amico, *Men of Respect* (1991)
	Puck, *A Midsummer Night's Dream* (1999)
Tuma, Radek	director, screenwriter, *Stredoletní noci sen* (2005)
Tuminelli, Giuseppe	Polonius, *Un Amleto di meno* (1973)
Turner, Florence	Banquet guest, *Macbeth* (1908)
	unknown role, *Romeo and Juliet* (1908)
	unknown role, *Richard III* (1908)
	Jessica, *The Merchant of Venice* (1908)
	Regan, *King Lear* (1909)
	Titania, *A Midsummer Night's Dream* (1909)
	Viola, *Twelfth Night* (1910)
	Ethona, *Indian Romeo and Juliet* (1912)
Turturro, John	Michael Battaglia, *Men of Respect* (1991)
Ueda, Masaharu	cinematographer, *Ran* (1985)
Ulanova, Galina	Juliet Capulet, *Romeo i Zhulietta* (1955)
Ün, Memduh	director, producer, *Yavas gel güzelim* (1963)
	producer, *Intikam Melegi – Kadin Hamlet* (1977)
Unkel, Rolf	composer, *Hamlet, Prinz von Dänemark* (1961)
Urban, Charles	director, *The Tempest* (1905)
Väänäen, Kari	Lauri Polonius, *Hamlet liikemaailmassa* (1987)
Valdés, Ariel García	Richard III, *Richard III* (1986)
Valli, Alida	Claudia Lesurf, *Ophélia* (1963)

Wade, Ginger	producer, composer & Benvolio Montague, *Rockin' Romeo & Juliet* (2006)
Wagar, Paul	director, producer, *Shakespeare's Merchant* (2003)
Wakhévitch, Georges	production designer, *King Lear* (1971)
	production designer, *Otello* (1973)
Walken, Christopher	Lieutenant McDuff, *Scotland, Pa.* (2001)
Wallace, Michael	composer, *The Tempest* (2007)
Wallace, Vincene	Nurse, *The Secret Sex Lives of Romeo and Juliet* (1969)
Wallace, Will	Sebastian, *The Tempest* (2007)
Walton, William	composer, *As You Like It* (1936)
	composer, *The Chronicle History of King Henry the Fift with His Battell Fought at Agincourt in France* (1944)
	composer, *Hamlet* (1948)
	composer, *Richard III* (1955)
Wang, Yuanyuan	choreographer, *Ye yan* (2006)
von Wangenheim, Gustav	Romeo Montekugerl, *Romeo und Julia im Schnee* (1920)
Warbeck, Stephen	composer, orchestrator, *Shakespeare in Love* (1998)
Ward, Mackenzie	Touchstone, *As You Like It* (1936)
Warde, Ernest C.	director & Fool, *King Lear* (1916)
Warde, Frederick B.	Richard III, *Richard III* (1912)
	Lear, *King Lear* (1916)
Wardwell, Geoffrey	Hortensio, *The Taming of the Shrew* (1929)
Warner, David	Lysander, *A Midsummer Night's Dream* (1968)
Warrier, Manju	Thamara, *Kaliyattam* (1997)
Washington, Denzel	Don Pedro, *Much Ado About Nothing* (1993)
Watson, Douglas	Gaius Octavius Thurinus, *Julius Caesar* (1953)
Wauer, William	director, *Die lustigen Weiber von Windsor* (1917)
Weaver, Chris	cinematographer, *King Lear* (1999)
Webb, Alan	Robert Shallow, *Campanadas a medianoche* (1965)
	Gremio, *The Taming of the Shrew* (1967)
	Earl of Gloucester, *King Lear*

417

418

	Cleopatra (1908)
	Marcus Junius Brutus, *Julius Caesar* (1908)
Williams, Eric	Hubert de Burgh, *Hubert and Arthur* (1913)
	Henry V, *King Henry V* (1913)
	Marcus Junius Brutus, *Brutus and Cassius* (1918)
Williams, Heathcote	Prospero, *The Tempest* (1979)
	himself, *Looking for Richard* (1996)
Williams, Zelda	Frankie, *Were The World Mine* (2008)
Williamson, Nicol	Hamlet, *Hamlet* (1969)
Williamson, Phillip	Lover, *The Angelic Conversation* (1985)
Willis, Edwin B.	associate settings artist, *Romeo and Juliet* (1936)
	set decorator, *Julius Caesar* (1953)
	set decorator, *Kiss Me Kate* (1953)
	set decorator, *Forbidden Planet* (1956)
Wilmer, Douglas	Marquis of Dorset, *Richard III* (1955)
	R. Cassius, *An Honourable Murder* (1960)
	Second Murderer, *Macbeth* (1961)
	Marcus Vipsanius Agrippa, *Antony and Cleopatra* (1972)
Wilson, Hal	Oyenkwa, *Indian Romeo and Juliet* (1912)
	King's Friend, *Cardinal Wolsey* (1912)
Wing, Jason	Duke of Clarence, *Richard III* (2005)
	Laertes, *Hamlet* (2007)
Winslet, Kate	Ophelia, *Hamlet* (1996)
Winters, Shelley	Pat Kroll, *A Double Life* (1947)
Witter, Jason	Romeo Montague, *Romeo & Juliet vs. The Living Dead* (2009)
Wirth, Franz Peter	director, *Hamlet, Prinz von Dänemark* (1961)
	director, *Was Ihr wollt* (1962)
Wise, Robert	director, producer, *West Side Story* (1961)
Wong, Russell	Yung Gan, *China Girl* (1987)
Wood, Ashley	Lysander, *Midsummer* (1999)

Wood, Natalie	Maria, *West Side Story* (1961)
Woodley, Lorraine	Lady Anne, *Richard III* (2005)
Wooland, Norman	Horatio, *Hamlet* (1948)
	Paris, *Romeo and Juliet* (1954)
	Sir William Catesby, *Richard III* (1955)
	Brutus Smith, *An Honourable Murder* (1960)
Worth, Irene	Goneril, *King Lear* (1971)
Worthington, Sam	Macbeth, *Macbeth* (2006)
Wright, Geoffrey	director, producer, *Macbeth* (2006)
Wu, Daniel	Prince Wu Luan, *Ye yan* (2006)
Wynn, Keenan	Lippy, *Kiss Me Kate* (1953)
Wyzniewski, Arno	Count Claudio, *Viel Lärm um nichts* (1964)
Yamada, Isuzu	Lady Asaji Washizu, *Kumonosu jô* (1957)
Yamashta, Stomu	composer, *Tempest* (1982)
Yanshin, Mikhail	Sir Toby Belch, *Dvenadtsataya noch* (1955)
Yelnik, Clémentine	The son, *La tragédie de Gonzague* (2002)
Yermolayev, A.	Tybalt Capulet, *Romeo i Zhulietta* (1955)
Yip, Timmy	art director, *Ye yan* (2006)
Yordan, Philip	screenwriter, *Joe MacBeth* (1955)
York, Michael	Lucentio Bentivolio, *The Taming of the Shrew* (1967)
	Tybalt Capulet, *Romeo and Juliet* (1968)
Yorke, Kathleen	Edward V, *Richard III* (1911)
Young, Clara Kimball	Penelope, *A Midsummer Night's Dream* (1909)
	Anne Boleyn, *Cardinal Wolsey* (1912)
Yuen, Gary	Vincent Chan, *Jiyuan qiaohe* (2000)
Yuen, Wo-Ping	executive producer, fight choreographer, *Ye yan* (2006)
Yuill, Jimmy	Captain Jamy, *Henry V* (1989)
	Friar Francis, *Much Ado About Nothing* (1993)
	Alexander, *Hamlet* (1996)
	Constable Dull, *Love's Labour's Lost* (2000)
	Corin, *As You Like It* (2006)
Yurdakul, Reha	Kasim Evren, *Intikam Melegi – Kadin Hamlet* (1977)
Yutkevich, Sergei	director, *Otello* (1955)
Z'Dar, Robert	Theseus, *William Shakespeare's*

420